MW00812830

The New York Times

EASY CROSSWORD PUZZLE OMNIBUS
VOLUME 7
200 Solvable Puzzles from the Pages of The New York Times

Edited by Will Shortz

ST. MARTIN'S GRIFFIN ☙ NEW YORK

THE NEW YORK TIMES EASY CROSSWORD PUZZLE OMNIBUS VOLUME 7.
Copyright © 2011 by The New York Times Company. All rights reserved.
Printed in the United States of America. For information, address
St. Martin's Press, 175 Fifth Avenue, New York, NY 10010.

www.stmartins.com

All of the puzzles that appear in this work were originally published in *The New York Times*
from October 29, 2007, to June 22, 2010. Copyright © 2007, 2008, 2009, 2010 by
The New York Times Company. All rights reserved. Reprinted by permission.

ISBN 978-0-312-59058-1

First Edition: August 2011

10 9 8 7 6 5 4 3 2 1

The New York Times

EASY CROSSWORD PUZZLE OMNIBUS
VOLUME 7

ACROSS

1 Started a cigarette
6 Sail supporter
10 Rooters
14 Left one's seat
15 Gumbo vegetable
16 Track shape
17 Allotment of heredity units?
19 Parks who pioneered in civil rights
20 Our language: Abbr.
21 Took the blue ribbon
22 Room to maneuver
24 Nuclear power apparatus
27 Top 10 tunes
28 Hole-punching tool
29 Slender cigar
33 Prefix with -hedron
36 Is false to the world
37 Get from ____ (progress slightly)
38 Battle of the ____ (men vs. women)
39 Stadium section
40 Studied primarily, at college
42 Holder of 88 keys
43 Caveman's era
44 Vintage automotive inits.
45 Tennis great Arthur
46 Mediums' meetings
50 Stewed to the gills
53 King Kong, e.g.
54 Lacto-____-vegetarian
55 Sitarist Shankar
56 Preacher's sky-high feeling?
60 Twistable cookie
61 Turn at roulette
62 Decaf brand
63 Give an alert
64 Direction of sunup
65 Sticky problem

DOWN

1 Hearty brew
2 Jim Carrey comedy "Me, Myself & ____"
3 Kingdom east of Fiji
4 Milk for all its worth
5 Pay-____-view
6 Travel by car
7 Closely related (to)
8 Sign at a sellout
9 Bikini wearers' markings
10 TV channel for golfers?
11 State frankly
12 Shuttle-launching org.
13 Murder
18 Delinquent G.I.
23 Greek H's
25 Pasta-and-potato-loving country?
26 Former rival of Pan Am
27 Safe place
29 Mischievous sprite
30 Director Kazan
31 Claim on property
32 Prefix with dynamic
33 Scots' caps
34 Coup d'____
35 Japanese P.M. during W.W. II
36 Mantel
38 Equine-looking fish
41 Take a siesta
42 Split ____ soup
44 Fishing line winder
46 Paid out
47 Nickels and dimes
48 Call to mind
49 Sunken ship finder
50 Furrowed part of the head
51 Dr. Zhivago's love
52 1964 Dave Clark Five song "Glad All ____"
53 Hertz rival
57 Mileage rating org.
58 Cleopatra's biter
59 Eastern "way"

by Fred Piscop

2

ACROSS
1 Peak
5 Chattered incessantly
10 TV horse introduced in 1955 . . . or a Plymouth model introduced in 1956
14 Partiality
15 Seeing red
16 Prime draft status
17 Drug-yielding plant
18 Opposite of serenity
19 Cartoonist Al
20 Scary sound from the ocean?
23 Park, e.g., in N.Y.C.
25 "Sting like a bee" athlete
26 Having seniority
28 Scary sound from a war zone?
33 Juillet's season
34 Kodiak native
35 Physics unit
36 Theory's start
37 Scary sound from a cornfield?
41 Splinter group
44 Motel-discount grp.
45 Sales slips: Abbr.
49 Galley implement
50 Scary sound from a steeple?
53 Tedious
55 Boot part
56 "Whew!"
57 Misspells, say, as a ghost might at 20-, 28-, 37- and 50- Across?
62 Abominate
63 African antelope
64 Hot rod's rod
67 ___ Lackawanna Railroad
68 Countryish
69 Boot part
70 Card game for three
71 Walk leisurely
72 Stealth bomber org.

DOWN
1 Charles Gibson's network
2 A.F.L.-___
3 Cane cutter
4 Biblical son who sold his birthright
5 Wavelet
6 Language whose alphabet starts alif, ba, ta, tha . . .
7 Child's caretaker
8 Suffix with hypn-
9 Part of a bottle or a guitar
10 Kind of point
11 Helpless?
12 Filled to the gills
13 Big fat mouth
21 Country just south of Sicily
22 Moo goo gai pan pan
23 Lawyers' org.
24 Kilmer of "The Doors"
27 ___ Irvin, classic artist for The New Yorker
29 Cowlick, e.g.
30 Fit for a king
31 Blunder
32 "Long ___ and far away . . ."
36 Creep (along)
38 Name that's an anagram of 27-Down
39 ___ de mer
40 Egyptian dry measure equal to about five-and-a-half bushels
41 Soak (up)
42 Tag for a particular purpose
43 Neighbor of Slovenia
46 Co. addresses, often
47 A duo
48 Crafty
50 Tournament pass
51 Like some music
52 Musically improvise
54 Sport utilizing a clay disk
58 Hospital shipments
59 Styptic agent
60 Part of a fishhook
61 Island with Waimea Bay
62 Gentlemen
65 Meadow
66 Shoemaker's helper, in a fairy tale

by Gary Steinmehl

ACROSS

1 "Lady Marmalade" singer ___ LaBelle
6 Musical phrase
10 On the briny
14 Birdlike
15 Poet ___ Khayyám
16 Butter slices
17 T. S. Eliot title character who measures out his life with coffee spoons
20 Not just recent
21 Muck
22 "The Simpsons" bartender
23 Light throw
26 Studio sign
29 Actress MacDowell of "Groundhog Day"
32 Really impressed
34 Geller with a spoon-bending act
35 Light golden lager
38 ___ Bator, Mongolia
39 Editor out to smear Spider-Man
42 Parti-colored
43 Dance class outfit
44 Quantity: Abbr.
45 Sheep cries
46 Rapids transits
50 A goose egg
52 Phobia
55 Unfortunate sound when you bend over
56 Hay storage locale
58 Saw-toothed
61 Vice president who once famously mashed "potato"
65 Come to shore
66 Baby bassoon?
67 War horse
68 Lyric poems
69 Puppy bites
70 Sexy nightwear

DOWN

1 ___ party (sleepover)
2 Frankie of "Beach Blanket Bingo"
3 Cultivated the soil
4 President who later served as chief justice
5 Initials on a cross
6 Where you might hear "Ride 'em, cowboy!"
7 Little devil
8 Distant
9 Lively '60s dance
10 Kitchen spill catcher
11 Brazil's largest city
12 And so on: Abbr.
13 "___ and ye shall receive"
18 CPR pro
19 Grocery offering
24 California city in a 1968 Dionne Warwick hit
25 Accumulation on the brow
27 Persia, today
28 ___ Tin Tin
30 Its first ad touted "1,000 songs in your pocket"
31 German article
33 Humorist Bombeck
36 Singsong syllables
37 Grain bundle
38 Beef quality graders: Abbr.
39 Guitarist Hendrix
40 747, e.g.
41 Be mistaken
42 La ___, Bolivia
45 Hit, as on the noggin
47 Worn at the edges
48 Like the Marquis de Sade or the Duke of Earl
49 Rapid
51 Unilever skin cream brand
53 Fireplace remnants
54 Necessary: Abbr.
57 Roger Rabbit or Donald Duck
59 Corrosion sign
60 Appraise
61 Female singer's 2001 album that debuted at #1
62 "Dear old" guy
63 Slugger's stat
64 Blouse or shirt

by Jeremy Horwitz

4

ACROSS

1 Home in an old warehouse district
5 Virus named for a river
10 Trans-Siberian Railroad stop
14 Peculiar: Prefix
15 U.S./Canada early warning syst.
16 City bond, for short
17 Eisenhower was one
20 Move unsteadily
21 Delon of "Purple Noon"
22 Cedar Rapids college
23 2:30, aboard ship
27 Dele undoers
29 Something new
30 Ho Chi Minh's capital
31 Boris Godunov, for one
32 Rove, with "about"
35 Full range
37 It's off the tip of Italy
40 Bad-mouth
41 ___ war syndrome
45 ___ plume
46 Chiang Kai-shek's capital
48 Mountain cats
49 Rests for a bit
52 Singleton
53 "Waiting for Lefty" playwright
54 Like Dickens's Dodger
57 Shortly after quitting time, for many
62 Forearm bone
63 Shul V.I.P.
64 Pizzeria fixture
65 Hot times in France
66 Befuddled
67 Try for a role

DOWN

1 Brit's elevator
2 Garfield's foil
3 Nickel
4 Slugging it out
5 ___'acte
6 Feathery wrap
7 Bobby of the Bruins
8 Dillydally
9 Fruity quencher
10 Brunch dish
11 Wall art
12 Symbol of slowness
13 Ceramists' baking chambers
18 Welcomes, as a guest at one's home
19 Catches red-handed
23 Jack Sprat's taboo
24 Hypotheticals
25 Rome's ___ Veneto
26 Blunders
27 Outbuilding
28 Vehicle with a medallion
32 Request for a congratulatory slap
33 Pierce player
34 Gray concealers
36 End-of-workweek cry
38 At a cruise stop
39 Be worth
42 A.P. competitor
43 "My Name Is Asher ___"
44 "For shame!"
46 Colorful fishes
47 Helper: Abbr.
49 Brimless cap
50 At least 21
51 "The Family Circus" cartoonist Bil
54 Home to most Turks
55 Iris's place
56 Libraries do it
58 Big Band ___
59 Turn state's evidence
60 "Sesame Street" channel
61 Honest ___

by John Underwood

ACROSS

1 Pear variety
5 Filthy place
11 Mardi ___
15 Paul who sang "Puppy Love"
16 Win over
17 Bringing up the rear
18 "Floral" film that was the Best Picture of 1989
21 Ran into
22 Some ales
23 Wilderness photographer Adams
24 Quit, with "out"
25 Glossy alternative
26 "Again!"
27 Gave utterance to
29 Customers
30 Celtic dialect
31 Regional dialect
34 "Floral" film of 2006 with Josh Hartnett and Scarlett Johansson
40 Cowboy contests
41 "SportsCenter" channel
43 Feudal workers
47 Traveling group of actors
49 Motown's Franklin
50 Newspapers, TV, radio, etc.
53 Teacher's favorite
54 "Get lost!"
55 System of government
56 La ___, Bolivia
57 "Floral" film of 1986 based on an Umberto Eco novel
60 Swedish soprano Jenny
61 Like some inspections
62 ___-friendly
63 "For" votes
64 Shorthand takers
65 Fictional detective Wolfe

DOWN

1 "You'll regret that!"
2 Written up, as to a superior
3 Easily startled
4 Cleveland cager, for short
5 Group of five
6 Bar of gold
7 Entire range
8 Slug, old-style
9 ___ and turn
10 1812, 2001, etc.: Abbr.
11 Quick look
12 ___ d'être
13 State with conviction
14 Shag, beehive, updo, etc.
19 "Woe ___!"
20 From Copenhagen, e.g.
26 Kazan who directed "On the Waterfront"
28 Grade between bee and dee
29 Atlantic swimmers
31 Cushions
32 Hole in one
33 W.B.A. decision
35 The Creator, to Hindus
36 Name repeated in "Whatever ___ wants, ___ gets"
37 Virgo's predecessor
38 Noncommittal agreement
39 One who's making nice
42 EarthLink alternative
43 To a huge degree
44 Jughead's pal
45 One of tennis's Williams sisters
46 Bleachers
47 Gives 10% to the church
48 Funnywoman Martha
50 Bullwinkle, e.g.
51 Spritelike
52 "Me, too"
55 Shut (up)
58 Calendar pgs.
59 Hurry

by Harvey Estes

ACROSS

1 Prefix with sphere
5 Assigned stars to
10 Thriving time
14 Jewish ritual
15 Visibly stunned
16 Humorist Bombeck
17 Ornery sort
18 Cutoffs fabric
19 Yemeni port
20 Striptease business?
23 Drive-thru convenience, perhaps
24 Having lunch, say
25 "___ to say this, but . . ."
26 Some auto deals
28 Stereotypical sandwich board diner
31 Young 'un
32 Younger brother, say
33 Knight's attendant
35 Wrestling business?
39 Former "Dateline NBC" co-host Jane
40 Beanery sign
43 Cockpit abbr.
46 Carefully arranged
47 Portugal's place
49 The March King
51 ___-Caps (Nestlé candy)
52 Row C abbr., maybe
53 Comb business?
58 Volcano known to locals as Mongibello
59 Dweller along the Arabian Sea
60 "Darn!"
62 Goatee site
63 Mullally of "Will & Grace"
64 ZZ Top, e.g.
65 Look after
66 Dummy Mortimer
67 Thanksgiving side dish

DOWN

1 "Dancing With the Stars" airer
2 One on a board
3 Jumble
4 ___ buco
5 Figure that's squared in a common formula
6 Go-between
7 Zesty flavor
8 Cast-of-thousands film
9 Floor model
10 Place for an umbrella
11 Tough time
12 Mafia code of silence
13 Unlike drone aircraft
21 Reason to cry "Alas!"
22 Some Japanese-Americans
23 Jungfrau or Eiger
27 Metro map feature
28 A singing Jackson
29 Bacchanalian revelry
30 Polar drudge
33 TV handyman Bob
34 Kind of diagram
36 The Pineapple Island
37 Expected in
38 Sauce for some seafood
41 Cratchit boy
42 Bummed out
43 Appearance
44 Not be able to stomach
45 Submit, as homework
47 Under consideration
48 Dizzy Gillespie's genre
50 Witness's place
51 School locator?
54 Pierre, François, etc.
55 Hood fighters
56 Parakeet keeper
57 Pseudo-cultured
61 Brillo alternative

by Fred Piscop

ACROSS

1 Bit of smoke
5 "Jeepers!"
11 Burton who produced "The Nightmare Before Christmas"
14 Popular plant gel
15 Native name for Mount McKinley
16 Long-distance number starter
17 Subversive group
19 Buddy
20 Four: Prefix
21 QB Manning
22 Repulsive
23 Soap or lotion, say
27 Searched
29 Gardner of Hollywood
30 Debtor's promise
31 Wise ones
34 Suspect's excuse
38 ___ Ness monster
40 Where you may find the ends of 17-, 23-, 52- and 63-Across
42 Social slight
43 Actor Hawke
45 Sirius XM medium
47 Three: Prefix
48 No ___, ands or buts
50 Furry burrowers
52 Notorious stigma
57 Umpteen
58 Fish eggs
59 Mullah's teaching
62 Traveler's stopover
63 Coveted film honor
66 Stocking's tip
67 Hardly hip
68 Drooling dog in "Garfield"
69 Evil spell
70 Freshman's topper
71 Spiffy

DOWN

1 Blow gently
2 Tennis champ Nastase
3 One who'll easily lend money for a hard-luck story
4 Fuel by the litre
5 U.S. health promoter: Abbr.
6 Auto last made in the 1930s
7 Shoreline opening
8 Newswoman Zahn
9 New York city Mark Twain is buried
10 What it is "to tell a lie"
11 Subject of discussion
12 With everything counted
13 Fracas
18 Flags down, as a taxi
22 Pharmacy containers
24 Vault
25 Ventriloquist Bergen
26 Big electrical project inits.
27 Mah-jongg piece
28 Underlying cause
32 Fed. air quality monitor
33 Marsh plant
35 Period between
36 Jefferson's first vice president
37 Curve-billed wader
39 Hirsute
41 Real sidesplitter
44 Org. for Colts and Broncos
46 Eye-related
49 Calm
51 Charlton of "The Ten Commandments"
52 Suffix with black or silver
53 It gets a paddling
54 Building add-on
55 Puccini opera
56 Pretend
60 Met highlight
61 Assemble
63 Fella
64 Hawaiian dish
65 ___ du Diable

by Lynn Lempel

ACROSS

1 Missing Jimmy
6 Hit the slopes
9 General feeling
14 Paula of "American Idol"
15 Chum
16 Take forcibly
17 Big spender's woe?
19 "Mule Train" singer, 1949
20 Bête ___
21 Gum arabic-yielding tree
22 Where to find the headings Books, Dolls & Bears, and Collectibles
25 Revolver toter?
27 The Ewings' soap
29 ___ Tin Tin
30 Letter-shaped support
31 Huge expanses
33 Clinic name
37 MasterCard-carrying ecclesiastic?
40 New York home of Rensselaer Polytechnic Institute
41 Give the boot to
42 Greene of "Bonanza"
43 Mark, as a ballot square
44 "Blah, blah, blah . . ."
45 Peter?
51 Deck wood
52 Country singer Milsap
53 Quick Pick game
55 Worse than bad
56 Where this puzzle's theme pairs would like to meet
60 Chain unit
61 Reproductive cells
62 Condor's nest
63 Tender spots
64 Prickly husk
65 Pasta sauce brand

DOWN

1 Witchy woman
2 Sapporo sash
3 Rx watchdog
4 1975 Barbra Streisand sequel
5 Chorus voice
6 Richard's first vice president
7 Superman's birth name
8 Under the weather
9 Spock, on his father's side
10 Asimov of sci-fi
11 LaCrosse carmaker
12 Bert's Muppet pal
13 Pickle portion
18 Some ballpoints
21 Imitative in a silly way
22 Papal bull, e.g.
23 Kiddie lit elephant
24 Olds discontinued in 2004
26 Developer's plot
28 "___ Blue"
31 Spa feature
32 Overhead trains
33 Reggie Jackson nickname
34 Think alike
35 Buttinsky
36 Vacuum maker
38 Library no-no
39 Supermodel Carol
43 "Trust No One" TV series, with "The"
44 Sermon ending?
45 Lacking couth
46 Self-help category
47 Due to get, as punishment
48 Toughen
49 Romantic message, in shorthand
50 Without face value
54 Pipe section
56 Cry out loud
57 Seam material
58 Rug, of a sort
59 Zodiac beast

by Larry Shearer

ACROSS

1 Clothing
5 It's arched above the eye
9 iPhone maker
14 Creme-filled cookie
15 Wine: Prefix
16 Burger side order
17 Bean-filled bag moved with the foot
19 Expire, as a subscription
20 Honor bestowed by Queen Eliz.
21 Farm unit
22 Bowling alley divisions
23 Postcard sentiment
25 Comedy club razzer
27 Simple
28 Electric cord's end
30 Where dirty dishes pile up
31 Say "Do this," "Do that" . . . blah, blah, blah
34 Border on
36 Prefix with classical
37 Like some hams
41 Fishing pole
42 Loads
43 Id's counterpart
44 Beverages in barrels
46 Fall
48 Statutes
52 Pop artist David
54 Bucharest's land
57 Gather, as information
58 Opposite of fall
59 Auto gizmo that talks, for short
60 Scarecrow's wish in "The Wizard of Oz"
61 2004 film "I ♥ ___"
63 ___ living
64 On the briny
65 Like a first-place ribbon
66 "What ___!" ("It's so dirty!")
67 Dakota ___ (old geog. designation)
68 Depletes, as strength

DOWN

1 "Get out of here!"
2 Where Saudis live
3 Nook
4 ___ choy (Chinese green)
5 Chocolate syrup brand
6 Stand on the hind legs, as a horse
7 "___ upon a time . . ."
8 Chinese cooking vessel
9 Insurance co. with a "spokesduck"
10 Throwing cream pies and such
11 Oil conveyor
12 Abated
13 180° from WNW
18 "That's great news!"
22 Peanut, e.g.
24 Out of ___ (not harmonizing)
25 Parts of cars with caps
26 Early MGM rival
29 ___ rest (bury)
32 Letters before an alias
33 Flax-colored
35 Dress (up)
37 3-D picture
38 "You don't say!," after "Well"
39 Actor Calhoun
40 Kind of nut
41 Stadium cry
45 Balls of yarn
47 Person comparing costs
49 Actress Lansbury
50 Use a paper towel
51 Gives some lip
53 Grandmas
55 Schindler of "Schindler's List"
56 ___ culpa
58 Subterfuge
60 Actress Arthur
61 Sombrero, e.g.
62 Kids' ammo

by Andrea Carla Michaels

ACROSS

1 In debt
6 Post-op locale
9 Bets build them
13 Workplace for some clowns
14 Melon exterior
16 Sign to heed
17 States confidently
18 Rice-shaped pasta
19 Late-night name
20 Number one #2?
22 Hunchbacked assistant
23 "All My ___ Live in Texas" (1987 #1 country hit)
24 Manorial worker
26 2 and 12, e.g., in dice
31 "I am such a dope!"
32 Bart's teacher, ___ Krabappel
33 Hen's home
35 Oslo is on one
39 Have-___ (poor people)
40 Traffic problem
42 Northamptonshire river
43 Yucky
45 Olympics blade
46 Toy with a cross frame
47 Dental problem calling for braces
49 Puts together hastily
51 Empty, as a stare
55 Baton Rouge sch.
56 Prefix with culture
57 Little woman?
63 Heist haul
64 Proceed slowly
65 Persian tongue
66 Cuzco native
67 Holding a grudge
68 "I surrender!"
69 Batik artist
70 In a funk
71 Manages to elude

DOWN

1 Like most folklore
2 Used a loom
3 Brainchild
4 Social misfit
5 Matthew or Mark
6 Hard porcelain
7 Magazine fig.
8 Loosen, as a parka
9 What a comedian might do before going onstage?
10 Alphabet ender
11 Carpentry joint part
12 Angry bull's sound
15 Apportioned, with "out"
21 Members of management
25 "___ Wiedersehen"
26 China's ___ Xiaoping
27 Dumpster emanation
28 Sermon preposition
29 Fish-shaped musical instrument?
30 Ivory, Coast and others
34 Made impossible
36 Alsace assents
37 Queue after Q
38 Tough to fathom
41 Most trivial
44 ___ Tomé
48 High-heel shoes
50 Really sorry
51 Not yet expired
52 Intense pain
53 Jim who sang "Time in a Bottle"
54 Missile sites
58 Ibsen's ___ Helmer
59 Hand, to Hernando
60 Rainbow shapes
61 Cruise stopover
62 Stamping tools

by Julie Ann Bowling

ACROSS

1 Part of a molecule
5 Supply-and-demand subj.
9 Pepsi and RC
14 Prom night transportation
15 Furry tunneler
16 Face-to-face exams
17 Alda of "What Women Want"
18 Othello's false friend
19 White-plumed wader
20 Profanity, e.g.
23 2007 film "___ and the Real Girl"
24 "Bonanza" star Greene
25 Sit behind bars
28 Memorial designer Maya ___
29 Cowboy boot attachment
32 Madonna title role
33 Flies off the handle
35 Mail carrier's beat: Abbr.
36 1995 Woody Allen comedy
39 Number before "ignition . . . liftoff!"
40 Bank robber's job
41 Dressed to the ___
42 Arctic floater
44 Suffix with meth-
45 "No Exit" playwright
46 Becomes frayed
48 Hand protector
49 Classic "Jeopardy!" category
54 Henhouse perch
55 Earthenware jar
56 College in New Rochelle, N.Y.
57 From days of yore
58 Bring up, as children
59 Be certain about
60 Saltine brand

61 Home of the invaders in Wells's "The War of the Worlds"
62 Snaky swimmers

DOWN

1 Self-pitying cry
2 Pinball foul
3 Sharif of "Doctor Zhivago"
4 Monument carved from a single stone
5 Settler from a foreign land
6 Snowman's eyes
7 Olympic gymnast Korbut
8 Nighttime advertising sign, maybe
9 ___ de Lion, epithet for Richard I
10 Church hymn accompaniers
11 Easily read type
12 Away from the wind
13 Lander at J.F.K., once
21 Football's Broadway Joe
22 Dead duck
25 Brit's service discharge
26 Sheeplike
27 Golfer named A.P. Male Athlete of the Year four times
28 Senior moment, e.g.
30 Pure-and-simple
31 Witherspoon of "Walk the Line"
33 Cloudburst
34 Beethoven specialty
37 Have a hankering
38 Off-road two-wheeler
43 Gird oneself
45 Indian instruments
47 Prudential rival
48 Grinding tooth
49 Extremity of the earth
50 "Not guilty," for one
51 Companionless
52 Hydroxyl-carbon compound
53 Toothed tools
54 Peri Gilpin's "Frasier" role

by Harvey Estes

12

The answers at 17- and 51-Across and 11- and 24-Down can all be defined by the same missing three-letter word. What is it?

ACROSS

1 Keen-edged
6 Gave in
11 ___-a-cake
14 Chomping at the bit
15 Last Olds made
16 Corrida cheer
17 *See blurb*
19 Cooking spray brand
20 "When hell freezes over"
21 Grouch
23 Not exactly insightful
26 Gung-ho sort
27 Minty drinks
28 Greg's sitcom mate
30 Oklahoma Indians
31 Some earrings
32 Slugger's stat
35 Hershey confection
36 Pasta is loaded with them
37 Skier's transport
38 "I do"
39 Four-page sheet
40 An ex of the Donald
41 Martini garnishes
43 Shiny fabric
44 Regal fur
46 Brilliantly colored parrots
47 Actress Gaynor
48 Scarlett of Tara
50 "Evil Woman" band, for short
51 *See blurb*
57 Cornhusker State: Abbr.
58 Special talent
59 Fashionably old-fashioned
60 Batiking need
61 Doughboys
62 Thoroughly enjoy

DOWN

1 Trice, informally
2 "2001" computer
3 In the past
4 Counterpart of bus.
5 Engagement contracts, briefly
6 Cut up
7 "I cannot tell ___"
8 Zig or zag
9 Directional suffix
10 For whom Sandy Koufax pitched
11 *See blurb*
12 Texas shrine
13 Tantalize
18 Come clean, with "up"
22 Smash into
23 Belly button type
24 *See blurb*
25 Summer shirts
26 Nukes
27 Facetious
28 Day of "Pillow Talk"
29 Boxcar rider
31 In the pink
33 Farm bundles
34 Neighbor of Turkey
36 Place to moor
37 "Later"
39 Like a picky eater
40 Like much of Poe's work
42 Designer Claiborne
43 ___ Lee cakes
44 Make corrections to
45 Life of ___ (ease)
46 Some big trucks
48 Mideast sultanate
49 Bumpkin
52 ___ lark
53 Arthur of "The Golden Girls"
54 Hall-of-Famer Mel
55 Play about Capote
56 Toy with a string

by Alison Donald

ACROSS

1 John ___, host of "America's Most Wanted"
6 "Jeopardy!" whiz Jennings
9 "Hey, you!"
13 ___ 2600 (classic video game console)
14 St. Louis landmark
15 Voice above a tenor
16 Appetizer with sweet and sour sauce
18 Gorilla watcher Fossey
19 Frightful female
20 Puccini heroine
21 Cheerful
22 Take turns
24 Dangler on a suitcase
26 Deadly long-tailed fish
28 Where you might get into hot water?
31 Schiaparelli of fashion
34 Cigarette substance
35 Interlocks
37 Bride's bounty
39 Meadow
41 Bird on birth announcement cards
42 Comes about
44 Wrigley's product
46 S&L conveniences
47 All U.S. senators until 1922
48 Monotonous voice
51 Birds flying in V's
53 Has confidence in
56 Beverly Sills and others
58 Young cod for dinner
60 F.D.R. job-creating measure: Abbr.
62 "Famous" cookie maker
63 Gangly guy
65 Fruit from a palm
66 "Don't hurt me!," e.g.
67 Straight up
68 Laid off, as workers
69 Wood in archery bows
70 Copenhageners, e.g.

DOWN

1 Do the laundry
2 Even, on the leaderboard
3 Slow, in symphonies
4 ___ Lanka
5 Merely suggest
6 Ray who created the McDonald's empire
7 Custardy dessert
8 Rink org.
9 City where Galileo taught
10 Goliath's undoing
11 Baseball's Musial
12 Broadway award
14 Weapons stash
17 "Oh, I see"
21 Eyelid nuisances
23 Romanov rulers
25 River blocker
27 One of the Allman Brothers
29 Straight-to-curly transformation, informally
30 Poses questions
31 Dutch city with a cheese market
32 Oral tradition
33 Make-or-break election bloc
36 Does' mates
38 Sí and oui
40 Home of the von Trapp family
43 Bro's sibling
45 Lamebrain
49 Get cozy
50 Prodded gently
52 Lessened, as pain
54 11- or 12-year-old
55 Rocket's realm
56 1920s art movement
57 Giant-screen theater
59 Backstage bunch
61 Tiny tunnelers
63 Mata Hari, for one
64 Top half of a bikini

by Lynn Lempel

14

ACROSS

1 Like some petticoats
5 Own up (to)
10 Bank with significant deposits?
14 Award for "Hot L Baltimore"
15 Harness parts
16 Writer ___ Stanley Gardner
17 Teen's response to a parent's "No"
20 Somme summer
21 Greek war god
22 Novelist Joyce Carol ___
23 Blacken
24 Pumpkin pie ingredient
26 Outdated
29 Musical Count
30 "Encore!"
31 Forest in "As You Like It"
32 By way of
35 Teen's response to a parent's "No"
39 & 40 Change of government
41 1973 #1 hit "___ an American Band"
42 Basketball position
43 Gushed
45 Subject to legal damages
47 Like badly worn tires
48 Peter of "Casablanca"
49 "Howdy!"
50 Batman and Robin, e.g.
53 Teen's response to a parent's "No"
57 Window section
58 Power problem
59 Mideast V.I.P.
60 Narrow cut
61 Wheels for big wheels
62 Folk singer Seeger

DOWN

1 Ear or leaf feature
2 Be next to
3 Mention, as in a court opinion
4 To date
5 Couples' destination?
6 Prevent through intimidation
7 Pageant title
8 Country lodge
9 General on a Chinese menu
10 Malign
11 Steaming
12 Movie-set light
13 Plural suffix with auction or musket
18 "Aren't you the comedian?!"
19 Lugging
23 "Moonstruck" actress
24 Point from which there's nowhere to go but up
25 Depletes, with "up"
26 Meteor shooting across the sky, maybe
27 Aphrodite's domain
28 Sketched
29 Kennel club listing
31 Tennis great Agassi
32 Panorama
33 Memo phrase
34 Like some cheeses
36 "Absolutely!"
37 ___ surgeon
38 Had to hand it to?
42 January birthstone
43 What the teen wishes the parent would do instead
44 Land office map
45 Hometown-related
46 Tehran resident
47 "Ex-x-xactly!"
48 Kissers
49 Havoc
50 "It's your ___"
51 Military group
52 Nasty sort
54 Hi-speed connection
55 Non's opposite
56 With it, once

by Gail Grabowski

ACROSS

1 ___ mater
5 Letter-shaped structural piece
9 Lesser-played half of a 45
14 Elementary particle
15 Vex
16 Gucci alternative
17 Upstate New York city and spa
20 Remote areas
21 Imp
22 Head for
23 The boondocks
24 Honeymooners' destination
28 Alternative to .com or .edu
29 Fix, as brakes
30 Jacob's twin
34 Track events
36 Asian New Year
37 Leaves port
38 Bygone U.S. gas brand
39 Mother ___, 1979 Peace Nobelist
41 Napkin's place
42 Former president of Harvard
45 Kodak, Pentax and Nikon
48 The "L" in S&L
49 Is wild about
50 Mythical island that sank into the sea
54 Comic who played Robin Williams's son in "Mork & Mindy"
56 Auto route from Me. to Fla.
57 1930s migrant
58 Smell ___ (be suspicious)
59 Groups of spies
60 Fails to keep pace
61 Without: Fr.

DOWN

1 "I ___ sorry!"
2 Hawaiian cookout
3 Homeowners' burdens
4 Like clocks with hands
5 Shipment to a steel mill
6 Home of the Cowboys, familiarly
7 "Sad to say . . ."
8 ___ judicata
9 Spread out ungracefully
10 Isle of Man's locale
11 Rumba or samba
12 Mystery writer's award
13 Swiss city on the Rhine, old-style
18 Dwellers along the Volga
19 Working stiff
23 French city where Jules Verne was born
24 Alaskan city where the Iditarod ends
25 Angers
26 Raises or lowers a hem, say
27 Passionate
31 Time before talkies
32 Banned orchard spray
33 Letter carriers' grp.
35 Broad-minded
37 Pago Pago resident
39 Garbage
40 Besmirches
43 Mountain ridges
44 Powerful rays
45 Louisianan of French descent
46 Get ___ of one's own medicine
47 Pre-stereo recordings
50 Paul who sang "Put Your Head on My Shoulder"
51 Tiny branch
52 Tehran's home
53 Concordes, briefly
55 "You've got mail" co.

by Richard Chisholm

16

ACROSS

1 Comment not to be taken seriously
5 ___ Marley's ghost in "A Christmas Carol"
10 Con game
14 Unwanted spots
15 Band together
16 Poi source
17 Response to a knock
19 29,035 ft., for Mt. Everest
20 Have a bawl
21 Designer label letters
22 Heap kudos on
24 "For instance . . ."
25 Empathize with
26 The important thing
31 A Chaplin
32 Sluggers' stats
33 Lhasa ___ (Tibetan dogs)
38 Doctor's query
41 Scattered about
42 Entre ___
43 Metropolitan ___
44 "Never!"
47 Some apartments
51 Uno + due
52 Apartment window sign
53 Kudrow of "Friends"
55 Mediterranean fruit
58 Both: Prefix
59 Discounter's pitch
62 Computer with an iSight camera
63 Have an ___ mystery
64 Plow pullers
65 Unit of force
66 Teammate of Snider and Hodges
67 Classic computer game set on a seemingly deserted island

DOWN

1 1975 Spielberg thriller
2 Eerie cave effect
3 One not associating with the likes of you?
4 Private eye, for short
5 Place to find auto parts
6 Have ___ with
7 Half of an E.P.A. mileage rating
8 Pony players' locale, in brief
9 Paging device
10 Incredible bargain
11 Where the San Andreas Fault is: Abbr.
12 "Ain't!" retort
13 Shaker's partner
18 Genesis patriarch
23 Convened again
24 "Can you believe this?" look
25 Come clean
26 Knocks the socks off
27 Alternative to a Twinkie
28 From the top
29 Steakhouse selections
30 Attach, in a way
34 Terrible twos, e.g.
35 Browse, as the Web
36 Sportscaster Hershiser
37 Hang around
39 Dickens's Drood
40 "Can I come out now?"
45 Armed conflict
46 Battleship shade
47 Sober
48 Rock opera with the song "Pinball Wizard"
49 Densely packed, in a way
50 Pour salt on, perhaps
53 Apollo's instrument
54 N.Y.S.E. debuts
55 Full of guile
56 Tees off
57 Fellow
60 Step on it
61 Soccer ___

by Alan Arbesfeld

ACROSS

1 Doorframe parts
6 Chinese-born American architect
11 Be a pugilist
14 Bide one's time for
15 Manicurists' concerns
16 Electrical unit
17 One who's always up for a good time
19 Coastal inlet
20 Out of bed
21 ___ Aviv
22 In the near future
23 Prefix with -lithic
24 ___ of students
26 President before D.D.E.
27 Background check for a lender
32 Jay-Z and Timbaland
35 Atop, poetically
36 ___ Speedwagon
37 Horizontally
38 Musical transitions
40 "What was ___ do?"
41 Bulls, rams and bucks
43 Goes to
44 Long, long sentence
47 "I know what you're thinking" claim
48 Mississippi's Trent
49 BlackBerry, e.g., in brief
52 Unretrievable
54 Illustration, for short
55 Husband of Isis
58 April 15 org.
59 Light hauler
61 Sgt., e.g.
62 Didn't go out for dinner
63 Gift recipient
64 Floppy rabbit feature
65 Issues an advisory
66 Edgar Bergen's Mortimer ___

DOWN

1 Where the Pokémon craze originated
2 Cognizant (of)
3 Nintendo brother
4 Kibbles 'n ___
5 Eyelid woe
6 Holiday ___
7 Drink that often comes with an umbrella
8 Olive stuffing
9 Airline to Ben-Gurion
10 Nantucket, e.g.: Abbr.
11 Bruce Springsteen's first hit
12 Akron's home
13 Marvel mutant superhero
18 Big name in fairy tales
22 Egyptian viper
25 Actor Harris and others
26 Regarding this point
27 TV's "___ Sharkey"
28 Send again
29 Place that often has picnic tables
30 Hollow-stemmed plant
31 Flip
32 Fence part
33 Play's start
34 "Nutty" role for Jerry Lewis
39 ___ Xers
42 Worker with genes or film
43 Bit of land in a river
45 Superlative suffix
46 Brenda Lee's "___ Around the Christmas Tree"
49 Trim, as branches
50 Kitchen gizmo
51 Questioned
52 Word that can follow the starts of 17-, 27-, 44- and 59-Across
53 Killer whale
54 Sandwich bread
56 Norms: Abbr.
57 Fe, to chemists
59 Furry foot
60 Little ___ (tots)

by Mark Sherwood

ACROSS

1 Sword handles
6 Worker's due
10 Wood-shaping tool
14 "One for My Baby" composer Harold
15 Horse course
16 One of nine in golf
17 "Merry Christmas" to the French
19 Antique autos
20 Tipple
21 Winter melon
23 "Atlas Shrugged" author Rand
24 Shooters' grp.
26 Genie holders
29 "Merry Christmas" to Danes
33 Spar verbally
36 "I can only ___ much"
37 Sch. named for a televangelist
38 Life stories on film
40 Leak fixer
43 Toss in
44 Not e'en once
46 Inspiring sisters
47 "Merry Christmas" to Spaniards
51 "Lemon Tree" singer Lopez
52 Third after delta
53 "Pow!"
56 Federer and Nadal
59 Collected
62 Hgt.
64 "Merry Christmas" to Italians
66 Two capsules, perhaps
67 Terrier sounds
68 Animated ogre
69 Cold war superpower
70 Sectional, e.g.
71 Makeup maker Lauder

DOWN

1 Muslim pilgrim
2 Kitchen drawer?
3 Visit from the Blue Angels, maybe
4 Readying for a drive
5 Cold-shoulder
6 Hit the jackpot
7 Guacamole ingredient
8 Greek earth goddess
9 Architects' annexes
10 Car safety device
11 Prized positions
12 Menagerie
13 U.S.N.A. grad
18 TV's Warrior Princess
22 Thrilla in Manila boxer
25 It had a notable part in Exodus
27 Blender setting
28 Pronounces poorly
30 Waikiki welcome
31 Lively wit
32 Chat room chuckle
33 Sailor's behind
34 Bill tack-on
35 Piety
39 It has headquarters at N.Y.C.'s Time Warner Center
41 Thurman of "Dangerous Liaisons"
42 Spa treatments
45 Make balanced
48 "The nerve!"
49 Benzoyl peroxide target
50 "Rats!"
54 Split up
55 Knock-down-drag-out
57 Corp. recruits, often
58 Continental currency
60 Move gently
61 Apollo astronaut Slayton
62 Campus e-mail suffix
63 Acapulco article
65 Supersecretive intelligence org.

by Nancy Salomon

ACROSS

1 Oodles
6 Wide as the ocean
10 Huffed and puffed
14 Seoul's land
15 Diva's song
16 Jacob's first wife
17 A magnet attracts it in a physics experiment
19 Between twice and never
20 Grand Coulee, e.g.
21 County seat NNW of Oklahoma City
22 Relieve
24 At a tilt
26 Praise
27 Tire filler
28 Divorces
32 Locale for a New York diva
35 What the number of birthday candles signifies
36 Olden times
37 Jinxes
38 Snooper's org.
39 Tomato-hitting-the-floor sound
40 Speed skater Heiden
41 Bamboozle
42 Sales pitches
43 Zilch
45 Carry the day
46 Crazy-sounding bird
47 Freighters' freights
51 One with a hook, line and sinker
54 Stuporous sleep
55 Doc's picture producer
56 Java neighbor
57 Star's marquee position
60 Genesis garden
61 Tall tale teller
62 Have a meal at home
63 Orange-flavored powdered drink
64 "Born Free" lioness
65 Medicinal amounts

DOWN

1 On the ___ (going to pot)
2 Deep pink
3 Enticing smell
4 TV room
5 Two-point plays in football
6 Legitimate
7 Parched
8 Envy or gluttony
9 Event before moving
10 Pre-transfusion procedure
11 Gave for a while
12 "To ___ his own"
13 Amusement park shout
18 Lifeless
23 "Yes, madame"
25 Some verbal abuse
26 Women's links org.
28 Paragon of virtue
29 One and only
30 ___ Mountains, Europe/Asia separator
31 Four-footed friends
32 Next
33 Medal winner for bravery
34 Escape route
38 Nickel or dime
39 Shot up, as inflation
41 Gleeful laugh
42 Hindu teacher
44 Misery
47 King ___ (dangerous snake)
48 Skips
49 Old TV comic Kovacs
50 Leo and Libra
51 Help illegally
52 Zilch
53 "Galveston" crooner Campbell
54 Inspectors of fin. books
58 "Black gold"
59 Neighbor of a Vietnamese

by Lynn Lempel

ACROSS

1 "Mamma Mia" group
5 Play chauffeur
10 Money to help one through a tight spot
14 Either of two directing brothers
15 All gone, as dinner
16 Mayberry boy
17 Daydreamer's state
20 Directional suffix
21 A choir may stand on it
22 Good thing
23 Sailor, colloquially
24 Digit in binary code
25 Joseph Conrad novella
34 Edward who wrote the play "The Goat, or Who Is Sylvia"
35 Pastor's flock
36 Rebellious Turner
37 Vintage autos
38 Kind of club that's a hint to this puzzle's theme
39 Prefix with lock or knock
40 ___-cone
41 Colonial settlement
42 Bobby Orr, notably
43 Vocational school instruction
46 Superannuated
47 Ring outcome, briefly
48 ___ pants (multipocketed wear)
51 Room plus, in a hotel
54 "Don't ___"
57 Common employment benefit
60 Cleveland's lake
61 Enlarge a house
62 Men-only
63 "The World of Suzie ___"
64 Sierra ___, Africa
65 Certain vanity plate for husband-and-wife cars

DOWN

1 Suffer from a charley horse
2 Transvaal trekker
3 Vanilla ___
4 "What else?"
5 "Meet the Fockers" co-star, 2004
6 Hamelin's problem
7 "___ Jury" (Spillane novel)
8 Zig or zag
9 S.A.S.E., e.g.
10 Relax, as rules
11 Berkeley Breathed comic strip
12 Lieutenant
13 Fit snugly
18 Really hot under the collar
19 Like Lincoln, in physique
23 Uno + dos
24 Straight: Prefix
25 Hard on the ears
26 "Maria ___" (Dorsey tune)
27 ___ to mankind
28 Taken wing
29 Intimidate
30 Station with a show
31 The blahs
32 Participated temporarily, as with a band
33 Police con
38 Victuals
39 Florence's river
41 Letter-shaped opening for a bolt
42 Harley rider
44 Links bend
45 Bring into harmony
48 Stick of gum, e.g.
49 Prefix with -postale
50 Common Seattle forecast
51 Slaw or fries, e.g.
52 Reverse, on a PC
53 "The shoe ___ the other foot"
54 A couple of chips, maybe
55 Injury reminder
56 Purchases for a shindig
58 ___ 9000, sci-fi computer
59 Bit of air pollution

by Adam G. Perl

ACROSS

1 Peeling knives
7 "See ya"
10 Katie Couric's network
13 Kansas city where Dwight Eisenhower grew up
15 Symbol of sturdiness
17 High hit behind the catcher, say
18 Do surgery (on)
19 End of a school Web address
20 Salves
22 "My life ___ open book"
23 Ward off
26 Safety item for a tightrope walker
27 Pep rally shout
28 Refused
30 Tallied up
33 Neurologist or orthopedist
36 Graceful swimmer
38 Nuptial agreement
39 Spotty
41 Tidy savings
43 Miss. neighbor
44 ___ of Man
46 Paths from here to there
47 Stretchy fabric
49 Self-assurance
51 Family
52 Vegetable that rolls
53 Looks to be
57 Treble's counterpart
59 Thorny parts of roses
61 III + IV
62 Miss terribly
64 Theory of the universe, or a hint to the starts of 17-Across and 7-, 10-, 35- and 40-Down
67 Scene at a natural history museum
68 Observed secretly
69 Summer hrs. in D.C.
70 One doing leg. work
71 Derisive looks

DOWN

1 Post or Trib
2 Residence
3 Shred
4 Aide to Santa
5 Old auto inits.
6 Rebuff
7 Prosperous place
8 Kennel cries
9 ___ out (barely make)
10 Extreme effort at weight loss
11 Alpha, ___, gamma . . .
12 Glimpsed
14 Twisty-horned antelope
16 Musical chord
21 Eye part
24 "Cómo ___ usted?"
25 Vientiane native
27 Abductors' demands
29 Eye part
31 Periphery
32 Lady and the Tramp, e.g.
33 Start a card game
34 Air France destination
35 Skilled marksman
37 Aviation-related prefix
40 Baloney
42 Inside of a paper towel roll
45 Sporting sword
48 One heeding the alarm clock
50 Symbols of meekness
54 Dodge
55 Petty
56 + and −
57 Ordered
58 Carbolic ___
59 A few
60 Nurses a drink
63 Lead-in to fetched or sighted
65 Card game with knocking
66 Spelling competition

by Lynn Lempel

ACROSS

1 Desktop folder, e.g.
5 John Candy's old comedy show
9 William of ___, known for his "razor"
14 Bay of Pigs locale
15 Rock's Mötley ___
16 He didn't give a damn
17 Fedora feature
18 Boot from office
19 Angora and merino
20 What you really saw?
23 Sonora snack
24 Pass by
28 What you really saw?
32 First secretary of homeland security
33 ___ Lingus
34 Quito's land: Abbr.
35 Co. that owns Parlophone records
36 Z's
40 Tolkien humanoid
41 Many want-ad offerings: Abbr.
43 Play for a sap
44 "I ___ amused!"
46 What you really saw?
50 "Super!"
51 N.R.A. part: Abbr.
52 What you thought you saw
58 Tiny hairs
61 "Scarface" star, 1932
62 Economy-___
63 Don't exist
64 Sidewalk stand drinks
65 Raison d'___
66 Sheriff's symbol
67 Abominable Snowman
68 Circus barker

DOWN

1 Minuteman, e.g.: Abbr.
2 Make perfect again
3 End piece?
4 "Hello" sticker
5 Burn with an iron
6 Defoe castaway
7 Keister
8 Challenge to Congress
9 Big Brother's creator
10 Bach work
11 Corp. V.I.P.
12 Turner Field locale: Abbr.
13 See 25-Down
21 Hall's singing partner
22 Pooped
25 With 13-Down, Pa. range
26 Grow sick of
27 Make into law
28 Part of a nun's habit
29 Blue-pencil wielder
30 Judge of sex and violence in films
31 Swarm member
32 Flinch, say
37 Peeved and showing it
38 Grp. helping those on shore leave
39 ___ hole in (corrodes)
42 Web recreation
45 Grade lowerers
47 Get wider
48 Refrigerator adornment
49 St. Francis's home
53 "If ___ be so bold . . ."
54 Pantyhose shade
55 Summon to court
56 Poet Pound
57 Fiddler's tune
58 It may have a medallion
59 Roth ___
60 Had charge of

by Malia Jackson and Noah Snyder

ACROSS
1 Bay State sch.
6 Juicy fruits
11 Target of many a boxing blow
14 Sophomore's grade
15 Old Testament prophet
16 "It's no ___!"
17 Good sign on a highway
19 Reverse of NNW
20 Dollar or Budget competitor
21 Like the season before Easter
23 Floated gently in the air
26 7 on a grandfather clock
28 Prefix with potent
29 Use a rasp on
30 Comment on, as in a margin
32 Expected
33 Org. for the humane treatment of pets
35 Bobby of the N.H.L.
36 Alcoholics Anonymous has 12 of them
39 Once around a track
40 Catnip and fennel
43 Safe box opener
44 White ___ (termites)
46 Cousin of a Keogh, briefly
47 Arizona's Petrified Forest dates from this period
50 Optimistic
53 Sups
54 "___ luck?"
55 Heavy hammer
56 Bear witness
58 Consequently
59 Fr. holy woman
60 Good sign on a candy box
66 Dark time, in poetry
67 Vice President Burr
68 Weights abroad, informally
69 Scores in the end zone, for short
70 Velocity
71 Appears

DOWN
1 Western tribe
2 "___ in Black," Will Smith film
3 &
4 Layers
5 Acted rudely while in a line, maybe
6 Academics' degrees
7 High's opposite
8 Grp. that entertains the troops
9 Magician in Arthurian legend
10 Hot Japanese drink
11 Good sign on a car trunk
12 Concurrence
13 Ineffectual one, slangily
18 Helpers
22 ___ Dame
23 Bankrolls
24 Be next to
25 Good sign on a lawn
26 Good sign at a motel
27 Not well-put
31 "That feels gooood!"
34 "Above the fruited ___"
37 Kind of porridge
38 The "S" in CBS: Abbr.
41 Boast
42 Fill the stomach of
45 Dish often served with 10-Down
47 Group of cups and saucers
48 Squealed (on)
49 Despotic ruler
51 Sets (down)
52 Nickname for Elizabeth
57 Places to be pampered
58 Manage, as a bar
61 Anger
62 Actress Caldwell
63 ___ de France
64 Suffix with official
65 Twisty curve

by Robert Dillman

24

ACROSS

1 Some charity fundraisers
6 Outspoken
11 Org. with a code
14 Singer Davis with the 1998 hit "32 Flavors"
15 Airplane seat choice
16 Old ___, London theater
17 Joie de vivre
19 Lab eggs
20 Accomplish
21 Star-related
23 Prank player
26 "South Park" kid
27 Preceder of Bell or shell
31 Speed-happy driver
33 Book in which the first Passover occurred
35 Castle protector
36 Middle-earth meanie
39 Teacher's charge
40 Paris's ___ Invalides
41 Colder and windier
43 "___ a Tramp" ("Lady and the Tramp" tune)
44 Singer Pinza
46 Popular setting for a wedding
47 Fantastically wonderful
50 Snare
51 Daughter of Czar Nicholas I or II
53 Arctic bird
55 Newswoman Katie
57 Diner sign filler
62 ___-la-la
63 Speaking manner
66 Go wrong
67 Proficient
68 O.K.
69 Newsman Koppel
70 Fix, as laces
71 This puzzle's theme

DOWN

1 ___ Strip (much-fought-over area)
2 British P.M. ___ Douglas-Home
3 Whip
4 Prefix with matter
5 Like wearing a seat belt, e.g.
6 Lombardy province or its capital
7 De-squeak
8 CBS forensic drama
9 "Our Gang" kid
10 Famous Virginia family
11 Lofty place for an academic
12 Pepsi vis-à-vis Coke
13 Symbol of justice
18 Racetracks
22 Bout decision
24 Didn't stay on
25 Kerfuffles
27 Part of M.I.T.: Abbr.
28 Highway toll unit
29 Its academy is in New London, Conn.
30 Some E.R. cases
32 ___ vez (again, in Spanish)
34 Preowned
37 Singer McEntire
38 Wheat, barley or beans
40 In ___ of
42 First drug approved to treat AIDS
45 90210, for Beverly Hills
46 Feeling of loss
48 Person obeying a coxswain
49 Significant
51 Four duos
52 Peter of "M"
54 Super stars
56 ___-Tass news agency
58 Court plea, informally
59 Tributary of the Colorado
60 Rent-___ (security person for hire)
61 Wraps (up)
64 Snare
65 Prefix with dermis

by Stella Daily and Bruce Venzke

ACROSS

1 Lascivious
5 Dopey or Doc
10 Say jokingly
14 Zone
15 More unusual
16 Great Salt Lake's state
17 Triumph, but just barely
19 Hawaiian island
20 Badminton court divider
21 Actor Ed of "Daniel Boone"
22 Declining in power
24 False fronts
27 God, to Muslims
28 Smug smiles
30 TV, slangily, with "the"
32 Legal wrong
33 Find a new purpose for
35 Org. with admirals
38 Fall off a beam, e.g.
42 Baseballer Mel
43 Ice cream holders
44 Fusses
45 Politico Gingrich
46 Marks that look like inverted v's
48 Pago Pago's locale
51 Less drunk
54 Graduates
56 Opposite of an intro, musically
57 Parisian yes
60 MasterCard rival
61 Momentarily forget (or get lucky in Scrabble?)
64 Barely earned, with "out"
65 Ship from the Mideast
66 Suffix meaning "little"
67 M&M's that were removed from 1976 to 1987 out of a health concern for a coloring dye
68 A ton
69 Command to a steed

DOWN

1 Home turf?
2 Shallowest Great Lake
3 Led off
4 Amount of hair cream
5 All soap operas, basically
6 Declined in power
7 Got up
8 Thing, in legal briefs
9 Unoccupied, as a theater seat
10 Popular newspaper puzzle subtitled "That Scrambled Word Game"
11 Online commerce
12 Finnish bath
13 Chicken piece
18 Talk idly
23 Biblical tower site
25 Comic Johnson
26 Cigar ends
28 Capital of Manche, France
29 No longer worth debating
31 "The Star-Spangled Banner" land
33 Leases
34 WNW's opposite
35 Sworn to tell the truth
36 Glaswegian, e.g.
37 Loch ___ monster
39 Atlantic or Pacific
40 At this moment
41 Swiss river
45 Wanderers
46 Trees whose wood is used for chests
47 United ___ Emirates
48 Lifeguard, at times
49 Similar
50 Meditated (on)
52 City between Gainesville and Orlando
53 Took a curtain call
55 Fox hit "American ___"
58 "Render therefore ___ Caesar . . ."
59 Scandinavian furniture giant
62 ___ de Janeiro
63 Actor Ayres

by Andrea Carla Michaels

ACROSS

1 Ooze
5 Neighbor of Kan.
9 Go after
14 Island dance
15 Do perfectly
16 Go online
17 Final notice?
18 Coastal flier
19 Take away little by little
20 Diana Ross musical, with "The"
21 They require signals
23 Neptune's domain
24 ___ carte
25 Number of operas composed by Beethoven
26 Play the slots, e.g.
28 Ohio university whose team is the Golden Flashes
34 Fancy flapjacks
37 Comstock ___
38 Touch with a hanky, say
39 Pro ___ (proportionately)
40 Slacks material
42 Facts and figures
43 Baseball bat wood
44 P P P, in Greek
45 Liechtenstein's language
47 Fibs
50 Stephen of "The Crying Game"
51 Beehive State native
52 Timeline division
54 Carpet fuzz
57 Publication that is the key to this puzzle's theme
62 Conk out
63 Tunesmith's org.
64 "That's a shame"
65 Exec's note
66 Peach pit

67 Treat with grandmotherly love, with "on"
68 Kitchen dial site
69 Sharpened
70 Proofer's mark
71 Takes as one's spouse

DOWN

1 Exhibits
2 Blake of jazz
3 1998 role for Cate Blanchett
4 Butter slice
5 N.B.A.'s Shaquille
6 Egyptian temple site
7 Airport delay?
8 Guinness of stage and screen
9 Make spotless
10 Big buzzer
11 Bug-eyed
12 Slaw, e.g.
13 Hydrocarbon suffixes
21 After the buzzer
22 "Oh, goody!"
27 Air quality grp.
29 Beethoven dedicatee
30 "Smoking or ___?"
31 Genesis duo
32 "Ciao!"
33 Israel's Abba
34 Sticking point?
35 Too hasty
36 Haul, slangily
41 ___ polloi

42 Rap's Dr. ___
44 Entered again
46 Part of Q.E.D.
48 New Orleans school
49 Hundred on the Hill
53 Bowling alley button
55 Pointed
56 Doers of drudgery
57 Track meet event
58 Regarding
59 Revered one
60 Little shavers
61 Jillions
65 Use a Lawn-Boy, e.g.

by Adam G. Perl

ACROSS

1 Baby's first word, in Italy
6 Commercials
9 Touches
14 Skip ___ (lose tempo)
15 Tennis do-over
16 Katmandu's land
17 ___ firma
18 Mai ___ (tropical drink)
19 "Yum!"
20 "Future Shock" author
23 Prefix with -lithic
24 Wetland
25 Antique restorer's efforts, for short
28 Late hunter of Nazi war criminals
34 Comedian Philips
35 Aria singer
36 Brewing coffee produces one
37 Designer Christian
39 Semesters
42 Muslim holy man
43 Shake hands (on)
45 Former senator Trent
47 ___ dye (chemical coloring)
48 "Sister Carrie" author
52 Airport schedule abbr.
53 The 1919 Treaty of Versailles concluded it: Abbr.
54 Directional suffix
55 Singing group suggested by the starts of 20-, 28- and 48-Across
61 Dragon Ball Z game company
64 ___ Solo of "Star Wars"
65 Actress Papas or Ryan
66 Thesaurus author
67 Superlative suffix
68 Girlish laugh
69 Bullwinkle, for one
70 Letter between pi and sigma
71 Actress Falco and namesakes

DOWN

1 ___ Hari
2 Brother of Cain and Seth
3 "___ Griffin's Crosswords"
4 Dolphins QB Dan
5 Finished
6 Choir voice
7 Like most users of sign language
8 Cadavers, slangily
9 Insect or radio part
10 Yogi, for one
11 FedEx competitor
12 Tit for ___
13 Crafty
21 Namely
22 Former auto executive Iacocca
25 Clarence of the Supreme Court
26 Kind of class for expectant mothers
27 Noisy shouting
28 Anesthetize, say
29 "Put me down as a maybe"
30 Tied down, as a boat
31 "___ changed my mind"
32 Country rocker Steve
33 Prefix with lateral
38 Old Olds car
40 "The ___ Squad" of '60s–'70s TV
41 Throat problem
44 First American to walk in space
46 Orkin target
49 Be in the red
50 Wealthier
51 Accustomed
55 ___ chic
56 Corned beef concoction
57 Absorbed by
58 Soda pop brand
59 Thigh/shin connector
60 Understands
61 Slot machine part
62 Excessively
63 In the past

by Michael Blake

28

ACROSS

1 Prominent feature of Dracula
6 Reunion group
11 Showman Ziegfeld
14 "Let's Make ___"
15 Search engine name
16 Designer Claiborne
17 It may end up in the gutter
19 In the style of
20 ___ acid (protein component)
21 Schindler of "Schindler's List"
23 Spy's device
26 Sweater style
29 Runs out
32 Slave girl of opera
33 Exploding stars
34 Fuel economy org.
35 City in Italia
39 What 17-, 26-, 50- and 60-Across have in common
43 Pageant accessory
44 Tony Soprano and cohorts, with "the"
45 Cheese hunk
46 One on a pedestal
48 Old timer?
50 Classic breakfast fare
54 Suffix with butyl
55 Reporting to
56 How-to presentations
59 ___ glance
60 Item on a set
66 Fix illegally
67 Disney mermaid
68 Sees red
69 Informal top
70 Center of power
71 Some retired racehorses

DOWN

1 Wonderful, slangily
2 Fuss
3 Partner of improved
4 Big bash
5 ___ to none (long odds)
6 Stellar swan
7 Part of a repair estimate
8 "Got it!"
9 Showman Hurok
10 Went at it alone
11 Cereal morsel
12 Purple hue
13 Country/rock's ___ Mountain Daredevils
18 Nick at ___
22 Tangled, as hair
23 Big tops
24 Lei Day greeting
25 Blacktops, say
27 Surveillance evidence
28 Fact fudger
30 Common union demand
31 Part of a min.
34 Flow back
36 Nostalgic tune
37 Mullally of "Will & Grace"
38 Fred Astaire's sister
40 Bow-toting god
41 Certain plea, for short
42 On one's ___
47 Skin-related
48 Makes hard
49 "Semper Fi" org.
50 Milk purchase
51 Loosen, in a way
52 Bit of wisdom
53 Parting word
57 Klutzy sorts
58 Dirty reading
61 "___ y plata"
62 Trader ___ (old restaurateur)
63 Rhea relative
64 Like Republican states on an electoral map
65 Braying beast

by C. W. Stewart and J. K. Hummel

ACROSS

1 "___ upon a time . . ."
5 Like a score of 10 out of 10
10 Speedy
14 "Star Wars" princess
15 Dated yet trendy
16 Knowing of
17 "See you again!"
20 Longtime CBS and NBC newsman Roger
21 Touchdown destination
22 Blacktops
25 Tricky curves
27 Bud's partner in comedy
28 Had dinner
29 ___ B'rith
30 Coarse file
31 "Veni, vidi, vici" speaker
34 The "R" of NPR
37 "See you again!"
41 Henry Blake's rank on "M*A*S*H": Abbr.
42 Many IM recipients
44 Letterhead design
47 "___ Green" (Kermit the Frog song)
49 Snooze
50 In the style of
51 Mah-jongg pieces
53 Domineering
55 The dole
57 Chief Norse deity
59 "See you again!"
64 Suffix with sock
65 Ship-related
66 Lawman Wyatt
67 Former Cub ___ Sandberg
68 Entrap
69 Where "you can do whatever you feel," in a hit 1978 song

DOWN

1 Outdated
2 Recent: Prefix
3 The Reds, on scoreboards
4 Words on a Wonderland cake
5 Steamed
6 Muffle, as a sound
7 U.F.O. fliers
8 Kind of well
9 Michaels of "Saturday Night Live"
10 "Happy Days" cool cat, with "the"
11 Country north of Namibia
12 Dictation takers
13 Shredded
18 Greyhound vehicle
19 TV spots
22 Grp. funding 19-Down in campaigns
23 Just slightly
24 Swerve
26 "Nobody doesn't like" her, in a slogan
29 ___-a-brac
30 Stir up
32 Lindbergh's classic flight, e.g.
33 Fitting
35 Actress Cannon
36 "How was ___ know?"
38 Duke or earl
39 Restroom door word
40 Chapters in history
43 Austin Powers, e.g.
44 Perry Mason, e.g.
45 Clinton cabinet member Hazel
46 Gasoline unit
48 Weather map line
51 Tic-___-toe
52 Cattle branding tools
53 Lighter and pen maker
54 Perfectly pitched
56 A polar bear might be found on one
58 Valley
60 Actress Mendes
61 '60s conflict site
62 Tolkien creature
63 F.D.R. initiative

by Dave and Tracy Mackey

ACROSS

1 Ashen
5 Decorative molding
9 Yellow shade
14 Gen. Robt. ___
15 "Look both ways before crossing," e.g.
16 Lax
17 In front of a hydrant, say
20 Notice for late ticket-buyers, maybe
21 "Waking ___ Devine" (1998 film)
22 Ignited
23 "Uh-oh"
27 Cool, to a cat
30 They might be near I.C.U.'s
31 Hair removal product
32 Tic-tac-toe loser
33 Atlanta university
36 Fran of "The Nanny"
38 School lady
39 Things hidden in 17-, 23-, 49- and 57-Across
41 Pawn
42 Loch Ness monster, e.g.
44 Dictatorial
45 Umberto who wrote "The Name of the Rose"
46 1998 song by the Goo Goo Dolls that was #1 for 18 weeks
47 Part of m.p.g.
48 Aurora's Greek counterpart
49 Publicists
54 Nafta signatory
55 Opposite of post-
56 Only Super Bowl won by the New York Jets
57 Business sessions that drag
63 Seed-to-be
64 Israel's Abba
65 French seas
66 Mythological reveler
67 Hair line
68 Zebras, to lions

DOWN

1 "Taste that beats the others cold" sloganeer, once
2 Morning waker-upper
3 "Vive ___!"
4 "Horrors!"
5 Directives
6 Father ___ Sarducci, longtime "S.N.L." character
7 Pipe joint
8 Epitome of slipperiness
9 Home of the Casbah
10 Castle defense
11 Ex-hoopster Manute ___
12 Course for a recent émigré: Abbr.
13 King in un palacio
18 Contestant's mail-in
19 The Oscars of magazine publishing
24 ___ Jean (Marilyn Monroe, affectionately)
25 Disrobe
26 Zinger
27 Ding Dongs competitor
28 Board members, for short
29 Looney Tunes pig
33 Maker of introductions
34 ___ Polo
35 Snacks dipped in milk
37 Dusting or taking out the garbage
39 "Yippee!"
40 Lake ___, outlet of the Maumee River
43 Racetrack tout
44 Father
47 Father, e.g.
50 Stab
51 Forty-___
52 Un gato grande
53 Girlish boy
54 Hard on the eyes
57 ___ Lobos
58 TV's Longoria
59 Kook
60 Opposite of "naw"
61 Wall St. hire
62 Little troublemaker

by Peter A. Collins

ACROSS

1 Black-bordered news item
5 Anne of "Wag the Dog"
10 Dull-colored
14 Internet connection at a restaurant or airport
15 Fanfare
16 Seized vehicle
17 Snoop
19 Height: Prefix
20 Steak that a dog might end up with
21 "Huckleberry Finn" author
22 Wet mascara worry
25 Felix and Oscar, with "the"
28 Bathroom powder
30 Wyatt of the Wild West
31 Magazine V.I.P.'s
32 1980s video game with a maze
35 Down, usually, on a light switch
38 Carouse
42 Golf peg
43 Boxed stringed instrument
44 "___ solemnly swear . . ."
45 Ax or awl
47 Judicial assertion
49 Symbol of purity
54 Figure of speech
55 Wall art
56 Mutual of ___
58 "Gotcha," to a beatnik
59 Want ad heading . . . or a hint to the starts of 17-, 25-, 38- and 49-Across
64 Queue
65 More than steamed
66 March Madness org.
67 Brain readings, for short
68 Parceled (out)
69 Safecracker

DOWN

1 To have and to hold
2 Life story, for short
3 Conditions
4 Men's fashion accessory
5 Submarine sandwich
6 Commercial prefix with Lodge
7 Informed, with "in"
8 ___ Solo of "Star Wars"
9 Flight board info: Abbr.
10 Use, as past experience
11 CliffsNotes version
12 "___ Love," 1957 #1 hit by 13-Down
13 Singer Pat
18 Brusque
21 The Blue Jays, on a scoreboard
22 Rung
23 Furious with
24 Pitcher of milk?
26 John Donne's "___ Be Not Proud"
27 Went by dugout
29 Passover bread
33 Spicy dish that may have a fire-alarm rating
34 Encountered
36 ___-Lay (snack company)
37 At the end of one's patience
39 Take-home pay
40 Squirm
41 Capitol's top
46 Bird that hoots
48 Crevice
49 Photographer's request
50 Peep show flick
51 Circular gasket
52 Go ___ for (support in time of need)
53 Overact
57 Copied
59 Huck's raftmate
60 Metal from a mine
61 Sno-cone filler
62 Re-re-re-remind
63 Respond to a really bad joke, maybe

by Ken Bessette

ACROSS

1 Olympics prize
6 "Zounds!"
10 "In your dreams!"
14 Vega of "Spy Kids" movies
15 Marilyn Monroe facial mark
16 It may be tempted
17 Reminisce about a nice facial outline?
20 "I'll take that as ___"
21 Cartoon villain Badenov
22 Gangsters' gals
23 Ambassador's forte
25 Nada
26 Sidney Poitier title role
27 Reminisce about spring cleaning?
33 "Daggers" look
35 Rap sheet letters
36 Trifling amount
37 Common breakfast fare
40 Tense subject?
43 Brit. record label
44 Catchword of 6-Down
46 Wise up
47 Reminisce about working in a restaurant?
52 Pool tool
53 Messenger ___
54 Starch-yielding palm
57 Santa ___, California city, county or river
60 Not spoken
62 Buddhist sect
63 Reminisce about a pig-out?
66 Census data
67 Jungle menaces
68 Minister's home
69 Physiques, informally
70 Cathedral area
71 Like dessert wines

DOWN

1 Corday's victim
2 Actress Verdugo
3 Like a blue state
4 Give the boot
5 Mild-mannered type
6 Lagasse of cooking shows
7 Big bully
8 "The Sound of Music" setting
9 "___ Rosenkavalier"
10 Be able to meet the expense of
11 Go yachting
12 "___ be a cold day in hell . . ."
13 Honoraria
18 U2 frontman
19 Skip
24 Time in a seat
26 Mark permanently
28 Middling grade
29 Heart chart, for short
30 People rival
31 Wing it?
32 Roll of the dice, maybe
33 Attendee
34 Poor, as an excuse
38 Having the resources
39 Postgraduate study
41 Boxer Laila
42 Department store department
45 Salsa percussion
48 Unlike this answer
49 Waikiki wingding
50 As a precaution
51 Follow, as a suspect
55 Honkers
56 Get-go
57 Kvetching sort
58 Toy block brand
59 Got 100 on
60 'Vette roof option
61 Parts of a drum kit
64 Home for Bulls, but not Bears: Abbr.
65 Like a new recruit

by Deb Amlen

ACROSS

1 Bounce to the surface
6 Botch
10 Sports equipment
14 Belittle
15 Least bit
16 Present opener?
17 Free health and dental care, and then some
20 List of test answers
21 Aviates
22 Limerick or sonnet
23 Luke's twin sister in "Star Wars"
24 Price ___ pound
25 Math symbol for extraction of a root
30 Pilot's stat.
33 Warnings
34 Entree in a bowl with beef or lamb, say
36 Pelvic bones
37 Boat propeller
38 Clark's crush on "Smallville"
39 "Hey, come back a bit"
42 Enter en masse
44 Where pigs wallow
45 In limbo
47 Wood-shaping tool
48 Nays' opposites
49 Flair
52 Peppermint ___ of "Peanuts"
54 Sombrero, e.g.
57 Eyeglass option for different distances
60 Early state in the presidential campaign
61 Reclined
62 Major artery
63 The Big Board: Abbr.
64 Doe's mate
65 Winona of "Girl, Interrupted"

DOWN

1 Pitcher's faux pitch
2 New York theater award
3 One often needing a change
4 Take advantage of
5 "Couldn't be better!"
6 Pertaining to a son or daughter
7 Ear or leaf part
8 Four Corners-area Indians
9 Prohibition
10 Errand runner
11 Dubai dignitary
12 Six-legged scurriers
13 Move skyward
18 Fake identity
19 Occurrence
23 Bygone Italian coins
24 Tour grp.?
25 Monsoon occurrences
26 Apportion
27 God or goddess
28 Brainy
29 Suffix with bombard
30 Trailblazing video game maker
31 His tomb is in Red Square
32 Banjo sound
35 Hits hard
37 Lummox
40 Like 16 vis-à-vis 15, agewise
41 Turk's topper
42 Home viewing for a price
43 Subscription period, often
46 Loathing
47 Aquatic plant life
49 Pirouette
50 "Iliad" setting
51 Cries after being burned
52 H.S. junior's exam
53 Where most of Russia is
54 Group of buffalo
55 Prefix with chamber
56 Ruler before 31-Down
58 Ernie of the 24-Down
59 Silver screen star Myrna

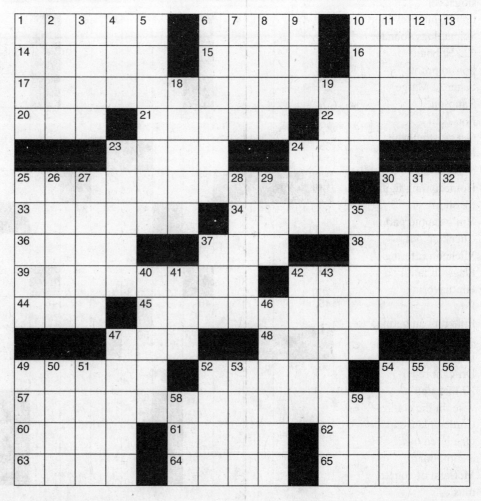

by Lynn Lempel

34

ACROSS
1 Puppies' plaints
5 Cobb of "12 Angry Men"
9 Icy look
14 Oratorio highlight
15 Di or da preceder in a Beatles song
16 Moves like sludge
17 "What ___ Did" (classic children's book with a punny title)
18 ___ Spee (old German warship)
19 Catcher's position
20 Enjoying an outing, of sorts
23 "Gets the red out" sloganeer
24 Italian auto, for short
25 Scientology founder ___ Hubbard
28 For no profit
32 Sister of Marge Simpson
36 Forsaken
38 Get ___ the habit
39 Enjoying an outing, of sorts
42 Homecoming figure, for short
43 Yin's counterpart
44 Checking out
45 Michelin offering
47 Flagston family pet
49 Gin flavoring
51 Edit
56 Enjoying an outing, of sorts
61 Like wild tigers
62 Drought relief
63 Hi Flagston's wife, in the comics
64 Garden plant support
65 One hired by a corp. board
66 McCann of country music
67 Cheated, slangily
68 One of "The Addams Family," informally
69 Comrade in arms

DOWN
1 Comic Smirnoff
2 Tehran denizen
3 Actress ZaSu
4 Greet cordially
5 Paul Bunyan, e.g.
6 River of Spain
7 Mideast airline
8 Port of Israel
9 Treat leniently, with "on"
10 Talkativeness
11 France's Côte d'___
12 Actor Stephen and kin
13 Renaissance family name
21 China's Zhou ___
22 Trolley sound
26 Gymnast Korbut
27 Ad infinitum
29 "The ___ Love" (R.E.M. hit)
30 British W.W. II-era gun
31 Chinatown gang
32 Exchange jabs
33 Former Connecticut governor Grasso
34 Speak well of
35 "I can't blame anyone else"
37 Latvia's capital
40 Fishing line material
41 Georg who wrote "The Philosophy of Right"
46 Trued up
48 Twist badly
50 Everglades wader
52 Home overlooking the sea, maybe
53 How some tuna is packed
54 Dexterity
55 Lamb or Bacon piece
56 ___ browns (diner fare)
57 Analogy part
58 Havana aunts
59 Kind of stand
60 Doesn't dally

by Victor Fleming

ACROSS

1 Boston orchestra
5 Seaboard
10 30 minutes, in the N.F.L.
14 Once more
15 God of the Koran
16 Mixed bag
17 X-rated dance
19 Miniature plateau
20 Top secret?
21 "Thar ___ blows!"
22 Something to cram for
23 Banjo picker Scruggs
25 Org. that publishes American Hunter
27 Some Caribbean music
30 Beach find
36 Referred to
39 ___ Speedwagon (1970s–'80s band)
40 Rotgut
41 "___ of Two Cities"
42 Fabergé collectible
43 Acquire, as a debt
44 ___ badge, boy scout's award
45 Dover's state: Abbr.
46 ___ jacket, 1960s fashion
47 Initial power source
50 One of a D.C. 100
51 401(k) alternative, for short
52 Oodles
55 Object of the actions suggested by the starts of 17-, 30-, 47- and 66-Across
58 "You've ___ Mail"
61 Lose all one's money in gambling
65 Thomas Edison's middle name
66 Pinto
68 Plane assignment
69 Ryan of "The Beverly Hillbillies"
70 Julia Roberts's role in "Ocean's Eleven"
71 Golfer's target
72 Krupp Works city
73 Alphabetize, e.g.

DOWN

1 It might be checkered
2 Not fooled by
3 Llama country
4 Slide, as a credit card through a reader
5 Supplies, as food for a party
6 Cheer for El Cordobés
7 "Ah, me!"
8 Part of a girl scout's uniform
9 Finis
10 1990 Macaulay Culkin film
11 The "A" in A-Rod
12 Kudrow of "Friends"
13 Cappuccino head
18 ___ brain (nitwit)
24 "Streets of ___" (classic cowboy song)
26 Bird that comes "bob, bob, bobbin' "
27 Little rascal
28 Ben Franklin, famously, in an electrical storm
29 Arcade game maker
31 Israeli desert
32 Sharp turn on a golf course
33 Sources of Scottish streams
34 Sky-blue
35 Twice-seen TV show
37 Competitor of "The 5th Wheel," in reality TV
38 Scare off
48 Chatterbox
49 Spoiled
53 Scrooge's cry
54 Dalmatian markings
55 Launder
56 Margarine
57 White House office shape
59 Crew's control?
60 Deadlocks
62 Cookie with a creme center
63 Stalingrad's land, for short
64 The "T" of S.A.T.
67 U-turn from SSW

by Randall J. Hartman

36

ACROSS

1 Its eye may be part of a witch's brew
5 Daddy-o
9 Sleep soundly?
14 Popular cornstarch brand
15 "___ my word!"
16 Prenatal sites
17 Low-fat, as beef
18 Not on time
19 Business on the Internet
20 Polishing machines at an Ithaca campus?
23 CPR giver
24 Opposite of throw away
25 Geometry symbols
28 Recipient of "G'day"
31 Puts into effect
35 Trustee group at an Atlanta campus?
38 Peel
39 Musical closings
40 Old Michael Jackson 'do
41 Zellweger of "Chicago"
42 In a bit
43 Thoroughfare at a New Orleans campus?
45 Broadway Joe
47 Flip out
48 U.F.O. crew
49 Fishing float
51 Swiffer, e.g.
53 Rental arrangement at a Milwaukee campus?
60 Letters that must be bought on "Wheel of Fortune"
61 Versifier
62 Kind of hygiene
63 Analyze in English class
64 Mental flash
65 Lice-to-be
66 Cross over?
67 Dance's partner
68 Let (up)

DOWN

1 Face powder ingredient
2 Lunchbox goody
3 Food thickener
4 John who wrote "Love built on beauty, soon as beauty, dies"
5 Can opener
6 October gem
7 What Texas hold'em tables hold
8 Take furtively
9 Volvo's home
10 Stationer's supply
11 Sharif of "Funny Girl"
12 Baseball stat
13 Night school subj.
21 Outstanding Comedy Series awards
22 Addiction
25 Pie nut
26 "___ roll!"
27 Sin city
29 Vegetarian's protein source
30 ___ Court (London tube station)
32 Paddled vessel
33 One of two choices on Halloween
34 Tournament favorites
36 Discovered by accident
37 A horse of a different color?
41 Towed items, sometimes
43 No ___ traffic
44 Conventioneer's wear
46 Close-fitting hats
50 French military hats
52 Nokia offering
53 Repast
54 Suffix with billion
55 Fuss
56 Adolescent
57 Melody for Dame Nellie Melba
58 Piper's followers
59 Ultimatum's ultimate word
60 N.Y.P.D. alert

by Sarah Keller

ACROSS

1 ___ Antoinette
6 Tallies
10 Series of scenes
13 Actress Blake or Plummer
15 Not having a stitch on
16 Letter before sigma
17 Lump in the throat
18 "Calm down!"
20 Neighbor of Scot.
21 Dabbling duck
23 Years and years and years
24 "Move!"
29 One-named Art Deco master
30 Stephen of "The Crying Game"
31 Bear in constellation names
34 Cap or helmet
39 "Pay attention!"
43 Cared for a home while the owner was away
44 Pink wine
45 Hang back
46 Sail support
49 "Lookie there!"
56 Like many a wiseacre's comment: Abbr.
57 Part of F.Y.I.
58 Lots of laughs
60 "Oh, be serious!"
64 Car model with a musical name
66 Metalliferous rock
67 Done with
68 Passes, as a law
69 Auction motion
70 Farewells
71 "Savvy?"

DOWN

1 Crew member
2 Honor ___ thieves
3 Poconos or Tetons
4 Write-___ (some votes)
5 Manuscript receiver
6 White, in Mexico
7 Owing
8 Banned insecticide
9 Caribbean, e.g.
10 "This way" sign
11 Dishes for fancy meals
12 ___-turvy
14 Native seal hunter
19 "Golly!"
22 Breakfasted, e.g.
25 Parts of an udder
26 Stew
27 Go like mad
28 "If I ___ hammer . . ."
31 "Yuck!"
32 Rock's ___ Speedwagon
33 Sutcliffe of the early Beatles
34 F.D.R. successor
35 Middle measurement
36 It may be puffed up
37 Sighs of contentment
38 Letter carrier's assignment: Abbr.
40 Hades
41 Golfer ___ Aoki
42 Heroic legend
46 Call to a calf
47 Blow ___ (become enraged)
48 Brawny
49 Not be able to swallow
50 When to celebrate el año nuevo
51 Schlepped
52 "Gimme ___!" (frequent Alabama cheerleader's cry)
53 Color specialists
54 "It's ___" ("There's no doubt")
55 ___-frutti
59 Cartoonist Thomas
61 High tennis shot
62 Some Christmas greenery
63 Doctor's quote
65 Scottish refusal

by C. W. Stewart

38

ACROSS

1 It's full of holes and traps
5 Gastric juices, e.g.
10 Remnant of a tattoo removal, maybe
14 Zone
15 Herb popular in Indian food
16 Staff note
17 Glam rocker's accessory
19 Jessica of "Fantastic Four" films
20 The "F" in the equation "F=ma"
21 Pat on the back, as a baby
22 Sleigh
23 Get up
25 Loathes
27 Usurer's victim
30 Throat condition
31 Parisian streets
32 Tiptop
35 Drained of color
38 "What ___ the odds?"
39 Dumps (on)
41 Guitarist's guitar
42 Succeed in life
44 It fills barrels
45 Freshly
46 Make believe
48 Espy
50 Like trees on a prairie
52 Hooch
54 "Mr. ___ risin'" (classic Doors lyric)
55 One always on the lookout for a deal
57 Hotel room posting
61 Wife of Osiris
62 Director's cry . . . or a statement about 17-Across and 11- and 29-Down
64 Longtime Yugoslav chief
65 Flood preventer
66 Surrounding glow
67 List ender
68 Play to the back of the audience
69 Longings

DOWN

1 Sailor's hook
2 Nabisco cookie
3 King who was the father of Cordelia
4 Moneybags types
5 Starting pitcher
6 Places to park
7 Saturate
8 New Look designer
9 Answer in anger
10 Overhead shots
11 Transparent packaging material
12 Color meaning "caution" on 13-Down
13 See 12-Down
18 Guitar ___ (hit video game series)
24 Oil-rich land
26 They're uplifting
27 Bummer
28 Money since 2002
29 Taco alternative
30 Coal bed
33 Extended family
34 Stereotypical tattoo
36 Company V.I.P.
37 Former speaker Gingrich
39 "Exodus" author
40 Long-gone bird
43 Kind of can
45 Eroded
47 Like caresses
49 Writer Pound
50 Beat, biblically
51 Take as a given
52 "Wonderful!"
53 Wedding band, maybe
56 Polite way to interrupt someone
58 Loyal
59 Pull in
60 Watering holes
63 "Get it?"

by Kevin Donovan

ACROSS

1 Stars and Stripes, e.g.
5 Places where lines meet
9 French greeting
14 ___ of Sandwich
15 Cause of a game cancellation
16 Unaccompanied
17 "Here he is now!"
20 Black card
21 Talks one's head off
22 French summer
23 Twinings selections
26 Sign before Virgo
27 Big Apple ave.
28 Be undecided
33 ___ Wednesday
34 Suds maker
35 Mounted, as a horse
38 Talking maybe a little too fast
40 Snapshot
43 Sgt. Snorkel's dog
44 Fable writer
46 No. on which a magazine's ad rates are based
48 Freudian one
49 Persist to completion
53 Prefix with center
55 Column's counterpart
56 Interstate entrance or exit
57 Fish after which a cape is named
58 Logic diagram
60 Long Island airfield town
64 Command center? . . . or where you might hear the starts of 17-, 28- and 49-Across
68 Nephew of Donald Duck
69 For whom the bell tolls, in a John Donne meditation
70 Numerical prefix with -ber
71 Bygone Montreal ball club
72 Quiet exercise
73 Remove from the freezer

DOWN

1 Admit (to), with "up"
2 Reindeer herder
3 Geometry calculation
4 "My pleasure"
5 Black power hairdo, for short
6 Dunderpate
7 The "C" in N.Y.C.
8 Divided 50-50
9 Dirge
10 Schooner fill
11 Billet-doux
12 Join
13 Old message system
18 Wails
19 Dueling sword
24 Perched on
25 Deposed Iranian
28 "Roots," for one
29 ___ of Wight
30 Message on a shipping crate
31 Geologic time unit
32 Pigeon's sound
36 Big elevator manufacturer
37 ___ too soon
39 Droid
41 Wedding cake feature
42 Killer whale
45 Republican, Democratic, Green, etc.
47 "Luann" or "Blondie"
50 Knight time?
51 A score
52 End result
53 French place of learning
54 Mail receiver, in brief
59 Repeat
61 ___ Ness monster
62 Itsy-bitsy bit
63 Winter truck attachment
65 God, in Italy
66 Brain scan, for short
67 Bounding main

by Ken Bessette

ACROSS

1 Where to tie the knot
6 "Bearded" bloom
10 Captain Hook's henchman
14 Exotic jelly flavor
15 "___ a deal!"
16 Boston suburb
17 Is pessimistic
20 Waterborne youth group member
21 "I agree completely"
22 Follows orders
24 Ballpark worker
25 Stuffed mouse, maybe
29 Diving bird
31 Intergalactic traveler
32 ___ shui
34 Hellenic H's
38 Is optimistic
41 Eliot of the Untouchables
42 Taj Mahal site
43 Hobby knife brand
44 Bearded grazer
45 Springing bounce in tall grasses, as by an animal, to view the surroundings
46 Garbage
50 A dwarf planet, now
53 Makes use of
55 Binging
60 Is apathetic
62 March plaything
63 "Hurry!"
64 Frolics
65 Sapphic verses
66 Attack, as with eggs
67 Attack with rocks

DOWN

1 Dark ___
2 Elegance
3 Bite-size appetizer
4 Forum greetings
5 Masked scavengers
6 One Time?
7 Like a bad dirt road
8 "___ bin ein Berliner"

9 Tom Jones's "___ a Lady"
10 Job openings
11 Gift of the Magi
12 Come after
13 Key in
18 Shakespeare's Sir ___ Belch
19 Captain Queeg's creator
23 Year-end temp
25 "Love and Marriage" lyricist Sammy
26 Natural emollient
27 A lot of a car valet's income
28 Buttonless shirts, informally
30 "Disgusting!"
32 Get all steamy

33 Flub
34 24/7 auction site
35 PC whiz
36 Regarding
37 Halt
39 "Go, team!" screamer
40 Whistle-blowers
44 Neuter, as a horse
45 Walk of Fame embedment
46 Screwy
47 Steer clear of
48 Cook in a wok, maybe
49 Scrabble pieces
51 Opposite of express
52 Not suitable
54 Start of a play to the quarterback
56 Storyline

57 San ___, Italy
58 Nascar airer
59 In ___ (actually)
61 China's Lao-___

by Eugene W. Sard

ACROSS

1 "I saw ___ sawing wood . . ." (old tongue twister)
5 Lawn base
8 Finally
14 Outlaws
15 "I won! I won!," e.g.
16 Amp toter
17 What President Washington said upon winning the lottery?
19 Professor's goal
20 "I've got a mule, her name is ___"
21 Once around the sun
22 Hidden valley
23 What flagmaker Ross said . . . ?
28 Colonial Franklin, familiarly
29 Cheer to a matador
30 Just watched
33 What Miss Molly said . . . ?
39 End in ___ (draw)
40 In a huff
41 Captain who said "Eat your pudding, Mr. Land"
42 What Galileo said . . . ?
44 "I can't ___ satisfaction" (Rolling Stones lyric)
45 "___ shocked . . . SHOCKED!"
46 Collide
47 What the Big Bad Wolf said . . . ?
55 Figure skater's jump
56 Rocklike
57 Clamor
59 Overhaul
62 What Noah Webster said . . . ?
64 Aftershock
65 Shepherd's locale
66 Nylons
67 High-school honey
68 Directional suffix
69 Ready for business

DOWN

1 Flows out
2 Request at a medical exam
3 Viewpoint
4 Put to good ___
5 Porch protector
6 "Rock of Ages" accompaniment
7 Hair colorers
8 Picasso output
9 Little piggy
10 Actress Jessica
11 Rated NC-17, e.g.
12 Fathers
13 Wee
18 Hand-wringer's words
24 Monk's home
25 Traffic noises
26 Merrie ___ England
27 Command to Rover
30 ___ Miguel, largest island of the Azores
31 Part of N.C.A.A.: Abbr.
32 Actor Robbins
33 Commercial prefix with phone
34 Row
35 "You're ___ talk!"
36 Rent out
37 Trio after K
38 "___-hoo!"
40 Slanted type: Abbr.
43 Sis or bro
44 Lightheaded
46 Novelist Melville
47 Witches' blemishes
48 Put forth, as effort
49 Flood stopper
50 Transporter across the Andes
51 Not cut up
52 HBO's "Real Time With Bill ___"
53 Lottery winner's yell
54 Convalescent home employee
58 Biblical place of innocence
60 Hip, in the '60s
61 Delve (into)
63 "Sez ___?"

by C. W. Stewart

42

ACROSS

1 MacDowell of "Groundhog Day"
6 #41 or #43
10 These may be coddled
14 Nickel and dime
15 Home to most Turks
16 Maul or awl
17 Providential
19 Mr. Peanut prop
20 Vogue competitor
21 Not 'neath
22 Walked like a tosspot
24 Disco ___ of "The Simpsons"
26 Conclude one's argument
27 Nary a penny
33 Gymgoer's pride
34 Portfolio contents
35 Carrot or radish
37 Ending with bed or farm
39 Mai ___
40 Cass and Michelle, in '60s pop
41 Does something
42 Like cows, to Hindus
44 Hieroglyphics serpent
45 In close pursuit
48 Double reed
49 One of two in "boxcars"
50 Never-before-seen
53 Be in hock
55 Follow closely
59 Pope from 440 to 461
60 Adds up . . . like this puzzle's theme?
63 "We try harder" company
64 Up to the task
65 Bracelet site
66 Thought before blowing out the candles
67 Tide type
68 Significant ___

DOWN

1 Ibuprofen target
2 Coward of the theater
3 "Don't touch that ___!"
4 Play the market
5 Suffix with Brooklyn
6 When stolen, it stays in place
7 Tech caller
8 Covet thy neighbor's wife, say
9 Dislikes, plus
10 "Yadda, yadda, yadda"
11 Slap shot success
12 Auctioneer's last word
13 Iditarod entry
18 Some are proper
23 Upper-left key
25 Wart cause, in folklore
26 Hit the hay
27 Gunslinger's mark
28 "___ a Nightingale"
29 Everything that's left
30 Get to
31 "___ is an island"
32 Done for, slangily
33 Org. with dens
36 Cough medicine amt.
38 Really wow
40 Early 17th-century year
42 One with a carrot nose, maybe
43 Tricky turns
46 U.K. honour
47 Full range
50 What "there oughta be"
51 Strauss of jeans
52 Cohort of Clark
53 State with a panhandle: Abbr.
54 Show grief
56 Hieroglyphics cross
57 Archipelago unit
58 Sly glance
61 "Honest" prez
62 ___ Paulo

by David Pringle

ACROSS

1 Ooze
5 La ___, Milan opera house
10 One-spot cards
14 "Not guilty," e.g.
15 Jeopardy
16 Phileas ___, who went around the world in 80 days
17 Like 39-Across's fans on his induction day?
19 Plenty
20 Uses a stool
21 Spy Mata ___
23 Warmongers
26 H.S. junior's exam
28 Old horse
31 Away from the wind
32 Layers
34 Letter before omega
35 "___ Bitsy Spider"
36 Waved one's arms at, as a cab
37 Place to wager on the 28-Acrosses: Abbr.
38 Goes bad, as fruit
39 Notable Army inductee of 3/24/58
40 Military no-show
41 Part of a gearwheel
42 Flexible
43 Land of Lima and llamas
44 French "a"
45 Makes very happy
46 Balletic bend
47 ___ and feather
48 Simplicity
49 Legendary Chicago Bears coach George
50 Singer ___ Anthony
52 One who makes a good first impression?
54 Derrière
56 Last movie 39-Across made before his Army stint
62 Dunce cap, geometrically
63 1975–78 U.S. Open champ Chris
64 Finger's end
65 Novelist Seton

66 Artist who liked to paint dancers
67 Hard journey

DOWN

1 Place to refresh oneself
2 Building wing
3 Wriggly swimmer
4 Openers for all doors
5 Good name for a Dalmatian
6 Corporate V.I.P.'s
7 Noah's ___
8 "Ally McBeal" actress Lucy
9 Some computer software checks
10 Light years away
11 Army officer who met 39-Across in 25-Down
12 Self-esteem
13 Last Army rank of 39-Across: Abbr.
18 What the "H" of H.M.S. may be
22 Not too much
23 Much-photographed event after 39-Across's induction
24 City with a Penn State campus
25 Where 39-Across was stationed overseas
26 First Army rank of 39-Across
27 Like seawater
29 Waldorf-___ Hotel
30 First movie 39-Across made after his Army stint
32 Defeated soundly
33 Actresses Shire and Balsam
40 Clear to all
42 Word before group or pressure
49 What the "H" of H.M.S. may be
51 Neighborhood
52 Indian tourist city
53 Police hdqrs.
54 Record label of 39-Across
55 Long, long time
57 "___ had it!"
58 Photo image, briefly
59 Rowboat mover
60 Made-up story
61 Antlered animal

by David J. Kahn

44

ACROSS

1 Philosophies
5 Former Fiesta Bowl site
10 Tortilla sandwich
14 Bring in from the fields
15 ___ squash
16 Breezy greeting
17 Gallic girlfriend
18 Blasé group of directors?
20 5, 7, 9, etc., for juniors' dresses
22 Dallas-to-Des Moines dir.
23 Change
24 TV, radio, newspapers, etc.
26 Double or triple, say
28 Tourmaline, e.g.
29 Read quickly
31 Smokestack emission
32 Mormon State
34 "Pomp and Circumstance" composer
36 Traditional paintings
40 Spend an afternoon in a hammock, e.g.
41 Musical beat
42 Exam for a future atty.
43 It can get under your skin
44 Under way
45 "Lohengrin" lass
46 Slowing, in mus.
48 Get ___ arms
50 Head lines?
51 Helmets and such
55 Exclude
57 Notwithstanding the fact that, briefly
58 Messenger material
60 Kickback
62 Lovely hotel accommodations?
65 Addict
66 Eye drop
67 "Li'l" one in the comics
68 Refinery waste
69 Abbr. on a business sign
70 It may go off on you
71 Partners of haws

DOWN

1 Bank offerings, for short
2 Arsenic or antimony
3 Farm-grown labyrinth?
4 Methamphetamine
5 "Running" amount
6 Business subj.
7 Wake at dawn?
8 Primp
9 Player next to a tackle
10 Pit in its entirety?
11 Lasso
12 Lew who played Dr. Kildare
13 Mexican father
19 Where spirits run freely?
21 "___ boom bah!"
25 Film material
27 Kind of artery
28 Waters south of the South, e.g.
30 Hebrew leader?
33 Mooing group of cattle?
35 Each
37 Key passage?
38 Light in a light show
39 Unaccompanied
47 "___ Rhythm"
49 It's south of S.D.
51 Swiftness
52 Actor Cary of "Twister"
53 Bothered a lot
54 Caribbean vacation spot
56 Dentist's advice
59 Fit to ___
61 Pieces of work?
63 Schnook
64 Fumble

by Steve Salmon

ACROSS

1 Sea creature that sidles
5 Group of eight musicians
10 Underhanded plan
14 Greeting in Granada
15 Get up
16 Toy block brand
17 Andy's partner in old radio
18 *Sci-fi barrier
20 *Newspaper article lead-in
22 Quenched
23 Big name in audio equipment
24 Martial artist Jackie
25 Result of a belly flop
28 *When the curtain goes up
32 Quiet spells
33 Bed board
34 Turf
35 Kind of history
36 Word that can precede each half of the answers to each of the eight starred clues
37 Performed ballads, e.g.
38 President pro ___
39 Go after bucks or ducks, say
40 Outpouring
41 *Wrestling move that puts an arm around someone's neck
44 Less bold
45 Slick
46 Corduroy ridge
47 Measly
50 *Secret communication location
54 *Mars Pathfinder, for one
56 Rouse from slumber
57 Regarding
58 Western flick, in old lingo
59 Farm measure
60 Abound (with)
61 One of a reporter's five W's
62 Annum

DOWN

1 Punched-out part of a paper ballot
2 Capital of Italia
3 Plenty
4 *Diamond game
5 Like a lout
6 Hag
7 Become bushed
8 PC bailout key
9 Golfer's opening drive
10 Flexible
11 Cousin of an onion
12 Gawk at
13 Sondheim's "Sweeney ___"
19 Scratch on a diamond, e.g.
21 Amount printed in red ink
24 Nautical map
25 Slow-moving mammal
26 Blender setting
27 South American wool source
28 Move with one's tail between one's legs
29 Actor and rockabilly crooner Chris
30 Three-card hustle
31 Yard worker's tool
33 Impertinent
37 *Indy 500 venue
39 "Yikes!"
40 Hawk, as wares
42 Business that may have gone boom and then bust in the '90s
43 Pre-euro money in 2-Down
44 ___ d'
46 Eucharist disk
47 H.S. junior's exam
48 Cathedral recess
49 Tardy
50 Corner, as a king
51 10K or marathon
52 Gumbo ingredient
53 House of Lords member
55 Pep squad shout

by Jeff Armstrong

ACROSS

1 Dress shirt closer
5 Four times a day, on an Rx
8 Person who doesn't put down roots
13 Had on
14 Acapulco article
15 State as one's view
16 Nitwit's swoon?
18 Nonsense, slangily
19 Torah holders
20 New York tribe defeated by the Iroquois
21 Exterior
22 Cartoon Chihuahua
23 On the house
24 Respect
25 Kind of eyes
27 Force (open)
28 Turn one way and then back
29 "A Tale ___ Cities"
30 Uncompromising sort
33 Regret some stupidity . . . with a hint to this puzzle's theme
37 Girls in the family
38 Watergate hearings chairman Sam
40 Univ. where "Good Will Hunting" is set
43 Suffix with neat or beat
44 ___ Conventions
45 Shabbily clothed
47 Rock star, e.g.
49 Speed (up)
50 Vinegar: Prefix
51 Pre-remote channel changer
52 R.E.M.'s "It's the End of the World ___ Know It"
53 Danger in dangerous waters
54 Spring in the air?
56 News groups
57 "Tastes great!"
58 "___ do for now"
59 Analyze the composition of
60 N.B.A. tiebreakers
61 Like some orders

DOWN

1 Promised to give up
2 Was attentive
3 Internet addresses
4 "Excellent!," in slang
5 Paper quantity
6 Type of 39-Down
7 Movie companion, maybe
8 Vibes not being picked up by anyone?
9 Painkiller since ancient times
10 "Uncle" of early television
11 Rages
12 Some tractors
16 Red River city
17 Houston hockey player
23 Doing credible work as a magician?
24 Mozart's "Madamina," e.g.
26 Verdon of "Damn Yankees"
27 Top exec.
30 Miner's tool
31 Hawaiian instrument, for short
32 Pulled apart
34 Gifts at Honolulu Airport
35 Push too hard, as an argument
36 Have it good
39 Belly part
40 Bad atmosphere
41 "
42 Steps (on)
44 Asian desert
46 Places in the heart
47 Contribution, as of ideas
48 Buildings near some cafeterias
51 Bout-ending slug
52 Mennen shaving brand
55 Shining

by Manny Nosowsky

ACROSS

1 See 48-Down
5 Stick in one's ___
9 Frank of the Mothers of Invention
14 Not loco
15 "___ and the King of Siam"
16 Decorate
17 Bess Truman or Barbara Bush
19 Snooped, with "about"
20 "You're ___ talk!"
21 Enclosure with a MS.
23 NNW's opposite
24 Hi-___ monitor
25 Question after the fact
29 Car bomb?
31 Old letter salutation
32 "God's Little ___" (Erskine Caldwell best seller)
34 Competitor of Dove or Camay
36 Prop for Picasso
40 Takes care of all possibilities
44 Pan-cooked brunch treat
45 Words after ". . . as long as you both shall live?"
46 "Mona ___"
47 Make the cut?
50 Funny DeGeneres
52 Grilling
56 "Shame on you!"
59 Crew's control?
60 One who indulges too much in the grape
61 French city famous for its mustard
63 Garbo of "Mata Hari," 1932
65 1990 Macaulay Culkin film
68 Ed of "Lou Grant"
69 The "U" in B.T.U.
70 Compete in the America's Cup
71 Bookcase part
72 Model Banks
73 Med school subj.

DOWN

1 In regard to
2 Where Bangor is
3 Put aside for later
4 Place for eggs
5 Iron Man Ripken of the Orioles
6 Genetic letters
7 ___ forth (et cetera)
8 Brother comic Shawn or Marlon
9 "Riders of the Purple Sage" author
10 Hullabaloo
11 Star's entourage
12 ". . . or ___ 9 for more options"
13 Peruvian peaks
18 Play with, as a Frisbee
22 Star Wars program, for short
26 Morays, e.g.
27 Hint
28 Fit to be tried?
30 More profound
32 U.N.C.'s athletic org.
33 Where streets intersect: Abbr.
35 "Sweet" age in ancient Rome?
37 Play by George Bernard Shaw
38 Superman's symbol
39 Meadow
41 Relatively low-temperature star
42 German river in a 1943 R.A.F. raid
43 Part to play
48 With 1-Across, infamous Ugandan dictator
49 Opposite of "At ease!"
51 Mother of Castor and Pollux
52 "Animal House" party costumes
53 Like winters in the Arctic
54 Ballroom dancer Castle
55 Foolish person, slangily
57 Braga of "Kiss of the Spider Woman"
58 Prepared to pray
62 She requested "As Time Goes By"
64 ___ Aviv
66 Bygone Russian space station
67 When a plane is due in: Abbr.

by Randall J. Hartman

48

ACROSS

1 Kaplan of "Welcome Back, Kotter"
5 Tally
10 Émile who wrote "Truth is on the march"
14 Is in hock
15 More than sore
16 Leave out
17 Ronald Reagan movie
20 Think tank products
21 Indy 500 inits.
22 Cuban boy in 2000 news
23 As a result
25 Chat room shorthand for "Here's what I think"
27 "Rule, Britannia" composer
30 Doris Day movie, with "The"
35 ___ Paulo, Brazil
36 Era-spanning story
37 Greg of "My Two Dads"
38 Honda with a palindromic name
40 Gradual decline
42 Cause of some food poisoning
43 2001 title role for Audrey Tautou
45 Wren or hen
47 ___ Irvin, longtime cartoonist for The New Yorker
48 Rock Hudson movie
50 Not fem.
51 Deuce beater
52 Bonkers
54 "___ is human"
57 Sandy island
59 Football's Fighting ___
63 Barbara Eden TV series
66 ___ St. Vincent Millay
67 Old newspaper sections
68 Touch-and-go
69 Support staffer: Abbr.
70 Map detail
71 Have-___ (lower economic group)

DOWN

1 Mongolian expanse
2 Impressed and then some
3 "Venerable" monk
4 Bequeathed property
5 Colgate competitor
6 Equestrian competition
7 Bonkers
8 A world without 71-Across
9 According to
10 Of the animal kingdom
11 First Dodge with front-wheel drive
12 Minnelli of "Arthur"
13 Like ___ of bricks
18 Suffix with bull or bear
19 Didn't act up
24 Work ___ lather
26 Flaubert's Bovary, e.g.: Abbr.
27 B.M.I. rival
28 "Spider-Man" director Sam
29 It's no short story
31 ___ the Hutt of "Star Wars"
32 Ancient meeting place
33 Maxim's target audience
34 Pioneering 1940s computer
36 Annabella of "The Sopranos"
39 "It's on me!"
41 Subject of a 1976 film "ode"
44 Stand-in for "you" in "Concentration"
46 "Flying Down to Rio" studio
49 Captain of industry
50 Informal greeting at a breakfast shop
53 Grp. known as the Company
54 "___ yellow ribbon . . ."
55 Bookie's quote
56 Coastal raptors
58 P.M. periods
60 Dope
61 Sort (through)
62 Attention getters
64 Hosp. procedure
65 Ballpark fig.

by Dave Mackey

ACROSS

1 Vampire's tooth
5 Playing marble
10 At any time
14 πr^2, for a circle
15 Engine
16 Lucy Lawless TV role
17 From ___ (completely)
18 Cheri formerly of "S.N.L."
19 Persia, today
20 Bidding impediment?
23 "Ooh, tasty!"
26 Enter
27 Streisand film about a Jewish girl masquerading as a boy
28 How sardines may be packed
30 Suffix with vocal
32 Enzyme suffix
33 Outdoor meal deterrent?
38 Gas brand with the slogan "Put a tiger in your tank"
39 Book after Daniel
40 Show ___ (attend, as a meeting)
44 Truth obstruction?
47 ___ Francisco
50 Inc., abroad
51 Lawn care brand
52 Garbage
54 Tipplers
57 The second "S" in MS-DOS: Abbr.
58 Metallic element's obstacle?
62 Small plateau
63 Singer Bryant
64 January to December
68 Humdinger
69 Odometer units
70 Nautilus captain
71 Chair or pew
72 Happening
73 Photo often taken after an accident

DOWN

1 Air safety org.
2 Murals and such
3 Opposite of paleo-
4 Mideast's ___ Strip
5 BP gas brand
6 Crime boss known as the Teflon Don
7 Had dinner at home
8 Bullring bull
9 "___ go bragh!"
10 Napoleon, on Elba or St. Helena
11 "The Two Gentlemen of ___"
12 Passes, as a law
13 Annoy
21 Aptly named tropical fruit
22 Computer memory unit
23 "Eek!"
24 Les États-___
25 Beaded shoes, informally
29 "Are you ___ out?"
30 "___ a man with seven wives"
31 Neuter
34 Casual conversation
35 Wrestling move
36 "___ live and breathe!"
37 German industrial valley
41 No ___ allowed (sign)
42 Hurting all over
43 Some boxing results
45 Grades 1 to 12, briefly
46 Mozart's "___ Fan Tutte"
47 Actor John of "Full House"
48 Dahl or Francis
49 Pregnancy symptom, frequently
53 Brainy
54 Photographer's request
55 Frequently
56 "Here's mud in your eye!," e.g.
59 Partner of rank and serial number
60 Prof's place: Abbr.
61 Wildcat
65 Suffix with musket
66 Doc's org.
67 Dodgers catcher Campanella

by Christina Houlihan Kelly

ACROSS

1 Like a cold fish
6 Final Four games
11 Item in a bucket
14 Lash ___ of old westerns
15 Bring shame to
16 Greeting at the Forum
17 *Myopic cartoon fellow
19 Drink from a snifter, e.g.
20 Garbage hauler
21 Rowlands of "Gloria"
22 Charlie of the Stones
24 Film terrier
26 Victoria Falls river
28 Fess up to
31 Boots, gloves, mask, etc.
33 Took off excess pounds
35 ___ huff
36 One way to run
39 Muesli morsel
40 Kind of exam, with a hint to the answers to the four starred clues
43 U2's home: Abbr.
44 Inuit's transport
46 Born, in France
47 Former Disney chief Michael
49 Home of the Scarlet Knights
52 Dangerous gas
53 Soft, colorful candy
55 "___ Flux" (Charlize Theron film)
57 Clear the blackboard
58 ___ de vie (brandies)
60 What icicles do
64 Japanese band
65 *Popular tune around Halloween
68 June honoree
69 "Golden" tune
70 Gave a beating to
71 U.S.N.A. grad: Abbr.
72 Chills out
73 Start-up costs, of sorts

DOWN

1 Beggar's cry
2 Not of the clergy
3 Approximately
4 Be more patient than
5 Agent's take
6 Just like
7 Israel's Abba
8 16 or Seventeen
9 Prefix with bar
10 "Prove it!"
11 *Plan hatcher
12 Former Disney chief Michael
13 Soda selection
18 Mil. unit
23 Simple rhyme scheme
25 ___ cell research
27 On top of things
28 Big deals
29 Call up
30 *Some ticket issuers
32 Passer of bad checks
34 Dog from Down Under
37 Treat that's sometimes dunked
38 "Show Boat" composer
41 Diving board locales
42 Muralist Joan
45 Clothes, informally
48 Sleep inducer of song
50 Richter scale blip
51 Pan-fries
53 Crystal-lined rock
54 Word before blight or sprawl
56 Program file extension
59 "___ stands . . ."
61 Angry outburst
62 "It makes sense to me"
63 Advanced degs.
66 Soccer stadium shout
67 ___ Dome (Colts' longtime home)

by Ken Bessette

ACROSS

1 Do some fall farmwork
5 Servings of corn
9 Windshield material
14 Auto shaft
15 Ladder rung
16 Actor Murphy of old westerns
17 Twelvemonth
18 Symbol of a new start
20 Low-growing tree found typically in rocky soil
22 Joined by treaty
23 Tax org.
24 Actress Longoria
25 Byways: Abbr.
26 Dangerous cargo
30 Does the butterfly, e.g.
32 Fugard's "A Lesson From ___"
33 It indicates the seconds on a clock face
37 Aussie jumpers
38 Three squares, e.g.
39 ___ Lackawanna (bygone railroad)
40 Small whirlwind
42 Carpenter's tool
43 "As You Like It" forest
44 Ransacked and robbed
45 Seer's gift, briefly
48 It's about 78% nitrogen
49 Butterfly catcher
50 Hasty glance
52 Stock transaction done at a loss for tax purposes
57 Old radio part
59 "Stronger than dirt" sloganeer
60 Commerce on the Web
61 Out of harbor
62 Visitors to baby Jesus
63 Drug-yielding shrub
64 "Hey!"
65 Once, long ago

DOWN

1 Sunbeams
2 Prez or veep
3 Banned spray on apple trees
4 Lima's land
5 Debutante's date
6 Book of maps
7 Smell horrible
8 Fat farm
9 Old-fashioned light
10 Pause
11 Red who fought oil well fires
12 Put in place
13 Does some spring farmwork
19 Forces at sea
21 Favoritism or discrimination
24 Actor Tom of "The Girl Can't Help It"
26 Difficult
27 Baseball's Felipe or Jesus
28 Places with exotic animals
29 Legendary Washington hostess Perle ___
30 Lover
31 Bookcase part
33 Cut apart
34 Asia's ___ Sea
35 Three's opposite on a clock face
36 Land owner's document
38 Steak order
41 Bram Stoker novel
42 Central part
44 Usher again
45 Roof's edge
46 Sudden outpouring
47 Pie nut
49 Local theaters, in slang
51 Go to rack and ___
52 Pantywaist
53 Unchanged
54 Not quite closed
55 Doesn't keep up
56 Number on an Interstate sign
58 Faucet

by Janet R. Bender

ACROSS

1 What a gal has that a gent doesn't?
6 Elephant of children's literature
11 Church perch
14 Correspondence sans stamp
15 Muscat resident
16 Mystifying Mr. Geller
17 Fishing trawler's haul?
19 Opposite of max.
20 Board of directors hiree
21 ___ Plaines, Ill.
22 Needed fixing, as a faucet
24 Suffix with east or west
25 Lukas of "Witness"
27 QB boo-boos: Abbr.
28 Seat of government's acquisitions?
32 Family cars
35 Whichever
36 1910s–'20s car inits.
37 Upturned, as a crate
38 Gallery display
39 Parade entry
41 Yeoman's agreement
42 Caesar of comedy
43 Big Easy team
44 Publisher's windfall?
48 Terra firma
49 Money maker
50 Celestial altar
53 Getting slick during winter
56 Funny Charlotte
57 Business owner's dreaded ink color
58 Jazz instrument
59 Salary for selling insects as food?
62 Big galoot
63 "Snowy" bird
64 Ryder rival
65 "That's a go"
66 Fakes out with fancy footwork
67 By itself

DOWN

1 Therefore
2 Mideast pooh-bah
3 Betray, in a way
4 Gambler's cube
5 Campaigner's greeting
6 Dwarf tree
7 Parisian pal
8 Wedding reception staple
9 How curses are exchanged
10 On the upswing
11 Works out with weights
12 Lake next to Avon Lake
13 Kiting necessity
18 Harvests
23 Sch. monitor
26 "American Idol" quest
28 Pink-slip
29 Industrious insect
30 Spiffy
31 Elbow-benders
32 "General Hospital," for one
33 New Age superstar
34 Throws in the trash
38 Run on TV
39 Add some meat to the bones
40 Fleur-de-___
42 Go off a diet big-time
43 Mount of the Ten Commandments
45 Forever and a day
46 Manipulated, as an election
47 Many Guinness listings
50 Loud, as a crowd
51 Twin of Romulus
52 Fred's dancing sister
53 "Look here, old chap!"
54 Part of Batman's ensemble
55 "The other white meat"
60 "Didn't I tell you?"
61 ___ Guevara

by Nancy Salomon

Note: 17- and 64-Across and 11- and 34-Down each conceals an article of clothing.

ACROSS

1 "Miss America" might be printed on one
5 Mafia bosses
10 "Ali ___ and the Forty Thieves"
14 Painterish
15 Japanese cartoons
16 Grandson of Adam
17 Boardinghouse sign
19 Perched on
20 Together
21 Canceled
22 Goes out in a game of rummy
23 Katmandu resident
25 Snarled mess
27 Old-time actress Turner
29 "Chill!"
32 Many conundrums have them
35 Sneak peek: Var.
39 Suffix with human or organ
40 Pitcher's stat
41 Making out . . . or a hint to this puzzle's four hidden articles of clothing
42 4:00 drink
43 Pages that aren't editorial matter
44 Open, as an envelope
45 Pod contents
46 Perfectly clear
48 Some creepy-crawlies
50 Vinegary
54 Slave
58 The "C" in T.L.C.
60 Openly declare
62 Eskimo home
63 ___ Romeo (car)
64 Halifax's home
66 Male-only
67 El ___, Spanish artist
68 Cooking fat
69 Sharpen, as skills
70 Church council
71 God of war

DOWN

1 Brand of kitchen wrap
2 Lifted off the launch pad, e.g.
3 Not stand completely erect
4 Church songbooks
5 Purrer
6 Soon, to poets
7 Stove light
8 Letter after phi, chi, psi
9 Not vacillating about
10 Snoopy, for one
11 Favoring common folk
12 Great benefit
13 Nile reptiles
18 Emmy-winning Ward
24 Permanently, as writing

26 Tour de France winner LeMond
28 Rainbow shapes
30 Between ports
31 Lennon/Ono's "Happy ___ (War Is Over)"
32 Sound of laughter
33 Language of Lahore
34 Daytona 500 enthusiast
36 ___ out a living
37 Lab bottle
38 Not yet burning
41 Michelangelo's David, e.g.
45 Shaded passageway
47 Time of advancing glaciers
49 À la mode
51 Zesty flavors

52 Old piano key material
53 Witches' group
55 Place to exchange "I do's"
56 Valley known for its chateaux
57 Laundry units
58 Bills and coins
59 Saxophone type
61 Texas city on the Brazos
65 Old prairie home material

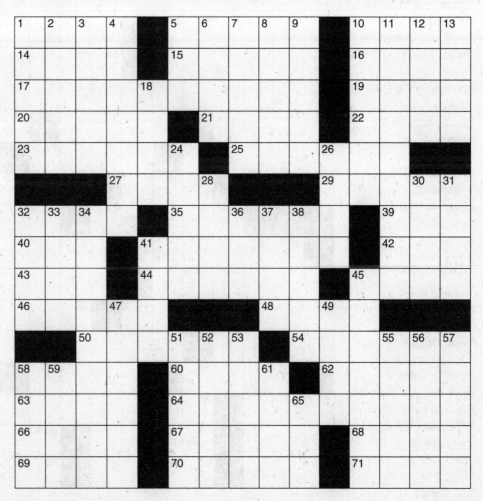

by Gary Disch

ACROSS

1 No stranger to the slopes
7 Bun
11 Sporty auto, for short
14 Tried one's hand (at)
15 Mongolia's home
16 Cigarette's end
17 Semiautobiographical Bob Fosse film
19 Tai ___ (meditative martial art)
20 "Saturday Night Live" bit
21 Schnoz
22 Creature from the forest moon of Endor
24 Country singer Tucker
26 Blacken on the barbecue
28 Laid up
30 "Brokeback Mountain" director Lee
31 "Well, ___-di-dah!"
33 "Lord of the Rings" studio
35 River along the Quai d'Orsay
37 Highlander's textile pattern
38 A.L. M.V.P. in 2003, 2005 and 2007
41 Trumpeted
42 Things to whistle
43 New Jersey's ___ Air Force Base
45 Bogey beater
46 Certain NCO
49 "Getting close"
50 Arizona birthplace of César Chávez
52 More cunning
54 It's a piece of work
56 Decisive defeat
58 Book after II Chronicles
59 Part of a coffee service
60 1970s joint U.S./Soviet space project
63 Sharp turn
64 Ilk
65 "___ Bells"
66 Suffix with modern
67 Former mates
68 Followed orders

DOWN

1 Daisy developed by Luther Burbank
2 Brand name in dog food
3 In neutral
4 Loco
5 "Yecch!"
6 Ancient land along the Dead Sea
7 Eastern prince
8 Resident of Japan's "second city"
9 Claiborne of fashion
10 Loll
11 Supporter of the House of Stuart
12 Namesake of a branch of Judaism
13 4, on a keypad
18 Modern dance music originating in Detroit
23 The Beatles' "I Am the ___"
25 Only son of Czar Nicholas II
27 Eye part
29 Cub's place
32 Hang on the line
34 Exactas and trifectas
35 Blood fluids
36 Summer hrs. along the Atlantic
38 The Rock
39 Georgia city or college
40 Drag performer with a wax likeness in New York's Madame Tussauds
41 Audi competitor
44 It was divided by the Iron Curtain
46 Alignment of the sun, earth and moon, e.g.
47 Punishing rod
48 Loco
51 Lawn diggers
53 Spaghetti western director Sergio
55 Actress Winslet
57 Hitler : Germany :: ___ : Japan
59 Gun in an action film
61 Eucharist vessel
62 Sis or bro

by Will Nediger

ACROSS

1 Meat featured in a Monty Python musical title
5 Alternatives to PCs
9 Popeye's creator E. C. ___
14 "Look what I did!"
15 "There oughta be ___!"
16 Singer Cara
17 Difficult burden
18 Many a stadium cover
19 Exxon competitor
20 Tourism bureau's offering
23 The matador's opponent
24 Totally cool, in '90s slang
25 Photo ___ (White House events)
28 It's swung at Wimbledon
32 J.F.K.'s successor
35 Ooze
36 1983 Barbra Streisand title role
37 Notes in a poker pot
39 It makes bread rise
42 Old-time wisdom
43 Kind of patch for a rabbit
45 Ark builder
47 Try to win, in romance
48 Pesky wasp
52 Communication means for the deaf: Abbr.
53 Cry when a light bulb goes on
54 Clears an Etch A Sketch, e.g.
58 It helps determine how much tax you owe the I.R.S.
62 Team leader
64 Venus de ___
65 Actress Spelling
66 Airs, in Latin
67 Suffix with switch
68 "The devil ___ the details"
69 King with a golden touch
70 Amount owed
71 Guitarist Atkins

DOWN

1 Vermont ski town
2 Group of experts
3 Like blue movies
4 Yale's bulldog, e.g.
5 Small amount of cash saved for an emergency
6 ___ vera
7 Pitch tents for the night
8 Says on a stack of Bibles
9 Time off from work with pay
10 Cleveland's lake
11 Become acquainted with
12 Lee who directed "Crouching Tiger, Hidden Dragon"
13 ___ Speedwagon
21 Miners' finds
22 Mercury or Saturn, but not Venus
26 Oil industry prefix
27 Canonized fifth-century pope
29 Born: Fr.
30 Classic toothpaste brand
31 Animation frame
32 Muammar el-Qaddafi's land
33 Makes yawn
34 Noted performing arts school
38 "My gal" of song
40 Party to the left of Dem.
41 Become established
44 Targets of Raid
46 Queen on Mount Olympus
49 A question of identity
50 Blocked, as radio broadcasts
51 Bit of strategy
55 Smidgen
56 Like "The Twilight Zone" music
57 Tour of duty
59 Univ. sports org.
60 Country whose name is an anagram of 10-Down
61 Unidentifiable mass
62 Film device, for short
63 Yves's yes

by Stella Daily and Bruce Venzke

ACROSS

1 Mag. sales info
5 Cat calls
10 Dutch cheese
14 Baseball's Matty or Felipe
15 First string
16 Danish-based toy company
17 Special Operations group
19 And
20 Makings of a hero, perhaps
21 Food giant that owns Ball Park Franks and Hillshire Farm
23 Domain
26 Tabula ___
27 Part of M.O.
30 Way back when
32 Welsh breed
35 Universal donor blood type, for short
36 Not susceptible
38 German article
39 Kilmer of film
40 Dr. ___ formerly of Death Row Records
41 Tiny amount
42 Coast Guard officer below Lt.
43 "Richard ___"
44 Busybodies
46 "Hey there!"
47 War correspondent Pyle
49 Asian holiday
50 Nun, in Nanterre
51 N.F.L. periods: Abbr.
53 "The Wolf in Sheep's Clothing" author
55 Takes to the police station
58 New Jersey college until 1995
62 Biblical brother
63 Highly pleasing
66 Impart
67 Brooke's longtime rival on "All My Children"

68 "Rule, Britannia" composer
69 "Beetle Bailey" dog
70 Capital suggested by the circled letters and by the starts of 17- and 63-Across and 11- and 29-Down
71 Fails to keep

DOWN

1 Scoundrels
2 Intestinal parts
3 Sushi bar offering
4 Dance
5 Capo's organization
6 Ike's W.W. II arena
7 Done, to Donne

8 1954 war comedy "Francis Joins the ___"
9 Dirty political tactic
10 Rio Grande city
11 TV angel portrayer
12 Fit of shivering
13 Jazzman Allison
18 University town near Des Moines
22 Ran
24 "Alas, poor Yorick!," e.g.
25 RKO competitor
27 Picture
28 Studio sign
29 Overdue
31 Beat in a Nathan's hot dog contest, e.g.
33 Supersharp knife
34 Violin or cello: Abbr.

36 Fury
37 "Illmatic" rapper
40 Batik artists, e.g.
45 1773 jetsam in Boston Harbor
46 Britney Spears, for one
48 "That's enough, I guess . . ."
50 Year before jr.
52 Allied
54 Cuban export
55 Heavenly circle
56 Help in mischief
57 Stout's Wolfe
59 Bushy do
60 Fontanne's stage partner
61 Publican's stock
64 Tyler of "Stealing Beauty"
65 Swelling reducer

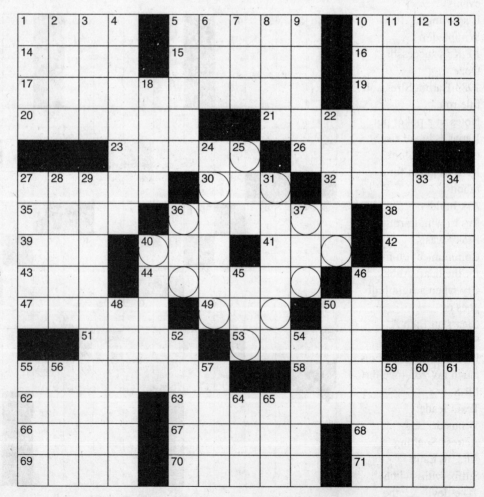

by Gary J. Whitehead

ACROSS

1 Exiled Ugandan Idi ___
5 Home of the N.F.L.'s Buccaneers
10 Nile reptiles
14 "This ___ be!"
15 Criminal's "a k a" name
16 Post-Christmas store event
17 Anglican body
19 "Wheel of Fortune" action
20 Former Roxy Music member Brian
21 Point a gun
22 Hornswoggled
23 Discover
25 Oration
28 Question when you can't tell two things apart
32 Number of Little Pigs
35 Egg layers
36 Kanga's kid in "Winnie-the-Pooh"
37 Shot in the arm
38 Duracell size
39 Like a score of 10 of a possible 10
41 Attys.' org.
42 Baseball glove
43 Not just mean
44 Jewish high holy day
48 Top secret?
49 The "I" of Canada's P.E.I.
53 Shady spot
55 Excellent service?
56 Whisper sweet nothings
57 Profound
58 Youth groups . . . with a hint to 17-, 28- and 44-Across
62 Autobahn auto
63 Chili con ___
64 Suit to ___
65 Seat for two or more
66 Has a bawl
67 Salon applications

DOWN

1 Needed a chiropractor, say
2 The Pine Tree State
3 Gold brick
4 To the ___ degree
5 South Seas getaway
6 Homecoming attendee, for short
7 Old space station
8 ___-10 Conference
9 Louisville Slugger wood
10 Per se
11 September birthstones
12 Ballet bend
13 E-mail command
18 Sign of prestige
22 Morning moisture
24 Flock females
25 Put away, as a sword
26 Something beaten at a party in Mexico
27 Letter before tee
29 ___ longue
30 Jacket
31 Fit to be a saint
32 Skiers' lift
33 Tramp
34 Entree carved by a chef
39 "I'll be right there!"
40 Roald who wrote "James and the Giant Peach"
42 Treasure seeker's aid
45 Fanfare
46 "Ben-___"
47 Specialized markets
50 Less than 90°
51 Prestigious prize awarded every December
52 Prescribed amounts
53 Commotions
54 Seized vehicle
55 "Rule, Britannia" composer
58 Agcy. that can fine TV stations
59 Crew's control?
60 Geller with a psychic act
61 Fall behind

by Randall J. Hartman

58

ACROSS

1 Perfect
6 Farm sound
9 Highly excited
13 Wispy clouds
14 Ash containers
16 Let go
17 Singers Clint + Patti
19 Couple in the news
20 Ache reliever
21 They may be sown
23 Fr. holy woman
24 It's jumped in a high jump
26 As high as you can possibly go
29 Pulitzer-winning biographer Leon
32 Singers Tom + Johnny
35 Where Kofi Annan earned his master's deg.
37 Says lovingly
38 Copacabana Beach locale
39 Classic film company . . . or a description of 17-, 32-, 46- and 65-Across?
43 Pharmaceutical watchdog grp.
44 Show subtitled "The American Tribal Love-Rock Musical"
45 "___ my shorts!": Bart Simpson
46 Singers Neil + Courtney
49 D.E.A. agent
52 "___ Deep" (1999 Omar Epps film)
53 Suffix with Caesar
55 Yale student
57 Midwestern tribe
60 Perched
63 Like Yul Brynner, famously
65 Singers James + Sly
67 Blue, in Bogotá
68 ___ Lee cakes
69 Poet Federico García ___
70 Prominent part of a Groucho disguise
71 "Wailing" instrument
72 Vows

DOWN

1 Cold war weaponry
2 Widen, as a pupil
3 Got rid of marks
4 Paths of pop-ups
5 Simile part
6 Accused's bad break
7 Uris hero
8 "Farm" dwellers
9 Vinegary
10 1960s sitcom with the catchphrase "Sorry about that, Chief"
11 Uplifting poem
12 Cameo, e.g.
15 Any ship
18 40-Down, e.g.
22 Heavenly
25 Cut again, as a turkey
27 Mother goddess in Egyptian mythology
28 Howe'er
30 British record label
31 John of "3rd Rock From the Sun"
33 Rocky hill
34 Bag with handles
36 Bluish hue
39 Tempura ___ (Japanese dish)
40 Vessel in "Twenty Thousand Leagues Under the Sea"
41 God, to Galileo
42 Where to board a train: Abbr.
43 Post-it note abbr.
47 Brain, slangily
48 Q-tip target
50 "So's your old man!," e.g.
51 Grip tightly
54 Sine qua ___
56 "An invasion of armies can be resisted; an invasion of ___ cannot be resisted": Hugo
58 They may be crunched
59 Lima ladies: Abbr.
61 Norway's capital
62 Ancient Greek walkway
63 No-smoking ordinance, e.g.
64 ___ dye
66 ". . . ___ mouse?"

by Caleb Madison

ACROSS

1 The pyramids, for pharaohs
6 "Hey . . . over here!"
10 PBS newsman Lehrer
13 "The Cat and the Curmudgeon" author Cleveland ___
14 Inventor Elias
15 Absolutely the best
16 Place not generating rent
19 Feeling tied up, as a stomach
20 Rock band follower
21 "The first ___, the angel did say . . ."
23 Worked at, as a trade
24 Guarantees that mean nothing
30 Point again, as a gun
31 Crimped, as hair
32 Hit CBS drama with two spinoffs
35 Formal entrance
36 Euphoric
38 Pretend to be, as at a Halloween party
39 Without a prescription: Abbr.
40 Pal for Spot or Rover
41 Increase
42 Win that brings little actual gain
46 Avis competitor
48 Post-it, e.g.
49 Brandy cocktail
52 Warms up again
57 Contents of guns used in training exercises
59 Offerings to the poor
60 Dust Bowl migrant
61 New York footballer
62 Bad: Prefix
63 Baby boomers' kids, informally
64 Groups of buffalo

DOWN

1 Rikki-tikki-___
2 Neighbor of Yemen
3 Make fun of
4 Kellogg's Raisin ___
5 Roget's listing
6 "Star Trek" weapon
7 Soak (up)
8 Booty
9 Ariz., e.g., before 1912
10 Portrayer of Frank Sinatra on "Saturday Night Live"
11 Concave belly button
12 Rationed (out)
15 Stubborn as ___
17 Feature of many a sports car
18 ___-turvy
22 Scuttlebutt
24 Therefore
25 Vegetarians avoid it
26 1998 Robin Williams title role
27 Common Father's Day gift
28 Off one's rocker
29 Climbing vine
33 Suffix with dino-
34 1960s Bill Cosby TV series
36 Baseball great Hodges
37 Words before "You may kiss the bride"
38 London hrs.
40 Group watched by Little Bo Peep
41 A pair of deuces beats it
43 Black cats and broken mirrors, by tradition
44 Whirlpool or tornado
45 Anatomical passage
46 Equally awful
47 Eli ___ and Company
50 Slip ___ (blunder)
51 Clean up leaves, e.g.
53 Actress McClurg
54 Food thickener
55 Care for, with "to"
56 Fleet that was permanently retired in 2003
58 ___ Tin Tin

by Mike Nothnagel

60

ACROSS

1 Break ground, in a way
5 Spill the beans
9 Come to an end
14 Boxcar hopper
15 After the buzzer
16 "The usual," e.g.
17 Active sort
18 Salem's state: Abbr.
19 Fare payer
20 Antlered salon employee?
23 Woodworker's groove
24 Actress Vardalos
25 Curly poker
28 Make darts, say
31 Lost bobcat?
34 Heebie-jeebies
36 Grab some Z's
37 Teed off
38 Train alternative
39 Vintner's valley
40 One with a pitch
43 Passé
45 Wildebeest who doesn't spare the rod?
47 Future alums: Abbr.
48 Approx. takeoff hr.
49 Here, in Haiti
50 Broadway musical with the song "Will I?"
52 Unwelcome porcine party attendee?
57 Crawfish's home
60 Tall story
61 Like some chatter
62 Continental divide?
63 Building extensions
64 Parks of Montgomery
65 Cops' rounds
66 European deer
67 Tiny amount

DOWN

1 Profs' degs.
2 Rioter's take
3 Toe the line
4 Word before class or war
5 Mrs. Bumstead
6 Slow movements, in music
7 "Up and ___!"
8 Showy blooms
9 Prom accessory
10 Toledo's lake
11 Throw in
12 Comprehend
13 Slip up
21 Big name in pet foods
22 Barnyard sound
25 Chatty avians
26 Even (with)
27 Nationals living abroad, informally
28 Genève's land
29 Wholly absorbed
30 Li'l fellow
32 Attacked by a jellyfish
33 Come to earth
35 Yemeni port
38 Something to slide on
41 Vail trails
42 Easily split mineral
43 Unity
44 Pulmonary organ
46 It's between the headlights
51 Rival of a 'Vette
52 Fur
53 Saintly sign
54 What wavy lines signify in the comics
55 As well
56 Gather in
57 Short do
58 1 or 11, in twenty-one
59 Roll call vote

by Billie Truitt

ACROSS

1 Irons or Woods
6 Iridescent gem
10 Classic clown
14 Old Big Apple restaurateur
15 Put blacktop on
16 Word repeated before "pants on fire"
17 Strap-on leg supports
19 Sister of Prince Charles
20 Reason for an R rating
21 Apple seeds' location
22 Film critic Gene
24 Without slack
25 Lady's partner
26 Cavalry cry
29 Experts with the ends of 17- and 55-Across and 10- and 24-Down
33 Eagle's nest
34 Cornmeal bread
35 Biblical flood survivor
36 Lame gait
37 Michelangelo masterpiece
38 Event proceeds
39 Fox's "American ___"
40 Away from the storm
41 Cancel, at Cape Canaveral
42 Rifle and revolver
44 Poisonous atmosphere
45 Part of a birthday celebration
46 Waste reservoir
47 Football refs
50 Mitchell who sang "Big Yellow Taxi"
51 "___ the season . . ."
54 "Peek-___, I see you!"
55 Mincemeat, e.g.
58 Gullet
59 Bones: Lat.
60 22-Across's longtime partner
61 Middle of many a steering wheel
62 Wed. follower
63 Things to salve

DOWN

1 Seeks info
2 Chaplin prop
3 "Jurassic Park" giant, informally
4 Poem often titled "To a . . ."
5 Chest protector
6 Some psychedelic designs
7 Show worry in the waiting room, maybe
8 "___ Maria"
9 Decreased
10 It sets things off
11 Sound piggish
12 Western writer Grey
13 Baseball's Hershiser
18 Rakish sort
23 Bank statement abbr.
24 Feat for Secretariat
25 Three wishes granter
26 Sacramento's state: Abbr.
27 Title heroine played by Shirley Temple in 1937
28 Knight's protection
29 Hawks' opposites
30 Goes up, up, up
31 Jazz great Art
32 "Come Back, Little ___"
34 ___ d'Or (Cannes award)
37 Appearing and disappearing feature on Jupiter
41 "Fresh as a daisy" and others
43 Org. that helps with tow service
44 Tax-exempt investment, for short
46 To date
47 2007 Masters champion Johnson
48 Longest Spanish river
49 Wild hog
50 Bach's "___, Joy of Man's Desiring"
51 Level
52 Legal memo starter
53 Some noncoms: Abbr.
56 Approximately: Suffix
57 Debt-incurring Wall St. deal

by Mark Sherwood

62

ACROSS
1 "Fall" guy
5 Three, it's said
10 Saks sack, say
14 Fries or slaw
15 Slot machine fruit
16 Enterprise alternative
17 E.S.L. class, perhaps?
20 Our base system
21 Word before fee or group
22 Main line
23 Harris's ___ Rabbit
24 It'll curl your hair
26 They're not original
29 Save for a rainy day
33 Diva's delivery
34 With 44-Down, "Wuthering Heights" actress
35 Title role for Will Smith
36 Seedy hangout across the Atlantic?
40 Web address ending
41 Down-and-out
42 Demon's doing
43 Bank receipts
45 Go to bat for
47 Makes verboten
48 Depend
49 Primp
52 Supreme Court count
53 Everyday article
56 Hip-hop critics?
60 Cookie with its name on it
61 Get off one's behind
62 Et ___
63 Hammer part
64 Meal with readings
65 1995 Physics Nobelist Martin L. ___

DOWN
1 Part of T.A.: Abbr.
2 Parcheesi pair
3 Mideast's Gulf of ___
4 Loo sign
5 Winds up
6 Direct, as for info
7 Actor Epps
8 Took all the marbles
9 Double-helix material
10 Puget Sound city
11 Frequent word from ham operators
12 TV control
13 "Cómo ___ usted?"
18 Lira's replacement
19 OPEC, e.g.
23 Kid you might feel like smacking
24 Kegger, e.g.
25 First name in scat
26 Did a 10K, e.g.
27 Eat away
28 Locker photo, maybe
29 Thrills
30 Give up
31 Chipmunk of pop music
32 Give up
34 Track team schedule
37 Out of one's mind
38 Ja's opposite
39 Go against
44 See 34-Across
45 Less astute
46 Gen. Robt. ___
48 Shampoo bottle instruction
49 Telephone on a stage, e.g.
50 Pink inside
51 Blunted blade
52 Reason to be barred from a bar . . . or the theme of this puzzle
53 Start to communicate?
54 "Aquarius" musical
55 Disney's "___ and the Detectives"
57 Carrier to Bergen
58 Opposite of post-
59 Bill (Bojangles) Robinson's forte

by Adam G. Perl

ACROSS

1 Calves' meat
5 Group of eight
10 Evil organization in "Get Smart"
14 Folkie Guthrie
15 Conductor Zubin
16 Shrek, for one
17 Knots
18 Keep an ___ (watch)
19 "Man, oh, man!"
20 Church bell ringer
22 Heater or repeater
24 Japanese maker of watches and calculators
26 Request
27 Weight of diamonds
30 Runs a cloth across furniture, say
32 Happy ___ clam
35 Event with ukulele entertainment
36 Revolutionary pattern of the moon
38 The "A" of A&E
39 Sex researcher Hite
40 Seep
41 Non-oil painting method
43 Fashion's ___ Saint Laurent
44 Stealthy
45 Soothed or smoothed
46 Treaty of ___-Litovsk, 1918
47 Guy's partner
48 "Ditto!"
50 TV Guide info
53 Shabby
57 Olympic sport from Japan
58 Lone Ranger's companion
60 Countess's husband
61 Upon
62 Available from a keg
63 The Beatles' "Lovely ___"
64 Beauty mark
65 View again
66 Iditarod vehicle

DOWN

1 Winery containers
2 Toledo's lake
3 "I'll take Potpourri for $200, ___"
4 The Civil War, for the Confederacy
5 Portents
6 1970s Dodgers All-Star Ron
7 What the starts of 22-, 36-, 41- and 50-Across comprise
8 Yours: Fr.
9 Predecessor of Katie Couric
10 Telly Savalas role
11 Golden ___ (senior)
12 City near Provo
13 "Oh yeah? ___ who?"
21 Grain in Cheerios
23 Gas brand in Canada
25 Some potatoes
27 Talons
28 Hearing-related
29 Dilapidated
31 Walked with a purpose
32 Upon
33 Assesses, as a situation, with "up"
34 "This is only ___"
36 Lazy person's stairs?
37 Trigger man?
42 Deciphered
46 It can be constricting
47 Search with the hands
49 Figure of speech
50 Jaguar or Mustang
51 Golden deity, say
52 Clock chime, e.g.
54 What a donkey gets at a children's party
55 Commedia dell'___
56 Trash bag brand
57 Musical free-for-all
59 ___ kwon do

by Barry Boone

ACROSS

1 Sci-fi's "Doctor ___"
4 PG or R
10 From the start
14 Suffers from
15 "The Tempest" king
16 "Later"
17 Like many planetary orbits
19 Clarinet type
20 Ebony, e.g.
21 Like
22 Ranch visitor
24 Uneaten part of an apple
26 Long March participants
29 Airer of Congressional proceedings
32 Bout stopper, for short
34 Far from wimpy
35 Question posed by a 1987 children's best seller
38 Fighter for Jeff Davis
39 Western pal
40 Sample
41 Open widely
42 Old spy org.
43 This puzzle's answer to 35-Across (spelled out four times)
45 Pub serving
47 A, in Austria
48 Composer Camille Saint-___
49 Indian oven
51 It turns the tide
53 Commotions
54 Equinox mo.
55 Bargain
59 Bargain event
61 Building seen on a nickel
64 Moselle tributary
65 French satellite launcher
66 West of "My Little Chickadee"
67 Gum globs
68 City with a view of Vesuvius
69 Do zigzags, maybe

DOWN

1 "That was close!"
2 Symbol of sanctity
3 Nobel Institute city
4 Grammy category
5 Rite site
6 Light perfume
7 Pizarro foe
8 Code-cracking org.
9 Israel's Meir
10 Maine's ___ National Park
11 1990s–2000s sitcom shrink
12 Absorb, as a loss
13 Wine and dine
18 It may be swiped
23 Man, in 68-Across
25 Canadian "loonie" denomination
26 Material used in casting
27 It's "mightier," in a saying
28 Gets over drunkenness, with "up"
29 Breakfast cereal pioneer
30 Cascades peak
31 Purchase of one who's looking for love
33 Whole-grain cereal brand
36 RR stop
37 Boxing Day mo.
41 Starbucks size
43 Langston Hughes poem
44 Bear, in Bolivia
46 Jersey parts?
50 Ottoman Turk leader
52 Speak one's mind
54 Salon sound
56 "Slippery" trees
57 Wings: Lat.
58 MGM mogul Marcus
59 Phila.-to-Miami dir.
60 Tow-providing org.
62 ". . . man ___ mouse?"
63 These, in Tours

by Pete Muller

ACROSS

1 50%
5 Goya's "The Naked ___"
9 Pet adoption org.
13 Jai ___
14 Yale of Yale University
16 Where a horseshoe goes
17 *Sightseer's guide
19 Plus
20 Passover meals
21 One of the U.S. Virgin Islands
23 Hooded jacket
26 Variety
27 1950, on a cornerstone
30 *Creation made with a bucket and shovel
35 "Are you in ___?"
37 Stinks to high heaven
38 D.D.E.'s political rival
39 Spanish wine beverage
41 Has high hopes
43 CPR provider
44 Shenanigan
46 Mall unit
47 *One who puts the pedal to the metal
50 River of Hades
51 Opposite of paleo-
52 ___ Gay (W.W. II bomber)
54 Quits yapping
58 British society magazine
62 Arizona tribe
63 *The worst player wins it
66 Cupid
67 Longtime Yankees skipper
68 Big do
69 Here today, ___ tomorrow
70 Saucy
71 "Split" soup ingredients

DOWN

1 They may be thrown into the ring
2 Skin soother
3 Praise
4 *Hose company hookup
5 Gentlemen: Abbr.
6 PC key
7 Beam in a bar?
8 Solvers' shouts
9 Predatory types
10 Ralph Lauren label
11 Mozart's "___ Fan Tutte"
12 Crazy like ___
15 Slight improvements in business activity
18 Songwriter Gershwin
22 Necklace fasteners
24 Sport in which belts are awarded
25 "Wheel of Fortune" purchase
27 Grandma ___, American folk artist
28 Muscle malady
29 Three-card scam
31 Church official
32 Fortuneteller's card
33 Suspicious
34 Beloved of Elizabeth I
36 Swaps
40 Iffy
42 Warning cry . . . or a hint to the beginnings of the answers to the five starred clues
45 "___ Mine" (Beatles song)
48 Whole
49 "Maybe later"
53 Once around the track
54 Retro cut
55 ___ sapiens
56 Second word in many a fairy tale
57 Inside info
59 Long, long sentence
60 Cornell of Cornell University
61 Vintage vehicles
64 Valuable rocks
65 "Man, it's cold!"

by Paula Gamache

ACROSS

1 Sportswriters' pick, for short
4 Serves at a restaurant
11 Masseur's workplace
14 "Look at that!"
15 Pennsylvania railroad city
16 Proof-ending abbr.
17 Oklahoma Indian
18 18th-century Parisian design
20 Scout's doing
22 Flyers' org.
23 Ocean motions
24 Joan at Woodstock
26 Slanty type: Abbr.
28 Beef cut
34 Charlton Heston role of 1956
35 Missouri river
36 Classic Jaguar
37 Holds the title to
38 ___ fatty acid
39 Board game turn
40 "___ Beso" (1962 hit)
41 Verbal flourishes
42 "The Republic" philosopher
43 Aggies' home
46 Rock's Clapton
47 Reagan's "evil empire"
48 1940s computer
51 The "one" of a one-two
53 Bumpkin
56 Surprises for buyers . . . or what 18-, 28- and 43-Across contain
60 ___ Ben Canaan of "Exodus"
61 Luau instrument, informally
62 In an imprecise way
63 Bronzed, at the beach
64 Govt. narcotics watchdog
65 Heavenly gateman
66 Silly Putty container

DOWN

1 State of mind
2 Privilege of those 18 and over
3 "Poetry Man" singer
4 Realm of Ares
5 Mourning of the N.B.A.
6 Prickly heat symptom
7 Shed item
8 Part of Ascap: Abbr.
9 "The Plastic ___ Band—Live Peace in Toronto 1969" (1970 album)
10 Tennis great Ilie
11 3 ft. by 3 ft.
12 Old Cosmos great
13 Sidewalk stand quaffs
19 Arcade flub
21 Broad valleys
25 Ambulance letters
26 Argumentative comeback
27 Glad rags
28 Use a divining rod
29 Kind of skiing
30 Violinist Stern
31 American in Paris, e.g.
32 "Go fly ___!"
33 Lotto relative
34 Big name in faucets
38 It's hailed by city dwellers
39 Web address punctuation
41 Bygone Toyotas
42 Qt. halves
44 Honey drink
45 Understated
48 Israel's Barak
49 Greek goddess of victory
50 Something to think about
51 "No way, ___!"
52 Play ___ (enjoy some tennis)
54 Mountain climber's grip
55 Word before snake or crab
57 "Just the opposite!"
58 Whistle blower, at times
59 Neighbor of Turk.

by Barry C. Silk

ACROSS

1 Hullabaloos
5 Wood for a model plane
10 Where eggs are laid
14 ___ I.R.A. (investment)
15 Arctic ___
16 Poison ivy symptom
17 Voice below soprano
18 Follow persistently, as a celebrity
19 One G
20 1960s weather song by Peter, Paul and Mary
23 Sacagawea dollar and others
24 Cuts into cubes
25 Secret matters
28 Wrigglers, to a fisherman
30 Co. honchos
31 Viewpoint
33 Star pitcher
36 1960s weather song by the Beatles
40 Bull or cow in the forest
41 Openly declares
42 Encircle
43 Dateless
44 Animals with brown summer fur
46 Clear jelly used as a garnish
49 "___ Gavotte," "My Fair Lady" tune
51 1960s weather song by the Cascades
57 Rani raiment
58 Prospero's servant in "The Tempest"
59 Mallorca or Menorca, por ejemplo
60 Red sky in the morning, e.g.
61 New Orleans's Vieux ___
62 Fur trader's fur
63 Eliot of the Untouchables
64 "To ___—perchance to dream": Hamlet
65 Back talk

DOWN

1 Qatari, e.g.
2 Barbie or Ken
3 Director Preminger
4 Cabinet for displaying wares
5 Neighbor of Croatia
6 Be part of, as a play
7 Isn't quite vertical
8 "S" shaker
9 Egyptian symbol of life
10 Lamebrain
11 Body of moral principles
12 British biscuit
13 Falling sounds
21 Charged particle
22 Archie's "dingbat"
25 Have rheumatic pains
26 Predigital film part
27 Bottle part that goes "pop!"
28 Voice below baritone
29 Six-legged worker
31 Cause of some urban coughs
32 "Ben-Hur" author Wallace
33 Home to more than half the world's population
34 Terse to the point of rudeness
35 Termini
37 Fish that's no longer in the sea
38 Eggs
39 Self-aggrandizing acts
43 Some '60s protests
44 Carry, slangily
45 Place for a Dr. Scholl's pad
46 Criminal burning
47 Humiliation
48 Combustible funeral structures
49 Burning
50 Cubic meter
52 Alternatives to PCs
53 Like traditional epic poetry
54 On the briny
55 Woes
56 Washington nine

by Ronald J. and Nancy J. Byron

ACROSS

1 Bride's title
4 Cry of success
9 Sudden influx
14 It keeps going and going . . .
15 Express one's point of view
16 Put to rest
17 In the style of
18 Furniture within easy walking distance of the kitchen
20 Actor Mos __
21 Takes care of
22 Jabbers
23 Give off
25 Beer ingredients
27 Start
31 Show of lowbrow taste
35 Show signs of an impending storm
39 Chevy S.U.V.
40 Pimpernel or prairie clover
41 __ colony
43 Cheer competitor
44 Quick on one's feet
46 Headed straight down
48 Popular thesaurus
50 African heavyweight, for short
51 Throb
53 Perennial teenage feeling
57 Overly self-assured
60 Popular place
64 Consumed
65 Invitation info . . . or two alternate endings for the starts of the answers to 18-Across, 10-Down and 24-Down
67 X
68 Going gray
69 Paradise for the parched
70 Feedbag bit
71 Some tartan garments

72 Lawman Earp
73 Apt. units

DOWN

1 Union general at Gettysburg
2 Geneva-based watchmaker
3 Major muddle
4 Much-needed help
5 Early Ron Howard role
6 Fork prong
7 Alehouses
8 Canines, e.g.
9 Precollege exam
10 Popular Sony product
11 Jessica of "Fantastic Four"
12 It's cheap, proverbially
13 Ogles
19 Corner piece
24 Spy who lives dangerously
26 Peach stone
28 Soak (up)
29 Tied, as a score
30 Pavarotti, for one
32 Weapon in a gang fight
33 What a programmer writes
34 Pay attention to
35 Blacken
36 Brand of blocks
37 Not a dup.
38 Done without due consideration
42 Island garland

45 List ender
47 Procedure in a paternity suit
49 It's usually over a foot
52 Give, as a grant
54 University of Florida mascot
55 Heating choice
56 Some desert dwellings
57 Mt. Rushmore's locale: Abbr.
58 Trio in a Christmas story
59 Electric or water co.
61 Dog command
62 Site of some Galileo experiments
63 Leave out
66 Lawyers in cabinets: Abbr.

by Steven Ginzburg

ACROSS

1 Annual sleigh driver
6 Walk like an expectant dad
10 Summit
14 Martian, e.g.
15 "Yeah, right"
16 Radar sign
17 Words to a fourth runner-up
20 R.B.I. or H.R.
21 Angers
22 "Casablanca" star, informally
23 Its symbol is Sn
25 Not him
26 Words to a third runner-up
34 Latin dance
35 Push out of bed
36 Pi's follower
37 Swiss artist Paul
38 Height's companion
39 Jack who pioneered late-night talk
40 Un : France :: ___ : Germany
41 Irked
42 Alice's cake instruction
43 Words to a second runner-up
46 Finish up
47 Chicago transports
48 Norse myths, e.g.
51 Warmth
54 Gave temporarily
58 Words to a first runner-up
61 Suffix with million
62 Florence's river
63 Ahead by a point
64 Borscht vegetable
65 Lawyer Dershowitz
66 Op-ed piece

DOWN

1 Tools with teeth
2 Disembarked
3 One of Columbus's ships
4 Science lab glassware
5 Year, in Madrid
6 Where ships dock
7 ___-bodied
8 Corp. kingpins
9 Martians, e.g., for short
10 What paper towels do
11 What paper towels do to a toilet
12 "La Bohème" soprano
13 Fencing sword
18 Skirt that exposes a lot of thigh
19 Film critic Roger
24 Boise's state: Abbr.
25 Word to a crying child
26 New Haven collegian
27 Signs for good or ill
28 Dentist's tool
29 Call in the Alps
30 Surpass
31 Poet's Muse
32 Killer whale that does tricks
33 Went 80, say
34 Distort, as data
38 Untamed
39 Salary indicators
41 Dentist's direction
42 Electric fish
44 Cups, saucers, sugar bowl, etc.
45 Presidential prerogative
48 Picket line crosser
49 "I cannot tell ___"
50 Al of "An Inconvenient Truth"
51 Throw
52 Sicilian volcano
53 Ever and ___
55 Inflated selves
56 "Peter Pan" dog
57 Deuce topper, in cards
59 Sheep's bleat
60 Actor's prompt

by Andrea Carla Michaels and Patrick Blindauer

ACROSS

1 Give a heads-up
5 Prefix with -syncratic
9 Valuable violin
14 Coup d'___
15 Birth place
16 French-speaking African nation
17 Hotel offering
19 Asteroid's path
20 Number of coins in the Fontana di Trevi?
21 Bow-taking occasion
23 In an obvious way
25 Early sixth-century year
26 Charisse of "Singin' in the Rain"
27 Blown away by
32 "Eso ___" (Paul Anka hit)
35 Love, Italian-style
36 Pal of Tarzan
37 Poker face
41 Mathematical proof letters
42 Novelist Zola
43 Armchair athlete's channel
44 In a calm way
46 Grier of "Jackie Brown"
48 Devoured
49 Dress store section
53 Cinema offering
58 Final: Abbr.
59 Like some committees
60 Flintlock need
62 Actress Aimée
63 Earth sci.
64 With "and" and 47-Down, Lawrence Welk's intro
65 Like ground around a tree
66 "Coffee, Tea ___?"
67 Something you can do to the starts of 17-, 21-, 37-, 53- and 60-Across

DOWN

1 Internet-on-the-tube company, formerly
2 Pong maker
3 Motel posting
4 To the ___ degree
5 "If asked, yes"
6 Bride's worldly possessions
7 "Since ___ You Baby" (1956 hit)
8 Syllables before "di" or "da" in a Beatles song
9 Has a tough time deciding
10 Friend of Peppermint Patty
11 "Waterloo" pop group
12 Slave away
13 Part of I.S.B.N.: Abbr.
18 Frozen dessert chain
22 Start of a challenge
24 Desktop graphic
27 Adequately, and then some
28 Seconds and then thirds
29 Place for a lectern
30 Each
31 Neighbor of 38-Down: Abbr.
32 Patio parties, briefly
33 General Robt. ___
34 ___ City (Baghdad district)
35 Leaf-to-branch angle
38 Home of Mammoth Cave
39 Arab chieftain: Var.
40 Teamster's rig
45 Have dinner in a restaurant
46 Us Weekly rival
47 See 64-Across
49 ___ Penh, Cambodia
50 Henry VIII's house
51 Jimmy Dorsey's "Maria ___"
52 Scatter, as seed
53 Jack who quipped "A funny thing happened to my mother one day: Me"
54 Fig. on a driver's license
55 When repeated, a train sound
56 Frozen waffle brand
57 Litigious sort
61 Roll of dough

by Barry C. Silk

ACROSS

1 Like students in the Head Start program
5 Nonplayer's spot in the dugout
10 "Out!" or "Safe!"
14 Sharpen, as a knife
15 Meat-contaminating bacteria
16 Double Stuf cookie
17 British pop group with a repetitive name
19 This-and-that dish
20 ___ quo
21 Reagan antimissile plan, for short
23 Geller who claims paranormal ability
24 The Lord
25 Kurdistan city on the Tigris
28 Traveler's route
31 Pillages
32 ___ Francisco
33 Termination
34 Filming site
35 On-ramp
42 Gratuity
43 Nipper the dog's company
44 "Now I get it!"
45 Mark who was a swimming phenom at the 1972 Olympics
48 Lipton employee
51 Welch's soft drink
53 ___ polloi
54 Dangler on an item for sale
55 Pen point
56 Signify
59 Spanish artist Joan
61 Unexpected wallet fattener . . . and what the circled words are
64 Far from land
65 Cavaradossi's love in a Puccini opera
66 Few and far between
67 Mock
68 Tale
69 Donations for the poor

DOWN

1 Grad school achievements
2 Defeat decisively
3 Maddening
4 Buster on the silent screen
5 Mattress sites
6 Bygone French coin
7 ". . . ___ a lender be"
8 Chic
9 Worshiper of Brahma
10 Trig ratio: Abbr.
11 Conductor Toscanini
12 Regard with lust
13 Reasons for special ed
18 Like the upper half of the Venus de Milo
22 In worse health
25 Umpteen
26 Chose from the menu, say
27 Smidgen
28 Sort of: Suffix
29 Mai ___ (rum cocktail)
30 Harvest
34 Rebounds or assists
36 URL starter
37 Shrink from age
38 March Madness org.
39 Not local or state
40 Fighter with Fidel
41 Audiologist's concern
45 High-ranking noncom
46 Kudos
47 "That's my opinion, too"
48 As well
49 "Uh, excuse me"
50 Mexican state bordering Arizona
52 Looks (through), as for information
56 June 6, 1944
57 Six years, for a senator
58 Peepers
60 Crew implement
62 Support grp. for the troops
63 Big maker of checkout devices

by Lynn Lempel

ACROSS

1. Kansas City university formerly known as College of Saint Teresa
6. Prefix with conference
10. Stds. important to the health-conscious
14. Gore who wrote "Lincoln" and "1876"
15. Eddie's character in "Beverly Hills Cop"
16. Commercial prefix with méxico
17. Retired general?
20. Surgeon's order
21. Speaker's place
22. Antlered animal
23. Part of the mailing address to Oral Roberts University
25. Field for Dem Bums
28. Was loud
31. Poetic work by Tennyson
32. Old cracker brand
35. University wall covering
36. Stringy
37. Late nobleman?
41. Grades 1–6: Abbr.
42. That: Sp.
43. "The Thin Man" terrier
44. Glass-encased item in "Beauty and the Beast"
45. Former Seattle team, for short
48. Residue locale
50. Set one's sights
55. Unit a little longer than an arm's length
56. Chest muscles, for short
58. "The Time Machine" race
59. Carillon call?
63. Groening who created "The Simpsons"
64. Together, in music
65. Egyptian peninsula
66. Sit (for)
67. Greek letters that look like pitchforks
68. Seven-year stretch

DOWN

1. "Stop!" at sea
2. Objets d'art
3. Unimprovable
4. Cobblers' forms
5. Optional hwy. route
6. 1970s Japanese P.M. Kakuei ___
7. W.W. II vet, e.g.
8. A majority of August births
9. Tolkien creature
10. Horse-racing devotees, slangily
11. Dressed to the nines
12. "___ you happy now?"
13. Sisters' org.
18. Hero to many
19. Library Lovers' Mo.
24. "___ Ben Adhem" (Leigh Hunt poem)
25. Big name in ice cream
26. Impatient sort
27. Done with a wink
29. Wisconsin town where the Republican Party was born
30. "Little" Stowe character
32. Signs of goodness
33. Giant glaciers
34. Catcher's location
38. Comfy spot
39. General on Chinese menus
40. Hoeing the garden, e.g.
41. Chronology segment
46. Urges
47. Word in many Perry Mason titles
49. "___ say!"
51. Fear-inspiring
52. How hermits like to be
53. Des Moinesian or Davenporter
54. Modest dresses
56. Opium poppies have them
57. Decorative sewing kit
59. Hi-fi component
60. Kung ___ chicken
61. Access, as a resource
62. 23-Across winter setting: Abbr.

by Ken Bessette

ACROSS

1 Mount ___, Ten Commandments locale
6 Normandy invasion town
10 Sweat opening
14 Writer Nin
15 Cupid
16 Genesis son
17 Antiterrorism legislation of 2001
19 Gun blast
20 Proverbial saver of nine, with "a"
22 Snake or alligator
25 Playful knuckle-rub
26 Eggs ___ easy
27 Suck-up
30 Pants part
31 Kentucky's ___ College
33 Try to strike
35 "My Cousin Vinny" Oscar winner
39 Word with Asia or Ursa
40 Ultimately become
43 Necessity: Abbr.
46 "Keep it simple, ___"
49 Earthen pot
50 Bet on a one-two finish
52 Dreamlike
54 Classic battles between the Giants and Dodgers, e.g.
57 "Beetle Bailey" bulldog
58 1986 world champion American figure skater
62 Pants part
63 "The Last Tycoon" director Kazan
64 "I was at a movie theater when it happened," e.g.
65 Highlands Gaelic
66 What gears do
67 Tyson or Holyfield

DOWN

1 Maple syrup source
2 Bull ___ china shop
3 Turner who led a revolt
4 Wind tunnel wind
5 "Lord, ___?" (Last Supper query)
6 Certain sofa
7 ___ II razor
8 ___ Ness monster
9 Recurring melodic phrase
10 Green Italian sauce
11 Like angels we have heard?
12 Dormmate
13 Think the world of
18 Greasy
21 Unbranded
22 Steal from
23 December 24, e.g.
24 Salon job
28 On the ball or on the dot
29 Sch. in Cambridge, Mass.
32 Record label for the Kinks and the Grateful Dead
34 Pavarotti performance
36 Working together
37 Trivial amount
38 Not doing anything
41 Diminutive suffix
42 Buddy
43 Tranquillity
44 New Hampshire prep school
45 Airline with a kangaroo logo
47 Book after Song of Solomon
48 It'll bring a tear to your eye
51 Equivalent of 10 sawbucks
53 Place to "dry out"
55 The "T" of TV
56 Diamond stats
59 Blend
60 President Lincoln
61 Madam's partner

by Bob Klahn

ACROSS
1 Option for a H.S. dropout
4 Yaks
8 Ford misstep
13 Dispense, as milk
14 Surrounding glow
15 Throw water on
16 Big name in athletic shoes
18 Still asleep
19 Site of a tkt. booth
20 J. Edgar Hoover's org.
21 "Enough, you're killing me!"
22 Prince
28 Singer Guthrie
29 Electronics giant
30 Reader of omens
31 Supermodel Carol
34 Defendant's plea, for short
36 Neither's partner
37 End of a Napoleonic palindrome
40 Mensa figs.
42 "Wiseguy" actor Ken
43 Mediterranean, for one
44 Boring routines
46 Laments
48 Rock's Better Than ___
52 Black-and-tan purebred
56 Bush's "___ of evil"
57 Priestly vestment
58 Sgt. or cpl.
59 Three-card con
61 Carrier with a shamrock logo
64 Slang
65 Bird with an olive branch
66 Zaire's Mobutu ___ Seko
67 "Fargo" brothers
68 Singles
69 "What ___ the chances?"

DOWN
1 Possible result of iodine deficiency
2 Provider of a pass abroad
3 Basketball's Erving, familiarly
4 Greta of "Anna Christie," 1930
5 I.R.S. scares
6 Article under a blouse
7 ___ Diego
8 Mrs. Woodrow Wilson
9 Patrons of the arts, perhaps
10 Court summons
11 Chicago-to-Pittsburgh dir.
12 Commanded
13 Turkish pooh-bah
17 Frequently, to a poet
21 Modes
23 Engine sound
24 Puff the Magic Dragon's frolicking place
25 Sufficient, for Shakespeare
26 Prefix with con
27 "To ___ is human . . ."
32 Dr. Kildare player Ayres
33 Pageant toppers
35 Corrida cry
37 Alienate
38 Synagogue
39 1930s heavyweight champ Max
40 Tax planner's plan, for short
41 On the ___ vive
45 Church groundskeeper
47 Go hungry
49 Clever comeback
50 Disqualify, as a potential juror
51 Got up from sleeping
53 Removes excess poundage
54 Monthly fashion issues
55 Category in which the single-season record is 191
59 Bub
60 Gold, in Guadalupe
61 Hubbub
62 Long, long time
63 Code-crackers' org.

by Andrea Carla Michaels

ACROSS

1 New ___, India
6 Massachusetts vacation spot, with "the"
10 "Yeah, sure!"
14 Like the outfield walls at Wrigley Field
15 Downwind, to a sailor
16 Musical finale
17 Red Sox stadium
19 Frozen waffle brand
20 Actor Omar
21 Precious Chinese carvings
22 Look through the cross hairs
25 ". . . ___ quit!"
26 Alpha's opposite
28 New York City's ___ Island
30 Makes believe
33 Peels, as an apple
34 Copper/zinc alloy
35 Cockney's residence
36 "Anything ___?"
37 "To Autumn" poet
38 Roman poet who wrote the "Metamorphoses"
39 Fed. biomedical research agency
40 "O Come, ___ Faithful"
41 Packing string
42 Watergate and Irangate
44 Bitterness
45 Everest or Kilimanjaro
46 Diving seabird
47 College credit units: Abbr.
48 Classic Alan Ladd western
50 Lacking any guarantee of being paid
53 Score the 3 in a 4-3 game
54 Seaside community NE of Boston
58 Natural balm
59 Actress Rowlands
60 House of Henry VII and Henry VIII

61 Fairy's stick
62 Stepped (on)
63 "Tosca" or "Thaïs"

DOWN

1 "What's the ___?" ("So what?")
2 Holiday preceder
3 China's ___ Yutang
4 Cuts with an ax
5 Potatoes from the Northwest
6 Blue Grotto's island
7 Jai ___
8 Make holes in, as for ease of tearing
9 Hair-raising cry
10 Period ending about 9000 B.C.

11 Peter who directed "The Last Picture Show"
12 Periphery
13 New Mexico city or county
18 A knitter might have a ball with it
21 "Cool your ___!"
22 Forest quakers
23 Like right-slanting type
24 "The Goodbye Girl" actress
27 Cafeteria, to a soldier
29 Football kicker's aid
30 Says grace, e.g.
31 Key of Beethoven's Ninth
32 Passover meals
34 Carillon site

37 Group investigated in "Mississippi Burning"
38 Have title to
40 Together, in music
41 Likes immediately
43 "Thanks, but I'm O.K."
44 Coach Adolph in the Basketball Hall of Fame
46 Comparable to a wet hen?
48 Picnic side dish
49 Spanish greeting
51 One billionth: Prefix
52 Medium bra size
54 "___ Pepper's Lonely Hearts Club Band"
55 "To Autumn," e.g.
56 Rocky peak
57 ___ la la

by Ed Early

ACROSS

1 Music played by Ravi Shankar at Woodstock
5 "There it is!"
10 Disconcert
14 Historic periods
15 Pianist Claudio
16 "I'll get right ___!"
17 Use of a company car, e.g.
18 Wherewithal
19 Emulates Lil' Kim or Lil Wayne
20 Fairy tale's start
23 Greeted, with "to"
24 Destination for a W-2
25 Thor Heyerdahl craft
28 That, to Tomás
29 "Exodus" author
32 "Brrrr!"
34 Grandpa's start
36 Plus
39 Adlai's opponent in '52 and '56
40 Rod's partner
41 Mom's start
46 "The Count of Monte ___"
47 Blueprint detail
48 Broadway's Hagen
51 Cooke who sang "You Send Me"
52 Indianapolis-to-New Orleans dir.
54 Like some patches
56 Legend's start
60 Balletic leap
62 Location of a starry belt
63 Cole Porter's "Well, Did You ___?"
64 Lab medium
65 Quitter's cry
66 It produces more than 20 billion bricks annually
67 Popular Microsoft product
68 Expressed disapproval
69 White blanket

DOWN

1 Period of rest
2 Gladiators' locales
3 Ice cream flavor Cherry ___
4 Made an inquiry
5 Anne Rice's Lestat, for one
6 Cookie with a floral design on it
7 Ahmadinejad's land
8 Island veranda
9 Where Schwarzenegger was born
10 W-2, e.g.
11 Bacterium that doesn't need oxygen
12 Address ending, informally
13 Some "Stargate SG-1" characters, in brief
21 Guttural refusal
22 Ideological beliefs
26 ___ vera
27 Pastoral composition
30 The G, W or B in G.W.B.
31 Followers of Guru Nanak
33 Grant in four Hitchcock films
34 Chinese cookers
35 Sob
36 Rudiments
37 Yuri's love in "Doctor Zhivago"
38 Curved saber
42 Start of a spider's description, in song
43 Barely beat
44 Condescended
45 Prefix with phobic
48 Not level
49 Trinidad's partner
50 Be that as it may
53 Gives a yellow flag
55 Law school newbies
57 Geek
58 Cafe proprietor in "Casablanca"
59 It's commonly filleted
60 Talk on and on, slangily
61 Sense of self

by Leonard Williams

ACROSS

1 C.S.A. soldier
4 Unconscious states
9 Sounds of bells or laughter
14 Grp. putting on shows for the troops
15 Journalist ___ Rogers St. Johns
16 Whodunit award
17 Rev. ___ (Bible ver.)
18 Like "Have a nice day"
19 Denizens of 45-Down
20 1934 title role for Ginger Rogers
23 8½"×14" paper size
24 "Yes, madame"
25 With 56-Across, Saint of Hollywood
27 The Depression and the cold war, for two
28 "This is only ___"
31 Bank acct. guarantor
32 "That's one small step for ___ . . ."
33 Candidate lists
35 1934 title role for Jeanette MacDonald
39 Emperor killed on the Ides of March
40 Fail to include
41 "Darn," more formally
42 Imam's faith
44 Bills and coins
48 Nonvegetarian sandwich, for short
49 Biol. or chem.
50 Slow, in music
51 1975 title role for Lynn Redgrave
56 See 25-Across
57 Base-clearing hit
58 Urban address abbr.
59 Uniquely
60 "Sesame Street" grouch
61 Brazilian hot spot
62 Stinky stream
63 Writer Zora ___ Hurston
64 New England's Cape ___

DOWN

1 What leaves do in the wind
2 Purim heroine
3 Barrio grocery
4 Plotters' plot
5 Jazzy Anita
6 Darn
7 Jai ___
8 Series of shots, as from warships
9 Lab's ___ dish
10 The "E" of N.E.A.: Abbr.
11 Accepted, as terms
12 Placid vacation vista
13 Soon-to-be grads: Abbr.
21 Phase hotter than liquid
22 Defeat by a stroke?
26 Window units, briefly
28 Song that begins "My country, 'tis of thee"
29 Part of a cigarette rating
30 Sign up
31 Furbys or yo-yos, once
32 Doc grp.
34 On fire
35 Sailor's yarn
36 Charles de Gaulle : Paris :: ___ : London
37 Twisty curve
38 Singer Sumac
39 What a hack drives
43 Drain furtively, maybe
44 Corp. biggie
45 Capital ESE of Istanbul
46 Enter
47 Dr. Seuss elephant
49 Like pantyhose
50 Peter of "M"
52 "___ kleine Nachtmusik"
53 Ask, as questions
54 Gym locale, for short
55 Get better
56 "No ___!" ("Stop!," in Spanish)

by Gilbert H. Ludwig

ACROSS

1 Requests for a saucer of milk, maybe
6 Film vixen Bara
11 Woebegone
14 Central courtyards
15 Sahara sights
16 Blubber
17 "2, 4, 6, 8, who do we appreciate?," e.g.
18 Competitive noshers' event?
20 Room under the roof
22 Iraq's second-largest city
23 One cured of a sleep disorder?
26 Cyberjunk
29 British Conservative
30 Demonic
31 Letter between eta and iota
32 Like some winks
33 Pupil surrounder
34 Transferred, as property
35 Sarcastic comment?
37 Glad rival in the kitchen
40 Shipshape
41 LP speed
44 Newspaper columnist Goodman
45 Cargo
46 Nautical leader?
47 Kazan of Hollywood
48 Brushoff from the Ottomans?
50 ___ Empire, conquered by Cortés
52 Doled (out)
53 Terrible-twos tantrums?
57 Hole-making tool
59 Round-faced flier
60 Daisylike bloom
61 Low-tech office recorder
62 Pint-size
63 Bassoonists' buys
64 On edge

DOWN

1 Apple on a desk
2 Biofuel option
3 Speaker's art
4 Cold and raw
5 French composer Erik
6 Super Bowl stat
7 Attila the ___
8 Tooth protector
9 Remodeler's planning
10 Seeks assistance
11 Like some tickets and Western pioneers
12 Rocket's path
13 Artificial color
19 Fraternity recruit
21 Church official
23 Parts of P.O. labels
24 Roman poet banished by Augustus
25 Acapulco agreement
27 Wolfed down
28 Loony
31 Sherpa shelter
33 Informed about
34 Headgear fit for a queen
35 Disreputable
36 Tap mishap
37 Last of 26
38 Indisposed
39 Easily bent
41 Goes back (on)
42 Sensible
43 Gangster group
45 Clear plastic
46 Discerning
48 On edge
49 Moonshine ingredient
51 Romanov ruler
53 What a violinist may take on stage, in two different senses
54 Amaze
55 Brother of Jack and Bobby
56 Most univ. applicants
58 Pop artist Lichtenstein

by Lynn Lempel

ACROSS

1 With 21-Across, begin from scratch
6 Heart of the matter
10 Hair untangler
14 Tithing portion
15 Great Lake touching four states
16 Cry to a matey
17 Zealous
18 Tailless cat
19 Emulate a mob
20 WNW's opposite
21 See 1-Across
24 Hot dog topping
26 Number of a magazine
27 Where to store a lawn mower
29 Entirely
33 Christmas ___ (holiday stamp)
36 Woodsy
40 Coffee, in slang
41 Move into the limelight
44 "___ was saying . . ."
45 Once did
46 Givers and receivers of alimony
47 Element of a doctrine
49 Sign from above
51 Recreation center posting
55 "Really!"
59 With 73-Across, be beaten by the rest of the field
63 Dump cleanup grp.
64 Gunk
65 It's "catchy"
66 Lets or sublets
68 Fail to mention
69 Something to whistle
70 Peeved, after "in"
71 7-6, 2-6, 6-4, e.g.
72 ___-specific (like the answers at 1-, 41- and 73-Across)
73 See 59-Across

DOWN

1 Have the wheel of a car
2 Tempt
3 Extremely well-behaved child
4 66 on a map, e.g.: Abbr.
5 Defeat soundly
6 Onyx and opal
7 Baghdad native
8 Nasal congestion locale
9 Sam Houston served as its president, senator and governor
10 Lurch from side to side
11 One of the states touched by 15-Across
12 Apollo 11 destination
13 Computer unit
22 Dissertations
23 Aztec or Mayan cities, today
25 ___ of Wight
28 Unit of force
30 Cleanser whose name comes from Greek myth
31 High-priced seating area
32 Performers Peggy and Pinky
33 Goals or assists
34 Simplicity
35 Related (to)
37 Bygone Ford
38 Nix, presidentially
39 Kitchen emanations
42 Such a jokester
43 Be inclined (to)
48 Totally loses one's cool
50 Nab in a sting operation
52 Tilts
53 Ho-hum feeling
54 Tilt
56 Dye in temporary tattoos
57 ___ nerve
58 Fritter away
59 What modest people lack
60 City south of the Bering Land Bridge National Preserve
61 "Go ahead!"
62 Writer James
67 Course for a future U.S. citizen, maybe: Abbr.

by Roger Baiocchi

ACROSS

1 "Casablanca" star, informally
6 Rio automaker
9 Legendary cowboy ___ Bill
14 Brings in
15 Dijon denial
16 Bejeweled topper
17 Mediocre F. Scott Fitzgerald novel?
20 Whopping
21 Gibbons of TV talk
22 Gas company that sells toy trucks
23 "Evil Woman" band, for short
25 Daisy ___, who went to Marryin' Sam
27 Mediocre place to scuba?
36 It merged with the WB to form the CW
37 Yarn buy
38 Atoll makeup
39 Bow-wielding god
41 Quick-witted
43 "Lovely" Beatles girl
44 Sony competitor
46 Cold war–era blast, in headlines
48 Mean mutt
49 Mediocre Steve McQueen film?
52 Unlock, to a bard
53 Kiev's land: Abbr.
54 Like a trim lawn
57 Unyielding
61 Asia's ___ Sea
65 Mediocre Jerry Lee Lewis hit?
68 In the ___ of life
69 Barbie's beau
70 Novelist Calvino
71 Zesty dip
72 Match part
73 Hose material

DOWN

1 "Little Women" woman
2 Honolulu's home
3 Kinnear of "Little Miss Sunshine"
4 "For sure!"
5 Suffix with journal
6 See 29-Down
7 Actress Skye
8 1998 animated film with a queen
9 Group that usu. meets at a school
10 "Take your pick"
11 Scope out, pre-heist
12 Planets or stars
13 Comes out with
18 Items of apparel for Dracula
19 Willing to go along
24 Barbell abbr.
26 ___ welder
27 Spare-room user
28 First name in book clubs
29 With 6-Down, ready to propose
30 Place to get clean
31 Cowpoke's rope
32 How mistakes are often marked
33 "All My Children" vixen
34 Thoroughly enjoy
35 S O S signal
40 Roget's listings
42 False start?
45 Alley ___
47 Terse reproof
50 Trillion: Prefix
51 Cunningly evil
54 Unruly dos
55 Gumbo vegetable
56 Banshee's sound
58 Types
59 High spirits
60 George Harrison's "___ It a Pity"
62 Omani money
63 Folkie Guthrie
64 Trotsky of Russia
66 Arthur of "Maude"
67 One of a snorkeler's pair

by David Kwong and Emily Halpern

ACROSS

1 Christmas drink
4 Little bit, as of color
7 ___ de plume
10 T.L.C. giver
13 1945 battle site with a flag-raising
15 Like waves on a shore
17 One offering kudos
18 Mountain climbers' tools
19 Books for jotting down appointments
21 Lendee's note
22 Pretentious
23 Hospital imaging devices
31 Author Wharton
32 Not rot
33 Hip-hop greetings
36 Cruise around the Web
39 Award won by Roger Clemens seven times
41 General on Chinese menus
42 Word before ring or swing
44 Miniature hooter
45 Burping and slurping in public
48 Moments, in brief
52 ___ Lingus
53 Places for antiwar slogans
61 Case for an otologist
62 Say "Sure, why not?"
64 Invites to a movie, say
65 Ralph who wrote "Invisible Man"
66 Florida island
67 Opposite of SSW
68 Nutritional stat.
69 ___ Dhabi, Persian Gulf port

DOWN

1 Biomedical research org.
2 "Man, that hurts!"
3 All used up
4 Dagger
5 Earhart who was the first aviatrix to fly solo across the Atlantic
6 Subatomic particle made of three quarks
7 Young of Crosby, Stills, Nash & Young
8 Killer whale
9 Big name in faucets
10 The 7-Up in a 7 and 7
11 Conspicuous
12 Like dorm rooms, often
14 Quarterback Namath
16 Yemen's capital
20 The Sex Pistols' genre
23 ¢
24 Juice drinks
25 Marshal ___, Yugoslavian hero
26 Ave. crossers
27 ___ change
28 The Common Market: Abbr.
29 Playa del ___, Calif.
30 Watch through binoculars, say
33 Christmas
34 Lollapalooza
35 Bilko and Pepper: Abbr.
37 A. A. Milne baby
38 Rock's ___ Fighters
40 Have the rights to
43 Lacking color
46 Scanty
47 Comic actor Tom
48 Command to Fido
49 Wipe out
50 Like the taste of some bad wine
51 Subway stops: Abbr.
54 Supply-and-demand subj.
55 Ostracize
56 French bean?
57 "The Lion King" daughter
58 Priest who raised Samuel
59 Sub ___ (secretly)
60 One looking down on the "little people"
63 Wildebeest

by Oliver Hill

ACROSS

1 Woodworking tool
5 Real-life scientist played by David Bowie in "The Prestige," 2006
10 Dwarf or giant, maybe
14 Perjured oneself
15 Work that begins "Sing, goddess, the wrath of Peleus' son . . ."
16 Older brother of Michael Jackson
17 Writer who created the character Vivian Darkbloom
20 Edgar ___ Poe
21 Suffer
22 Keep ___ on
26 Spleen
27 Singer who nicknamed himself Mr. Mojo Risin'
32 Sine ___ non
35 Words said with a nod
36 Unwakeful state
37 Newspaperman Harold
39 The 40 of the Top 40
40 "Saturday Night Live" bits
42 End of an illness?
43 Mr. T series, with "The"
45 Inter ___
46 "Toodles!"
47 Talk smack about
48 Author/illustrator who used the pseudonym Ogdred Weary
51 Caustic cleansing agent
52 Stagger
53 Unidentified man
57 Upper crust
62 What the clues for 17-, 27- and 48-Across all contain
66 Teeming (with)
67 Besmirch
68 Shake alternative
69 British gun
70 Adlai's 1956 running mate
71 Revolutionary car part?

DOWN

1 Thomas ___ Edison
2 Salmon garnish
3 Fervor
4 Snorri Sturluson work
5 Newsman Russert
6 With 10-Down, ABC series starring Jonny Lee Miller
7 Walter Scott title
8 Superboy's crush
9 Samuel Barber's "___ for Strings"
10 See 6-Down
11 "Kon-___"
12 All-inclusive
13 Travel the country
18 Preoccupied with
19 Carried
23 They may be drawn with compasses
24 Tom who wrote "The Greatest Generation"
25 Akin
27 Fanatics wage it
28 Last Supper query
29 Doles (out)
30 Badlands sight
31 "Saturday Night Live" genre
32 Doha's land
33 Hook up
34 Analyze, as ore
38 Don Corleone
41 Marquis de ___
44 "The Great Gatsby" gambler Wolfsheim
49 Lower the allowed electrical capacity of
50 Narrow valley
51 Three-star officer: Abbr.
53 Location of Olympus Mons
54 Still alive
55 Out's opposite
56 Brief holiday?
58 One-L person, in an Ogden Nash poem
59 Big movie fan's option?
60 Distinguish
61 Dirección from which the sun rises
63 Cambridge sch.
64 Suffix with ethyl
65 The shakes, for short

by Joon and Caroline Pahk

ACROSS

1 Feeling bloated
6 Eyeliner boo-boo
11 "Don't tase me, ___!"
14 Make amends (for)
15 Bizarre
16 Experiment site
17 Psychologically manipulated
19 I
20 Lawman Wyatt
21 "The Andy Griffith Show" boy
22 Cowboy's greeting
24 End of a student's e-mail address
26 Town shouters
28 Place to play twenty-one
31 Jewish mystical doctrine
34 Formulaic
37 "Long ago and ___ away . . ."
38 Furnace output
39 Western treaty grp.
40 Car with a logo of four rings
41 Lubricate
42 Put-upon
46 Out, as a library book
48 Smooth and lustrous
49 At an angle
52 Galas
53 Norwegian coastal feature
55 Car that comes with a driver
57 Opera set along the Nile
61 ___ Vegas
62 Like players in pin-the-tail-on-the-donkey
65 Likely
66 Helpers
67 Rationed (out)
68 Crosses out
69 Silly birds
70 Escalator parts

DOWN

1 Comic Kaplan
2 Gillette razor
3 Go out of sight, as gas prices
4 Criticizes, perhaps unfairly
5 Craving
6 Ivory or Coast
7 "If ___ be the food of love, play on": Shak.
8 Onetime dental anesthetic
9 "___ you sleeping?"
10 Fiery-tempered sort, they say
11 Loses it
12 Ayn who wrote "Atlas Shrugged"
13 Follow orders
18 Cause for stitches
23 Globe
25 Racket
27 "Rocks"
28 Make aware
29 No matter what
30 Stench
32 Weighed down
33 Desertlike
34 When repeated, a toy train
35 Way cool
36 AOL and others, in brief
40 Demands much (of)
42 Pocketbook
43 Termite look-alike
44 Free from
45 "Xanadu" grp.
47 Rower's need
50 Omit in pronunciation
51 Eats by candlelight, say
53 Source of linen
54 Mock
56 Retailer's goods: Abbr.
58 Unemployed
59 Bottomless
60 Tosses in
63 "This puzzle is really, really hard," e.g.
64 Takes too much, for short

by Thomas Heilman

ACROSS

1 Just for guys
5 Rice dish
10 Colleague of Clark at the "Daily Planet"
14 Oscar winner Kedrova
15 Amorphous critter
16 Ultimatum's end
17 State firmly
18 Musical genre for Destiny's Child
19 Concert halls of old
20 TV game show that places spouses at risk?
23 "Crocodile Rock" singer John
24 Fresh talk
25 Chemical in Drano
27 Belittle, slangily
28 Toe the line
32 Chocolate trees
34 Red Bordeaux
36 Outback avians
37 TV game show that quizzes oenophiles?
40 Morales of "NYPD Blue"
42 Lease signer
43 Winter topper
46 Hawaii's state bird
47 Hood's pistol
50 Do-over at Wimbledon
51 Pint-size
53 Reads closely, with "over"
55 TV game show that eliminates coy contestants?
60 Super server
61 ___ to (in on)
62 Nair competitor
63 "Comin' ___ the Rye"
64 First name in TV talk
65 Gabor and Longoria Parker
66 Colon, in an emoticon
67 Not the sharpest pencil in the box
68 Place for a blotter

DOWN

1 Left rolling in the aisles, as an audience
2 Copenhagen's ___ Gardens
3 Native Alaskans
4 Reclusive Greta
5 A comb makes one
6 "If ___ suggest . . ."
7 Last name in TV talk
8 Co-panelist of Cowell, once
9 It's sold by the yard
10 Sainted fifth-century pope
11 Former inamorato or inamorata
12 "Peekaboo" follower
13 Neptune's realm
21 ___ Gay (W.W.II bomber)
22 New Deal org.
26 Pothook shape
29 Lawman Masterson
30 Once, once
31 Aden's land
33 Coin whose front was last redesigned in 1909
34 In vogue
35 Newcastle's river
37 "Don't move— I'll go for help"
38 Hardly ruddy
39 All thumbs
40 Night school subj.
41 Lacking details
44 "How cute"
45 Espied Godiva, e.g.
47 Show sorrow
48 Trojan War hero
49 "You should have known better"
52 Country rocker Steve
54 Had title to
56 Cupid's Greek counterpart
57 Ceramist's oven
58 Times to revel
59 January 1 song word
60 Broke bread

by Ray Fontenot

ACROSS

1 Univ. military program
5 Samsung and Sony products
8 In unison
13 Type that leans: Abbr.
14 Hurry
15 High point of a story
16 *1981 film starring William Hurt and Kathleen Turner
18 If all goes exactly according to plan
19 Peter Pan lost his
20 Thomas ___ Edison
22 Fed. auditing agency
23 List ender: Abbr.
25 *Hoopster's complete miss
27 A/C meas.
30 Night before a holiday
31 Encl. with a manuscript
32 *Z, alphabetically
35 "Livin' La ___ Loca"
39 Former Montreal team
40 Sea, to Debussy
41 Like Robin Hood's men
42 Trace of smoke
43 *Painted highway divider
45 Amo, ___, amat
47 Collection of scenes
48 Call for help
49 *Touchdown site
52 Sticky stuff
54 Here-there link
55 Eye part
57 Setting for many a fairy tale
61 Title girl in a 1983 Kool & the Gang hit
63 Jerry Garcia fan . . . or what each part of the answers to the starred clues can take
65 Sedated, perhaps
66 Follower of Mar.
67 Adolescent outbreak
68 Poet William Butler ___
69 Moms
70 "Say ___" (pourer's request)

DOWN

1 Barbecue dish
2 From a different perspective, in chat room lingo
3 "Look what I did!"
4 Outlaw partner of Bonnie
5 Motion made by fans in a stadium
6 By way of
7 ___ good example
8 Hitching posts?
9 Bro or sis
10 The end, to Euripides
11 Vocally twangy
12 Shower with praise
15 Expensive topping served with a tiny spoon
17 Monopoly purchases
21 Team game with infrared-sensitive targets
24 "I'll try to think of something . . ."
26 Cut at an angle
27 Missed, as a chance
28 Ride that's hailed
29 Mail carrier's grp.
33 November birthstone
34 Countdown start
36 Bearded flower
37 Early 007 foe
38 Affirmative votes
41 "The Wind in the Willows" amphibian
43 Sail material
44 High-m.p.g. vehicles
46 Hershey's bar with coconut
49 Take pleasure in
50 Nary a soul
51 Euripides' genre
53 "Shucks!"
56 Funnyman Sandler
58 Engineers' school, briefly
59 Lois of the "Daily Planet"
60 Place of bliss
62 Take-home pay
64 Org. monitoring industrial wastes

by Paula Gamache

ACROSS

1 Admirer of Beauty, with "the"
6 Sing like Ella Fitzgerald
10 Genesis victim
14 Longtime G.E. chief with the best seller "Jack: Straight from the Gut"
15 Mrs. Dithers in "Blondie"
16 1950s–'70s Yugoslav leader
17 Loud, as a crowd
18 Place for a roast
19 Not duped by
20 "Huh?"
23 And others of the same sort: Abbr.
24 Circle section
25 Comment after 20-Across
34 Not just once
35 Word from the crib
36 Etiquette maven Vanderbilt
37 Restrain, with "up"
38 Andrea Bocelli deliveries
40 Sicilian spewer
41 Male gobbler
42 Say "one club," say
43 Like something communicated with a wink and a nod
44 Comment after 25-Across
48 MSN rival
49 Lode load
50 Comment after 44-Across
59 ___ Inn
60 Wild cat
61 Rodeo contestant
62 Neutral shade
63 The "U" in 21-Down
64 Puccini opera
65 In the public eye
66 Head of France?
67 Like a cigar bar

DOWN

1 N.Y.C. theater district, for short
2 One of the Saarinens of Finland
3 Baseball's Moises
4 "The Lion King" villain
5 Bases loaded
6 Burn with an iron
7 Place to moor a boat
8 See 58-Down
9 Big mugs
10 "A.S.A.P.!"
11 Cherry variety
12 Caesarean rebuke
13 Chicago district, with "the"
21 Abbr. on an appliance sticker
22 "___ la Douce"
25 Desert flora
26 "Ha! That's ___ one!"
27 One of the Judds
28 Litter cry
29 Minneapolis suburb
30 Fine bond rating
31 "But of course!"
32 ___ vincit amor
33 Jane of "Father Knows Best"
38 Well said
39 Tape deck button
40 Have a bite
42 ___ about (roughly)
43 Opera, ballet and so on
45 Bygone Japanese car name
46 Until now
47 Dernier ___
50 When 12-Down was uttered
51 Valentine decoration
52 Stringed instrument of old
53 Letter in a mysterious inscription
54 Throw off
55 Appear ominously
56 ___ facto
57 Chicken part that's good for soup
58 With 8-Down, source of an ethical dilemma

by Harriet Clifton

ACROSS

1 Opposed to
5 Leg part below the knee
9 Come from ___
13 Have as a definition
14 Tour of duty
15 Singsong syllables
16 Be very potent
18 Londoner, e.g., for short
19 "Seats sold out" sign
20 Singer Ronstadt
21 "Pet" annoyance
22 Social hierarchy
24 Shout before "Open up!"
27 Toronto's prov.
28 Neighbor of Yemen
29 Capital of Bolivia
32 Engine additive brand
35 Very best puppy or kitten
39 Pig's place
40 Moth-repellent wood
41 Lower-priced spread
42 RR stop
43 Burr and Copland
45 Miscellaneous coins
51 Dark
52 "Steppenwolf" writer Hermann
53 Fuss
56 Squad
57 Got ready to kiss
59 Tent floor, maybe
60 Lucy's pal on "I Love Lucy"
61 Go ballistic
62 Kill
63 Requirement
64 Ed with the 1967 hit "My Cup Runneth Over"

DOWN

1 Concert equipment
2 Within easy reach
3 Stuffed tortilla
4 What a quill may be dipped in
5 Reeked
6 Language of India
7 Of an old Andean empire
8 To the ___ degree
9 Physicist Einstein
10 Got along
11 Dead's opposite
12 "Consumer Reports" employee
14 Zest
17 Baldwin of "30 Rock"
21 Kind of scheme that's fraudulent
22 Like the sky at dawn or sunset
23 Aim
24 Boston ___
25 Leave out
26 Like some delicate lingerie
29 Inc., in England
30 "I get it!"
31 The "p" in m.p.g.
32 Normandy town in W.W. II fighting
33 College freshman, usually
34 Experts
36 Eight-piece band
37 Accomplishment
38 Ripped
42 Meager
43 Photographer Adams
44 Ripening agent
45 Strokes on the green
46 Hollywood's Ryan or Tatum
47 Barton of the Red Cross
48 Water park slide
49 "Men in Trees" actress Anne
50 Inquired
53 Father of Cain and Abel
54 Hill you might drive a buggy over
55 Chooses, with "for"
57 Quill, sometimes
58 Eisenhower years, e.g.

by Andrea Carla Michaels and Michael Blake

ACROSS

1 Smidgens
5 Corp. recruits
9 Bill of fashion
14 Home of Zion National Park
15 The New Yorker cartoonist Peter
16 In town
17 Antique, antiquely
18 Formal frock
19 Extreme
20 Rose
23 Bill from the govt.
24 Angler's accessory
25 Lionel Richie's "You ___"
26 A/C meas.
27 Nebraska native
29 Sang like a bird
31 Tends tots
33 PC key
35 Base cops
36 Rose
41 Co. in a 2001 merger with Time Warner
42 Charisse of "Silk Stockings"
43 Fill fully
45 Waiters' aides
49 Moping
51 U.S.M.C. barracks boss
52 Case worker: Abbr.
53 "Go ahead, ask"
55 Host a roast, say
57 Rose
60 Suggest
61 Garr of "Tootsie"
62 Designer for Jackie
64 More agreeable
65 Precipitation that can leave dents
66 Abraded
67 Enclosures with MSS.
68 Mideast carrier
69 Runs, hits or errors

DOWN

1 Batman and Robin, e.g.
2 Monopoly avenue
3 Put down
4 Cover of night?
5 Travelers to Bethlehem
6 Some spears
7 Peace Nobelist Sadat
8 One begins "Shall I compare thee to a summer's day?"
9 Symptom of hypothermia
10 1970 Kinks hit
11 Honest-to-goodness
12 "Nausea" author
13 Cracked up at a comedy club
21 Former automaker that manufactured trucks in W.W. II
22 Its capital is Hamilton
23 SuperStation inits.
28 Hunter's cry
30 D-Day carriers: Abbr.
32 Volvo rival
34 Sleuth, informally
37 Natural alarms
38 What 1938's "The War of the Worlds" broadcast set off
39 Most trusted knight of King Arthur
40 Yadda yadda yadda
44 Help wanted abbr.
45 They're relayed in relays
46 Heaven on earth
47 Unmovable ones
48 Give relief
50 ___ Leppard
54 Jermaine ___, six-time N.B.A. All-Star
56 "I want in" or "I want out" indicators, maybe
58 Common arthritis site
59 Window part
63 Comprehend

by Nancy Salomon

ACROSS

1 Siestas
5 Greek letters that resemble pitchforks
9 Vibrant
14 Lyrical, like a Pindar poem
15 "___, Brute?"
16 Actor Sal of "Exodus"
17 "Shhhh!" prompter
20 Hersey's "A Bell for ___"
21 Top to go with shorts
22 Present but not visible
24 Words before fix or flash
25 Actress Farrow
28 180° from WNW
29 Kitschy
32 Herb who played "Tijuana Taxi"
34 "Take your time"
36 Otherwise
37 "Shhhh!"
40 Bride's ___ of honor
42 Tax paid at port
43 Idiot boxes
46 Three Little Pigs' foe
47 Sign of a hit show
50 Precollege hurdle, for short
51 Fishing stick
53 "Pay attention!"
55 Like oranges and tangerines
58 Piece of garlic
59 "Shhhh!" response
63 "What's Love ___ Do with It" (Tina Turner #1 hit)
64 Rock's ___ Pop
65 Ice in the sea
66 Pondered
67 Close to
68 Snick and ___

DOWN

1 Key on an old register
2 Nike competitor
3 "Ecce homo!" utterer Pontius ___
4 Where it's happening
5 Chest muscle, for short
6 Leave in, to an editor
7 "How sweet ___!"
8 Japanese food
9 Unconcerned with ethics
10 Light tune
11 Not Rep. or Dem.
12 Victory sign
13 Ages and ages
18 Sarge, for one
19 Actress Lollobrigida
23 Old salts
25 Blend
26 1040 org.
27 Had something
30 Mixed breed
31 "I don't believe it!"
33 B'way showing
34 Naked
35 Sandwich that requires two hands
37 "Gorillas in the ___"
38 Not just might
39 Place to work
40 Rushmore and Rainier: Abbr.
41 Actress Gardner
44 Camera stand
45 Drunkards
47 Like some kisses and bases
48 Paul with a midnight ride
49 Antsy
52 Sink outlet
54 Hunks of concrete
55 Refer to
56 Prod
57 Nintendo rival
59 "Grand Hotel" studio
60 "See ___!"
61 U.S.N. officers
62 Damascus's land: Abbr.

by Andrea Carla Michaels

ACROSS

1 Dudley Do-Right's org.
5 Hoof protector
9 "Lost" airer
14 Airline that flew the humanitarian Operation Solomon
15 Place to park a car
16 India's second-largest city
17 Newspaper V.I.P.'s
20 Sprang up
21 Bone-dry
22 Many a corner office holder, for short
23 Laundry pen, e.g.
27 Yankee nickname starting in 2004
28 Lingo: Suffix
29 Tiny brain size
32 Bingham of "Baywatch"
35 Letters on Endeavour
39 Exodus 20 subject
43 Choral voice
44 Keep on file
45 Big laugh
46 Deck cleaner
49 Half of Mork's sitcom sign-off
51 User's guide
59 It might be stuck in a log
60 English prince's alma mater
61 Division of an epic poem
62 12th–15th century European tongue
66 Moves slowly
67 On the summit of
68 Insignificant
69 Logic
70 Part of CNN
71 Hoo-ha

DOWN

1 Chart again
2 County north of Limerick
3 Feudal estate
4 ___-screen TV
5 ___-fi
6 Attila or one of his followers
7 Company newsletter
8 Chicago-based film reviewer
9 Avia alternative
10 "You ___!" ("O.K.!")
11 What a mouse ran up, in a rhyme
12 Midafternoon
13 Sun blocker
18 Adjust for
19 "Thin" coin
24 What's expected
25 Wax-coated cheeses
26 Actress Russo
29 Bake sale holder, maybe: Abbr.
30 Sushi fish
31 Pantry invader
33 Mouse chaser
34 Hole-___
36 Whichever
37 Alphabetic trio
38 Invite (out), say
40 Order to Rover
41 Fraction of an ounce
42 Threat
47 Threat ender
48 Tampa/St. ___
50 Deprives of weapons
51 Accelerates, with "up"
52 One who's persona non grata at home
53 Got nourishment from
54 ___ Ryan, a k a the Ryan Express
55 Equivalent of 20 fins
56 Not yet realized
57 Arcade game pioneer
58 One averse to mingling
63 Person who's always feeling down in the mouth?: Abbr.
64 "Holy moly!"
65 Modern dashboard attachment, for short

by Stanley Newman

ACROSS

1 Party to remember
5 Guys' dates
9 Frankie of the Four Seasons
14 Town east of Santa Barbara
15 Fencing blade
16 Ancient Mexican
17 Madcap
18 Informal greeting
19 Elbow
20 Cranky street performer?
23 Sup
24 Name typed in to log on
28 Act obsequiously
32 Escapes, slangily
34 Opposite of WSW
35 Spaceship inhabitant
36 U-boat
38 Baltimore oriole : Maryland :: ___ : Hawaii
39 Tattered
40 Popular plant "pet"
41 Heaviest iron in a golfer's bag
43 Puts a worm on, as a fishhook
44 From ___ Z
45 Facetious cry of understanding
46 Pass, as time
47 Waste at a treatment plant
49 ___-mo
50 Don Juan, e.g.
57 Urge
60 April 1st event
61 Et follower
62 "Guys and Dolls" song with the lyric "Call a lawyer"
63 Against
64 Gusto
65 Dirty campaign tactic
66 Tall one or cold one
67 Actor Montand

DOWN

1 Classic clown
2 Open just a little
3 Crooned
4 Informal greeting
5 Trinket
6 Into pieces
7 Denim pioneer Strauss
8 Beheld
9 Actress Hudgens of "High School Musical"
10 Sky hue
11 English "Inc."
12 Chicken drumstick
13 Sno-cone base
21 Like many Las Vegas signs
22 "Person" in a crash test
25 Send a second time
26 Igloo inhabitants
27 Lower the value of, as currency
28 Dorothy's home in "The Wizard of Oz"
29 Olive oil component
30 Sift
31 Miffed, with "off"
32 "Unhand me!"
33 Spanish paintings
36 Moves aimlessly, with "about"
37 March Madness org.
39 Tailor again, as a skirt
42 Oregon Trail traveler, e.g.
43 Soviet ___
46 Panacea
48 Odor
49 Maryland or Hawaii
51 "Moby-Dick" captain
52 Zero
53 Unclear
54 Hgt.
55 Get higher
56 Horse food
57 Road curve
58 Dubble Bubble, e.g.
59 "Golly!"

by Oliver Hill

ACROSS

1 Filter's target
5 Not much
9 Answers a party invitation
14 Big Apple neighborhood
15 Stuff of legend
16 Rankled
17 Anybody . . . and the missing clues for 30-, 48- and 63-Across
20 "Cut me some slack!"
21 On the ___ vive
22 Assign an NC-17, say
23 Singer Lisa with the 1994 #1 hit "Stay"
25 Monopoly payment
27 Sans ice
30 ???
35 Ctrl+___+Del
36 Firebug
37 1980s TV's "Remington ___"
38 Tequila source
40 N.B.A. Hall-of-Fame nickname
42 Ball of yarn
43 Ring figures?
45 Its HQ is in Brussels
47 Trawler's equipment
48 ???
50 Order in a bear market
51 Slugger Moises
52 Domesticated ox in India
54 Wally's little bro
57 Org. with an e-file option
59 "Don't bother"
63 ???
66 Teen, maybe
67 Daddy-o
68 Relaxation
69 ___ apple
70 Online auction site
71 MapQuest suggestions: Abbr.

DOWN

1 Jet-setters' jets, once
2 Hundred Acre Wood denizen
3 "Oy vey"
4 Old car that was famously available in black, black . . . or black
5 Middle Ages pseudoscience
6 ___ choy
7 2008 campaign issue
8 Fire insurance?
9 "Go, team!"
10 1960s TV series with numerous spinoffs
11 Designer Wang
12 Role
13 Ocular woe
18 Equal: Prefix
19 Loses on purpose
24 Shakespeare, e.g.
26 Bananas
27 Org. co-founded by W. E. B. Du Bois
28 Composer heard at graduations
29 ColecoVision rival
31 Michaels of "S.N.L."
32 Carolyn who wrote Nancy Drew mysteries
33 Architect Saarinen
34 Barbra Streisand title role
36 Blossom element
39 "Sex-x-xy!"
41 Rap star who co-owns the New Jersey Nets
44 One who bites the bullet
46 Wee
49 Area in a grand tour
50 Person in a solarium
53 ___ constrictor
54 The Crimson Tide, to fans
55 City along the Chisholm Trail
56 "___ Karenina"
58 Name-dropping sort
60 Coup d'___
61 End of an ultimatum
62 Goes platinum?
64 Mos. and mos.
65 Escape from the rat race

by Patrick John Duggan

ACROSS

1 "I needed it by yesterday!"
5 Slightly
9 Cat sounds
14 Daffy
15 Exploding star
16 TV opera "___ and the Night Visitors"
17 Completely nude
19 Pago Pago's home
20 Clarinetist Shaw
21 Pass, as legislation
23 Larry King's channel
24 J. R. of "Dallas"
26 It makes good scents
28 Fearsome snakes
31 Prophet of I and II Kings
33 "The Simpsons" shopkeeper
34 Be harshly bright
36 Persia, today
39 "Les Misérables" fugitive
41 Feeling all excited
44 Fashion magazine founded in France
45 Big name in office equipment
47 Cauliflower ___
48 Treating unkindly
51 Name that one logs on with
53 Alternative to a paper clip
55 Cities with wharves
57 Rocky peak
58 Dog strap
60 Sell via the Internet
64 Catawampus
66 All-male gathering
68 Birds flying in a V formation
69 Scarlett O'Hara's plantation
70 Poe story, e.g.
71 Bother persistently
72 Greek war god
73 90° pipe joints

DOWN

1 "Dark Angel" star Jessica
2 Making the mouth pucker, say
3 The "A" of I.R.A.: Abbr.
4 More dawdling
5 Literary olio
6 Turnstile coin
7 Eye-for-an-eye seeker
8 Anti-art movement
9 Angel hair and penne
10 Thurman of "Kill Bill"
11 Bygone Dodge S.U.V.
12 Alps-to-Arles river
13 Bias
18 Like music in a candle shop, maybe
22 CBS forensic series
25 Cuba, por ejemplo
27 Goatee's place
28 Bats' place
29 Down Under gemstone
30 "Buy buy buy" time on Wall Street
32 Meadows
35 Working without ___
37 Jai ___
38 Guy with his nose always stuck in a book
40 Humvee forerunner
42 Military stint
43 Marching synchronously
46 Elton John or Britney Spears
49 Completely wrong
50 Maiden name preceder
52 Lord and lady's home
53 Thespian's platform
54 Where sailors go
56 Chicago air hub
59 "The Thin Man" pooch
61 Kazakhstan's ___ Sea
62 "___ do" ("That's fine")
63 Caustic solutions
65 That, in Chihuahua
67 Regular, plus or super

by Sharon E. Petersen

94

ACROSS

1 Car parker
6 Show hunger, in a way
11 Snaky shape
14 Fight site
15 Revealing woman on TV?
16 TV control abbr.
17 Grouch who's plenty mad?
19 "___ were you . . ."
20 ___ limits (election issue)
21 Exhaust
22 Abbr. before a name on an envelope
23 Always, in poems
25 Perennial loser
27 Pipsqueak under cross-examination?
32 Bird in the "Arabian Nights"
33 ___-Ball (arcade game)
34 20 Questions turn
37 Some brews
39 Daisy Mae's man
42 Coffeemaker style
43 They're outstanding
45 Agitated state
47 Ear: Prefix
48 Wee lad feted by the Friars?
52 Resistance to change
54 Sushi fish
55 What nomads do
56 Shows with pavilions
59 Takeout sign?
63 Class
64 Burned-out goofball?
66 Sault ___ Marie, Mich.
67 "Goodnight" girl of song
68 Assault on Troy, e.g.
69 Ship's pronoun
70 Weather station's need
71 Choice words?

DOWN

1 Seemingly limitless
2 Comic Johnson
3 Goat's look
4 Glossy finish
5 Cap with a pompom
6 Blockbuster rentals
7 Talladega 500, e.g.
8 Torrent
9 Even (with)
10 "Chocolate" dog
11 First lady played by Madonna
12 The first letter of "circle" (but not the fourth)
13 Move furtively
18 "That's it!"
22 Clear ___ (hard to understand)
24 Loop transports
26 Beatnik's "Get it?"
27 Mortarboard tosser
28 Cameo, e.g.
29 Party warmer-upper
30 She's coming out
31 Brains
35 As originally placed, after "in"
36 "You missed a ___!"
38 Blow hard
40 Wrap up
41 Best for picking
44 Did nothing
46 Golf ball's perch
49 Western mountain chain, with "the"
50 Proceeded along the tarmac
51 Second man to walk on the moon
52 March marchers
53 Nick of "Affliction"
57 Federico of the Clinton cabinet
58 Baltic feeder
60 Barely managed, with "out"
61 Block brand
62 One making a visual assessment
64 Yule tree
65 "The Star-Spangled Banner" land

by Michael Langwald

ACROSS

1 Wild-eyed and crazy
6 Mutual of ___ (insurance giant)
11 With 66-Across, where this puzzle's circled things can all be found
14 ___ Gay (W.W. II bomber)
15 Religious doctrine
16 Bucharest's home: Abbr.
17 Sacred song
18 Shoves (in)
19 ___ pro nobis (pray for us: Lat.)
20 "Cat ___ Hot Tin Roof"
21 Proceed effortlessly
24 African desert
26 Respect that one deserves, in slang
27 Mount on which Noah landed
29 Fly into the wild blue yonder
30 Insurrectionist
31 "Are you ___ out?"
33 Subj. that includes monetary policy
37 Conger, for one
38 Tire irons loosen them
41 Actress Gardner
42 Guinness who played Obi-Wan Kenobi
44 Song sung around Christmas
45 April, May and June, e.g.
47 Russia/China border river
49 Hidden from view
50 ___-ski
52 Masonry tool
54 1972 hit for the Spinners
56 Airport info: Abbr.
59 Teachers' grp.
60 Steak variety
61 Bandleader Shaw
63 Suffix with north or south

64 Related to an arm bone
65 Defer (to)
66 See 11-Across
67 Rings, as a church bell
68 Tender spots

DOWN

1 Office note
2 Soon, poetically
3 Less competent
4 ___ de France
5 Multipurpose
6 Go down, so to speak
7 "I just met a girl named ___" ("West Side Story" lyric)
8 Santa ___ (hot winds)
9 The Titanic's was Southampton
10 Michael ___, Cochise player in 1950s TV
11 Scouting group
12 Centers of steering wheels
13 Online pub.
22 Lab maze runner
23 Oral history
25 "You ___ So Beautiful"
27 Sector
28 Film unit
29 James Brown's genre
31 Hunchbacked assistant of horror films
32 Opposite SSW
34 Ensued
35 Through with
36 Political cartoonist Thomas

39 Having no practical application
40 Winter "no school" times
43 Low-___ diet
46 N.Y.C.'s Madison ___
48 Join (with)
49 Scam
50 Old Olds
51 Texas city just north of Dallas
52 Having melody and harmony
53 Contrite ones
54 Mother of Don Juan
55 Jaffe who wrote "Five Women"
57 Stir (up)
58 Cincinnati team
62 ___ Grande

by Peter A. Collins

ACROSS

1 In-box clogger
5 Secluded valleys
10 Intent look
14 To boot
15 Race with handoffs
16 Barrel of laughs
17 One risking arrest
19 Environs
20 "___ pig's eye!"
21 Farm size measure
22 One of eight Eng. kings
23 The "V" in K.J.V.
25 Trousers feature
28 Madison Ave. worker
29 Some seers read them
32 In medias ___
34 Gun lobby org.
35 Phone no. abbr.
36 Sink items
40 Geol. or astron.
42 Stephen of "Michael Collins"
43 ___ polloi
44 Trattoria offering
48 Twist, as a wet cloth or a neck
52 Beat but good
53 Had for dinner
55 Part of an iceberg that's visible
56 "Like me"
58 Egg cells
59 Frame of mind
61 Where 17-, 29-, 36- and 44-Across often wind up
63 Author Rice
64 Santa ___ Derby (annual horse race)
65 Stretch out on a sofa, say
66 Razz
67 Note on a Chinese menu
68 Nosegay

DOWN

1 Drool, basically
2 Made smooth
3 Teeming, as with bees
4 Group with enforcers, with "the"
5 Painter El ___
6 Found out, British-style
7 Actress Sommer
8 Glasgow denials
9 Neighbor of Isr.
10 First-class
11 Radio hosts' medium
12 Actress Caldwell
13 When a flight is due in: Abbr.
18 Two-time Oscar winner Luise
22 Bard's "before"
24 Calcutta wrap
25 Lock horns
26 "___ sells"
27 Superlative finish
30 Conclude by
31 "Exodus" hero
33 Throat ailment
36 Sound after a hang-up
37 So far
38 Query to a brown cow
39 Home of County Clare
40 N.Y.C.-to-Miami dir.
41 Balancer of the books, for short
45 Quiet aircraft
46 Bygone school dance
47 Numbskulls
49 "Same goes for me"
50 Dickens output
51 Very cool, in slang
54 Dog collar attachment
56 ___ Domini
57 It keeps things on the level
59 Capt.'s superior
60 Unnamed person
61 Author McEwan
62 Peak seen from Zurich

by Richard Chisholm

ACROSS

1 It may get a licking after lunch
5 Charged, as particles
10 "Immediately!," in the operating room
14 Choose
15 Said letter by letter, British-style
16 One of 18 on a golf course
17 Actress Spelling
18 One who embroiders a waste conduit?
20 Police weapons that immobilize suspects
22 Drug that's smoked in a pipe
23 On the safe side, at sea
24 Despots
26 Sketcher of a bureau compartment?
30 Caesar or Cicero
31 Drunk's sound
32 Facts and figures
36 Had lunch, e.g.
37 Ph.D. recipient
41 Hoover, informally
42 Chromosome part
44 Many, many moons
45 Ham it up
47 Presenter of a bathroom stall?
51 "The __ Falcon"
54 And others: Abbr.
55 Mideast chief: Var.
56 Shipping hazards in the North Atlantic
60 One pulling a tall structure?
63 Chimney buildup
64 "Just a little off" at the barber's
65 Put up with
66 Dial __ (telephone sound)
67 Meeting: Abbr.
68 Sal of "Rebel Without a Cause"
69 Distort

DOWN

1 Withdraws, with "out"
2 Hilariously funny thing
3 Hosiery hue
4 Pacific island in major W.W. II fighting
5 Main bank vis-à-vis currency
6 Unlocked
7 The first "N" of CNN
8 __ du Diable
9 Middle: Abbr.
10 Astronaut Alan
11 Bring, as a disabled car to a garage
12 Native on the Bering Sea
13 Contract provisions
19 Hurting
21 Secluded valleys
24 Head's opposite
25 Org. promoting leadership and growth for females
26 Engage in a street auto race
27 Memorization method
28 "You said it, brother!"
29 French wine region
33 State openly
34 London's __ Gallery
35 Whiz at tennis serves
38 Corporate V.I.P.'s
39 Hockey legend Gordie
40 Get-off-drugs facility
43 Holds in high regard
46 Bothers
48 München mister
49 Many men's hairlines do this
50 Not mono
51 Actor Damon and others
52 Love Italian-style
53 Annual telethon host Jerry
56 Triumphant cry
57 Piece next to a knight
58 "Going, going, __!"
59 One-dish meal
61 Scottish cap
62 Geisha's waistband

by Sharon Delorme

ACROSS

1 "___ and the Night Visitors"
6 Gasohol, e.g.
10 Peacemaker's goal
14 Jason jilted her
15 Part of ABM
16 Baseball exec Minaya
17 Wide receiver Michael, nicknamed "the Playmaker"
18 Lo-cal
19 Keeping the eyes and ears open
20 Particle-detecting device
23 "The Nazarene" novelist Sholem
24 Saturn model of 2003–07
25 Polygon calculations
28 Western topper
30 Outback bird
32 However, briefly
33 Canal locale
34 Glass of public radio
35 Auto roof option
36 "Sic semper tyrannis!" crier
41 Coughs up, so to speak
42 Tip of a wingtip
43 Wildcatter's find
44 J.F.K. posting: Abbr.
45 Raven's call
46 Be subjected to
50 Belgian treaty city
52 Singer DiFranco
53 Go for a part
54 Chemistry class poster, perhaps
58 Winter Palace figure
60 Fr. ladies
61 Organic compounds
62 Rustler's target
63 Carpet feature
64 The 40 of "the back 40"
65 Tattooist's stock
66 Classic R&B record label
67 Home of Barack Obama's father

DOWN

1 Early Commodore computers
2 Most trifling
3 "Dear Abby" offering
4 Grows more intense
5 Swim meet division
6 Atlanta gridder
7 Bargainer at strike talks
8 Caesarean rebuke
9 Property claim
10 Word before tie or lunch
11 Almond-flavored liqueur
12 Airport rental
13 Give it a go
21 Abbott and Costello movie based on a Ziegfeld musical
22 Cross shape
26 "There'll be ___ time . . ."
27 Jayvee player, maybe
29 Creator of a branch division?
30 Bard's "before"
31 Like Knights Templar
34 Hurricane of 2008
35 Zero ___
36 Computer image file format
37 Courtroom recitation
38 Franklin D. Roosevelt's birthplace
39 Part of PRNDL
40 Bit of eBay action
45 N.F.L. line position: Abbr.
46 For all, as a salon
47 Having new vigor
48 Shipboard kitchen
49 Ukrainian port city
51 Dweebs
52 Journalist ___ Rogers St. Johns
55 Little mischief-makers
56 Not include
57 Weather-resistant wood
58 A.L. or N.L. city, in brief
59 Meditative sect

by Allan E. Parrish

ACROSS

1 Blood type, briefly
5 "___ Miz"
8 Source of all the tender words in this puzzle?
14 "The Sopranos" airer
17 The "Z" of DMZ
21 Slow-cooked entree
23 Oregon city
24 Body parts that may be pierced
26 8-Across issuer
29 Neither's partner
30 Tear
31 German direction
32 Flow back, as the tide
33 Retired flier
35 Motto of 26-Across found on the 8-Across
41 Mornings, briefly
44 Water of Oise
45 Emergency PC key
47 It led to a 1773 Boston "party"
48 "That hurts!"
51 "That feels so-o-o good!"
53 Symbol of 26-Across found on the 8-Across
57 Sage
58 Symbol of 26-Across found on the 8-Across
61 What gave the Hulk his powers
62 Stunt legend Knievel
63 Fort Knox feature
64 Ryan of "Love Story"
65 Marked, as a box
66 Holler
67 ___ Lingus
68 Lorna of fiction

DOWN

1 Choose (to)
2 Yokohama drama
3 Somme summer
4 Lowly soldier
5 Dragon's ___ (early video game)
6 Ballpark fig.
7 Uncompromising
8 Tyrant
9 Opposite of safe
10 N.Y.C. landing site
11 Tennis umpire's cry
12 "Wheel of Fortune" buy
13 Club Med, for one
14 Weights
15 Word repeated before "black sheep"
16 "Coffee, Tea ___?" (1960s best seller)
17 "The Greek" of film
18 ___-Wan Kenobi
19 I.B.M. competitor
20 Spanish pronoun
22 "Bed-in" participant with Lennon
25 Beirut's land: Abbr.
27 Archaeological operation
28 The Buckeyes, for short
33 Clear kitchen wrap
34 "Guys and Dolls" song
35 Mountaineer's tool
36 ___ Decimal System
37 Forgo, as one's rights
38 Three-legged support
39 Immune system lymphocyte
40 "Tippecanoe and ___ too"
42 Nearsighted "Mr."
43 Where dos are done
44 Breakfast brand for a toaster
45 List-ending abbr.
46 Lithuania or Estonia, once: Abbr.
49 Praiseful poem
50 Join with a blowtorch
52 Roll call response
54 Doc bloc
55 Affirmative at sea
56 Psychedelic drug
58 "Be Prepared" org.
59 Had a meal
60 "Without further ___..."

by Patrick Blindauer

100

ACROSS

1 Telly watcher
5 Companion of Snow White
10 Cry out loud
14 PC pop-up
15 "Boléro" composer
16 One of Pittsburgh's three rivers
17 Ice cream holder
19 Pull hard
20 Whacked, in the Bible
21 Monk's hood
23 "You can't mean me!?"
24 Lion in "The Lion King"
27 Classic clown
29 "Then what happened?"
32 Diagram of nutritional needs
36 Responses to bad calls
38 Cousin of a bassoon
39 Actress Emma Roberts, to Julia Roberts
40 Many pizza slices, geometrically
42 Hear about
44 Large in scale
45 Ashe Stadium org.
47 Volcano in Verne's "Journey to the Center of the Earth"
48 Community of Web journals
51 Old J.F.K. lander
52 Chow ___
53 End of an iffy statement
55 Ring hit
57 Theater mogul Marcus
59 Bother persistently
63 The works
65 Six-colored puzzle
68 Langston Hughes poem
69 Actress Christensen of "Traffic"
70 Isle of poetry
71 Weak
72 Baker's 13
73 Sounds of disapproval

DOWN

1 Upscale autos
2 Photocopier tray capacity, maybe
3 Google users seek it
4 Massachusetts university
5 Rap's Dr. ___
6 W.W. II-era female in uniform
7 Guacamole base
8 Gambling mecca
9 Passed quickly
10 Part of EGBDF
11 Occasions to cry "Eureka!"
12 "Brown bagger"
13 Mischievous Norse god
18 Explorer Ericson
22 ___ Doone cookies
25 ___ court (law school exercise)
26 Rises suddenly, as a buoy
28 Where Ali dethroned Foreman
29 Focus of the Manhattan Project, briefly
30 For dieters
31 Short-lived economic expansion of the late 1990s
33 Snowball hurler
34 Desktop images
35 Trim, as meat
37 Looie's underling
41 Cause of a blown engine, maybe
43 Get through hard work
46 Movies, TV, Broadway, etc.
49 Sawed logs, so to speak
50 How long it takes canyons to form
54 "Be silent," in music
55 One corner on a Monopoly board
56 Lead-in to a congratulatory cry
58 100 cents
60 Wise one
61 Kind of
62 Sawbucks
64 Playwright Akins
66 Former White House moniker
67 Bob Dole's state: Abbr.

by Kevin G. Der

ACROSS

1 No-frills
6 Alternative to buttons on a jacket
11 Proof finale
14 Stewpots
15 Small flock of birds
16 ___ Today
17 Caribbean area where pirates plundered
19 After-hours bank convenience
20 "The Sweetheart of Sigma ___"
21 Tic-tac-toe win
22 Poet Nash
24 Harrison Ford's "Star Wars" role
27 Fermented apple juice
29 Sherlock Holmes adventure, in brief
33 Truth ___ (interrogation injection)
36 Annual coll. basketball competition
37 Interceptions or yards rushing
38 Oaf
39 Translucent dessert
41 Turner who sang "We Don't Need Another Hero"
42 With competence
43 "Based ___ novel by . . ."
44 Outspoken, as a critic
45 Faux Chinese dish
49 Jupiter's Io and Callisto
50 Dunk
54 Rant and rage
56 French friend
57 ___ lane (commuters' aid)
58 S.O.S ___
59 City on the Penobscot River
64 Firefighter's tool
65 Skin cream additives
66 Relating to an arm bone
67 Zero, in soccer
68 ___ incognita
69 Hero's acclaim

DOWN

1 Painter of "The Garden of Earthly Delights"
2 Beta preceder
3 Assassinated
4 Suffix with Freud
5 CBS forensic drama
6 Academy, e.g.
7 Hurler Hideo
8 Gardner who was once married to Frank Sinatra
9 Louvre Pyramid architect
10 Ecclesiastical councils
11 Kind of equation graphed as a parabola
12 Italy's Villa d'___
13 Censure
18 The heel is attached to it
23 Diamond or ruby
25 Prepare in advance of
26 Physicist Georg
27 Rattlesnake's shape
28 Enthusiastic about
30 Postnuptial relative
31 Mom's mom, e.g.
32 Footnote abbr.
33 Healing formation
34 Dresden's river
35 Someone to emulate
39 Sen. McCain
40 Grandson of Adam
44 Get-up-and-go
46 Hand-to-hand fighting
47 Brunch cocktail
48 Kuwaiti pooh-bah
51 Heavyweight zoo attraction, for short
52 Sub's navigational aid
53 "___ Breath You Take" (#1 hit by the Police)
54 Reach across
55 Alternative to the subway
56 Teen-___
60 It's poured in pints
61 ___'easter
62 Serving of root beer
63 100%

by Anthony J. Salvia

ACROSS

1 Rolling Stones drummer Charlie
6 Netting
10 One of the S's in U.S.S.
14 ___ water (facing trouble)
15 Pollster Roper
16 Sizable sandwich
17 Nancy Drew author Carolyn
18 Y's guys?
19 Epps of TV's "House"
20 With 59-Across, highway that goes through the 15 places indicated in this puzzle, in order, north to south
22 Ice Capades venue
23 Kind of deck for a fortuneteller
24 Asset in answering the question "Does this dress make me look fat?"
26 Bruce or Kravitz
29 Traditional Christmas sentiment
33 Needing directions
37 Con's opposite
38 "Dueling ___"
39 Declare openly
40 Longtime "S.N.L." announcer Don
42 Lawman Wyatt
43 Do lexicographical work
45 Phoenix cager
46 Strong cart
47 Harsh Athenian lawgiver
48 Online health info site
50 Cole Porter's "Well, Did You ___?"
52 College town near Bangor
56 Final Four org.
59 See 20-Across
63 Mideast missile

64 ___-Tass news agency
65 In the year ___ Lord . . .
66 Movie lioness
67 Nintendo rival
68 "The Boy Who Cried Wolf," e.g.
69 Half of an E.P.A. rating
70 Before, once
71 Skedaddles

DOWN

1 User-edited online reference
2 Concerning
3 Letter before iota
4 Copier additive
5 Unsaturated alcohol
6 Convene
7 Jazz's Fitzgerald
8 Old Walter Berndt comic strip about a teen
9 Old Testament prophet
10 Abridged
11 Hot-rod engine, briefly
12 Tehran's land
13 Much-criticized Congressional spending
21 Treeless plain
25 Expert with I.R.S. returns
27 Gun lobby inits.
28 Like Loki or Thor
30 Slightly open
31 Mrs. Dithers in "Blondie"
32 Catch sight of
33 Cheryl of TV's "Charlie's Angels"
34 On the high side, as a guess

35 Couch
36 Every 12 hours
38 Bit of wit
41 Make a knight
44 Follower of Oct.
48 Like sheets after bleaching
49 Use a towel
51 Biscotti flavoring
53 Butcher's byproducts
54 Weeper of myth
55 Small egg
56 Minute part of a min.
57 251, in old Rome
58 Neighbor of Switz.
60 Carps, carps, carps
61 Part of Q.E.D.
62 "___ Tú" (1974 hit)

by Lucy Gardner Anderson

ACROSS

1 Tempest
6 Those, in México
10 Mimicked
14 Energetic almost
   to a fault
15 Save for later
   viewing
16 As a result
17 "___ my case"
18 Nile queen,
   informally
19 "Seeing red" feeling
20 Prickle in Alaska?
22 2008 film about a
   hunchbacked lab
   assistant
23 Leader overthrown
   in 1917
24 Mrs. Truman
25 Ruby, for one
26 Opened a bit
28 W.W. II arena
30 Lawyers' grp.
33 Computer character
   set, for short
36 Simmered dish in
   California?
38 Take a new path . . .
   or a hint to 20-, 36-,
   41- and 57-Across
41 Chair in Maine?
42 Pawns
43 Easter egg coloring
44 Gov. Landon,
   who lost to F.D.R.
45 Film figure with
   fangs, for short
47 Aphorism
49 Leaping insect
51 Kit ___ (candy bars)
55 Butter servings
57 Scream in Alabama?
59 Prefix with lateral
60 Pop singer Brickell
61 Multitude
62 Paul of "Knocked Up"
63 Bald people may
   wear them
64 Singer John

65 "The Danny ___
   Show" of the 1960s
66 Narrow opening
67 Sting

DOWN

1 Time in the
  army, say
2 Neophytes
3 Puccini production
4 Curb
5 "You do the ___!"
6 Artist working on glass
7 Missile holders
8 Manager
9 In the near future
10 Eagle's home
11 Hardheaded
12 Frozen waffle brand

13 Active person
21 Not yet decided,
   on a sched.
25 "You fell for it!"
27 Interlocking puzzle
29 Mao ___-tung
31 "Everything will
   ___" ("Don't worry")
32 Plant bristles
33 Scored 100% on
34 One-horse carriage
35 Examined example
36 Punning and such
37 Capital on the
   Baltic Sea
39 Lamprey ___
40 Flower in Wordsworth's
   "I Wandered Lonely
   as a Cloud"

45 Abhor
46 Cheerleader's cheer
48 Parenthetical remark
50 Mario's brother in
   Nintendo's
   Mario Bros.
52 Line from the heart
53 English royal
   house after York
54 Medical tube
55 Fringe benefit
56 Blue hue
57 Stitches
58 The Beatles' "___ a
   Woman"

by Daniel Raymon

104

ACROSS

1 Many fund-raisers
6 Electrical coil inventor
11 Seattle-to-Las Vegas dir.
14 Oversleeper's need
15 Parolee, e.g.
16 All ___ day's work
17 P
20 "___ With a View"
21 Warren of the Supreme Court
22 PO
28 Future J.D.'s
29 It may be cupped or cuffed
30 Jazz singer Laine
31 Kind of tea
35 Topeka hrs.
38 POL
41 Cries of pain
42 They may make you cry
43 "___ hardly believe it!"
44 ___, amas, amat . . .
45 Contradict
46 POLK
53 Myanmar neighbor
54 Relatives of nieces
55 POLKA
62 Sugar Loaf Mountain site, briefly
63 Poppy product
64 Five o'clock shadow remover
65 ___ Lingus
66 Impertinent
67 Space shuttle gasket

DOWN

1 It's dispensed from a hose
2 Remodeled Clay?
3 Lenient
4 Public hangings?
5 Dirty tricks on the campaign trail
6 :50
7 Shower with praise
8 Dolt
9 Online chuckle
10 "Wheel of Fortune" purchase
11 Instrument played by George Harrison
12 Bergen dummy
13 Jumping the gun
18 Suffix with ranch
19 Eye drop
22 Boxer Graziano, formally
23 Holiday visitor, maybe
24 #2's
25 "The Time Machine" race
26 The squares of "three squares"
27 Event for Cinderella
31 Making the dean's list, e.g.
32 QB Manning
33 Sigma preceder
34 Big box
35 The four seasons, e.g.
36 Where Rioja wine comes from
37 Doctrine
39 Heavy volume
40 Like a game heading into extra innings
44 Reply to "Are not!"
45 Champs-Élysées sight
46 Plant life
47 Jack of "The Great Dictator"
48 Helicopter part
49 City of Light
50 ___ T. Firefly, Groucho's role in "Duck Soup"
51 Any Hatfield, to a McCoy
52 MapQuest quests?: Abbr.
56 Jackson and Derek
57 Air quality org.
58 Driveway topper
59 Submachine gun
60 Dijon denial
61 Work unit

by Randall J. Hartman

ACROSS

1 Korbut who was a sensation at the 1972 Olympics
5 Like animals in a zoo
10 Fissures
14 Tidy
15 Subside
16 ___ of measure
17 Husband of a countess
18 Rigatoni or spaghetti
19 Something to wish upon
20 Aerosol tanning?
23 Daft
24 Fable writer
25 John, Paul, George or Ringo
28 Traditional paintings
30 ___ Spumante
31 Buffalo hockey player
33 Korean automaker
36 Tiffany showroom?
40 With "of" plus 49-Down, momentous time
41 Railroad station
42 ___ tide
43 Tweety ___ of Warner Bros. cartoons
44 Overindulgence
46 Molded jelly
49 Broadcaster
51 Babble incoherently?
57 Sassy
58 Lerner's partner for "Camelot"
59 Inside info
60 Otherwise
61 Pesos : Mexico :: ___ : Turkey
62 Poker declaration
63 Dodger or Met, for short
64 Bias
65 Theater award

DOWN

1 Change for a five
2 Jump
3 Teri of "Close Encounters of the Third Kind"
4 Europe/America separator, with "the"
5 Truman who wrote "Breakfast at Tiffany's"
6 Sternward
7 Bloated, as the stomach
8 "___, Brute?"
9 College official
10 Spews, as lava
11 Those voting nay
12 Instrument for Rachmaninoff
13 Throat ailment
21 Brynner who starred in "The King and I"
22 1690s Massachusetts witch hunt locale
25 Statue's support
26 "Monday Night Football" channel
27 Not much
28 Death notice, for short
29 Lyricist Gershwin
31 Real-life org. seen in "Bullitt"
32 "Much ___ About Nothing"
33 Midleg joint
34 Actress Lupino and others
35 Egyptian snakes
37 Proclamation
38 "___ the land of the free . . ."
39 By deferred payment
43 Not sweet
44 Author Hemingway
45 Illiterates' marks
46 Colorado resort
47 Participate in a bee
48 Derby prize
49 See 40-Across
50 Des Moines native
52 Building additions
53 Stir up, as the waters
54 Baseball's Hideo
55 Twirl . . . or a cryptic hint to 20-, 36- and 51-Across?
56 Start of a counting-out rhyme

by Andrea Carla Michaels and Michael Blake

106

ACROSS

1 Place for a dictionary
6 In pursuit of
11 Asian holiday
14 Skater-turned-actress Sonja
15 Sculpted figure
16 "Xanadu" band, to fans
17 Dickens lad
19 Align the cross hairs
20 Itinerary word
21 Motorcyclist's wear
22 Rental ad abbr.
23 Takes out surgically
26 Red dye
28 Small equine
32 ___ nous
35 Thurman of "Gattaca"
36 W.W. I fighter plane
37 MGM's lion
38 Activity exemplified in the '60s by the ends of 17-, 28-, 48- and 64-Across
42 Summer, in Sèvres
43 Caesarean rebuke
45 Last article in the Constitution
46 Grant portrayer on TV
48 Weightlifter's lift
52 Oscar winner Marisa
53 From one side only, in law
57 AOL, e.g., for short
58 Norman of the Clinton and Bush cabinets
62 Hole-making tool
63 Brandy label letters
64 Rum/vodka cocktail
67 Wriggly fish
68 Singer/actress Lenya
69 Lets loose
70 NNW's opposite
71 Showy display
72 Take a sip of

DOWN

1 Action on a crowded subway
2 Double ___ (DNA structure)
3 Computer that debuted in 1946
4 Actress Tyler
5 Attorney's charge
6 Swear to
7 Poultry
8 Far from pudgy
9 Latin 101 verb
10 Went bad
11 Unwraps in a hurry
12 Rule out
13 "The Tomorrow Show" host
18 South Korea's first president Syngman ___
24 Mount Carmel's locale: Abbr.
25 Lawn mower's spot
27 Photo ___ (media events)
29 Readily comprehended
30 "What a good boy ___!"
31 Bert Bobbsey's twin sister
32 Nonrequired courses
33 Red ink entries
34 Indian carving
39 Frank Sinatra's wife before Mia
40 "Collages" novelist
41 "The World According to ___"
44 Oil-rich land: Abbr.
47 Jamaican music
49 Hardly clumsy
50 Trendy travelers
51 Proctored event
54 Landscapers' tools
55 Call from a nest
56 "Family Ties" mother
59 ___-Z (zippy Camaro)
60 N.L.R.B. part: Abbr.
61 "Cómo ___ usted?"
65 Frequently, to bards
66 New Deal inits.

by Allan E. Parrish

ACROSS

1 "Green ___" of 1960s TV
6 Spoiled kid
10 Bossy's offspring
14 Fill the crevices of, as a window frame
15 Capital of Italia
16 Zero-shaped
17 Etiquette expert writes messages online?
19 Device for a plow team
20 Thieves' locale
21 Moist, as morning grass
22 Dog : barked :: cat : ___
24 Frees (of)
25 Poverty
26 Singer speculates?
31 Eliminate the stubble
32 Pupil's surrounder
33 ___ & Tina Turner Revue
35 Misjudges
36 Princess who helped Jason
38 Tel ___
39 Ballot marks
40 When repeated, a Samoan city
41 Ingrid Bergman or Bjorn Borg
42 Artist clears the bases?
46 Food, informally
47 Actress Lupino and others
48 Many Halloween costumes
51 Cross-country ___
52 Grain in Cheerios
55 Announcement for the head of a queue
56 Actress searches?
59 Skater's jump
60 "___ and out"
61 Bar legally
62 Decrease, as the moon
63 Rover's "hands"
64 Hotel offerings

DOWN

1 Scored perfectly on
2 Arrived
3 Damage beyond repair
4 90° pipe turn
5 Jump from a plane
6 Read a little here and there
7 Pink, as cheeks
8 Gal. or qt.
9 One of the six states of Australia
10 Cousin of the gray wolf
11 Declare openly
12 Great Salt ___
13 Skipped town
18 Foot: Prefix
23 Wraps up
24 Guns, as an engine
25 Had on
26 One "tamed" in Shakespeare
27 Ankle bones
28 To whom a husband leaves an estate
29 Potomac, for one
30 Loses control on a snowy road, say
31 Gender
34 Cain and Abel's mother
36 Bobbysoxer's hangout
37 They're subject to inflation
38 Inspires reverence in
40 Warm-up exam for future collegians
41 See 53-Down
43 Butterfinger candy bar maker
44 Parkgoers with backpacks
45 Chief Norse god
48 Chew (on)
49 Six: Prefix
50 Plow team
51 Whole lot
52 Aware of
53 With 41-Down, nuclear device
54 Recipe measures: Abbr.
57 Actress Longoria
58 G.I. uplifter

by Susan Gelfand

108

ACROSS

1 Summer drinks
5 ___ the aisle (bipartisanly)
11 Like William Howard Taft
14 Actress Polo who played a presidential candidate's wife on "The West Wing"
15 Wilderness home
16 Ginger ___
17 Early November occasion in the U.S.
19 Zero
20 Singer Mann
21 The Blue Jays, on scoreboards
22 Ribicoff and Lincoln, familiarly
23 Dropped a size
26 Forestall
28 Corrode
29 Actor Rob who played a presidential aide on "The West Wing"
31 Italian battery pioneer
32 It went up in the 1960s
35 Inaugural ball holder
36 What many Americans will do on 17-Across (as hinted at by highlighting all the V's in this puzzle's answer)
38 Where the "Mona Lisa" hangs
41 Leaves early, as an office
44 Cause for celebration: Abbr.
45 ___ cava
46 Japanese moolah
48 Deprive, as through a loss
50 "View of Toledo" painter
53 I.R.S. workers
54 Jr.'s Jr.
56 "Holding Out for ___" (1984 Bonnie Tyler hit)
57 Cereal bit
58 Sights at polling places
61 35 is the minimum one to be U.S. president
62 New York lake
63 7/4/1776, for one
64 Sen. Kennedy
65 Most likely to raise eyebrows
66 Iowa college town

DOWN

1 Relaxed
2 Samson's undoer
3 Religious recluse
4 "Attack, Rex!"
5 ___ Baba
6 Co. captain?
7 Tirade
8 High, in a way
9 Beatles drummer
10 Nondairy milk source
11 Water pump turner
12 Not recognizable by
13 Kennedy-era launch
18 President pro ___
22 Long-legged shorebird
24 Beethoven dedicatee
25 "___ Stop" (Bill Clinton theme song)
27 Mrs. Perón
30 Zigzag
33 Musicians John and Christine
34 Baby buggy?
35 Outspoken
37 Barn topper
38 Researcher's wear
39 Short, as an article
40 Not yet having gone before an M.P.A.A. board
42 It involves reading letters out loud
43 Hide
45 Hidden
47 Hangmen's needs
49 Article of food
51 Gossip
52 "The Mary Tyler Moore Show" spinoff
55 "Would ___?"
58 Bad sound at a campaign rally
59 Takes too much, briefly
60 "Mom" in a heart, maybe, for short

by Peter A. Collins and Joe Krozel

ACROSS

1 Like the air around Niagara Falls
6 Counterpart of comedy
11 Feed seed
14 Entertain
15 Smidgens
16 Actress Peeples
17 Open-textured cotton fabric
19 AOL or MSN
20 Stayed out of sight
21 Allergic reaction
22 Fillet of ___
23 Gift-giver's urging
25 Showed boredom
27 Impressive grouping
30 Possible result of slamming on the brakes
31 Señor's "Positively!"
34 Without a guarantee of condition
36 Battery terminal
39 List-ending abbr.
40 "___ or plastic?"
42 F.B.I. agent
43 Scarfs (down)
45 Folk singer Seeger
46 E-mail command
47 Uses a pew
49 Relief from the sun
51 Alpine dwelling
53 Discourages
57 Marathon, e.g.
58 Say, as the Pledge of Allegiance
62 By way of
63 Feel feverish
64 The start of 17-Across or 11- or 33-Down
66 A/C meas.
67 Make amends
68 Clear the blackboard
69 Bro or sis
70 Capital of Oregon
71 Descartes and others

DOWN

1 Like a he-man
2 Beatnik's "Got it"
3 Napped leather
4 Mao ___-tung
5 Polite affirmation
6 What high rollers roll
7 Part on stage
8 Completely, after "from"
9 Shipboard pals
10 Cigarette's end
11 Russian church feature
12 An usher walks up and down it
13 Sealed up, as a package
18 Lure into a crime
22 Backyard apparatus for kids
24 Manicurist's tool
26 Letters before an alias
28 "Rush!" on an order
29 "Holy cow!"
31 Use needle and thread
32 "What was ___ do?"
33 Jazzy Latin dance site
35 Third son of Adam and Eve
37 Actor Aykroyd
38 Bring to a halt
41 Entertain with a tale
44 Sault ___ Marie
48 Rock layers
50 More profound
51 Grouchy sorts
52 Port-au-Prince's land
54 Perrier rival
55 Get the soap out
56 Wise ones
59 Environmental sci.
60 Dunce cap, geometrically
61 Talked-about twosome
64 Profs.' helpers
65 Opposite of post-

by Gail Grabowski

110

ACROSS

1 Agile for one's age
5 Athletic conference members: Abbr.
9 Heyerdahl who wrote "Kon-Tiki"
13 Opposite of windward
14 Sonneteer, e.g.
15 Herman who wrote "The Caine Mutiny"
16 Siren's sound
17 Almost-sacrificed son in the Bible
19 Crazy about
20 ___ Alley
22 1930s quints' name
24 Potemkin mutiny city
25 Crucifix inscription
26 Late singer Sumac
29 OP's forerunners
31 Tennis player
33 Part of a ship's bow
37 Pop's ___ Pop
39 Central computer
40 Old war story
41 Food stat
42 Sprang up
43 Heaps
44 Fats Domino's "It's ___ Love"
45 Sand formations
46 "You said a mouthful!"
48 European eruption site
50 Mystery writer Josephine
51 Sgts. and cpls.
53 Shining
58 Low-cost, in slang
60 Company that introduced NutraSweet
61 Injure
63 Gobsmacks
65 Terrible ___
66 Choir voice
67 The Everly Brothers' "Let ___ Me"
68 Cars from Korea
69 Places
70 Blacken
71 Artist Warhol

DOWN

1 Took care of
2 Highland pattern
3 Wife of un roi
4 Kennel cries
5 Backbone-related
6 Fortune 500 listings: Abbr.
7 Going straight to Antarctica, say
8 Result of an ink spill
9 Romulus or Remus
10 Bliss before the hard part begins
11 Tagged on a diamond
12 "Citizen Kane" studio
18 Unsophisticated, as humor
21 Inquired
23 Never, in Nürnberg
27 Pool stroke
28 Poker amounts
30 Spanish Surrealist
32 Like some streets
33 Try to strike
34 Unaccompanied
35 Chicago, with "the"
36 "Miss Universe" holder
38 Walk or trot
42 "Time is money," for one
44 Certain rec centers
47 Air Force ___
49 Sadat's predecessor
52 ___ nerve
54 ___ Gravas, role on "Taxi"
55 Field Marshal Rommel
56 Heaps
57 Complicated, as a divorce
59 Dr. providers
61 Prefix with practice
62 Pie ___ mode
64 Org. for Raptors and Hawks

DIAGONAL

1 Disappearing
12 Proceeding with little effort

by Nancy Salomon and Larry Shearer

111

ACROSS

1 Animal foot
4 Swiss peaks
8 Smaller than small, in dress sizes
14 Slugger's stat
15 Neil Armstrong made a giant one for mankind
16 "8 Mile" rapper
17 Takes too much, briefly
18 One-named singer of "Smooth Operator"
19 Gem measures
20 Demand legal restitution after injury
23 Outer: Prefix
24 Pentax competitor
25 Subtle auction bid indicator
28 Forum wrap
30 Oui's opposite
31 KitchenAid alternative
33 Seek compassionate treatment
36 Big talker
40 Lots and lots
41 What drought victims might do
45 Ration out
46 Aquarium wriggler
47 Intent look
51 "Rescue me!"
52 Shenanigan
54 Remain unsettled
56 Take unnecessary risks
60 Test of one's mettle
62 Perched on
63 Tractor-trailer
64 Place to begin to connect the dots
65 Coagulate
66 Free ___ bird
67 Seven-person band
68 Bills you might break 20s into
69 They generally run east-west in Manhattan: Abbr.

DOWN

1 Plain writing
2 Kidnap
3 Not fooled by
4 In addition
5 Get the hang of
6 Expense account no-no
7 Talk about
8 Ice cream nut
9 Online periodical, for short
10 Almost any part of the Michelin Man
11 All tangled up
12 Asian New Year
13 Bad ___ (German spa)
21 London forecast
22 Like the earliest Beatles recordings
26 Way back when
27 Calendar components
29 Rearward, at sea
31 In the midst of
32 Kind of school
34 Sense of self-importance
35 Le ___ Soleil (Louis XIV)
36 Transcript figs.
37 Guthrie who sang "Alice's Restaurant"
38 Tortilla chip topper
39 Caveat on a party invitation: Abbr.
42 Western gambling mecca
43 Take back, as a statement
44 Not too much
48 "The Simpsons" storekeeper
49 Football referees, informally
50 Sign up to serve
52 Note a half step up from G
53 Sing like Bing
55 Artist known for dance scenes
57 Transmitted
58 The shrew in "The Taming of the Shrew"
59 Chooses
60 Photo ___ (P.R. events)
61 ___ v. Wade

by Paula Gamache

112

ACROSS

1 Touch base again
6 Ukraine, e.g., formerly: Abbr.
9 The gamut
13 1940s–'50s politico Stevenson
14 "Don't look ___!"
15 Lois of the Daily Planet
16 Sporty 1980s Pontiac
17 Police stop
19 Beverage often served with sugar or lemon
20 Oreo maker
22 "Get my point?"
23 Remedy for failed courses, maybe
26 Powwowed (with)
27 Lacking pizazz
31 Playful mammal
34 Cardinal vis-à-vis Illinois, Indiana or Ohio
37 Wray of "King Kong"
38 Innocents
39 BMW or MG
40 Military capability
43 "You don't know ___!"
45 Lazy types
46 "Pow!"
47 Wheeled toy
54 Clairvoyant's gift, briefly
57 Labors over
58 Engine part
59 What 17-, 23-, 34-, 40- and 47-Across are each composed of
61 France's ___ Polytechnique
63 Back of the neck
64 James of "The Godfather"
65 "___ is an island"
66 Pinnacle
67 Fair Deal president, for short
68 ___ list

DOWN

1 Ohio political dynasty
2 Farewell
3 Glimmer
4 Former Mideast inits.
5 NASA program that explored the outer planets
6 One who never cries "Ow!"
7 #1 hit
8 British in the Revolutionary War
9 Without exception
10 New Mexico town or county
11 Formerly
12 The Cowardly Lion's Kansas counterpart
14 Wall St. figures
18 Trailblazer Daniel
21 Elementary class with crayons
24 Mrs. abroad
25 Isr. neighbor
28 Flaky mineral
29 Modern-day Persia
30 Capts.' subordinates
31 Wastes
32 Follower, as in espionage
33 Novice
34 Dated
35 It's not required for casual Fridays
36 It's south of Eur.
38 A pretty capable person
41 When a plane is due to take off: Abbr.
42 Kind of ID
43 Pour drinks
44 U.K. record label
46 Maidenform product
48 Old Apple computers
49 Sport shoe feature
50 Part of P.T.A.: Abbr.
51 Bouquet of roses
52 Mideast's ___ Heights
53 Utopias
54 11,000-foot Italian peak
55 Tit for tat . . . or tat for tit
56 Bishop of Rome
60 Bewitch
62 Iowa college

by Richard Chisholm

ACROSS

1 Event involving burning and looting
5 Competent
9 Not completely shut, as a door
13 Remove wooden pins from
15 Study just before a test
16 Created
17 Gardener's gift
19 Military no-show
20 Electric eye, e.g.
21 Rain cover
23 Big slice of history
24 Measure of national economic health
27 Cane cutter
31 Don Juan type
32 Norway's capital
33 Walk-___ (small parts)
35 Appears to be
39 Come to a compromise
43 Skedaddle
44 Outer: Prefix
45 River near the Sphinx
46 Butterfly catchers
49 Chin beards
51 "Call ___ sometime"
55 Brouhaha
56 ___ good example
57 Dine at a restaurant
62 Halter attachment
64 Rhyming word game
66 Hay bundle
67 Buffalo's lake
68 Go inside
69 Norway's patron saint
70 Start of a counting-out rhyme
71 Blah

DOWN

1 Toupees, slangily
2 Memo starter
3 Ready for business
4 Summer shirts, informally
5 Alas, in Augsburg
6 No gentleman
7 Hedy of "Samson and Delilah"
8 Womb occupant
9 Doctors' grp.
10 Chatted
11 Love to bits
12 "Stop worrying!"
14 Garden statuette
18 Spiral seashell
22 First of 12 popes with a religious-sounding name
25 Shipped off
26 Has no obligation to
27 Pops' partners
28 "Wait just ___!"
29 Queen of the 45-Across, for short
30 Definitely a day for air-conditioning
34 "That's all ___ wrote"
36 Actress Falco
37 French miss: Abbr.
38 Envisions
40 Agenda details
41 Veteran, perhaps
42 Mr. ___ (Lucy's TV boss)
47 Giggle
48 Lampoon
50 Yawning or visibly astonished
51 Reclusive actress Greta
52 Just right
53 "There!"
54 Arrested
58 Old-fashioned food containers
59 Not fooled by
60 Maui music makers
61 Newbie
63 Carson City's home: Abbr.
65 Ignition starter

by Billie Truitt

ACROSS

1 "Amerika" novelist
6 Apt. area measurement
10 "Shut your ___!"
14 Something you click to open
15 "Treasure Island," e.g.
16 Singer McEntire
17 Trial jury?
19 "Young Frankenstein" hunchback
20 ___ and outs
21 Writer Oscar
22 Heart beater in bridge bidding
23 Wine telemarketer?
25 Detective played by Peter Lorre
28 Word before Miss or Opry
29 Iranian money
30 Lone Star State duties?
37 Ecol. or biol.
38 Kind of pass that might get you backstage
39 Shout from Scrooge
40 Late-night talk show host's principles?
45 American Beauty, for one
46 ___ Flanders, neighbor of Homer Simpson
47 Some charge cards, informally
49 Slyly popping a breath mint, e.g.?
55 In the air
56 Kept the engine running
57 "What have we here?!"
60 Mrs. Dithers of "Blondie"
61 Sammy's backup singers?
63 Radioer's word
64 Land o' the Irish
65 Honda division
66 Line from the ankle to the waist, say
67 Stag or stallion
68 "Mmm-mmm!"

DOWN

1 Hat for a French soldier
2 "You said it, brother!"
3 Ones waiting for autographs, e.g.
4 Sedona maker
5 Totally mistaken
6 Bathroom division
7 Session after a lecture, informally
8 Old maker of baseball cards and bubble gum
9 ___ Aviv
10 Not quite in the majors
11 Kingly
12 "Welcome to my humble ___"
13 Tool for someone on KP duty
18 Test for a sitcom
22 Margarita garnish
23 Sanders, Klink or Mustard: Abbr.
24 Dow Jones listings: Abbr.
25 Richie's mom, to the Fonz
26 Puerto ___
27 Primary
31 Stowe heroine
32 Mark, as a ballot
33 Mil. address
34 GameCube competitor
35 Simplicity
36 The Rolling Stones' "___ a Rainbow"
41 Myrmecologist's box
42 "Very cool!"
43 Atlanta-based federal health org.
44 Hoopsters Archibald and Thurmond
45 VCR button
48 Noon
49 Mexican restaurant orders
50 "___ Lucy"
51 Grammy-winning pianist Chick
52 Miss America headwear
53 Tylenol rival
54 "Crazy" singer Patsy
57 Egg, biologically
58 Damage
59 "The Star-Spangled Banner" start
61 Barack Obama, e.g.: Abbr.
62 Site of an oxygen tent, in brief

by Caleb Madison

ACROSS

1 Actress Moorehead
6 Trayful of cookies, e.g.
11 J.F.K.'s successor
14 Minimum
15 One of the dancing Astaires
16 Commitment to pay
17 The Divine Miss M
19 Balsam, e.g.
20 John Cougar Mellencamp's "R.O.C.K. in the ___"
21 Baseball scores
22 Hardly ever
24 Actress Griffith
26 Leers at
27 Birth mother's helper
31 "Git!"
34 Some jeans
35 Menagerie
36 Came to the ground
37 Jesse of the 1936 Olympics
39 Jerome who composed "The Last Time I Saw Paris"
40 Rob on the street
41 ___ the Terrible
42 Waits patiently
43 Connected on only one side, as a town house
47 Turn away
48 Crew members
52 Declaration ending "or else!"
54 Rheumatism symptom
55 Order at the Pig and Whistle
56 Court
57 Change abruptly, or what the insides of 17-, 27- and 43- Across do?
60 Shoemaker's tool
61 Poetic Muse
62 Covered with ivy
63 "Get it?"
64 ___ motion (start)
65 Manicurist's tool

DOWN

1 The Beatles' "Revolver" or "Help!"
2 Ones flying south for the winter
3 Birth-related
4 Paris's Gare de l'___
5 Chest part
6 The "B" of 11-Across
7 Uses the "+" function
8 Number on a bus. card
9 Religious groups
10 Announces
11 Not reduced, as some illustrations
12 Bring to 212°
13 "12 angry men," e.g.
18 California's ___ Woods
23 VCR button
25 Study of the body: Abbr.
26 Storm clouds, to some
28 "Maria ___," 1941 #1 hit
29 Golf cry
30 Long times
31 ___ Club (discount store)
32 Game with Colonel Mustard and Mrs. Peacock
33 Complex procedure
37 Famous part of Rossini's "William Tell"
38 Power unit
39 Baby goats
41 Has thoughts
42 Deprive (of)
44 "___ Got a Secret"
45 Thing from which a butterfly emerges
46 Chemistry Nobelist Otto
49 Portland's home
50 "___ Gantry"
51 Impoverished
52 "___ the night before Christmas . . ."
53 Hockey great Gordie
54 Not pro
58 Mouse's big cousin
59 Barely shining

by Eric J. Platt

ACROSS

1 Ships' complements
6 Org. that defends the Bill of Rights
10 *Sound of . . . an explosion*
14 On the level
15 *. . . thunder*
16 One of Scotland's Inner Hebrides
17 Fireplace
18 *. . . a mother with noisy kids*
19 ___ Pictures (entertainment company)
20 Indispensable
22 *. . . a toy train*
24 *. . . a raindrop in a puddle*
26 Comical Costello
27 Cuba, e.g., to Cubans
28 Looked up to
32 *. . . a table tennis ball (with 45-Across)*
35 Not enough room to swing ___
37 Prefix with dactyl
38 Not worth a ___
39 *. . . brakes*
41 All the sounds in this puzzle together?
42 *. . . a basketball through a basket*
44 "La Bamba" actor Morales
45 See 32-Across
46 Dermal art
48 "Right now!," to a doctor
50 *. . . a knock on a door*
51 *. . . Road Runner*
55 *. . . grease in a deep fryer*
59 Destine for, as oblivion
60 Count ___ of Lemony Snicket books
61 Run for it
63 Egypt's Nasser
64 It follows first, second and third
65 *. . . a porker*

66 Classic British Jaguar
67 Columnist's column
68 Judge
69 Test track features

DOWN

1 *. . . champagne glasses*
2 Zellweger of "Jerry Maguire"
3 Ham-and-___ (incompetent sort)
4 Boar
5 Braces (oneself)
6 *. . . a surprised German*
7 *. . . a hen*
8 Mascara's place
9 Maintain
10 Serving with ham and gravy
11 *. . . a circusgoer*
12 ___ account (never)
13 B.L.T. ingredient
21 Fond ___, Wis.
23 Get-up-and-go
25 Mother-of-pearls
28 Relaxed
29 Second serve, for example
30 "___ Brockovich"
31 *. . . a doorbell*
32 *. . . a cheater in class*
33 Place name before and after City
34 "Bonne ___" (French wish at bedtime)
36 Two-time loser to D.D.E.
39 Little ham?
40 Quoted
43 Attacked from above
45 "McHale's Navy" craft
47 Select
49 Highest point in an orbit
51 Ford and Bush adviser Scowcroft
52 TV trophies
53 Day's march
54 The ends of the earth
55 London entertainment district
56 *. . . a person sitting down*
57 Pathetic
58 "On the Waterfront" director Kazan
62 Squeeze (out)

by Matt Ginsberg

ACROSS

1 Fill to excess
5 "___ la vista, baby"
10 Milky white gem
14 Earth Day subj.
15 Less cordial
16 Hoarfrost
17 Many a mall outlet
19 Slaughter in the Baseball Hall of Fame
20 Scout master?
21 California's Big ___
22 "Just kidding" signals
23 The "Na" in NaCl
25 Citizen Kane's estate
27 Nose-in-the-air type
29 Tooth covering
32 "Hey, over here!"
35 Instruction book
38 Dude
39 Land to build a house on
40 What the starts of 17- and 62-Across and 11- and 34-Down may each be a piece of
41 A conceited person has a big one
42 ___ de Cologne
43 Not yet taken care of
44 Gait faster than a walk
45 Devoted
47 Arthur of tennis
49 Dons
52 Muscle/bone connector
56 Now, in Nogales
58 By way of
60 Polo who visited Cathay
61 Dangerous shark
62 Place to keep a report
64 Get ready, for short
65 ___ tube
66 Carrier of coal from a mine
67 Filly's father
68 Swimmer Debbie who won three golds at the 1968 Olympics
69 Upper house members: Abbr.

DOWN

1 Religious splinter groups
2 Possible reaction from getting a cold shoulder?
3 ___ fro
4 Nose-in-the-air type
5 ___ and hers
6 Isn't idle
7 Sitting Bull or Crazy Horse
8 ___ cotta
9 "___ we having fun yet?"
10 Frozen potato brand
11 A.T.M. access code
12 Not a good way to run
13 Subtracted by
18 Verb accompanier
22 In a weak manner
24 Instants
26 Most at hand
28 Madam
30 Therefore
31 Plunder
32 "Not guilty," e.g.
33 Fly high
34 Five-card or seven-card game
36 Prefix with classical
37 Radius neighbor
40 Ruling group after a coup
44 Renters
46 The Continent
48 Powerful auto engine
50 Sheeplike
51 Fool
53 Rapper with a professional title
54 Neptune's realm
55 Standards
56 Concert equipment
57 Mata ___
59 "A Death in the Family" author
62 What a "swish" basketball shot doesn't touch
63 "It's c-c-cold!"

by Sarah Keller

118

ACROSS

1 Indo-Europeans
7 Hot night out, perhaps
11 Prospector's aid
14 Largest city on the Illinois River
15 Privy to
16 Stein filler
17 Traditional Christmas dessert
19 Conglomerate whose N.Y.S.E. symbol is the same as the company's name
20 Elhi grps.
21 Bulldozes
23 Red bird with black wings and tail
29 Word that can precede or follow "first"
30 Congregational area
31 They can be split or charged
32 Traditional January event
37 Lincoln's home: Abbr.
38 Take marks off
39 Took gold
40 1999 Tom Hanks film, with "The"
43 Simple disguise
45 See 62-Across
46 Fur for a stole
47 Home remedy for skin irritations
51 Medieval tale
52 Baldwin of "30 Rock"
53 Smashable tennis shot
54 Shade close to azure
61 Team ___
62 ___ of Constantine (landmark in 45-Across)
63 Mother of Calcutta
64 At any time, to a bard
65 Spreadsheet fill
66 Area between curbs

DOWN

1 "Killer" PC program
2 Theist's subj.
3 Whom "Uncle Sam wants"
4 Get ready for war
5 Parts of baby bottles
6 Browns, as meat
7 "Say that thou ___ forsake me . . .": Shak.
8 Singer DiFranco
9 Cargo unit
10 Carve on, as a monument
11 Indian corn
12 Take in or let out
13 Strokes . . . or ones stroked
18 "Can't Help Lovin' ___ Man"
22 A long, long time
23 "Language that rolls up its sleeves, spits on its hands and goes to work," per Carl Sandburg
24 Provide party food
25 Sun-dried brick
26 Lens holder
27 Ouzo flavoring
28 ___ the Great of children's books
32 More twisted, as humor
33 "2001" computer
34 Mark time
35 Michaels of "S.N.L."
36 East ___ (certain Londoner)
38 Jane Austen novel
41 Lead-in to while
42 Steno's staple
43 Shelf support
44 Dorothy's aunt and others
46 Chooses
47 Bullwinkle, e.g.
48 Open, as a gate
49 Russian villa
50 Grp. once led by Arafat
51 Game associated with the starts of 17-, 23-, 32-, 40-, 47- and 54-Across
55 All alternative
56 Deed
57 December exclamation
58 Actress Remick
59 Function
60 Partake of

by C. W. Stewart

ACROSS

1 Copycat
5 Alternative to MasterCard and Visa, informally
9 "Aw, quit your joshin'!"
14 Hatcher of "Desperate Housewives"
15 Spy from within
16 Erie Canal city
17 Secular
18 Poet Ezra's favorite desserts?
20 Give in (to)
22 Have a gander
23 It transcends sight, hearing, smell, taste and touch
24 City with ships at docks
26 Christmas carol
28 Eye parts
30 In need of a nap
34 Main part of a knife
37 When said three times, a film about Pearl Harbor
39 Taboo
40 Skin of a fruit
41 Hollywood's Dennis or Randy
42 Magician Henning
43 Prefix with present
44 Officials who cry "Yer out!"
45 River to the Caspian
46 Activity in a darkened room
48 Become established
50 Lady's man
52 Attempt at getting a tan
56 Bank offerings, briefly
59 Prefix with phobia
61 Belgrade's land
62 Essayist Charles's favorite entree?
65 Opposite of dry, as hair
66 Sky-blue
67 Slanted type: Abbr.
68 Not scheduled to compete
69 Impressionist Edgar
70 Voice quality
71 Minus

DOWN

1 Book often stored horizontally
2 War's opposite
3 Jong who wrote "Fear of Flying"
4 Writer Anne's favorite dessert?
5 Electric current unit
6 Call to a calf
7 Hebrew month
8 Gas in arc lamps
9 Purse the lips, with "up"
10 Depot: Abbr.
11 QB's cry after a string of numbers
12 Perfect tennis serves
13 Stinging flier
19 Thingamajig
21 Antiwar advocate
25 Actress O'Neal
27 Writer Jack's favorite entree?
29 Afternoon TV fare
31 Winter coat material
32 Like a bug in a rug, according to an expression
33 Exercise with crossed legs
34 Parker ___ (game co.)
35 Lemon-___ (Kool-Aid flavor)
36 Tennis's Kournikova
38 Reacts to yeast
41 Satisfy, as thirst
45 Plant with tendrils
47 Puts an end to
49 Tug-of-war
51 Stubbornness or kindliness, e.g.
53 Put up with
54 Money drawers
55 President after Grant
56 Decked out (in)
57 Stupefy
58 Contentedly confident
60 Aware of
63 Playtex product
64 State west of Mo.

by Susan Gelfand

120

ACROSS
1 Workplace stds. enforcer
5 Something a cat doesn't like
9 Place to live
14 Mimicry expert
15 "Peek-___!"
16 Lox holder
17 Kindergarten tune, with "The"
20 Soda shop freebie
21 Procter & Gamble best seller
22 Some motel prohibitions
23 Narc's org.
25 Gen. Bradley
27 Entrance to a botanical display
33 Rap sheet letters
35 Hindu title of respect
36 Standby passenger's salvation
37 Neighbors of Croats
40 Firefighter's tool
42 "Bye Bye Bye" boy band
43 Declares void
45 W.W. II arena
47 "Do ___ favor"
48 Gift that almost killed Snow White
52 Low grades
53 Simple shirt
54 Burn treatment
57 U.S. 1 and others: Abbr.
60 Tease
64 What the ends of 17-, 27- and 48-Across each represent
67 Some lounge combos
68 "Goodness gracious!"
69 Curved trajectories
70 Sporty Chevy, for short
71 Unruly crowds
72 Alder or elder

DOWN
1 Bunglers
2 Petty dispute
3 Frau's partner
4 Military flotilla
5 Mixologist's workplace
6 Somewhat
7 Actress Collette
8 "Oh, goody!"
9 Civil War nickname
10 Unwanted publicity
11 Curved molding
12 Shoulder muscle, briefly
13 Right-angle joints
18 Ornamental jug
19 Charles Atlas, for one
24 Words from sponsors
26 Oodles
27 Bouquet ___ (herb bundle)
28 Time worth remembering
29 Didn't allow
30 "What did I do to deserve this?"
31 Super-duper
32 Org. that once used the slogan "In Service for the Girls of the World"
33 "Without delay"
34 Numbers game
38 Stop for a motor coach
39 Plumlike fruit
41 Plane's landing stat
44 Hägar the Horrible's hound
46 Say no, with "out"
49 Think the world of
50 Durable do
51 Eagerly accept
54 When Hamlet dies
55 It's handed down from generation to generation
56 Forget to include
58 As a result
59 Sign of healing
61 Teri of "Tootsie"
62 Enough, for some
63 Big Board letters
65 Fair ___ (copyright issue)
66 Some E.R. cases

by Gail Grabowski

ACROSS

1 Sidewalk Santa worker, e.g.
5 Bugler's bedtime tune
9 Vagrant
14 Felipe or Moises of baseball
15 Sahara irrigator
16 Site of the Ho Chi Minh Mausoleum
17 First in a John Updike novel series
19 Confess (to)
20 Twin Mary-Kate or Ashley
21 Deface
23 Info on a pill bottle
24 Batsman at a wicket, say
28 Spunk
29 Give forth
30 Turn down
31 Tree popular in street names
33 Gross
37 "The loneliest number," in a Three Dog Night song
38 "Get going!," and a hint for the starts of 17-, 24-, 51- and 62-Across
41 Little Jack Horner's dessert
42 Zest
44 Hydrotherapy provider
45 Places for holsters
46 Bedouin, e.g.
49 Long-necked waders
51 Holder of an unfair trial
55 "Oh, woe!"
56 Fish-sticks fish
57 Hearty steak
60 Breads with pockets
62 Umbrellalike fungus
65 Theodore Roosevelt, to Eleanor
66 Humorist Bombeck
67 Extremities
68 Giggly laugh
69 Channel for football and basketball games
70 Out with the fleet

DOWN

1 Root used for poi
2 Carrier to Tel Aviv
3 Crowded, frenzied gatherings
4 Middle school stage, commonly
5 Grenade filler
6 Balloon filler
7 Large feather
8 House mate?
9 However, briefly
10 Numbers yet to be crunched
11 Vex
12 Computer attachment
13 Peter the pepper picker
18 "What's ___ for me?"
22 Meas. of engine speed
25 Queenly role for Liz
26 Large brown algae
27 Bits of fluff
28 Restaurant posting
30 One enrolled in obedience school
32 Washington and McKinley: Abbr.
34 Receptacles for tobacco chewers
35 A large part of a waitress's income
36 "Right on!"
38 Israeli dance
39 Grp. in which many of the leaders wear robes
40 Othello's undoer
43 Household downsizing event
45 Chamomile product
47 Rocket trajectory
48 Little foot warmer
50 Boring routines
51 Done for
52 Skirt with a flare
53 "But of course!"
54 Signs of decay
58 Knotty swelling
59 Designer Schiaparelli
61 Visit
63 Unit of electricity
64 Vice president Quayle

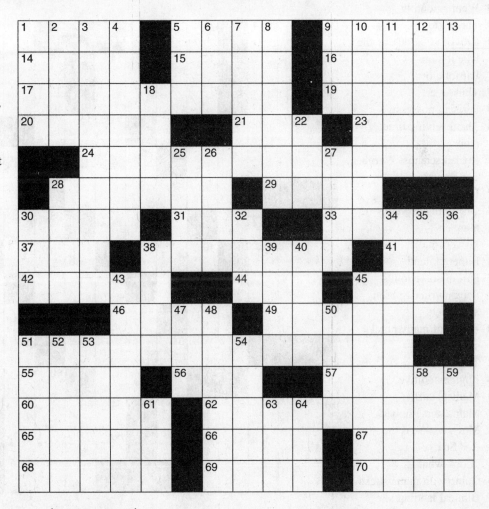

by Lynn Lempel

122

ACROSS

1 A Turner
4 Plopped (down)
7 Critic, at times
12 Seine sight
13 Oklahoma city
15 "Boom" preceder, in song
16 Unit of cell phone usage: Abbr.
17 Actress Conn
18 Snare again
19 The Wizard of Menlo Park
21 Start of a Latin 101 conjugation
23 Liquid meas.
24 Staff again
25 Show utter disrespect for
28 Went smoothly
30 Three trios
34 City of 100,000+ or the lake it's on
37 Patriotic org.
38 Thin layer
39 Parisian possessive
40 Thanksgiving time: Abbr.
41 Rocket scientist Wernher ___ Braun
42 Firm up
43 One with absolutely no manners
45 "Awesome!"
46 Limerick land
47 Part of some joints
48 Screenwriter Ephron and others
50 Policy of many hotel shuttles
52 Title giver
56 Engine additive
59 Medical suffix
60 Main course only
61 Moses vis-à-vis the Red Sea
64 "Look what ___!"
66 Game with matchsticks
67 Biblical landing site
68 Eat by candlelight, say

69 Whitney after whom Whitneyville, Conn., is named
70 Pave over
71 Univ. aides
72 Badge flasher: Abbr.

DOWN

1 Stove feature
2 Skip over
3 Shade of blue
4 Arizona locale famous for its red rocks
5 Have ___ with (know well)
6 Prescription abbr.
7 "Norma ___"
8 Technique
9 Rain check?
10 Part of Q.E.D.
11 Criticizes
14 It's a wrap
15 Easy pace
20 MS. enclosure
22 Season opener?
25 Balkan native
26 ___ even keel
27 Monique ou Dominique
29 Object of many screams
31 Not final, at law
32 Cabinet dept.
33 Gallery on the Thames
34 Coup d'___
35 Descartes who thought "I think . . ."
36 Hasn't left
38 City in California or New Jersey

40 iPod type
41 Actor Kilmer and others
44 "___ Dieu!"
45 Made good on, as a loan
46 Those, in Madrid
48 Unfavorable
49 Battery poles
51 Libel, e.g.
53 Dug
54 Ancient Roman magistrate
55 "Please ___" (invoice request)
56 Fight, but not all-out
57 Weight allowance
58 Backside, slangily
60 Jazz singer Simone
62 La preceder
63 Ring setting
65 Dah's counterpart

by Joe Krozel

ACROSS

1 Make believe
6 Barton who founded the American Red Cross
11 School grp.
14 Yo-Yo Ma's instrument
15 Alphabetically first name in the Bible
16 Harry Potter's best friend
17 Rain source
18 It might consist of 9♠ 9♦ 9♣ and 10♥ J♥ Q♥ K♥
20 Speedy two-wheelers
22 ___-frutti
23 "Pulp Fiction" co-star ___ L. Jackson
25 Something often stubbed
26 Yankees/Red Sox matchup, e.g.
29 Has being
30 Primo
31 Sn, chemically speaking
34 On the nose
35 Series of scenes
36 Make over
37 Massachusetts' Cape ___
38 Want badly, with "for"
40 95 things posted by Martin Luther
42 Candidate for a Tony
44 Andy Warhol genre
47 Dominant dogs
48 "Star Trek" lieutenant
49 Who often "did it" in a whodunit
51 L'eggs product
53 Game with a bull's-eye
57 Annoy
58 Duck that'll get you down?
59 "I'll have the ___"
60 ___ États-Unis
61 Monopoly cards
62 1¢

DOWN

1 Radio monitoring org.
2 Snakelike fish
3 U.N. agcy. awarded the 1969 Nobel Peace Prize
4 Most morose
5 "Absolutely"
6 Steve of "The Office"
7 Extol
8 An octopus has eight
9 CD-___
10 "Whenever"
11 Military aircraft engine maker ___ & Whitney
12 Kemo Sabe's companion
13 Actress MacDowell
19 Enormous
21 Pod contents
23 Anglo-___
24 Like half of Istanbul
25 Prohibition
26 Second round of testing
27 Tied up, as skates
28 Understood
31 Inventor Nikola
32 Inventors have them
33 Snoopy
35 "Now I understand!"
36 Say another way
38 In formation
39 Barracks bed
40 Like an N.B.A. center
41 Much ballyhooed
42 TV character who says "Don't have a cow, man!"
43 Tends, as plants
44 Tutee
45 Chicago air hub
46 Petty gangsters
49 Portend
50 Played for a sap
52 Hightail it, old-style
54 Something 18-, 26-, 42- or 51-Across might have
55 Sunbathe
56 Wily

by Kevin Donovan

124

ACROSS
1 Pretense
5 Big name in grills
10 Youngster
14 Actress Petty
15 Light on one's feet
16 Commuter option
17 Slugger Rodriguez
18 Foaming at the mouth
19 Nocturnal hunters
20 Incentive aimed at golden agers
23 Massachusetts tourist spot
24 Bit of work
25 Powerful Pontiac
26 Key element
31 Chocolate-coated candy
35 Hubbub
36 Before too long
37 Laptop key
38 Margarine
39 Modern navigational aid, for short
40 1949 Orson Welles film
44 Easy dupes
46 Thoroughfare
47 School of thought
48 Designed to increase traction
52 Ivan Turgenev novel . . . and a hint to 20-, 31- and 40-Across
56 Squander
57 Ammo unit
58 Sicilian hot spot
59 Norse trickster
60 In readiness
61 Power co.
62 Clinical study
63 Marathon handout
64 Look to be

DOWN
1 Reduce drastically, as prices
2 Needing darning, maybe
3 Fight site
4 Adding, as an ingredient
5 Samurai, e.g.
6 Antiquated exclamation
7 Nickname of Israel's Netanyahu
8 Some Ivy Leaguers
9 Insignificant amount
10 Slop container
11 Sign of fatigue
12 "Braveheart" getup
13 Overhead RRs
21 Not duped by
22 Tolkien brutes
26 Most of Santa's mail
27 Creep (along)
28 Conceal in the hand
29 "What's the big ___?"
30 Midday
31 Sporty cars, briefly
32 Potentially offensive
33 Light snack
34 Humbly patient
38 He devised the Trojan horse
40 Nonsense, to a Brit
41 Where touch typists begin
42 "Hmmm . . ."
43 Cape Town currency
45 Chowderhead
48 Jack of "Twin Peaks"
49 Tony winner Lenya
50 Certain navel
51 Song of David
52 Arctic mass
53 "Thumbs-up" responses
54 Barrett or Jaffe
55 Spades, for example
56 Diner order, briefly

by Doug Peterson

ACROSS

1 Brown eyes or curly hair
6 Surrender
10 House in Spain
14 Cry of exasperation
15 Salve ingredient
16 Boxer Muhammad and family
17 $500
20 Stoops
21 Not knowledgeable in the ways of the world
22 Prefix with plunk or plop
23 Collection of information in tabular form
25 $5,000
30 Gladden
31 Sort of: Suffix
32 "___ du lieber!"
35 Exactly . . . or where to find 17-, 25-, 43- and 57-Across?
40 China's Chiang ___-shek
41 Tricked
42 Questioned
43 $10,000
47 Not to be missed, as a TV show
50 ". . . boy ___ girl?"
51 Pester
52 Divided in appropriate amounts
57 $1,000
60 Swampy ground
61 Snakes that constrict
62 U.S./Mex./Can. commerce pact
63 Years and years
64 Rodgers and Hart's "___ It Romantic?"
65 Nervous

DOWN

1 Fancy marbles
2 Banister
3 Singer Guthrie
4 Ice house: Var.
5 Stocky
6 Kodak product
7 Majestic shade trees
8 Only one of the Seven Dwarfs to wear glasses
9 Hair-raising cry
10 Ancient Palestine
11 "___ well" ("Don't worry")
12 Kitchen utensil with a mesh
13 So far
18 Sound before "Your, um, fly is open"
19 Take ___ account
23 Waiter's serving
24 Tennis's Arthur
25 Bozo
26 Inter ___ (among other things)
27 Bearers of gold, frankincense and myrrh
28 Biblical suffix
29 "Same for me"
32 Paul who sang "Diana"
33 Middling grades
34 Jekyll's counterpart
36 Undress with the eyes
37 Alaskan city near the Arctic Circle
38 Dance craze of the '90s
39 ___Kosh B'Gosh
43 Hotpoint products
44 "___ sow, so shall . . ."
45 What the weary get, it's said
46 Can. division
47 Molten volcanic material
48 Strip, as a ship
49 Cause unrest?
52 Bit of strategizing
53 Shepard who walked on the moon
54 President just before Wilson
55 Med. specialists who might treat tonsillitis
56 June 6, 1944
58 Hitter's stat
59 "I Spy" co-star Bill, familiarly

by Mark Feldman

126

ACROSS

1 Christine's lover in "The Phantom of the Opera"
5 Onetime science magazine
9 Philosopher with a "razor"
14 "___ Lama Ding Dong," 1961 hit for the Edsels
15 Paper purchase
16 Best-selling author Bret Easton ___
17 "The Lord ___ shepherd . . ."
18 Only common word in the English language with the consecutive letters MPG
20 Wild animal track
22 Command to a person holding a deck of cards
23 ___ lily
24 What colors may do in hot water
26 Moves back, as a hairline
28 . . . ADQ . . .
31 Carney of "The Honeymooners"
32 Catch some Z's
33 "This tastes horrible!"
37 Really ticked
39 Circus stick
42 "Comin' ___ the Rye"
43 Actress Winona
45 Captain for 40 days and nights
47 "___ approved" (motel sign)
48 . . . KSG . . .
52 "I don't want to hear about it!"
55 Perform really badly
56 Golfer Isao
57 Escape clauses, e.g.
60 Pair of lenses
62 . . . ZKR . . .
65 Cheese sold in red paraffin
66 Cowboy star Lash, who taught Harrison Ford how to use a bullwhip
67 Boat in "Jaws"
68 Trick
69 Rub out
70 Butterfly catchers' needs
71 German admiral Maximilian von ___

DOWN

1 Goddess of discord
2 . . . SPB . . .
3 Burned ceremonially
4 Walloped but good
5 "The Lord of the Rings" baddie
6 Lake ___, created by Hoover Dam
7 ID
8 Bestow
9 Not 'neath
10 Narrowly spaced, as the eyes
11 Aware, with "in"
12 All-Star Danny who played for the 1980s Celtics
13 PC platform released in 1982
19 Mirth
21 Necessary: Abbr.
25 Pairs
27 What Evita asked Argentina not to do for her
28 Fur
29 First anti-AIDS drug
30 Freshen, as a stamp pad
34 Fettered
35 . . . NKC . . .
36 Romance/suspense novelist Tami
38 Rubble, e.g.
40 The "L" in L.A.
41 Marks with graffiti
44 Baseball summary inits.
46 The middle part of 44-Down
49 Crazedly
50 One of about 100 billion in the human brain
51 Snakes
52 Expensive fur
53 Arctic or antarctic
54 "Seven Samurai" director Kurosawa
58 Tucker out
59 Zen Buddhism, e.g.
61 Right-hand man for a man with no right hand
63 Capital of Zambia?
64 Tankful

by Matt Ginsberg

ACROSS

1 Bit of sunlight
4 Effrontery
8 Make equal, as the score
14 Ram's mate
15 Sting, in baby talk
16 Piece of luggage
17 ___-o'-shanter
18 Likely result of pollution along a beach
20 "You ___ wrong!"
22 Peach ___ (dessert)
23 Title bear of 1960s TV
26 Says "Come on, try harder!," say
30 Classic theater name
31 "Le Coq ___"
33 Height: Abbr.
34 "___ Marlene" (W.W. II song)
37 Half of dos
39 Charles Nelson ___, longtime "Match Game" panelist
41 Receptacle for some donations
44 1910s–'20s flivver
45 Make equal, as the score
46 Simplicity
47 Postpone, with "off"
48 Center of a simile
50 Peeved state
52 Crush, with "on"
54 "It's so good," in Paris
59 Bewildered
61 Milan's home
62 Lenten treat
67 Edge
68 Mount where Noah landed
69 President before Wilson
70 Adam's madam
71 Sags
72 "Scat!"
73 Filming locale

DOWN

1 Change the price on at the store
2 In the know
3 The "heel" of the Arabian Peninsula
4 Leave the band and strike out on one's own
5 Exclamation before "How cute!"
6 52, in old Rome
7 "___ at 'em!"
8 Good's opposite
9 Abigail of "Dear Abby"
10 Sir Edward who composed "Pomp and Circumstance"
11 Point on a 13-Down
12 "Made in the ___"
13 Writing implement
19 Darn, as socks
21 Walk purposefully
24 Rejoices
25 ___ means (not at all)
27 Emperor after Nero
28 ___ Island (onetime immigrants' arrival point)
29 Broadway songwriter Jule
32 China and environs, once, with "the"
34 Swellings
35 Has left the office
36 Caused
38 Mel who was #4 at the Polo Grounds
40 "Aha!"
42 Nonsense
43 Sound of crowd disapproval
49 King beaters
51 Really digs
53 Prefix with economics
55 Certain bridge positions
56 Reveals
57 Martini go-with
58 Citi Field player, for short
60 Bar habitués
62 Owned
63 Bobby who was #4 at Boston Garden
64 Chinese "way"
65 "Humbug!"
66 Sci-fi saucer

by Richard Chisholm

128

ACROSS

1 Pop music's Cass Elliot and Michelle Phillips
6 Wander aimlessly (about)
9 ___ America
13 Frigidaire competitor
14 Debuts on the N.Y.S.E.
16 Court records
17 Member of Sherwood Forest's "merry band"
19 Existing
20 First pro team to play on artificial turf
21 Calif. barrio area
23 Pale as a ghost
25 Company stationery
27 ___ Na Na
28 Old console using Game Paks, briefly
29 Scrap for Spot
30 Turkish title
31 Antique shop item
33 Humiliate
35 Prince Charles, beginning in 1952
41 Blackmailer's evidence
42 Heavenly hunter
43 One signatory to Nafta
46 Belmont Park action
47 Moon jumper of rhyme
49 Claiborne of fashion
50 Cramped spot, slangily
53 Soil: Prefix
54 Fire up
55 Five Nations tribe
57 Blacktop, e.g.
58 Poker player's dream . . . and a hint to the ends of 17-, 25-, 35- and 50-Across
62 ___-European languages
63 "Judge Judy" figure
64 Elzie ___, Popeye's creator
65 Woad and anil, for two
66 Take a shot
67 Snacks often eaten inside out

DOWN

1 Prefix with ware or content
2 Bordeaux buddy
3 Seductive W.W. I spy
4 Unable to sit still
5 Margarita go-with
6 Action figures for boys
7 Words after "deaf as" or "dumb as"
8 Cry accompanying a head slap
9 Cattail's locale
10 Summer refresher
11 "Hogan's Heroes" setting
12 Brand used in 10-Down, maybe
15 Show contempt for
18 Writer ___ Stanley Gardner
22 Gallery event
23 "The Apostle" author Sholem
24 Elisabeth of "Leaving Las Vegas"
26 "Hamlet" soliloquy starter
28 Opposite of everything
32 N.Y.C.'s original subway line
33 Sounds of relief
34 Go astray
36 Just for ___
37 Place for a béret
38 Auto dashboard indicator
39 Pinot ___
40 Automaker Ferrari
43 Log-on name
44 Dresden's state
45 Skee-Ball site
47 One who sings to the cops
48 Like Nash's lama
51 Pranks
52 More coquettish
53 Irene of a Sherlock Holmes story
56 "In that case . . ."
59 "Git!"
60 ___ Paulo, Brazil
61 Four-baggers: Abbr.

by Sharon Delorme

ACROSS

1 V.I.P.'s vehicle
5 Cry one's eyes out
9 Sudden impulse
13 Tracking dog's clue
14 Double-reed instrument
15 Glistened
16 *Backwoods locale
18 Parts of parkas
19 Averages
20 Colorful shawls south of the border
22 ___ Rica
24 Nintendo competitor
25 Spike who directed "Crooklyn"
26 Fireplace residue
27 *Particle with no electric charge
30 Commercials
31 Obstruction, as in a pipe
33 1950s prez
35 Boozers
36 Outbuildings
38 Sleeping, most likely
42 Golf peg
44 Place to buy a dog or dog food
46 Badminton court divider
49 *Stew made with paprika
51 L.A. campus
52 Ending on a campus e-mail address
53 Anglo-Saxon writing symbol
54 Monteverdi opera hero who descends into Hades
56 Marches in protest outside a workplace
58 Tiny flourish on a letter
60 Liability's opposite
61 Gush (over) . . . or sounds shared by the answer to each starred clue
65 "Crazy" birds
66 Hawaiian garlands
67 To the ___ of the earth
68 B&B's
69 "Fiddlesticks!"
70 Immediately, to a surgeon

DOWN

1 High tennis hit
2 Altar vow
3 *Apollo 11, 12 or 13, e.g.
4 "Ready ___, here . . ."
5 Ka-blam!
6 "Sesame Street" lessons
7 Stir-fry cooker
8 ___ of two evils
9 Cowboy's "Stop!"
10 *Commotion
11 Truly
12 Bungles, with "up"
15 Got smaller
17 Guzzled
21 Selfish sorts
22 Taxis
23 Nobel Peace Prize city
24 Church bell holder
28 Tactfully remove from a job
29 "Yuck!"
32 Winter hours in Minn.
34 Sup
37 U.S. anti-trafficking grp.
39 *Teased hairdo
40 Gaelic
41 Art ___ (1920s–'30s style)
43 Long-feathered wading birds
45 Lacking its wool coat, as a sheep
46 Katmandu native
47 The "Ed" of Con Ed
48 *Home of the University of Arizona
50 Still on the market
55 Roller coaster and bumper cars
57 Male companions for Barbies
58 Branch of Islam predominant in Iran
59 Sunrise direction
62 Above, poetically
63 Tooth decay-fighting org.
64 F.D.R.'s successor

by Lynn Lempel

130

ACROSS

1 Composer Kurt
6 Basketball backboard attachment
10 It's the truth
14 "Are not!" retort
15 Dame who's a hoot
16 Jacob's twin
17 View from the Oval Office
19 Madams' partners
20 Grab ___ (eat on the run)
21 Wrecks beyond repair
23 Stay-at-home ___
25 Premium Scotch whiskey
28 Sportscaster Hershiser
30 Sip from a flask
31 Greeted the morning
32 First-rate
35 Tandoori-baked bread
37 Event featuring sports stars of yesteryear
42 Not a copy: Abbr.
43 New York's ___ Square
45 "Your 15 minutes of fame ___!"
49 Litter box visitor
51 Sushi bar soup
52 Pastry sold at pizzerias
56 Safety device eschewed by the Flying Wallendas
57 Levels of society
58 Like an unborn baby's position
60 10 C-notes
61 Make an abrupt change . . . and a hint to this puzzle's theme
66 Passbook amts.
67 Smooth, as the way
68 Kovacs of early TV
69 Word after Bay or gray
70 Eyelid woe
71 Aid in pulling an all-nighter

DOWN

1 It was hell, to Sherman
2 Punk rock subgenre
3 "You're on!"
4 Leopold's 1920s co-defendant
5 Mr. Spock's forte
6 Found on this page
7 Like a "Ripley's Believe It or Not!" item
8 Cyclops eye count
9 Trousers
10 Addams Family uncle
11 Panini cheese
12 France's Bruni-Sarkozy and others
13 Bit of a fight
18 Greece's capital, in its airport code
22 Tropicana fruit
23 ___ Holliday
24 Folkie Guthrie
26 Partner of oil
27 On ___ with (equal to)
29 Drug sold on blotting paper
33 Visit while on the road, as a motel
34 Broadcast
36 ___ Wednesday
38 Prey for owls
39 Biceps' place
40 The rest of the U.S., to Hawaiians
41 "You're something ___!"
44 Preceder of com or org
45 #2 in a prosecutor's office: Abbr.
46 Newsman Dan
47 Chunnel's home
48 Patriotic chant
50 Chewy coating for an apple
53 Says while choking
54 Tennis do-over
55 Three-star U.S. Army officer
59 Commercial prefix with "flot"
62 Busby or derby
63 Wall creeper
64 Ipanema's locale
65 "___ who?"

by Gary Cee

ACROSS

1 John of colonial Jamestown
6 The first "A" in N.A.A.C.P.: Abbr.
10 Bag
14 "Tosca," for one
15 "Get out of here, fly!"
16 Surrounding glow
17 Completely uses up, as a credit card, with "out"
18 Dana Scully's sci-fi partner
20 Prowling feline
22 Nissan sedan
23 Letter-shaped, threaded fastener
24 Washed-up person
25 Course in which to conjugate "amo, amas, amat . . ."
27 "We ___ please"
28 Dull pain
29 Autumn
31 When repeated, bygone newsboy's cry
35 Con's opposite
36 Mystery quality . . . or what 18- and 55-Across and 3- and 32-Down have?
38 Snakelike fish
39 H. Ross ___, candidate of 1992 and 1996
41 Party giver
42 U.S. military vet
43 Ancient Greek city with a mythical lion
45 Learn secondhand
47 Having insurance
50 Large, at Starbucks
51 Twigs for baskets
52 "If I may . . ."
55 Owner of the farm where Woodstock took place
57 Contest submission
58 Writer James
59 Vases
60 Have the wheel of a car
61 Transmit
62 Jab between the ribs, say
63 Mob

DOWN

1 Capital of Italia
2 Milky white gem
3 "Superman" villain
4 Something for nothing
5 Start of a billboard catchphrase meaning "close to the highway"
6 Equally plump
7 Photographed
8 "Red" or "White" baseball team
9 Courteous rejection to a woman
10 House style with a long pitched roof in back
11 Actor Murphy of old westerns
12 Middle of an Oreo
13 Designer Donna
19 Coat named for an Irish province
21 Steep drop-off
24 Sword handles
25 Northern Scandinavian
26 Field unit
27 It acquired Reynolds Metals in 2000
30 Sighed with satisfaction
32 Cowboy who sang the title song from "High Noon"
33 ___ Park (Queens neighborhood)
34 A, in Arabic
36 Nissan S.U.V.
37 None of the above, on a survey
40 Like two jacks in a deck of cards
42 Take away from, as profits
44 Goof
46 Tangle up (in)
47 Unconscious states
48 Missouri river or Indian
49 Reindeer teamed with Prancer
50 Esther 8:9 is the longest one in the Bible
52 Play a practical joke on, slangily
53 Talking horse of '60s TV
54 Brontë's Jane
56 Miracle-___ (plant food)

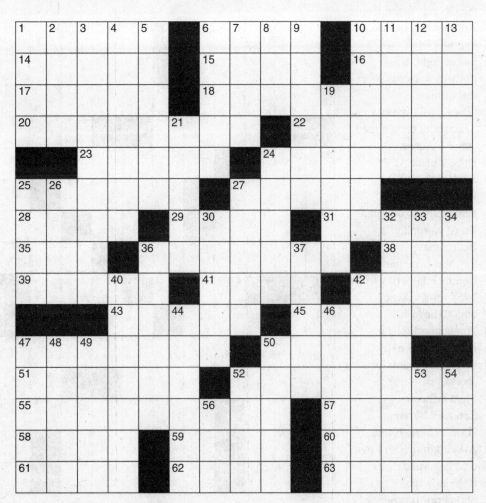

by Mike Nothnagel

132

ACROSS

1 Mountains
6 "Shall I compare thee to a summer's day?" has five of these
11 "Spare" thing at a barbecue
14 Eskimo
15 Instrument played with a bow
16 Gate guess: Abbr.
17 Solid with four triangular faces
19 Scoundrel
20 Lone Star Stater's northern neighbor
21 Unnamed person
23 Part of a word: Abbr.
25 First chief of staff in the Obama White House
28 Alternative to an iron, in golf
30 Sword fight, e.g.
31 Midway between sober and drunk
32 "Dies ___" (hymn)
33 Seat where people may sing 32-Across
34 Knee's place
35 Start of the Bible
37 Post-W.W. II demographic, informally
41 Bit of wordplay
42 Boar's mate
43 x, y and z, in math
44 Commercial writers
47 1958 sci-fi classic, with "The"
48 Population fig., e.g.
49 High muck-a-muck
52 Lifesaving team, for short
53 Most difficult
54 Loretta who sang "Don't Come Home A-Drinkin' (With Lovin' on Your Mind)"
56 Cobbler's tool
57 Shouter of this puzzle's circled sounds

62 "Didn't I tell you?"
63 John Lennon's "Instant ___!"
64 Explosive
65 Word repeated after "If at first you don't succeed"
66 Bird of prey's dip
67 Previously, in poetry

DOWN

1 Quarry
2 Suffix with propyl
3 Help in buying a car
4 Captain for Spock and McCoy
5 Series of steps between floors
6 "___ been there"
7 Reinforcements
8 Tiny bit to eat
9 Flower
10 Redwood City's county
11 Win back, as losses
12 Online music mart
13 By a hair
18 First thing usually hit by a bowling ball
22 Riddles
23 Big swallow
24 Days of ___
26 Colors
27 Kitten's plaint
29 Part of a pool for diving
34 Like an offer that's under actual value
36 Places for tanning
37 Idiot

38 Reach as far as
39 500 sheets
40 Old trans-Atlantic speedsters
42 Driver's caution to reduce speed
44 Shocked
45 Bureau part
46 Jacob whose ghost appears to Scrooge
47 Fernando ___, painter of plump figures
50 "Nonsense!"
51 Carrion consumer
55 Innocent
58 Popular music style
59 Popular music style
60 Go wrong
61 ___ v. Wade

by Chuck Deodene

ACROSS

1 U.S. disaster relief org.
5 Crackle and Pop's companion
9 "___ la vista, baby!"
14 Lumberjacking tools
15 Gondolier's need
16 Thespian
17 Jeopardy
18 Step after "write"
19 Baseball catcher's position
20 Spring egg distributor
23 Cartoonist Browne
24 Verdi aria "___ tu"
25 Gasoline additive
28 Wad of gum
30 Jetsam's partner
34 One who leaves money under a pillow
37 Fork part
38 Cove
39 "Yoo-___!"
40 Beauty parlor
41 Greenish-blue
42 Head of a major toy outfit
44 Largest city in Pakistan
46 "Big Love" airer
47 Depot: Abbr.
48 Greek letter X
49 Kind of date for an expectant mother
51 Ripley catchphrase that's apropos to 20-, 34- and 42-Across
59 "Keep your ___ the prize"
60 E-mail woe
61 Band's schedule
63 Disagree (with)
64 Heavy book
65 Poet Pound
66 Sloppy
67 Adam and Eve's first residence
68 Landlord's check

DOWN

1 Distant
2 Lighted sign above a door
3 Net
4 Posed, as questions
5 Mention
6 Agrees nonverbally
7 Disembarked
8 ___ Best of the pre-Ringo Beatles
9 Owner of Scrabble
10 Result of a "not guilty" verdict
11 Gobsmack
12 Means ___ end
13 Pretentious
21 Start of prime time, generally
22 Depend (on)
25 Adhere
26 Skater Harding
27 From the extreme north and south of the earth
29 Persian-founded faith
30 Possible sign of rabies
31 George Eliot's "___ Marner"
32 Provide ___ (allow to escape)
33 Group for geniuses
35 Stubborn
36 Charged particle
40 Search high and low
42 Prison weapon
43 What situps tighten up
45 Biden's predecessor as vice president
50 Write in
51 Smile from ear to ear
52 Rochester's beloved governess
53 Pants parts
54 Villa d'___
55 Apple MP3 player
56 Domesticated
57 Seep
58 Chance to play in a game
62 Mafioso informer

by Andrea Carla Michaels and Kent Clayton

134

ACROSS

1 With 73-Across, former New York governor
6 Enter unannounced, with "in"
11 Military mess workers, for short
14 Improve
15 Lucy's friend on "I Love Lucy"
16 W.W. II female
17 Gila woodpeckers nest in them
18 Layers of paint
19 ___ crossroads
20 Start of a quote by 1-/73-Across
23 Rank below cpl.
25 Not talking
26 What Fred Ott did in the first movie to be copyrighted
27 Crème ___ crème
29 Astronaut's work environment, for short
31 Actress Turner
32 Put down, as an uprising
34 Not ___ eye in the house
36 Brits call it "the pond": Abbr.
37 Middle of the quote
41 "Gimme ___ ding!"
44 ___ gin fizz
45 Fires
49 Memo starter
51 Win the World Series in four games, say
54 Perlman of "Cheers"
55 Sign painter's help
57 Crosses (out)
59 ___ McMuffin
60 End of the quote
63 Prefix with cycle or sex
64 Ancient Aegean region
65 Surgeon's assistant
68 ___ City (Las Vegas nickname)
69 Standing at attention
70 Trojan War epic
71 "___ Te Ching"
72 Drawer holders
73 See 1-Across

DOWN

1 Start of many a Scottish family name
2 Flu fighters: Abbr.
3 One of the three green R's
4 Call ___ question
5 Hatred
6 Turned out
7 Basic building block
8 Gershwin composed one "in blue"
9 Blow one's top
10 Elmer the Bull's mate
11 December celebration
12 "Beware the fury of a ___ man": John Dryden
13 Iran-Contra, e.g.
21 Slangy response to "Why?"
22 Hair goop
23 Instantly, for short
24 Fire: Fr.
28 Matterhorn, e.g.
30 ___ show (carnival attraction)
33 Part of U.C.L.A.
35 Casual greetings
38 "Hamlet" setting
39 Water-skiers' holds
40 Former Mideast inits.
41 Emotion conveyed by wrinkling one's nose
42 Willa Cather's "My ___"
43 Golfer Lee
46 "Toodle-oo!"
47 Unit of gunpowder
48 Slump
50 Cincinnati-to-Pittsburgh dir.
52 Ones living abroad
53 Each
56 "I can't remember if I ___" ("American Pie" lyric)
58 ___ the Hedgehog (video game)
61 Paper cut, e.g.
62 Navigator on the Enterprise
66 Uncle ___
67 Old Tokyo

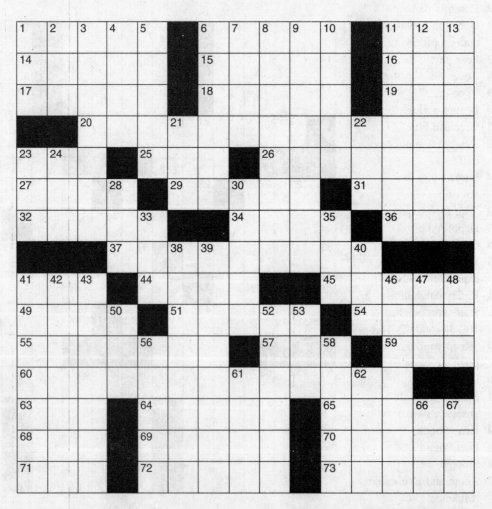

by Barry Boone

ACROSS

1 Actor's representative
6 Group of actors
10 Eye desirously
14 Copy machine powder
15 German king who became an early Holy Roman Emperor
16 Whoppers
17 Rushed, as a decision
18 Throat soother
20 Gin-touting Whitney
21 I.M. provider
22 Slanted
23 Time just after sunset
27 Almost any element whose name ends in -ium
29 12th graders
30 Class for U.S. citizens-to-be
32 "___ you kidding?!"
33 Three: Prefix
34 Letter after sigma
35 Alan who directed and starred in "Betsy's Wedding"
36 Where dishes may pile up
39 Give off
41 Motorists' org.
42 Lowest-ranking G.I.
43 Paper Mate product
44 "Larry King Live" channel
45 Sneaky types
49 Latino's Yankee buddy
51 Go in without a suit
53 Rulers until 1917
55 "What's more . . ."
56 All ___ day's work
57 Problem-solving research institute
59 Shade of yellow
61 Slime
62 Boundary
63 "Winnie-the-Pooh" writer
64 Cheers for the matador
65 Warty hopper
66 Newspapers collectively

DOWN

1 Parthenon's site
2 Only soccer player who can throw the ball
3 Junior naval officer
4 Kind of profit or loss
5 Take a stab at
6 Hot winter drinks
7 Ring-shaped island
8 Disco guy on "The Simpsons"
9 "Animal House" garb
10 Radio blast from the past
11 Chitchat at a sweet sixteen sleepover
12 Ballerina's tight-fitting attire
13 Meeting of the minds, for short?
19 WWW letters
21 From Niger or Nigeria
24 Bandleader's "Let's go!"
25 Wrongful act
26 Low in fat
28 "Back to the Future" actress Thompson
31 Discontinue for now
34 Black or green drink
35 Restless
36 Really big, as a mattress
37 Brinker with storied skates
38 Nobelist Pavlov
39 Clean Air Act org.
40 18-Across ingredient
44 It's popped on New Year's Eve
45 Sent an eye signal
46 Fit for consumption
47 White sale items
48 Bowling scores inferior to strikes
50 Places to make 48-Down
52 Roo's mom in "Winnie-the-Pooh"
54 "Do not change," to an editor
57 Likewise
58 Hustle and bustle
59 Measure of electric current
60 Onetime space station

by Lynn Lempel

ACROSS

1 "Attack, Fido!"
6 Lose firmness
9 Greeted at the door
14 Ahead of time
16 Excruciating pain
17 Happen
18 Hefty volumes
19 Western writer Wister
20 Make a pick
21 Guaranteed to happen
22 Aussie outlaw ___ Kelly
23 First cable series to win an Emmy for Outstanding Drama
27 Drag show accessory
28 "Your Moment of ___" ("The Daily Show" feature)
29 Globe: Abbr.
30 Visitor from beyond the solar system
33 Titan, to 9-Down
35 Director Kazan
36 Process involving illegal drug profits, say
39 Prima donnas have big ones
40 Falco of 23-Across
41 Feelings, informally
42 What a high jumper jumps
43 Original N.Y.C. subway line
44 Coop denizen
45 Flip side of the Beatles' "If I Fell"
49 500 mg., say
52 ___ May Clampett of "The Beverly Hillbillies"
53 ___ in queen
54 One seeking damages
55 Like some tabloid headlines
57 Retreat in fear
59 In pursuit of
60 Carpool, say
61 With 63-Across, name associated with the starts of 17-, 23-, 36-, 45- and 57-Across

62 Bug planter
63 See 61-Across

DOWN

1 Squelch
2 Extremely impressed
3 Like dry mud on cleats
4 Paradise
5 Three-time title for Yogi Berra, in brief
6 Potions professor at Hogwarts
7 Ad agcy. clients
8 "I didn't know that!"
9 Second-largest planet in the solar system
10 Ancient market
11 1960s movement rejecting traditional gender roles
12 Suffix with labyrinth
13 Albany is its cap.
15 Hilo hello
21 Shell out
23 Lead role on 23-Across
24 Form of oxygen with a sharp odor
25 Speak one's piece
26 Catches, as fly balls
27 Domesticated insects
30 Unicellular organism
31 Boston airport
32 "___ form a more perfect Union . . ."
33 Long-running "S.N.L." rival
34 Arles assent
35 "___ Brockovich"
37 Jim Croce's "bad, bad" Brown

38 At any time
43 "Let me help with the dishes"
44 "Steppenwolf" author
46 Perjurer's admission
47 Provide with gear
48 Good at home repairs
49 Like Mayberry
50 Big name in balers and harvesters
51 Elizabeth of cosmetics
54 Funny Mort
55 It's practiced on "The Practice"
56 Transport for a 30-Across
57 $200 Monopoly properties: Abbr.
58 Rebs' grp.

by Alan Arbesfeld

ACROSS

1 ___ wool (soft material)
6 Heart or kidney
11 Inc., in England
14 Delta alternative, once
15 Rent
16 Lyricist Gershwin
17 Like a story that can't be believed
19 Mink or ermine
20 It's just below the thigh
21 Fall birthstone
22 Streamlined
24 Spouse's servile words
26 Fancy items worn around the neck
27 Military strategy during the 2003 invasion of Iraq
32 ___ the Hutt ("Star Wars" villain)
36 Ad-___
37 Currier's partner in lithography
38 Jazzy Fitzgerald
39 Veep's superior
41 Profound
42 Greek H's
43 Battery for a camera or phone
44 Late
45 Subject of a 1950s "revolution"
49 Classic cigarette brand
50 Novels, e.g.
55 1945 conference site
57 Skye, e.g.
59 Hairstyle that may have a comb stuck in it
60 Sports Illustrated's Sportsman of the Century
61 Prepare to use a rifle
64 "___ Miz"
65 Spacecraft's path
66 Golden Globe winner Nick
67 Abbr. after a phone no.
68 One-footer, say, in golf
69 Much of Chile

DOWN

1 Like a rabbit's foot or four-leaf clover
2 Together
3 Spiked clubs
4 Rode a Schwinn, e.g.
5 Mrs., in Madrid
6 Veteran
7 Singer McEntire
8 France before it was France
9 "Talking" done with the hands: Abbr.
10 Mandela of South Africa
11 Candy with a hole in the middle
12 T on a test
13 Gloomy
18 Ark builder
23 "Well, look at you!"
25 Spanish "that"
26 Newborn
28 Cloudless
29 Spherical cereal
30 Marijuana, slangily
31 Glimpse
32 Give a Bronx cheer
33 Midrange voice type
34 Secretly ban from employment
35 Score after dribbling, say
39 Huff and puff
40 "Gnarly!"
44 Special attention for a patient, in brief
46 Like a clock with hands
47 Recently
48 Property claim
51 Eagle's grasper
52 "Too rich for my blood"
53 Give a grand speech
54 Junctures
55 Where the Clintons got law degrees
56 Trebek who says "And the answer is . . ."
57 Long-range weapon, for short
58 0% fat, say
62 ". . . ___ quit!"
63 Code of life

by James Mulhern and Ashton Anderson

138

ACROSS

1 Gulf of ___, off the coast of Yemen
5 Animal acquired from an animal shelter, say
8 Coins a nickname for
12 Eyelike windows
13 QB Manning
14 China's Zhou ___
16 With 2-Down, group with the only James Bond theme to hit #1
17 Okra feature
18 With 10-Down, flashy jewelry
19 Ones who stand above the crowd?
21 International alliance
23 Eastern royal
24 Cuban base in the news, in brief
26 Petri dish gel
27 IHOP drinks
29 Silent hellos and goodbyes
31 Daniel of the old frontier
34 A.P. transmission
38 ___ for Africa
39 With 25-Down, start of a nighttime nursery rhyme
41 Not used
42 Dress shirt accessories
44 Wear away
46 Bright double star in Orion
47 Former Japanese prime minister Taro ___
48 "Put a tiger in your tank" brand
51 On the ball
53 Arctic seabird
57 Italian ice cream treat
59 Emphatic refusal
61 With 50-Down, #1 hit of 1969
62 Prodigal ___
64 With 54-Down, intro to a joke
65 Flew into ___ (got furious)
66 License plate
67 Cover ltr. accompaniers
68 Smartphone introduced in 2002
69 Sellout sign
70 Fake at the rink

DOWN

1 High-end Honda division
2 See 16-Across
3 Great joy
4 Bilbao boy
5 Coke competitor
6 "Do Ya" rock grp.
7 High and low water lines
8 Credit card balance, e.g.
9 Let loose
10 See 18-Across
11 Nick who comes at night
12 Scent
15 Media exec Robert
20 They line up between centers and tackles: Abbr.
22 Orwell's "1984" or Clarke's "2010"
25 See 39-Across
28 Martial artist who starred in "Romeo Must Die"
30 Fencing weapons
31 Tampa Bay footballer, briefly
32 The Buckeyes, for short
33 Klutz
34 Menus with reds, whites and rosés
35 Lennon's "Two Virgins" partner
36 Newsman Koppel
37 Run a tab
40 City near Manchester
43 French cheese
45 Cash who sang "Black Cadillac"
47 20s dispenser
48 She, in Sicily
49 Sudden burst
50 See 61-Across
52 Rock star whose name is spelled out by the middle letters of 16-, 18-, 39-, 61-and 64-Across
54 See 64-Across
55 Donald Duck, to Huey, Dewey and Louie
56 "All systems go" signals
58 Nabisco cookie
60 Squeezed (by)
63 Sculling propeller

by John Farmer

ACROSS

1 Former British rule in India
4 "Bon appetit!"
9 With 46-Down, 1969 album by the 38-Across
14 Yoko ___
15 Spitting nails, so to speak
16 "We're more popular than Jesus now," famously
17 Luau dish
18 Athlete trying to pass the bar?
20 Novelist Ferber
22 It may be worn around the neck at a convention
23 Enters again, as text
25 Egyptian god of death
29 In custody
30 "Nowhere ___" (1966 hit)
32 Where eggs hatch
33 This and this
35 Of the congregation
36 Concert receipts
37 Pallid
38 Group with the four circled members
41 ___ Jones industrials
42 Israeli carrier
44 Big fibs
45 The Supremes and others
47 Sitarist Shankar
48 "Gonna ___ with a little help from my friends"
49 "Open 24 hours" sign, maybe
50 Hitchcock film with a shower scene
52 Injured
55 Silencer?
58 Sketched
59 Toxic herbicide
63 Metal on its way to a refinery
64 Not so good
65 Had
66 Business for Shell or ExxonMobil
67 Like a fuzzy computer image, informally
68 Sound akin to "Harrumph!"
69 Funnyman Brooks

DOWN

1 Cowboy with a lariat
2 Battery terminal
3 Head out to sea, say
4 Quick swim
5 Pressed, as clothes
6 Festive events
7 Short news piece
8 Campbell of "Party of Five"
9 Light blue shades
10 Like eyes seemingly about to pop out
11 Droid
12 Summer in Paris
13 "___ Blues" (song on the White Album)
19 Immediately
21 Yes votes
24 Commoner, for short
26 Library area
27 "How much ___ much?"
28 Mulligan and others
30 One to whom "Ahoy!" is directed
31 Isn't well
33 Dweeb
34 Longtime N.F.L. coach nicknamed Papa Bear
35 Lion's den
39 Corrida charger
40 Long part of a rose
43 Driver's ID
46 See 9-Across
49 Noodge
51 Despises
52 "Beats me!"
53 Like a coincidence that raises the hair on the back of your neck
54 Live (in)
56 Mavens
57 ___ tennis
59 Piercing tool
60 Slime
61 Mess up
62 Summer hours in N.Y.C.

by Ben Pall

140

ACROSS

1 Eucalyptus
8 Not easily tricked
11 Typewriter type
15 Cast a spell over
16 "Time out" hand signal shape
17 Jennifer Lopez's show, for short
18 Introduced to the mix
19 With 64-Across, everything considered
21 Use deep massage on
22 Donated
24 Toothpaste that Bucky Beaver once pitched
25 PC introducer of 1981
27 Where the North Slope slopes
30 Oscar-winning "American Beauty" writer
34 With 43- and 48-Across, everything considered
38 Habit-kicking program
39 "I have no preference"
41 Adriatic, e.g.
42 Stuntman Knievel
43 See 34-Across
44 Having similar properties
45 Actress Long of "Are We There Yet?"
46 Howard who announced "Down goes Frazier!"
47 Pullover style
48 See 34-Across
50 Avoid, with "from"
52 Oust from office
54 Internet access option, for short
55 Melvin of the Nixon cabinet
58 Droner, usually
60 Luke Skywalker's mentor
64 See 19-Across
67 The "O" of Jackie O.
69 Word after gray or Bay
70 Return addressee?: Abbr.
71 Phrases with "as a" in the middle
72 Quad building
73 Pedal next to the brake
74 Gets the better of, slangily

DOWN

1 First or neutral
2 "Go back" computer command
3 The year 1450
4 After "in," and with 44-Down, everything considered
5 "Way cool!"
6 Riddle
7 Sicilian hot spot
8 "Delphine" author Madame de ___
9 Call in tennis
10 Up to now
11 Tin that inspired the Frisbee
12 Inkling
13 Stamford's state: Abbr.
14 Capt. Pierce player
20 Backpacking sort
23 Traveling bag
26 Consumer protection org.
28 For a short time
29 Molt
30 Gladiators' venue
31 Ira who wrote "Rosemary's Baby"
32 Leading
33 Rent payer
35 Out of whack
36 German binoculars maker
37 Long and lean
40 Converse with
43 They carry a charge
44 See 4-Down
46 Publisher ___ Nast
47 #2's, for short
49 City near Raleigh
51 Like paradise
53 Bottomless pit
55 Washerful
56 Early do for Michael Jackson
57 Way of old Rome
59 Parks who wouldn't sit still for injustice
61 Capital on a fjord
62 Prie-___ (prayer bench)
63 Deputy: Abbr.
65 Use a spade
66 Coach Parseghian
68 Soul: Fr.

by Victor Fleming and Bonnie L. Gentry

ACROSS

1 Sunset direction
5 ___ sign (=)
10 Tempe sch.
13 State as fact
14 Breast-fed
16 Vigor
17 Latvia's capital
18 186,000 miles per second
20 Child's friend
22 Breastbones
23 Central points
24 Nonsense singing
25 Not making any sounds
32 Left-handed Beatle
33 Fetes
34 Prefix with skeleton
35 Not too soft, as pasta
38 Clearasil target
41 Sing like Bing Crosby
42 Taboo
43 Seabird native to the Galápagos Islands
49 "My bad!"
50 Worms, for a fisherman
51 Reveal
54 Only American League player to win a batting crown without hitting a home run
58 French novelist who had an affair with Frédéric Chopin
60 ___ noire
61 60-min. periods
62 Chic
63 "I can't believe ___ the whole thing!"
64 Fast jet, for short
65 ___ Rizzo, Dustin Hoffman role
66 Word that can follow the ends of 18-, 25-, 43- and 58-Across

DOWN

1 Twist out of shape
2 Blackhearted
3 Dreamcast game company
4 Amount of food at a cafeteria checkout
5 Intertwine
6 "Cut that out!"
7 Feel the ___
8 Cigarette's end
9 "___ Go Crazy" (#1 Prince hit)
10 Hasty glance
11 Perceived to be
12 Supply with more recent info
15 Summer clocks are set to it: Abbr.
19 Mexican moolah
21 "Après ___ le déluge"
25 Mimic
26 "Wailing" instrument
27 Status ___
28 15-percenter
29 ___ Fernando Valley
30 PC key
31 Fannie ___ (home financing group)
35 Terrier's bark
36 London lavatory
37 Scooby-___
38 Where to see elephants and elands
39 Schubert's Symphony No. 8 ___ Minor
40 Many an item in Santa's bag
41 ___ Romero, onetime player of the Joker
42 Zilch
43 Tree branches
44 Recluses
45 Like Brahmins in the caste system
46 Old U.S. govt. investments
47 Cool cat
48 Inexpensive pen
52 ___ Pepper
53 Deborah of "The King and I"
54 Diatribe
55 Derrière
56 Jazzy James
57 Bawl
59 Adriatic or Aegean

by Oliver Hill

ACROSS

1 City near the Great Sphinx
6 Mine treasure
9 Macaroni shape
14 Steve who was called Steverino
15 Turkish headgear
16 Golden egg layer of story
17 Rod in a henhouse
18 Magical powder
20 French lady friend
21 Peeved
22 1980s soap opera set at a winery
26 Fury
29 Blue literature
30 Blue hue
31 Cuts with light
34 Homecoming returnees, for short
35 1950s–'60s sitcom that ran on all three networks
40 Tale of Troy
41 Alfred P. ___ Foundation
42 Papyrus plant, e.g.
43 Plucks, as eyebrow hairs
48 Prefix with biology
49 Occasion for pumpkin picking
53 Almost
55 Killer whale
56 Part of a morning routine . . . or a literal hint to 18-, 22-, 35- and 49-Across
59 Knock the socks off
60 Not deigning to consider
61 ___ goo gai pan
62 Turn away
63 Ate in high style
64 Drink with a head
65 Fits one inside the next

DOWN

1 Wine container
2 Six-time baseball All-Star Sandy
3 Repetitively named Philippine province
4 Take out surgically
5 Ottawa's prov.
6 Take out
7 Show again
8 Net mag
9 1-Across is its capital
10 Mine treasure
11 Chic shop
12 C.I.A. forerunner
13 Not yet firm, as cement
19 Univ. dorm supervisors
23 Like some smoothly running machines
24 Tenn. neighbor
25 Wine containers
27 Jamaica exports
28 Atlantic Seaboard states, with "the"
30 Priest's robe
32 Blowup: Abbr.
33 Truth, old-style
34 Ed who played Lou Grant
35 Order after "Aim!"
36 The "A" in A-Rod
37 Get stewed
38 Duped
39 Guitar pedal effect
44 Change over time
45 Homes (in on)
46 Front car in a motorcade
47 Turns on, as a car
49 Not real
50 It might mean "I want a treat!"
51 Andean animal
52 "Disinfect to Protect" brand
54 Christmas light site
56 George Thorogood stutter "B-B-B-B-___ . . ."
57 A sac fly earns one
58 Nail spot
59 Wave a palm frond at, say

by Jonah Kagan and Victor Fleming

ACROSS

1. ___ Club (discount chain)
5. Pain
9. Country adjacent to the Dominican Republic
14. "Quickly!," on an order
15. Runaway victory
16. More peculiar
17. Blended fruit-flavored drinks
20. Available from a keg
21. Opposite of naughty
22. Hawaii's Mauna ___
23. Christmastime
25. Old-time singer Julius
29. "Jumpin' Jehosaphat!"
31. News anchor Williams
34. Highlands hillside
35. ___ tai (cocktail)
36. Oodles
37. Nothing fancy
39. "Woof!," e.g.
40. Tummy muscles
41. Peacock's distinctive feature
42. Past, present or future
43. TV character who says "It's 1 a.m. Better go home and spend some quality time with the kids"
47. Shorthand pros
48. Before long
49. 1970s Dodgers All-Star Ron
52. Harbor vessels
54. Thrust out
56. Words after the starting syllables of 17-, 29- and 43-Across
60. Oven setting
61. Wide-mouthed pitcher
62. What high rollers roll
63. Golf score of two under par
64. Pea holders
65. ". . . ___ and not heard"

DOWN

1. Give permission
2. Unanimously
3. A Gabor sister
4. Cowboy boot feature
5. Wily
6. High-priced
7. What you can do if you don't know the words
8. British prep school
9. Flapjack
10. Stick (to)
11. Uganda's ___ Amin
12. Summer shirt, for short
13. Org. with a 4/15 deadline
18. Silky synthetic fabric
19. Squirter at an auto garage
24. Mummifies
26. Financial adviser Suze
27. Roebuck's partner in retailing
28. Look-___ (twin)
29. Owns
30. Bush spokesman Fleischer
31. Sense of tedium, with "the"
32. C-3PO or R2-D2
33. Informal reply to "Who's there?"
37. Collect $200 in Monopoly
38. 52, in old Rome
39. London's Big ___
41. Reason for a 911 call
42. Lone Ranger's companion
44. Call for
45. Combined, as assets
46. Recovers from a bender, with "up"
49. Physics Nobelist Marie
50. Draw out
51. Modern locale of ancient Sheba
53. Rung
55. Country mail rtes.
56. Lincoln, informally
57. Gun rights org.
58. Woofer?
59. Duet number

by Ed Sessa

144

ACROSS

1 Guitarist Paul
4 Sportscaster Albert
8 Singer Baker
13 Humorist Buchwald
14 Comedian Anderson
15 Philosopher Diderot
16 First lady McKinley
17 Director Welles
18 Comedian Sykes
19 Mezzo-soprano Resnik
21 Poet Teasdale
23 Author Fleming
24 Actress Carter
26 Statesman Sharon
28 Director Kubrick
31 Author Waugh
32 Actor Feldman
33 Baseball player Yastrzemski
35 Humorist Bombeck
39 General Bradley
40 Designer Ellis
41 Newsman Huntley
42 Tennis player Sampras
43 Country singer Bryan
44 Dancer Castle
45 Economist Smith
47 Actress Bening
49 Political adviser Hughes
51 Civil rights figure Parks
52 Novelist Radcliffe
53 Keyboardist Saunders
56 Skier McKinney
60 Actress Zellweger
62 Composer Copland
64 TV writer/host Serling
65 Nurse Barton
66 Soap actress Kristen
67 Actress MacGraw
68 Poet Ginsberg
69 Basketball player Archibald
70 Newspaper editor Bradlee

DOWN

1 Place to hibernate
2 Earth, in Essen
3 Unaccompanied
4 A pep talk may boost it
5 Neighbor of Ger.
6 Carriers of water to los océanos
7 ___ cava
8 Pop-up-producing program
9 Cultural grant org.
10 Certain navel
11 Kind of basin
12 Dumb ___ ox
14 In need of company
20 The body's balance regulator
22 Good news on Wall Street
25 Lecture hall
27 Good Humor product
28 Old English bard
29 No light reading
30 "I smell ___"
31 Overdue debt
34 Genesis craft
36 Orator's skill: Abbr.
37 Puzzle completion?
38 Perfectly, after "to"
40 Creator of shavings
44 Bonkers
46 Humiliate
48 Zero
49 Mournful ring
50 Yearly record
52 Old Spanish treasure chest
54 Parade stopper
55 Follower of "ooh" or "tra"
57 Spirited horse
58 Credits listing
59 Tennis edge
61 Bard's "before"
63 Abbr. after many a general's name

by Joe Krozel

ACROSS

1 Prefix with dextrous
5 Musketeer with Porthos and Aramis
10 Bart Simpson's brainy sister
14 Detach from a source of dependence
15 Musical beat
16 Desertlike
17 Acupuncture, e.g.
20 Goes "A-a-a-choo!"
21 Tickles the fancy
22 Go up
23 The "A" in P.T.A.: Abbr.
24 Furnace, e.g.
29 "___ side are you on anyway?"
31 Good name for a Dalmatian
32 "___ about had it up to here!"
33 Male deer
34 Surface again, as a driveway
36 Extended family
37 1980s sitcom with an extraterrestrial
38 One-person performance
39 "___ you glad?"
40 Rough-terrain cyclist
44 Helper
45 Oklahoma city
46 Bolts (down)
49 Two-page ads
53 Samoan or Fijian
56 Quod ___ demonstrandum
57 Andrea ___, ill-fated ship
58 Writer Émile
59 TV's warrior princess
60 What to call Spain's Juan Carlos
61 15-percenters: Abbr.

DOWN

1 Fills with wonder
2 Like taking candy from a baby?
3 First, second or third, on a diamond
4 Bank accrual
5 Motionless
6 More uptight
7 "Well, let me think . . ."
8 Unlock, to a bard
9 Popular teen hangout 50+ years ago
10 Gap in a manuscript
11 Pupil surrounder
12 Trig function
13 Fruit beverages
18 Web mag
19 "No more for me"
23 Mighty Dog competitor
24 Greek port where Prince Philip was born
25 ___ Martin (James Bond car)
26 Bathroom floor installer
27 Former Indiana senator Bayh
28 Payment in Monopoly
29 "Kapow!"
30 Circle of angels?
34 Where a hot dog stand may stand
35 "Night" author Wiesel
36 Sideboard
38 Not flexible, as muscles
39 Director Kurosawa
41 Airport near Tokyo
42 Nickname for Elizabeth
43 Live, as a football
46 X-ray ___ (novelty item)
47 Have concern
48 Open up ___ of worms
50 Work like ___
51 Shoulder muscle, briefly
52 Mmes., in Madrid
54 Rank above maj.
55 Abbr. on a clothing sale item

by Tim Darling

ACROSS

1 Lamebrain
5 Kind of TV now converted from digital
11 Wood-shaping tool
14 Gas brand in Canada
15 Where to dock a Sea Ray
16 Monk's title
17 Zealous sort whose schedule may include 27-, 50- and 64-Across
19 Cyclotron bit
20 Weapon using high-arcing ammo
21 Morale booster
22 Early second-century year
23 Desktop picture
25 Japanese dramatic form
26 Suffix with chlor- or sulf-
27 See 17-Across
31 Head honcho
32 Spitfire-flying grp.
33 Rapper Kanye
34 Tax investigator, for short
36 Port of old Rome
38 A/C fig.
40 Spin doctor's concern
43 Golf innovator Callaway and bridge maven Culbertson
45 She-bears, south of the border
47 Barker
48 Like bad losers
50 See 17-Across
53 Printers' measures
54 London facility
55 Greek counterpart of Mars
56 Blond shade
57 River of Florence
59 Material thing
63 "Mamma ___!"
64 See 17-Across
66 Off-road transport, for short
67 One unlikely to compromise
68 Fuel from bogs
69 Word in alumnae bios
70 Big name in small swimsuits
71 Many-axled vehicle

DOWN

1 Appear to be
2 Golf's ___ Aoki
3 Roman Cath. title
4 Word with justice or license
5 Cynical Bierce
6 Scot's denial
7 ___ Sea (Amu Darya's outlet)
8 Kind of will
9 What a flamingo might stand on
10 Country's Brooks
11 Devotee
12 Sci-fi automatons
13 Class clowns, e.g.
18 Monticello or Saratoga
24 Crash-probing agcy.
27 Old hand
28 Refrain syllables
29 Item in a man's medicine chest
30 10th-century Holy Roman emperor
31 Emeril catchword
35 Loaded onto the wrong truck, say
37 Spot in the Seine
39 McCain's alma mater: Abbr.
41 55-Across, e.g.
42 I, to Claudius
44 Save for a rainy day
46 Go along with
48 One on deck
49 Like some job training
51 Novelist ___ de Balzac
52 Movie camera lens settings
54 Northern Scandinavians
58 Mayberry boy
60 "Gotcha"
61 Orioles or Cardinals
62 Bigfoot's Asian cousin
65 Tripper's turn-on

by Steve Dobis

ACROSS

1 Willy Wonka creator Dahl
6 Vessels at marinas
11 Boeing 737, e.g.
14 Golfer Palmer, informally
15 Parts to play
16 Firefighter's tool
17 Humor publication since 1952
19 Many a first grader's age
20 What generals command
21 Parks of civil rights fame
22 Educ. institution
25 Docs-to-be
28 Selected
30 Dorm overseers, for short
31 Seniors' org.
32 All-encompassing
38 Tricky operation for extending a plane's flight
41 Causing the most wolf whistles, perhaps
42 To be, to Henri
43 Tit for ___
44 Brides' walkways
46 Lionel products
52 N.Y.C. summer hrs.
53 Ammonia has a strong one
54 Mame on Broadway
56 Fix, as a fight
57 Dirty campaign tactic
62 Take to court
63 Win by ___
64 Actress Shire of "Rocky"
65 Ambulance letters
66 "That's enough out of you!"
67 Nonstop

DOWN

1 Computer capacity, for short
2 ". . . man ___ mouse?"
3 +
4 Peru's largest city
5 "Goodness gracious!"
6 Cornrow, e.g.
7 Falls through the cracks?
8 "He's making ___ and checking . . ."
9 The number at left + 1
10 NNW's opposite
11 Leader of the Argonauts, in myth
12 Be
13 State on the Rio Grande
18 F.B.I. operatives
21 Fixes, as a shoe
22 Rascal
23 Committee leader
24 Mob
26 Language derived from Hindustani
27 7/20/69, for one
29 Splash, as grease
32 Charlemagne's domain: Abbr.
33 Some tech grads
34 Sternward
35 Bibliographical datum
36 When right turns are often allowed
37 Spew out
39 Venetian's lang.
40 Film director Martin
44 Dead set against
45 Really digs
46 Samuel with a code
47 Hatred
48 Venetian rulers of old
49 Dangerous gas
50 "Moi, ___" ("Me, too": Fr.)
51 Cove
55 Former New York archbishop Edward
57 Big ___ (Golden Arches offering)
58 39-Down article
59 ___-de-France
60 Anaïs ___, "Delta of Venus" author
61 Travel aimlessly, with "about"

by Sarah Keller

148

ACROSS

1 Material for informal jackets or skirts
6 Building block brand
10 City on the Arno
14 "Gentlemen Prefer Blondes" writer Loos
15 Like slander, as opposed to libel
16 Bartlett's abbr.
17 Attendant at a '50s dance?
19 Occupy the throne
20 Animals farmed for their fur
21 Goodyear's Ohio headquarters
22 Personnel concern for Santa?
26 Tuckered out
27 Mule of song
28 Tofu source
29 List-ending abbr.
31 Item made from 20-Across
33 Goofs
36 Hosiery hue
37 One given away by her father, often
39 Secluded valley
41 Washed-up star
43 Grammarian's concern
44 Mandlikova of tennis
45 Krazy ___ of the comics
47 Miami-to-Boston dir.
48 Street urchins
51 Acupuncturist?
54 Pakistan's chief river
55 All lathered up
56 Injure, as the knee
57 Addicted to shopping?
62 Walk wearily
63 The brother in "Am I my brother's keeper?"
64 Item in "Poor Richard's Almanack"
65 Places for props
66 Many adoptees
67 Curtain fabric

DOWN

1 Morse T
2 Brian of ambient music
3 Sip from a flask
4 Response to "Who's there?"
5 Henri who painted "The Dance"
6 Subdued in manner
7 Shake an Etch A Sketch
8 Needle-nosed fish
9 Jolly ___ Saint Nick
10 Ads aimed at hikers and picnickers?
11 Toughen, as to hardship
12 Athenian lawgiver
13 With regard to
18 Inner: Prefix
21 "Chop-chop!," on a memo
22 To be, to Brutus
23 Gate fastener
24 Botanist's study
25 Pinochle lay-down
30 Gift in a long, thin box
32 Money for liquor?
33 Break a commandment
34 Botanist's study
35 Musical repetition mark
37 Gridder Roethlisberger
38 Collect, as rewards
40 Not e'en once
42 Jazz combo member
43 Ideal, but impractical
45 Rounded hills
46 63-Across's father
48 Cirrus cloud formations
49 A spat covers it
50 Dostoyevsky novel, with "The"
52 It might have a single coconut tree
53 Singer Lauper
57 Explorer's aid
58 Actor Vigoda
59 Aykroyd of "Ghostbusters"
60 Swelled head
61 La-Z-Boy spot

by Robert A. Doll

ACROSS

1 Actor Washington who once played Malcolm X
7 Org. for women on the links
11 Karl Marx's "___ Kapital"
14 Mountain climber's tool
15 Got ___ deal (was rooked)
16 Mind reader's "gift"
17 One word that precedes "pit," one that follows it
19 Had a bite
20 Antlered animal
21 Grieves
22 Cereal advertised with a "silly rabbit"
23 "Slipped" backbone part
25 "Don't tell ___ can't . . . !"
26 Sounds during medical checkups
27 One word that precedes "key," one that follows it
33 By eyesight
36 Long-nosed fish
37 Scottish refusal
38 Infant bodysuit
39 Countryish
41 "Let's call ___ day"
42 W.W. II female
44 Pregame morale builder
45 One word that precedes "play," one that follows it
48 Suffix with pont-
49 Cartoonist Chast
50 With 13-Down, "super power" glasses
54 Ostrich or owl
56 Buckaroo ___ (movie character)
59 Plains tribe
60 Insect with a queen
61 One word that precedes "hard," one that follows it
63 "___ bin ein Berliner"
64 Prepare cookies or chicken, e.g.
65 Egyptian temple site
66 "Love ___ neighbor . . ."
67 ___-bitsy
68 Evaluate

DOWN

1 Chopped into small cubes
2 Food-poisoning bacteria
3 Prominent giraffe parts
4 Ringo's drummer son
5 Test
6 NBC host Jay
7 Famed tar pits whose name is Spanish for "the tar"
8 Clipping, as shrubs
9 Guys' mates
10 Hole-making tool
11 Start of a Christmas letter
12 ___ Spumante (wine)
13 See 50-Across
18 Ventriloquist's prop
22 However, informally
24 Singer Kristofferson
26 Sudden
28 ___ Kenobi of "Star Wars"
29 Fat substitute brand
30 Risk taker
31 Train track part
32 What a swabbie swabs
33 Invalidate, as a check
34 Fascinated by
35 Fit for sailing
40 Hellish river
43 Music store fixtures
44 Order from Domino's
46 Silent assent
47 Braying animal
51 TV sports broadcasting pioneer Arledge
52 Book of maps
53 "Sunny" egg parts
54 Worms in a can, e.g.
55 ¹⁄₃₆ of a yard
56 Gravy vessel
57 Paul who wrote "My Way"
58 Actress Lupino and others
61 Slugger's stat
62 B&O and Reading: Abbr.

by Patrick Merrell

150

ACROSS

1 Hipster's jargon
5 Shrewd
10 Yank's foe
13 Black, to bards
14 Outranking
15 "A ___ bagatelle!"
16 *Did a dog trick
18 Toiling away
19 The Wildcats of the Big 12 Conf.
20 Took charge
21 Rebounds, shooting percentage, etc.
22 *One who's often doing favors
27 Tylenol alternative
29 Martínez with three Cy Youngs
30 ___-Rooter
31 Shrimp-on-the-barbie eater
33 Fancy dresser
36 *Affordable, as an apartment
38 *Tugboat rope
40 "Bed-in" participant Yoko ___
41 Most dangerous, as winter roads
43 Pullers in pairs
44 "You can't teach ___ dog . . ."
45 Sprinkle holy water on
46 *Aldous Huxley novel
51 Hawkeye State native
52 "___ on parle français"
53 Mangy mutt
56 Door-busting equipment
57 *Bar patron's request for a refill
61 "Dang it!"
62 Al ___ (pasta order)
63 Italian wine region
64 ID with two hyphens
65 Mythical lecher
66 School attended by 007

DOWN

1 So-and-so
2 Nigerian natives
3 "B," maybe, in an encyclopedia
4 Photo lab abbr.
5 Officer-to-be
6 "Humble" dwelling
7 White House Web address ending
8 Eden exile
9 "___ out!" (ump's call)
10 Mark down for a sale, say
11 Verdi aria
12 ___ Wetsy (old doll)
15 San ___ (Bay Area county)
17 Additional
21 Hinge holder
23 Songwriter Novello
24 Rotational speed meas.
25 Homes for 46-Down
26 ___-proof (easy to operate)
27 Guthrie who sang about Alice's Restaurant
28 Nut case
31 Cornice support
32 Of service
33 Salaries, e.g., to a business owner
34 Leftmost compartment in a till
35 Parker products
37 German indefinite article
39 Lounge around
42 Part of P.E.I.: Abbr.
44 Salt's "Halt!"
45 Creamy cheese
46 Things hidden in the answers to this puzzle's six starred clues
47 Zoo noises
48 "Gimme a break!"
49 Quick with the zingers
50 Autumn shade
54 "Render ___ Caesar . . ."
55 Horse halter
57 PC pop-ups
58 Teachers' org.
59 Neighbor of Que.
60 Singer Corinne Bailey ___

by Peter A. Collins

ACROSS

1 Tiddlywinks or tag
5 Leftover cloth bit
10 Moon-landing vehicles, for short
14 The Bard of ___ (Shakespeare)
15 Michelangelo masterpiece
16 "Peter Pan" pirate
17 Reaction of a sore loser
19 Boxer Oscar ___ Hoya
20 Bosom buddy
21 ___-hour traffic
23 Lung protector
24 Food from heaven
25 Head honcho
27 Shelley's "___ to the West Wind"
28 Cartoonish baby cry
30 Gives in (to)
31 Scotch and ___
33 Rioter's haul
36 Triumphant cries
37 Be productive . . . or what the answers at 17-, 25-, 53- and 63-Across do?
40 Hate
43 Highlands denials
44 Sounds of amazement
48 Country music's Tritt
50 Mattress problem
52 "Just kidding!"
53 They protect car buyers
56 City NW of Orlando
58 Reactions to adorable babies
59 Accessory that might say "Miss Universe"
60 "The ___ Bunch" of 1970s TV
61 AARP part: Abbr.
63 Select the best and leave the rest
66 Earl ___ tea
67 Seoul's home
68 Melville work set in Tahiti
69 Brontë's Jane
70 Boiling indication
71 Puts in stitches

DOWN

1 Windbag's output
2 Guacamole need
3 Lamented the loss of
4 Energy company that filed for bankruptcy in 2001
5 Energetic for one's age
6 Org. in "The Bourne Identity"
7 Copy, for short
8 Enjoyed immensely
9 Elapse
10 '60s hallucinogen
11 Valuable green stone
12 Bill & ___ Gates Foundation
13 "Chilean" fish
18 Munch on like a mouse
22 Jean-Bertrand Aristide's country
24 May and June: Abbr.
25 Locust tree feature
26 "That's swell!"
29 Lobster ___ Newburg
32 From the beginning, in Latin
34 Arthur Miller's "Death ___ Salesman"
35 Lock of hair
38 Brockovich and Moran
39 It's between Can. and Mex.
40 On the loose
41 Anheuser-Busch, for one
42 Pet with cheek pouches
45 Words after stop or turn
46 "My heavens!"
47 RR stop
49 Pants that are dressier than jeans
51 Graphically violent
54 ___ in the dark
55 Question of location
57 Mafia bosses
60 Stoker who created Dracula
62 It may have made a blonde blonde
64 Stephen of "The Crying Game"
65 Bout enders, briefly

by Paula Gamache

152

ACROSS
1 Pooh-pooh, with "at"
6 Way up a ski slope
10 School zone warning
14 TV signal component
15 Beatles meter maid
16 Topper for Charles de Gaulle
17 *Antishoplifting force
20 Roll-call call
21 D.C.'s Pennsylvania, e.g.
22 Antiseptic element
23 Early James Bond foe
25 With 46-Across, be angry . . . or what you can do inside the answers to the six starred clues
26 *Marching band percussion
30 Lower chamber of Russia's parliament
34 In a cautious way
35 Excuse maker's word
36 X __ xylophone
37 Satan's doings
38 State of confusion
39 Verge
40 Word with a handshake
41 Shell game spheroid
42 Hold tight
43 Some annexes
44 *Rims
46 See 25-Across
47 Prospector's strike
48 Financially solvent
52 E-mail attachment, for short
53 MasterCard alternative
57 *Textbooks for instructors
60 Nagging desire
61 In a snit
62 Subject of much Mideast praise
63 Pigskin supports
64 Manly man
65 Missouri Indian

DOWN
1 Window part
2 Just adorable
3 __-Eaters (shoe inserts)
4 *School evacuation exercises
5 A McCoy, to a Hatfield
6 "Key Largo" Oscar winner Claire __
7 Orthodontist's concern
8 Wolfed down
9 Most risqué
10 Losing streak
11 Jeans maker __ Strauss
12 Ready for business
13 Like an oracle
18 Foppish dresser
19 Tip of a wingtip
24 Reunion group: Abbr.
25 Full of oneself
26 Nobel or Celsius
27 Orange feature
28 Popular typeface
29 W.W. II sea menace
30 *Evel and Robbie Knievel, for two
31 Taking habitually
32 Cut into tiny bits
33 Hippies' crosses
38 Hatfield/McCoy affair
39 Ran in the wash
41 Anne Bradstreet, for one
42 Spring bloomers
45 Said "bos'n" for "boatswain," e.g.
46 When repeated, gung-ho
48 Engaged in a 38-Down
49 Big bash
50 Add a kick to
51 Phil who sang "Draft Dodger Rag"
52 Chile's northern neighbor
54 Seat of Allen County, Kan.
55 Hang-up
56 1975 Wimbledon winner
58 Pure baloney
59 "__ Te Ching"

by C. W. Stewart

ACROSS

1 Go back and forth in deciding
6 Traffic tie-ups
10 Hit hard
14 Common cause of food poisoning
15 Qatari ruler
16 Melville novel
17 Alaska boondoggle in 2008 campaign news
20 Eliot's "Adam ___"
21 Roman 552
22 Put a spell on
23 Relative of an ostrich
25 Part of a mushroom
27 Place to get gas
33 Minds
34 Tue. follower
35 Having ___ of fun
37 Yukon S.U.V. maker
38 Very hot and dry
42 Uno + due
43 Reach across
45 '60s–'70s service site
46 Molecule parts
48 Full-size Fords
52 Quaker pronoun
53 Where Obama was born
54 Texas A & M player
57 Summit
59 Degrees for corp. execs
63 Gets ready to crash
66 Cotton unit
67 State north of Ill.
68 MetLife competitor
69 Still sleeping
70 Suffix with major
71 Bygone anesthetic

DOWN

1 Jack who played Sgt. Friday
2 Plot unit
3 Null and ___
4 Getting on in years
5 Semi-tractor trailer
6 Trans-Atlantic air traveler's woe
7 Mine, in Marseille
8 Reverend
9 Sellout sign
10 Western part of the Czech Republic
11 "Don't leave home without it" card
12 Achy
13 Cleared weeds, say
18 Genesis garden
19 Hone
24 Snake's sound
26 "Didn't I do great?!"
27 Clouds (up)
28 1980s hardware that used Microsoft Basic
29 Old Renault
30 Beturbaned seer
31 10th-century Holy Roman emperor
32 ___ Jean Baker (Marilyn Monroe)
36 Eliot of "The Untouchables"
39 "The Diary of ___ Frank"
40 Lose one's temper
41 Sodium hydroxide, to a chemist
44 Observed
47 Dizzy Gillespie's instrument
49 Cry on a roller coaster
50 Force
51 Vehicle with a medallion
54 "Dancing Queen" group
55 Snatch
56 Near-hurricane-force wind
58 Part of P.O. or P.S.
60 The Wife of ___ (Chaucer character)
61 Teen affliction
62 One of seven in the Big Dipper
64 Stockholm's land: Abbr.
65 Fannie ___

by Ron and Nancy Byron

ACROSS

1 Ear part
5 Date with an M.D.
9 Restaurant chain whose logo features a western hat
14 Gumbo vegetable
15 Carson predecessor
16 Long-legged fisher
17 Germy dessert, to a five-year-old?
19 "Hello, Don Ho!"
20 Part of S.W.A.K.
21 Greek god of war
23 "Are you ___ out?"
24 Bird known for making baskets
26 Best Supporting Actor for "Cocoon"
28 Not many
30 Grub consumed around the dinner table?
33 Sasha and Malia's father
35 Prayer's end
36 No-brainer in school
37 Meditation syllables
38 It might be fixed or frozen
43 Picket line crosser
45 October blooms
46 One who's daft about archaeology?
51 Cornstarch brand
52 Sound before a blessing
53 Pitcher Satchel
55 Peter the Great, for one
56 [Oh, my stars!]
59 Twenty : English :: ___ : Italian
62 No longer sick
64 X, to a pirate?
66 "___ having fun yet?"
67 Hard-core followers, in politics
68 "Garfield" canine
69 Good name for a lingerie salesman?
70 Zenith
71 Prefix with phone

DOWN

1 "Livin' la Vida ___"
2 "Enough already!"
3 Young chickens suitable for dinner
4 Erodes
5 Monkey's uncle?
6 Mango alternative
7 Ark unit
8 Genealogy chart
9 Cry of discovery
10 Help from a bullpen
11 Rodeo horse
12 Start of a pirate's chant
13 Caught in a trap
18 Mideast land since 1948: Abbr.
22 "Dollar days" event
25 ___ Bridge, connecting Manhattan, Queens and the Bronx
27 Mocking birds?
28 Prez on a penny
29 Air safety grp.
31 "West Side Story" shout during "The Dance at the Gym"
32 Sends an OMG or LOL, say
34 Tokyo-based synthesizer maker
37 Big galoot
39 Parent in the wings, perhaps
40 Play to the balcony?
41 Bit of energy
42 General on Chinese menus
44 Drano target
45 One of the eight states bordering Tenn.
46 Influential moneybags
47 "And I'm the queen of England"
48 Yellow
49 Cunning
50 Stand against
54 It climbs the walls
57 Pop group whose name is coincidentally a rhyme scheme
58 Ivory, e.g.
60 Math subj. with many functions
61 Big furniture retailer
63 Susan of "L.A. Law"
65 Many a cowpoke's handle

by Patrick Blindauer and Rebecca Young

ACROSS

1 Not striped, as a billiard ball
6 Apple or quince
10 With 18-Across, the Tour de France, for one
14 Diagonal line, on a bowling score sheet
15 Carrier to Tel Aviv
16 Applications
17 Extend, as a subscription
18 See 10-Across
19 Profound
20 Game show catchphrase #1
23 When a plane or train is due, for short
24 Come out of a coma
25 Buenos Aires's country: Abbr.
28 Golf course pitfall
31 Medieval martial art
35 Ford auto, briefly
37 Game show catchphrase #2
39 Corporate raider Carl
41 Sign before Virgo
42 Neighbor of a petal
43 Game show catchphrase #3
46 Repetitive learning technique
47 Prisoner
48 H.S. junior's hurdle
50 Thoroughfares: Abbr.
51 Save, in a way, as some shows
53 However, briefly
55 Game show catchphrase #4
61 Moccasin decoration
62 Salvador who painted "The Persistence of Memory"
63 Halloweenish
65 Ricelike pasta
66 Analogous (to)
67 Les ___-Unis

68 Comic book heroes originally called the Merry Mutants
69 Identify
70 Krispy Kreme offering

DOWN

1 Belarus or Ukraine, once: Abbr.
2 Org. with many Mideast members
3 Turner who was known as the Sweater Girl
4 Actress Cara
5 Early New York governor Clinton
6 Lima's locale
7 Oil of ___
8 Noisy bird
9 Raise
10 Big Super Bowl advertiser, traditionally
11 "So that's it!"
12 Nautical bottom
13 Clairvoyant's claim
21 Taverns
22 Green-lights
25 Firenze friends
26 What a drone airplane may do, for short
27 Former Texas senator Phil
29 "___ Lang Syne"
30 Before surgery
32 Cosa Nostra leaders
33 Hilton rival
34 Man and Wight
36 Two-timed
38 Things two-timers break

40 "Reward" for poor service
44 Reno resident, e.g.
45 Western mil. alliance
49 Kind of movie glasses
52 Japanese port
54 Shelley's "___ the West Wind"
55 Four years, for a U.S. president
56 Fog or smog
57 Slight, as chances
58 Merlot, for one
59 Charter member of 2-Down
60 In ___ (as originally located)
61 Practice pugilism
64 Superlative suffix

by Adam Cohen

156

ACROSS

1 #1 position
5 According to
10 I.R.S. figures: Abbr.
14 Coal cart
15 Handed (out)
16 First Indian tribe met by Lewis and Clark
17 Bird watcher's accessory
19 The Crimson Tide, familiarly
20 Week-___-glance calendar
21 What a coach driver holds
22 2, for one
23 Trace of color
25 Tide or Cheer
28 Beetles sacred to ancient Egyptians
30 Language suffix
31 Prefix with content
32 "___ recall . . ."
33 One of five in "Julius Caesar"
34 ___ d'Ivoire (African land)
35 Essential part necessary for fulfilling a goal . . . or what 17-, 25-, 48- and 57-Across all have?
39 Droids
40 Flee
41 ___ de Cologne
42 Winter hrs. in Bermuda
43 Peace, in Peru
44 Compresses, informally
48 Symbol of life
51 Ones in a gaggle
52 "So long"
53 Demolish
55 Young fellow
56 Certain iPod or skirt
57 Cheesy Mexican snack
60 Knievel on a motorcycle
61 Smarty
62 Working without ___
63 Actor Beatty and others

64 Wuss
65 What a jack-of-all-trades is master of, supposedly

DOWN

1 Baseball statistics
2 "Everyone's a ___"
3 Procrastinator's response
4 Rock music subcategory
5 Together, on musical scores
6 Sphere and cube
7 Smoothing tool
8 Suffix with election
9 Things with shoulders: Abbr.
10 Edna Ferber novel
11 Young starlet's promoter, maybe
12 Propose for election
13 Where Starbucks was founded
18 Ironing line
22 Rap's Dr. ___
24 There are about 28.35 of these in an ounce
26 Georgia ___
27 High regard
29 Place for a petri dish
33 Sign at a convenience store
34 Save the Whales, for one
35 Plummet
36 Got
37 Disconcert
38 Measured

39 "Who Let the Dogs Out" group
43 Score components: Abbr.
44 Equilibrium
45 "Absolutely not!"
46 ___ Institute, California retreat center for alternative education
47 Tranquilize
49 Stirs
50 Neighborhoods
54 Wacky
57 Ones making handoffs, for short
58 Geller with supposed psychic powers
59 McEwan or McKellen

by Zoe Wheeler

ACROSS

1 Placed on a wall, as a picture
5 "It is ___ told by an idiot . . .": Macbeth
10 Went in haste
14 Butterlike spread
15 [See grid]
16 High-protein food often found in vegetarian cuisine
17 Lollapalooza
18 Make up for, as sins
19 Duos
20 The "P" in P.T.A.
22 Wrigley Field or Camden Yards
24 Facts and figures
26 Envision
27 "The racer's edge"
30 Boulder's home: Abbr.
32 Took for a trial run
37 In the poorest of taste, as a novel
40 Nozzle connector
41 Exactly what's expected
44 Sir ___ Guinness
45 Device that measures gas properties
46 Ankle-related
49 Classical opera redone by Elton John
50 180° from NNW
51 ___ cit. (in the place cited)
53 "Deadly" septet
55 Geometric curve
60 Cinco de Mayo party
64 "Washingtons"
65 "Thank you, Henri"
67 Tex's sidekick
68 Luau instruments, for short
69 [See grid]
70 Having length and width only, briefly
71 Vessel in "Cast Away"
72 Creation that's almost human
73 Concorde fleet

DOWN

1 Hula ___
2 Radius's neighbor
3 ___-do-well
4 Like an unfortunate torero
5 Slaughterhouse
6 Onesie wearer
7 Lots
8 Singer Horne and actress Olin
9 Shoelace hole
10 Internet address opener
11 Early state in presidential campaigns
12 Get an ___ effort
13 Dawn's opposite
21 Cheese-covered chip
23 Stan of Marvel Comics
25 Prince Valiant's wife
27 March 17 honoree, for short
28 Syllables in a gay refrain
29 Gadget for someone on K.P. duty
31 Milo of "Ulysses"
33 Elisabeth of "Leaving Las Vegas"
34 Legal wrongs
35 Mountain road features
36 Plow manufacturer
38 Certain NCOs
39 Actresses Garr and Hatcher
42 Systematized, as laws
43 Resident on the tip of the Arabian Peninsula
47 Tirana's land: Abbr.
48 Appeared on the horizon
52 Easy to understand
54 Back-to-school mos.
55 Preside over the tea ceremony
56 Paul who wrote "My Way"
57 Snorkeling site
58 Kind of prof. or D.A.
59 Ship in search of the Golden Fleece
61 Old sayings
62 Harness race gait
63 Comments further
66 151, in old Rome

by Holden Baker

158

ACROSS

1 This plus that
5 Breath freshener
9 In the style of: Suffix
14 First razor with a pivoting head
15 Child of invention?
16 Boast of
17 *Mark the transition from an old year to the new, maybe
19 Restaurant owner in an Arlo Guthrie song
20 Mercenary in the American Revolution
21 ___ Hawkins Day
23 "Enough already!"
24 Like a post-fender-bender fender
27 Common paper size: Abbr.
28 Concept in Confucianism
30 ___ extra cost
31 Burping in public, e.g.
34 Place for a hot pie to cool
35 Billboard
36 Roth ___
37 *Measure with strides
40 Fellows
41 Backgammon pair
43 Pub projectile
44 An Astaire
46 Questions
47 Stat for Babe Ruth: Abbr.
48 Uno + due
49 "Come on!"
51 Neighbor of Macedonia and Montenegro
54 Get in touch with
56 Slob's opposite
58 Factory
60 *New neighbors event
62 Italian bowling game
63 "___ and the Real Girl" (2007 film)
64 Irritate
65 Some are practical
66 Chichi
67 Interval on a scale

DOWN

1 "Brandenburg Concertos" composer
2 Oklahoma Indians
3 Object of Teddy Roosevelt's "busting"
4 Millennium Falcon pilot in "Star Wars"
5 Where trapeze artists meet
6 Runaway bride's response?
7 Partner of improved
8 What bronzers simulate
9 Circumvent
10 California's ___ Valley, known as "America's salad bowl"
11 *Period of contemplation
12 Dad's bro
13 Summer in Montréal
18 First-rate
22 Name widely avoided in Germany
25 Georgia of "The Mary Tyler Moore Show"
26 "Death Be Not Proud" poet
28 Wedding cake layers
29 Oodles and oodles
31 ___ basin
32 Pop up
33 *Reverse a position
34 Permanent reminder
38 Like single-purpose committees
39 Jill's portrayer on "Charlie's Angels"
42 Heart and soul
45 Ones who owe
48 Itty-bitty
50 Entrances to exclusive communities
51 "Hägar the Horrible" dog
52 Arctic native
53 Airplane seating request
55 "Hi, José!"
57 Hang on to . . . or a word that can precede either half of the answer to each starred clue
58 Common sandwich for a brown-bagger
59 W.C.
61 3, 4 or 5, usually, for a golf hole

by Paula Gamache

ACROSS

1 Harold of "Ghostbusters"
6 "Stainless" metal
11 Krazy ___
14 "Alas and ___"
15 "You gotta be kidding me!"
16 Misery
17 They're choosy about what they chew
19 Quaint lodging
20 12 months from now
21 Dressed in lab attire
23 Morning droplets
24 Use a Singer machine
26 ___ vera
27 Mach 1 breaker
29 "Ben-___"
31 Siberian city
34 Certain Indonesian
37 Sensational 1990s–2000s talk show host
39 Walled city near Madrid
40 Blown-up photo: Abbr.
41 Many-___ (large, as an estate)
42 Popular online reference
44 Couples (with)
45 Drink at a sushi bar
46 AOL alternative
47 Round about the belly
48 Concerning, on a memo
50 Miracle-___ (garden care brand)
52 G.I. grub
55 Speaker's stand
58 Say "Holy cow!" or "Hot dog!"
61 ___ of Good Feelings, 1817–25
62 Walt Disney creation
64 Tire fill
65 Sell online
66 Nash who wrote "I don't mind eels / Except as meals"
67 "On ___ Majesty's Secret Service"
68 Small baked desserts
69 Interminably

DOWN

1 Swift
2 1950s Dior dress style
3 Bird important in Mayan symbology
4 Very unpleasant
5 ___ terrier
6 Trap
7 Tyke
8 Providers of sheep's milk
9 Politician's add-on
10 Disinfectant brand
11 Store on TV that sells KrustyO's cereal
12 Super-duper
13 Care for, with "to"
18 Sunup direction
22 Beat Generation persona
25 Annoying complaining
27 Noteworthy
28 Lose it
30 The Bruins of the N.C.A.A.
32 ___-Ball (arcade game)
33 Some colorful sneakers
34 Highest-grossing film before "Star Wars"
35 Adidas alternative
36 "It Must Be Him" singer, 1967
37 Ruby and scarlet
38 "___ Rock" (Simon & Garfunkel hit)
43 Retired, as a female professor
47 Cunning
49 Convened anew, as the Senate
51 Projector items
52 Bea Arthur role
53 No longer in bed
54 Alter, as text
55 Sister of Rachel
56 Upstate New York's ___ Canal
57 Raleigh's home: Abbr.
59 "Get the lead out!"
60 The Olympic rings, e.g.
63 Collection of items for a modelist

by Scott Atkinson

160

ACROSS

1 Brainy Simpson
5 Try, as a case
9 In pieces
14 A Grimm beginning?
15 Lui : him :: ___ : her
16 First unelected president
17 Suffix with dino-
18 Fabrications
19 Faintest residue
20 Outcome of many a boxing match . . . or 38- and 36-Down
23 Sniggler
24 St. Louis Blues org.
25 One in the hand?
28 Pig's home
29 Corn units
33 Venerate
35 It's sometimes good to get back to them
37 Wood-shaping tool
38 Interstates . . . or 60-Down and 65-Across
43 "Yikes!"
44 Three-ingredient treats
45 Well-thought-out
48 "___, you noblest English . . . !": "Henry V"
49 ___ favor
52 Something to roll over, briefly
53 Brit. reference
55 Weeper of mythology
57 Crushed by sorrow . . . or 5-Across and 63-Down
62 Greek porticos
64 Skateboard trickster's track
65 Partner of means
66 Nail-biting
67 Modern storage units, briefly
68 "Aha!"
69 Early Icelandic literary works
70 U.S. Open's ___ Stadium
71 Drag racing org.

DOWN

1 The second number in a record
2 Peevish
3 Mulder's "X-Files" partner
4 Cliffside nest
5 Didn't give away
6 Author Wiesel
7 A Baldwin brother
8 Sticky stuff
9 Fifth-century emperor remembered as the epitome of cruelty
10 Expert in match play, for short?
11 "The West Wing" actor who played Arnold Vinick
12 Camcorder button abbr.
13 Uno + due
21 Tire pattern
22 Theater admonition
26 Snug as a bug in a rug
27 Flock females
30 Enzyme suffix
31 Clears (of)
32 Ordinary schlub
34 Statutes
35 Wait
36 Priory of ___ (group in "The Da Vinci Code")
38 Tenth: Prefix
39 Noted lab assistant
40 Tramp
41 Miracle-___
42 Temporary tattoo dye
46 Hangmen's tools
47 Shatner's "___ War"
49 Soapmaking stuff
50 One following directions
51 Exodus locale
54 Skin: Suffix
56 Golfer Hale ___
58 Tabula ___
59 Scottish rejections
60 Daily temperature stat
61 Otherwise
62 Fr. holy woman
63 Slugger Williams

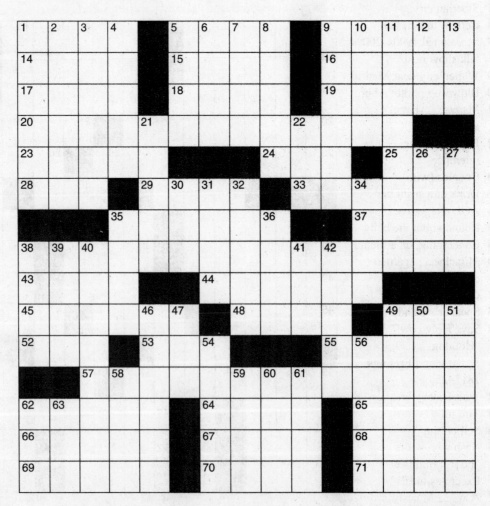

by Alex Fay

ACROSS

1 Harvard and Wharton degs.
5 ___ Millions (multistate lottery)
9 *With 68-Across, lingerie model's asset
13 Continental coin
14 Starting on
15 Prefix with iliac
16 *It may end up in a chop shop
18 Outerwear for an operagoer
19 On the job
20 Equipment in craps
22 Caustic drain opener
23 It means nothing
25 Own up to one's sins
27 *What you drop uncooked spaghetti or a tea bag into
32 Accepted, as a proposal
33 Gives in
37 Old Navy libation
38 Word describing the answer to each of the starred clues
40 Drink through a straw
41 Assembly of 100
44 Caviar or frogs' legs
47 *Bloody Mary seasoner
49 Mount ___, California observatory site
52 Where the Blues Brothers got their start, familiarly
53 Him: Fr.
54 Affirmative votes
56 "But what to do?!"
61 Popular pain reliever
63 *Supplier of electricity to subway trains
65 Sister's daughter
66 Scouting outing
67 Shaving mishap
68 See 9-Across
69 Imitates
70 Change for a five

DOWN

1 Mini-plateau
2 Thing in an ashtray
3 Lined up, after "in"
4 All alone
5 ". . . one giant leap for ___": Neil Armstrong
6 PC bailout key
7 Egg on
8 Sahara's place
9 Gal in an old song standard
10 Élève's school
11 Dentistry photos
12 Joins, as oxen
15 Start of an act
17 Bert's Muppet buddy
21 Mass-market fragrance maker
24 Width's opposite: Abbr.
26 Citrus soft drink introduced in the 1960s
27 Diamond bases
28 Grimm figure
29 Cast-___ stomach
30 Smooth, in music
31 "Whose ___ these are I think I know": Frost
34 Hawaiian wingding
35 800, to Caesar
36 Kind of terrier
39 Private eyes, for short
42 Husk-wrapped Mexican dish
43 Online auction house
45 Capital of England, to Parisians
46 Stranded in the middle of the ocean, say
48 Franklin known as the Queen of Soul
49 Alternative strategy if things don't work out
50 The "A" in A/V
51 Existed
55 Frigate or freighter
57 River through Florence
58 Cause for a game delay
59 Cursor movers
60 Fraternal group
62 Slippery, as winter sidewalks
64 Prez after Give 'em Hell Harry

by Paula Gamache

162

ACROSS

1 Warm-up for the college-bound
5 Vena ___ (blood line to the heart)
9 Victory overcoming 100-to-1 odds, e.g.
14 Prefix with sphere
15 Horatian verses
16 ___ del Rey, Calif.
17 Shiite leader
18 Lead-in to tiller
19 Put a duty on
20 Chocolate candy from Portugal?
23 Gist
24 Missing link, possibly
28 Milne hopper
29 "___ grip!"
31 "Don't Bring Me Down" grp.
32 African nomad who hasn't had a thing to drink?
36 Rep. rival
37 Mississippi senator Cochran
38 Generous ___ fault
39 Small amount
40 Tummy muscles
41 Lively Indian dance?
45 ___ polloi
46 "High Hopes" lyricist Sammy
47 Pizza ___
48 French schools
50 Fill and then some
54 Drum that's under all the others?
57 No. 2 in the statehouse
60 See 61-Across
61 Molecular 60-Across
62 How a bride and groom leave the altar, metaphorically
63 60-Across of computer memory
64 "Treasure Island," for one
65 Lecher

66 Required element in many figure skating competitions
67 Lead-in to while

DOWN

1 Lover: Suffix
2 They're followed by the finals
3 Heap up
4 Filled with trees
5 Pipe material for Frosty the Snowman
6 Acrobat software maker
7 Presidential "no"
8 "___ of the Sun" (Jack London novel)
9 Feeling well
10 Vehicle that taxis

11 Instrument for Kenny G
12 Part of a storm or a potato
13 Small amount
21 ___ about (approximately)
22 Diminish
25 French red wine
26 Prince Valiant's wife
27 "What God has joined together, let ___ put asunder"
29 What a lame joke might elicit
30 Israeli statesman Abba
32 Lesley of "60 Minutes"
33 "Wow!"
34 Like the A B C's
35 Prepare a commemorative plate, say
39 Very close friend

41 Freeze up
42 Condé ___ (magazine publisher)
43 Movable article of personal property
44 Garage occupant
49 Black key material
50 Whack, biblically
51 Fragrant oil
52 What a poor workman blames, in a saying
53 Irish patriot Robert
55 Marching band instrument
56 Common cameo stone
57 The Shangri-___ ("Leader of the Pack" group)
58 Airport screening org.
59 "___ milk?"

by Robert Cirillo

ACROSS

1 Collegiate digs
5 Baby's first word, maybe
9 Provide with funds, as a college
14 Emmy-winning Falco
15 Milky gem
16 ___-Dade County
17 What a dirty person has
20 ___ Gandhi, pioneering female leader
21 Sch. in Baton Rouge
22 Become less bright, as the moon
23 Refrigerated
25 Go down a slippery slope
27 What an embezzler has
33 Hair-raising
35 City where Joan of Arc was burned
36 Espionage org.
37 "If all ___ fails . . ."
38 Feudal workers
39 Machines on cotton plantations
40 Tennis serve requiring a do-over
41 Coffee for before bed
42 Long, arduous walks
43 What a well-connected applicant has
46 Eccentric
47 Aids for disabled cars
48 Kid's summer getaway
51 Bit of Dobbin's dinner
54 Exam taker
58 What a dreamer has
61 Passion
62 Tartar sauce ingredient
63 The "U" in I.C.U.
64 Manage to avoid
65 Blossom supporter
66 "Toodle-oo"

DOWN

1 Actress Moore
2 Valhalla god
3 Orange or watermelon cover
4 Health program for seniors
5 Gazillionaire Trump
6 Suitable
7 Roald who wrote "James and the Giant Peach"
8 Pub quaffs
9 Australia's unofficial national bird
10 Lamebrain
11 Input for computers
12 Portent
13 Telegram
18 Literary twist
19 Oohs and aahs (over)
24 Lacking a stopover, as a flight
26 Documentary filmmaker Burns
27 Simply must
28 Singer Jones whose father is Ravi Shankar
29 Spot for eating curds and whey
30 Far less friendly
31 Connection
32 Fair maiden
33 Freudian concern
34 Egypt's last ruling Ptolemy, familiarly
38 Forward, as mail
39 Fill with disgust
41 "The butler ___ it"
42 Low-tech hair dryer
44 Honcho
45 Techie's company
48 Paper ballot punch-out
49 Prefix with dynamic
50 Grass-roots org. that fights alcohol abuse
52 Devices you can bank on, briefly
53 "Take ___!"
55 Deli salad fish
56 Fix up, as text
57 "Cómo ___ usted?"
59 Fury
60 Cyclops' distinctive feature

by Lynn Lempel

ACROSS

1 ___ Canaria Island
5 Low man in the choir
9 Too sentimental
14 Frosty coating
15 Tetra- doubled
16 Smoked or salted
17 Hipster's "Understood!"
18 Mekong River land
19 Brainstormer's output
20 Larva-to-adult transition
23 Idle repairman's employer, in ads
24 Egg pouches
25 "___ pig's eye!"
28 ___, zwei, drei . . .
30 Sports show-off
32 Dawn goddess
35 Be monogamous, among animals
38 Mont Blanc, e.g., to locals
40 Windows program suffix
41 Either "Fargo" co-director
42 Leader on the field
47 Solidify, like Jell-O
48 Main lines
49 Ways to go: Abbr.
51 Sound of rebuke
52 Composer Bartók
55 Use Google, e.g.
59 Spam or sausage . . . or a hint to the starts of 20-, 35- and 42-Across
62 Manuscript sheet
64 Big Ten or Big 12 org.
65 Glass piece
66 Ill-mannered sorts
67 Underworld V.I.P.'s
68 Kerfuffles
69 "Golly!"
70 Stick around
71 Refusenik's refusal

DOWN

1 Brothers' name in children's literature
2 "___ Crooked Trail" (Audie Murphy western)
3 Peaceful relations
4 Cancel
5 Italian city after which a deli offering is named
6 "___ in every garage"
7 Subway map points
8 Skater Cohen
9 Clip out, as a coupon
10 BMW competitor
11 Spanish fortresses
12 Pod item
13 Rushing stats: Abbr.
21 Incapacitate
22 ___ Rios, Jamaica
26 Checking account come-on
27 Worker in real estate, e.g.
29 Assembly instructions part
31 Pampering, for short
32 Really bother
33 Nondairy spreads
34 Ignition system device
36 Phone no. add-on
37 Cause of quaking
39 Defib operator
43 Freight train's "office"
44 "Wait just ___!"
45 "Like taking candy from a baby!"
46 It may be urgent
50 Yangtze River boat
53 A library does it
54 Fancy neckwear
56 "___ or not . . ."
57 Vacation rental craft
58 Mushroom cloud maker, for short
60 Bar mitzvah or bris
61 Yemen's capital
62 Sitcom diner waitress
63 Response from the awed

by Paul Hunsberger

ACROSS

1 Smart ___ (wise guy)
5 Persian tongue
10 Roadies carry them
14 Sandwich spread
15 Sandwich spreads
16 Ark builder
17 Bakery fixture
18 Nickname for Andrew Jackson
20 Island east of Australia
22 Says hello to
23 Treasure chest
27 Trap
28 Mao ___-tung
31 The "R" in RCA
32 Shorebird
33 Depressed urban area
35 Former vice president Quayle
36 Word that can precede the starts of 18-, 20-, 53- and 58-Across
39 Smart ___ (wise guy)
42 Any member of a classic punk rock band
43 Morales of "La Bamba"
47 ___ New Guinea
49 Brian of Roxy Music
50 What the nose picks up
51 Pharaoh's realm
52 Dreary
53 Dangerous thing to be living on
58 First prize at a fair
61 Force felt on the earth, informally
62 Civil rights pioneer Parks
63 Cockpit occupant
64 Zippo
65 Aid and ___
66 Make ___ (do some business)
67 Carrier to Tel Aviv

DOWN

1 Surrounded by
2 Shirley's friend in 1970s–'80s TV
3 Goggles and glasses
4 People's worries
5 Jesters
6 It means everyone to Hans
7 Comedian Foxx
8 TriBeCa neighbor
9 "Beauty ___ the eye . . ."
10 Turkey's capital
11 Neigh : horse :: ___ : cow
12 Number on a golf course
13 Wallflower-ish
19 Lemonlike fruit
21 Dined
24 Like 1, 3, 5, 7, etc.
25 By way of
26 Long stretch of time
28 Parts of a bride's attire, for this puzzle
29 ___ Hall Pirates (1953 N.I.T. champs)
30 Prefix with -centric
33 "Today" rival, for short
34 1-1 or 2-2, e.g.
37 Daniel Webster, for one
38 Opal or topaz
39 Gorilla
40 What mattresses do over time
41 007, for one
44 Original
45 Oakland's county
46 Law-breaking
48 Optimistic
50 Caesar whose forum was TV
52 Al ___ (cooked, yet firm)
54 Kelly of morning TV
55 Sluggers' figs.
56 Syllables before "di" or "da" in a Beatles song
57 Winter coat material
58 Push-up provider
59 High tennis shot
60 Have no ___ for

by Steve Dobis

166

ACROSS

1 Camera openings
10 Wooden shoe
15 Patron of the hearts?
16 Weather of a region
17 Fidgety
18 "What's it all about, ___?"
19 Too much of e-mail
20 They lift kites
22 Bouquet holder
25 Half of the tai chi symbol
26 And other women: Lat.
30 Day's end, to a poet
31 Grappling site
34 "Come and get it" signals in the Army
36 Candied, as fruits
38 Org. that approves trailers
39 Is a maître d' for, say
41 Hibernia
42 Busybody
44 Service leaders in the service
46 See 59-Down
47 "Ready or ___ . . ."
49 Like most promgoers
50 Wildebeest
51 Grant
52 Song whose title is repeated before and after "gentille" in its first line
56 John who wrote "My First Summer in the Sierra"
60 Sainted 11th-century pope
61 References
65 Having plenty to spare
66 Den mothers
67 Wedding invitation encls.
68 Geographical features . . . or what the circled squares in this puzzle represent

DOWN

1 Dollar competitor
2 Sensory appendage
3 First name of the First Lady of Song
4 500 sheets
5 Blast producer
6 Colorado tribe
7 Narrow inlet
8 Come after
9 Trickle (through)
10 Halloween activity
11 Edgar ___ Poe
12 "Back to the Future" bully
13 Not mention
14 Caddie's bagful
21 Tint
22 Trader ___ (restaurant eponym)
23 Some batteries
24 Grade of beef
26 Outstanding Miniseries and Outstanding Drama Series
27 Conical dwelling
28 Yoga position
29 Exam with sections known as "arguments," for short
30 Brideshead, for one
31 Mrs. Arnold Schwarzenegger
32 Getting an A+ on
33 Uptight
35 "Well, ___-di-dah!"
37 Meager
40 Hightailed it
43 Extensions
45 Founding father Richard Henry ___
48 No longer fashionable
50 Slyness
51 Salsa singer Cruz
52 "Lackaday!"
53 Champagne Tony of golf
54 "Well, that was stupid of me!"
55 Like most N.B.A. players
56 Prefix with -zoic
57 CCCP, in English
58 Line-___ veto
59 With 46-Across, Antarctic waters
62 Cambodia's ___ Nol
63 "Tristan ___ Isolde"
64 3, on a telephone

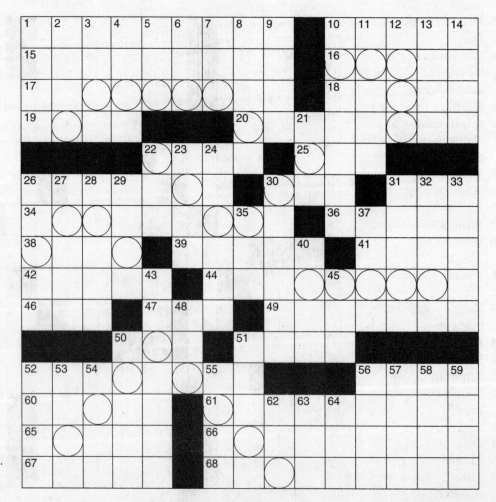

by Joanne Sullivan

ACROSS

1 1996 candidate Dole
4 "10 ___ or less" (checkout line sign that grates on grammarians)
9 The real ___
14 When a plane is due in, for short
15 Nerve
16 [Crossing my fingers]
17 ___ center (community facility)
18 Unrealized gain on an investment
20 Suffix with cyclo- or Jumbo
22 Braga a k a the Brazilian Bombshell
23 "Bah, humbug!"
24 Merely suggest
26 SSW's opposite
28 Letters on an ambulance
29 Detective, in slang
32 Give up, as rights
34 Evergreen
36 Fancy
40 "That's ___ haven't heard!"
42 "Jaws" menace
43 Wished
44 Good luck charms
47 Charles Dickens pseudonym
48 Kuwaiti leader
49 Kettledrum
51 Buddy
53 Mesh
55 Facet
58 Guthrie with a guitar
60 Pat of "Wheel of Fortune"
63 Mountain lift
64 They measure the tonnage of trucks
67 Singer Yoko
68 W.W. II bomber ___ Gay
69 Outdo
70 Giant great Mel
71 Copenhageners, e.g.
72 Tending to ooze
73 Flattens in the ring, for short

DOWN

1 Train sleeping spot
2 Former "S.N.L." comic Cheri
3 1676 Virginia uprising
4 Little devil
5 Woman presiding at a banquet
6 Giant fair
7 Appearance
8 Small finch
9 Former Russian space station
10 Take an ax to
11 Photo-filled reading matter in the living room
12 Poppy product
13 Reported Himalayan sightings
19 Cosmetic applied with a damp sponge
21 To the ___ degree
25 What to say to a doctor with a tongue depressor
27 Snakelike fish
30 Terse critiques
31 Path down to a mine
33 Talk over?
34 In favor of
35 Once ___ blue moon
37 Costing nothing, in Cologne
38 Wedding vow
39 ___ Percé tribe
41 Company called "Big Blue"
45 "Am ___ your way?"
46 Atlanta-based sta.
50 Well-put
51 Manhandled
52 Indoor game site
54 Tex-Mex sandwiches
56 Poetic chapter for Ezra Pound
57 Gaits between walks and canters
59 Look at amorously
61 Tarzan's woman
62 On the sheltered side
65 Contains
66 Word repeated in Mad magazine's "___ vs. ___"

by Brendan Emmett Quigley

ACROSS

1 *"In like a ___ . . ."
5 Voice below soprano
9 Goat-men in a Rubens painting
14 Capital once called Christiania
15 *Kook
16 Welles of film
17 Lone Star State sch.
18 *Godsend
19 Go from ___ worse
20 Choreographer Twyla
22 Greek gathering spot
24 *Doofus
25 Married woman, in Madrid
27 Author Silverstein
29 *Dud
31 Wood finish
34 Pub crawler
37 Minimal amount
39 Andean animal
40 Period described by the clues and answers to 1- and 72-Across (which are the start and end of a word ladder formed by the answers to the 10 asterisked clues)
43 Actor Williams of "Happy Days"
44 Gala night duds
45 Govt. ID
46 Handy man?
48 *Jim's gift in "The Gift of the Magi"
50 Looped handle, in archaeology
51 Look over
55 *Provide for free
57 ___ Brasi, enforcer in "The Godfather"
61 Cathedral areas
62 Absorbed the loss
64 *Sleepaway, e.g.
66 Sunday best, e.g.
67 Sea eagles
68 *Tiffany treasure
69 "Casablanca" heroine
70 "I beg to differ!"
71 Parts of una década
72 *". . . out like a ___"

DOWN

1 Lummoxes
2 "This ___ life!"
3 Ingredient in some potato chips
4 "Easy!"
5 Priest's robe
6 Going places?
7 Trolley warning
8 ___ occasion (never)
9 Della's gift in "The Gift of the Magi"
10 Title heroine of a Strauss opera
11 Mint green?
12 Say ___ (reject)
13 Name-dropper, perhaps
21 Draws out
23 Pale wood
26 Grace period?
28 Steering committee?
30 Nuts
31 Betraying no emotion
32 Gremlins and Hornets of old autodom
33 Songwriter Sammy
34 Partnerless, as at a party
35 "This can't be!"
36 Provider of a dead giveaway?
38 ___ Na Na
41 Sweet, gooey sandwiches
42 Dud
47 "Fly the friendly skies" co.
49 São Paulo's land, to natives
52 Throat dangler
53 Great shakes?
54 Sign abbr. meaning "founded in"
55 "It's News to Me" columnist Herb
56 Others: Sp.
58 The Bruins of the N.C.A.A.
59 James of "Thief"
60 Bullets
63 General on a Chinese menu
65 Second afterthought in a letter: Abbr.

by Elizabeth C. Gorski

ACROSS

1 Capitalized, as a noun
7 Tapioca source
14 Raw material for a steel factory
15 Draws in
16 Home of the U.S. Air Force Academy
18 Adam and __
19 Chimney grime
20 Fit __ (be perfect on)
21 State that was once a republic
24 Letters after epsilons
27 Vampire slayer of film and TV
33 Brit's goodbye
36 Nephews' counterparts
37 Once around the track
38 Service charge
39 Santa __ winds
40 Stetson or sombrero
41 Comes into play
43 Writers of i.o.u.'s
45 City in 21-Across
48 Big name in video arcades
49 Literature Nobelist William Butler __
53 Chester Arthur's middle name
56 "Mad Money" network
59 Slime
60 Comedic inspiration for Robin Williams
65 Leave high and dry
66 Eroded
67 Take another sip of
68 Bread bakers' buys

DOWN

1 Show to be true
2 Watch with a flexible wristband
3 John Lennon's middle name
4 __ favor (Spanish "please")
5 Big slices of history
6 Make over
7 Social divisions in India
8 Swiss peak
9 Camera type, for short
10 "I have no problem with that"
11 River of Florence
12 Bright northern star
13 Aide: Abbr.
14 Rapper/actor on "Law & Order: SVU"
17 Seeping
22 Honest __ (presidential moniker)
23 Overabundance
25 Path for a mole
26 In a cordial way
28 Big Spanish celebration
29 Enemy
30 Sound heard in a canyon
31 Front's opposite
32 Old trans-Atlantic jets, for short
33 Animal's nail
34 Mata __ (W.W. I spy)
35 Of sweeping proportions
39 Tooth doctors' org.
42 Musical group with its own 1977–81 TV show
44 Mao __-tung
46 Esoteric
47 Huckleberry __
50 Representative
51 Law school course
52 Middling
53 Not quite shut
54 Ear part
55 Sci. course for a doctor-to-be
57 Street through Times Sq.
58 Give as an example
61 Six-point scores, for short
62 Just off the grill
63 Teachers' union, in brief
64 "__ the season to be jolly"

by Stanley Newman

170

ACROSS

1 Telltale sign
7 Stick in one's ___
11 Paid no attention to
13 Protection
15 With 23-Across, famous "opening" line
17 Heavy coats
18 Respectful acts
19 Rapper ___ Rida
20 Says "Nice job!" to
23 See 15-Across
28 "Given the situation . . ."
29 Alberto VO5 product
30 With 35-Across, source of 15-/23-Across
32 Support for an ear of corn
34 "Olympia" artist
35 See 30-Across
37 Belief system
38 Like 10, but not X
40 15-/23-Across location
46 "England hath long been mad, and scarr'd ___": Richmond in "King Richard III"
47 Lost soldier, briefly
48 Hall providing entertainment
51 "Dear" columnist
52 Creator of 30-/35-Across
56 Family name in early violin-making
57 "Our Miss Brooks" star of 1950s TV
58 Like two peas in ___
59 Emphasize

9 Spellbound
10 Cinematic scene-changer
11 Chewy confection
12 Captain Cook landfall of April 1769
14 His or her: Fr.
16 Comes up short, say
20 Suggest
21 Restraint
22 Amount of money that can be raised?
24 "What will you ___?"
25 "Zounds!"
26 Depend (on)
27 Yellowstone roamer
30 –
31 "I didn't know I had it ___!"

32 Knucklehead ___, Paul Winchell dummy of old TV
33 Lab ___
34 Alex Doonesbury's school, for short
35 Lawyer's assignment
36 Silver coin of ancient Greece
38 Open-air lobbies
39 Fix, as a boot
41 ___ blaster
42 Classic tale in dactylic hexameter
43 Some Iraq war reporters
44 Cuba ___ (rum highballs)
45 Store, as supplies

48 Org. that promotes sugarless gum
49 Blue-skinned deity
50 Jacket fastener
51 Suffix with Frigid-
53 Hosp. hookups
54 Acquire
55 Raucous laugh syllable

DOWN

1 Tiny biological channel, as in the kidney
2 Aligned
3 Waterman products
4 Weird
5 ___ dog (Chinese breed)
6 Playfulness
7 Not so stormy
8 Go over and over, as arguments

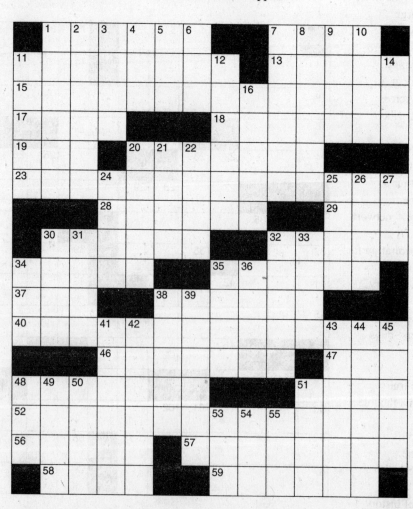

by Jeffrey Wechsler

ACROSS

1 Sank, as a putt
6 What bird wings do
10 Usually deleted e-mail
14 Item stuffed with pimento
15 Suffix with zillion
16 Living ___ (what an employer is asked to pay)
17 Two steeds?
19 πr², for a circle
20 Somewhat
21 One signing with a landlord
23 Groove
24 Industrialist J. Paul ___
25 Pants ending just below the knees
29 Small whiskey glass
32 Hang around for
33 $$$
34 Boat propeller
37 "Cheers" barfly
38 Isolated hill
39 "___ cow!"
40 In the style of
41 Hearty enjoyment
42 Small error
43 Poor, depressed neighborhood
45 Rodeo ropes
46 Hank whose home run record was surpassed by Barry Bonds
48 ___ de toilette
49 Intelligence
51 Move to another country
56 Cuts off, as branches
57 Two water slides?
59 Dull hurt
60 Bug-eyed
61 Sewing machine inventor Howe
62 Like a buttinsky
63 Deep-six
64 Harking back to an earlier style

DOWN

1 Arizona tribe
2 "The Good Earth" heroine
3 Italian currency before the euro
4 Actresses Mendes and Longoria
5 Point off, as for bad behavior
6 In legend he sold his soul to the devil
7 Queue
8 The "A" in MoMA
9 Cockroach or termite
10 Al Jolson classic
11 Two scout groups?
12 Player's rep
13 Full of substance
18 Cross to bear
22 Like omelets
25 Biblical water-to-wine site
26 Missing roll call, say
27 Two charts?
28 Salt's place on a margarita glass
29 Word-guessing game
30 Wild about
31 "Wow, I didn't know that!"
33 Event not to be missed
35 "Not to mention . . ."
36 Dark loaves
38 "However . . ."
39 Is afflicted with
41 Mannerly guy
42 Lopsided win, in slang
44 Rocking toy, in tot-speak
45 Of the flock
46 Lion in "The Chronicles of Narnia"
47 Oil company acquired by BP
48 Online publications, briefly
50 Small argument
51 Greek Cupid
52 Govern
53 Going ___ tooth and nail
54 Go like hell
55 Old U.S. gas brand
58 "Fourscore and seven years ___ . . ."

by Fred Piscop

172

ACROSS

1 One "in the woods"
5 Troop group: Abbr.
8 Tiny light that's here and gone
12 Classic door-to-door marketer
13 Manufactured
15 Radames's love, in opera
16 Something that swings
17 Keyboard key
18 Manual reader
19 Show ___
20 Stand-up comic's material
21 Film bomb of 1987
23 "You can't make me!"
25 Sch. with home games at Pauley Pavilion
26 Speediness
27 Kwame ___, advocate of pan-Africanism and the first P.M. of Ghana
31 Stewed to the gills
33 Pronto
34 Half-off event
35 Lucy of "Kill Bill"
36 Period of low activity
39 Bamboozle
40 Sell
42 Buff thing
43 Figure-skating figures
45 Dressed to the nines
47 Computer data acronym
48 Makes public
49 Gasoline additive
52 What 3-, 13-, 14- and 28-Down may be
55 Soft white cheese
56 Program file-name extension
57 Puppy's plaint
58 Farm letters?
60 Votin' no on
61 Poet laureate Dove
62 Ryan in Cooperstown
63 Newsman Roger
64 Pizazz

65 The Cards, on scoreboards
66 Low ratings

DOWN

1 Disney fawn
2 To have, to Henri
3 Tippler
4 Remnant
5 ___ jumping
6 Plops down
7 Ballantine product
8 German design school founded in 1919
9 Grocery shopper's aid
10 It's a thought
11 Catherine ___, last wife of Henry VIII
13 Donkey, for one

14 "How many months have 28 days?," e.g.
20 Zest
22 Professional's camera, for short
24 Too heavy
25 Cancel
28 Rat-a-tat-tat weapon
29 Very much
30 Chickens that come home to roost
31 Hollywood or Sunset: Abbr.
32 Place
33 Third degree?
37 Dandy sorts
38 Nouveau ___
41 Expressionless

44 Scala of "The Guns of Navarone"
46 Fizzle
47 Formerly common rooftop sight
50 Water or rust
51 Makes advances?
52 Instrument in ancient Greek art
53 Trompe l'___
54 Utah ski resort
55 Big swig
59 Cyclades island
60 ___, amas, amat . . .

by Paula Gamache

ACROSS

1 J.F.K.'s predecessor
4 Thesaurus creator
9 Roil, as the waters
14 Film critic Reed
15 Embarrass
16 Licorice flavoring
17 All around, as on a trip
20 Common cold cause
21 Spanish bulls
22 Suffix with disk
23 Young and feminine
26 Money on a poker table
29 "Hel-l-lp!"
30 Dashing actor Flynn
31 Ho-hum sort
32 "Remember the ___!"
33 Horse color
35 TV show with many doors
38 Last words of "Green Eggs and Ham"
39 Get by logic
40 "___ a fool to . . ."
41 Passover meal
42 Caboodle's partner
45 Sleepless princess' bane
46 Heat detector, e.g.
48 Walk a hole in the carpet, maybe
49 River of Arles
51 Richard's partner in the Carpenters
52 Move into first place in a race
57 Pillowcase accompanier
58 Celebrate boisterously
59 Sense of self-importance
60 Rice field
61 Rascal
62 Fellows

DOWN

1 Herds
2 Danny of "Throw Momma From the Train"
3 Applies, as pressure
4 Stadium cheers
5 Kabuki sash
6 Guy's date
7 Night school subj.
8 Buddy Holly's "___ Be the Day"
9 "The Treasure of the Sierra ___"
10 Reverse, as an action
11 Scattering of an ethnic group
12 Internet connection faster than dial-up
13 "___-haw!" (cry of delight)
18 Street, in Paris
19 "There is ___ in 'team' "
23 Former Texas senator Phil
24 "___ la Douce"
25 First-year players
27 Pitcher Hershiser
28 ___ Aviv
30 "Born Free" lioness
31 Title before Rabbit or Fox
32 End in ___ (come out even)
33 More secure
34 German/Polish border river
35 Stow, as cargo . . . or an anagram of the last word of 17-, 35- or 52-Across
36 Started out (on), as a journey
37 Prefix with skeleton
38 Tiniest drink
41 Contemptuous looks
42 N.B.A.'s ___ Abdul-Jabbar
43 Period of advancing glaciers
44 Sinew
46 Like Santa's suit after going through the chimney
47 Letter holder: Abbr.
48 Chum
50 Follow, as advice
51 Seaweed used as food
52 Recipe amt.
53 "That's brilliant!"
54 ___ center (community facility)
55 Energy inits. in the South
56 Bottom line?

by Andrea Carla Michaels

174

ACROSS

1 Vapors
6 Trades
11 Alternative to La Guardia or Newark, in brief
14 Travis who sang "T-R-O-U-B-L-E"
15 Picasso or Casals
16 Peyton Manning's brother
17 Try a North Atlantic fish for the first time?
19 Jamaican term of address
20 Afternoon hour
21 Rhino relatives with long snouts
23 & 25 "I'll alert ___": Hobson, in "Arthur"
28 French girlfriend
29 Bind with a belt
31 Ekco or Farberware?
34 Notions, in Nantes
36 Old photo color
37 Part of F.B.I.
40 Turning down
44 Like a visit from Benedict XVI, e.g.
46 Middle of the abdomen
47 Registers for a meditation class?
52 Big rig
53 Its capital is Muscat
54 Defendants enter them
56 Hunk
57 Airplane seating request
60 Houston baseballer
62 They're checked at checkpoints, briefly
63 Store photographer?
68 Code-breaking org.
69 "Hill Street Blues" actress Veronica
70 Augusta's home
71 Fast sports cars
72 Cornered
73 ___-Detoo . . . or, when read in three parts, a hint to 17-, 31-, 47- and 63-Across

DOWN

1 Co. with a blooming business?
2 Spoon-bending Geller
3 1960s sitcom with a talking palomino
4 Engrave glass with acid
5 Nor'easter, for one
6 Big name in small swimwear
7 Hell, to General Sherman
8 "Dancing With the Stars" network
9 Secret plan
10 Scotch's partner
11 Aunt known for her pancakes
12 Old European gold coin
13 Sex authority Alfred
18 Prez's #2
22 Melonlike tropical fruits
23 Letters said with a shout
24 Camouflage
26 The "I" in 23-Down
27 Got a perfect score on
30 Where to find the diving board
32 Unlock, in poetry
33 Wisc. neighbor
35 Ladies of Spain: Abbr.
38 Storekeeper on "The Simpsons"
39 Dweller above the Arctic Circle
41 "Eureka!"
42 Nautilus captain
43 Insincerely eloquent
45 I.M. snicker
47 A.A.A. activity
48 Surrounded by
49 "The Wizard of Oz" setting
50 Paltry
51 Miss America accessory
55 Leaf opening
58 Workers' protection agcy.
59 "Say again?"
61 Lion's warning
64 Govt. book balancer
65 Podded plant
66 British musician Brian
67 ___ Speedwagon

by Kurt Krauss

ACROSS

1 Wash very hard
6 "The racer's edge"
9 Chart anew
14 Hot love interest
15 ___-la-la
16 Former Mrs. Trump
17 Elvis Presley feature
19 Mamie Eisenhower feature
20 Tooth specialist's deg.
21 At the peak of maturity, as an apple
23 Shoulder muscle, informally
24 Author Ferber
25 Formidable opponents
27 Scads
30 Clad
32 Insolent
34 Tach readings
35 Drinker's road offense, for short
38 Fixed as a target . . . or a hint to four pairs of intersecting answers in this puzzle
42 Commercials
43 Appear to be
44 Its capital is Sana
45 Sugary drink
48 Apartment dweller's payment
49 Clothing
52 Move, in Realtor-speak
54 Opposite of freeze
55 Spanish devil
57 T in a fraternity
60 Willie Nelson feature
62 Betty Boop and Superman features
64 France's longest river
65 Asian New Year
66 Weapon in Clue
67 Step into
68 Grp. that opposed the Vietnam War
69 Not ___ (middling)

DOWN

1 Dirty Harry's employer: Abbr.
2 Dirt clump
3 Ewes' mates
4 Caller of strikes and balls, for short
5 Abraham Lincoln feature
6 Pull into
7 T on a test
8 Cousins of carrots
9 Tease
10 Got around
11 Jon Bon Jovi and Tina Turner features
12 It's measured in degrees
13 They may be sordid
18 Actress Merrill
22 Contract provisions
24 Impress, as in the memory
26 Like a net
27 Part of Istanbul is in it
28 Real estate
29 What tagging a runner and catching a fly ball result in
31 Give a shellacking
33 "___ no?"
35 Coin with F.D.R.'s profile
36 Bird that perches with its tail erect
37 George Harrison's "___ It a Pity"
39 Surrendered
40 They see things as they are
41 Prefix with dynamic
45 Lampoon
46 Circles, as the earth
47 Throw things at
49 Mosey along
50 Juan of Argentina
51 Pippi Longstocking feature
53 Rapunzel feature
56 Parroted
57 Chi-town paper, with "the"
58 ___ Romeo
59 Preowned
61 Architect Mies van ___ Rohe
63 Game with Skip and Draw 2 cards

by John Dunn

ACROSS

1 Explorers on a hwy., e.g.
5 ___ soup (starter at a Japanese restaurant)
9 Cops, in slang . . . or a hint to this puzzle's theme
14 Made quickly, as a meal
16 Indo-European
17 Up-to-date
18 Singer Bonnie
19 Gas bill unit
20 Gershwin's "Concerto ___"
22 Medical research agcy.
23 Brut or Paco Rabanne
28 Physical reactions?
31 Pro wrestling move
32 Informal British term of address
33 Schreiber of "X-Men Origins: Wolverine"
35 New Haven collegians
37 Gold-medal gymnast Comaneci
41 Browning opening line preceding "Now that April's there"
44 1900 Puccini premiere
45 Look
46 Site of Zeno's teaching
47 Civil War prez
49 Natasha's refusal
51 Whichever
52 Be indebted to the I.R.S.
57 Jap. computer giant
58 Took home the gold
59 Spirit of a group
63 "Welcome to Maui!"
65 Willa Cather novel
69 "So what else ___?"
70 Computer setup to facilitate instant messaging
71 Mary's upstairs neighbor, in 1970s TV
72 Floored it
73 Lover boy?

DOWN

1 Sultan of ___ (Babe Ruth)
2 "No way, no how"
3 Gambling or drinking
4 Fungus production
5 Sea, to Cousteau
6 Civil rights advocate ___ B. Wells
7 Light from above
8 Eye-related
9 Widespread
10 Nest egg for old age, in brief
11 Competing
12 Have dinner at home
13 Words before rocks, ropes or run
15 Alternative to Nikes
21 Eggy drink
24 Beekeeper of filmdom
25 Some Surrealist paintings
26 Distinguished
27 Egg shapes
28 Gazillions
29 Bygone cracker brand
30 Squash match units
34 Lexicon contents, for short
36 "Adios!"
38 Facts and figures
39 Privy to
40 The Beatles' "___ in the Life"
42 Gilda Radner character
43 Ariz. neighbor
48 Prefix with friendly
50 Wee
52 Broadcasting now
53 Like the name "Bryn Mawr"
54 ___ Lodge
55 Door handles
56 Inscribed pillar
60 Prince, e.g.
61 Roughly
62 Former fast jets
64 "I knew a man Bojangles and ___ dance for you . . ."
66 Young dog
67 Chemical suffix
68 Like 1, 3, 5, 7 . . .

by Elizabeth C. Gorski

ACROSS

1 Going for broke, as a poker player
6 Goatee, for one
11 Corp.'s head money person
14 Sarge's superior
15 ___-Detoo of "Star Wars"
16 Flight board abbr.
17 Campus/off-campus community, collectively
19 Bone that's part of a "cage"
20 iPhone downloads
21 Composer Stravinsky
22 Peru's peaks
24 Majority Muslim in Iran
26 Declaration that may be followed by "So sue me"
27 Confederate flag
31 Roasting rods
34 Med. group
35 Place for ChapStick
36 Charged particle
37 John Lennon's lady
41 Environmentalist's prefix
42 "Believe It or ___!"
43 Daisy ___ of "Li'l Abner"
44 Hat for a military specialist
46 Extreme pessimism
51 Job for a roadside assistance worker
52 Tater Tots maker
55 No longer vivid
56 ___ bene
58 Oompah band instrument
60 Lincoln, the Rail-Splitter
61 Damage from ordinary use
64 ___ de France
65 Where a wedding march ends
66 River mouth feature
67 Dem.'s foe
68 Triangular road sign
69 1950s Ford flop

DOWN

1 Resort near Snowbird
2 Figure skating figures
3 Boast of some shampoos
4 "No use arguing with me"
5 PBS funder
6 Nag to death
7 As a result
8 Suffix with origin
9 Part of an airplane seat assignment
10 Disney's ___ Duck
11 Seller of coupes and sedans
12 Chinese side dish
13 Heavenly bodies
18 Old-time actress Talbot or Naldi
23 Penpoint
25 Teeny, informally
26 Listen ___ (hear via eavesdropping)
28 Protected, as the feet
29 "I love," in Latin
30 Parking space
31 Perform on "American Idol," e.g.
32 Place to "rack 'em up"
33 Unable to dig oneself out
38 Muscat's land
39 It's north of Okla.
40 Melancholy instrument
45 Sent out, as rays
47 Fall behind financially
48 Chicago alternative to O'Hare
49 Senile sort
50 Algerian port
53 Face-offs with guns or swords
54 Lessen
55 Without a cloud in the sky
56 ___ the Great of children's literature
57 Grueling grilling
59 Asia's shrunken ___ Sea
62 "The Book of ___" (2010 film)
63 Ike's monogram

by Nancy Salomon

178

ACROSS

1 Establishments with mirrored balls
7 Snacked
10 In a state of 10-Down
14 Involve
15 South of South America
16 Help the dishwasher, perhaps
17 In a precise manner
18 It's directly below V-B-N-M
20 Turn in many a children's game
21 Relative of a raccoon
22 Bark beetle's habitat
23 Highway safety marker
27 Caballer's need
28 No ___ sight
32 Away from home
35 Unwelcome financial exams
39 French river or department
40 Punch in the mouth, slangily
43 Westernmost of the Aleutians
44 Alice's best friend on "The Honeymooners"
45 Honor society letter
46 "___ never believe this!"
48 "___ first you don't succeed . . ."
50 Homecoming display
56 Pompous fool
59 Cut down
60 Cuts down
62 Cold treat that can precede the last word of 18-, 23-, 40- or 50-Across
64 Menu selection
66 Not dry
67 Full house sign
68 Pig, when rummaging for truffles
69 Diva's delivery
70 Newspaper staffers, in brief
71 Fleet of warships

DOWN

1 Rooms with recliners
2 All thumbs
3 Flight segment
4 Forty winks
5 Olive product
6 Tricky
7 Part of P.G.A.: Abbr.
8 Rapper ___ Shakur
9 Sister of Clio
10 Feeling when you're 10-Across
11 Taunt
12 Birthstone for most Libras
13 Start, as of an idea
19 French filmdom
21 Remnant of a burned coal
24 Verbal brickbats
25 Tennis "misstep"
26 Plenty, to a poet
29 Icicle feature
30 Narrow winning margin
31 Classic soda pop
32 Give the go-ahead
33 "Do ___ others . . ."
34 South African Peace Nobelist, 1984
36 "It ___" (reply to "Who's there?")
37 Prepared for takeoff
38 [Well, see if I care!]
41 Actor Robert of "I Spy"
42 Give out cards
47 Bert of "The Wizard of Oz"
49 Indian percussion
51 Witherspoon of "Legally Blonde"
52 Cy Young, e.g.
53 Visual sales pitches
54 Line from the heart
55 Tammany Hall "boss"
56 Elton John/Tim Rice musical
57 Mark for life
58 Place for a cab
61 It's repeated after "Que" in song
63 Tax preparer, for short
64 Diamond stat
65 Neither's partner

by Sarah Keller

ACROSS

1 As a result
5 Handed (out)
10 Furry creature allied with Luke Skywalker and the Jedi knights
14 ___ of students
15 Deadly virus
16 Caster of spells
17 "My deepest apologies"
20 They go into overtime
21 Coffee orders with foamy tops
22 Actress Gardner and others
23 Deceptive talk, in slang
24 Soup ingredient from a pod
27 Worker's pay
28 Car navigational aid, for short
31 Had home cooking
32 Place for the words "Miss USA"
33 Margarita garnish
34 "No idea"
37 Actor's pursuit
38 Elvis ___ Presley
39 Emmy category
40 Opposite of NNW
41 Federal agent investigating taxes, informally
42 Pop maker in a nursery rhyme
43 Witches' ___
44 Sound gravelly
45 Nixed by Nixon, e.g.
48 Diversions . . . as hinted at by the ends of 17-, 34- and 52-Across
52 "Let's take that gamble"
54 And others: Abbr.
55 "Live Free ___" (New Hampshire motto)
56 Quadri- times two
57 "Star ___," biggest movie of 1977

58 Mexican dollars
59 Having everything in its place

DOWN

1 Cut and paste, say
2 Notes after do
3 Golden ___ Bridge
4 So-called universal donor blood
5 Skin-related
6 Theater awards
7 Arcing shots
8 90° turn
9 Vampire's undoing
10 Act with great feeling
11 Witch's blemish
12 Meanie
13 Frequently misplaced items
18 Large gully
19 Put money in the bank
23 Golden Fleece pursuer
24 Hideouts
25 Set of guiding beliefs
26 Author Zora ___ Hurston
27 Car with a big carrying capacity, informally
28 Lavish parties
29 Feather in one's cap
30 Super bargain
32 Scarecrow stuffing
33 Recycled metal
35 Try to impress in a conversation, say
36 "___ Fideles"

41 BlackBerry rival
42 Bathes
43 Plays tenpins
44 3:5, e.g.
45 It's afforded by a scenic overlook
46 Jazzy James
47 Peter the Great, for one
48 Highest degrees
49 They're often double-clicked
50 "Cómo ___ usted?"
51 32-card game
53 III in modern Rome

by Ian Livengood

180

ACROSS

1 Biblical strongman
7 Two cents' worth
10 Anti-D.U.I. org.
14 Climber's chopper
15 Sports org. with a tour
16 Skin care brand
17 Place to freshen up
19 Rock legend Hendrix
20 Display of grandeur
21 French-speaking African nation
22 Sport involving a chute
25 "Unforgettable" duettist Cole
31 Caen's river
32 Like clocks with hands
33 Tot's repeated questions
34 ID with two hyphens
37 Britney Spears's debut hit
40 Early Beatle Sutcliffe
41 Fully convinced
42 Joins
43 Hatcher with a Golden Globe
44 Disassembles, as a model airplane
45 Elite military group
49 On one's toes
50 Treatment with carbon dioxide
57 Prefix with star or bucks
58 Classic Miles Davis album . . . or a hint to the start of 17-, 22-, 37- or 45-Across
60 "___ Almighty" (Steve Carell movie)
61 Tattooist's supply
62 Characteristics
63 Bumper blemish
64 "Pick a card, ___ card"
65 Most achy

DOWN

1 Nurses, at the bar
2 Rent-___ (private security guard)
3 Whimper like a baby
4 One-named Nigerian songstress
5 Paul Bunyan's Babe and others
6 Dorky sort
7 Hybrid utensil
8 Way back when
9 Sweet potato
10 Desert with Joshua trees
11 Suspect's story
12 Friend of Pythias
13 Flopping at a comedy club
18 Ascended
21 Root used in some energy drinks
23 Start of a pirate's chant
24 Practice go-round
25 Catches, as a perp
26 Med school subj.
27 Forbidden-sounding perfume
28 Prince ___ Khan
29 Least strict
30 Pay no heed to
33 Subj. of a U.N. inspection, maybe
34 In ___ (as placed)
35 "Peter Pan" pirate
36 Loch ___ monster
38 Director Kazan
39 Up to, in ads
43 Iron-fisted boss
44 ___ car dealer
45 Identified
46 Tylenol alternative
47 Lacking meat, eggs, dairy, etc.
48 Like Abe Lincoln, physiologically
51 Goes bad
52 Early Jesse Jackson hairdo
53 Way up the slope
54 Netman Nastase
55 Contract loopholes, e.g.
56 Digs of twigs
58 Spectra automaker
59 B&B, e.g.

by Alex Boisvert

ACROSS

1 Noisy bird
6 "___ the night before . . ."
10 Exhilaration
14 Ninth planet no more
15 Days of King Arthur's Round Table, e.g.
16 Any brother in "Animal Crackers"
17 Broadway lyricist/composer who wrote "I Can Get It for You Wholesale"
19 Amo, amas, ___
20 Opposite of melted
21 Make ___ for (advocate)
22 California wine county
26 Whoop
28 Buddhist sect
29 Gas log fuel
31 Certify (to)
33 Virginia-born Pulitzer Prize novelist of 1942
36 Actress Cannon
37 Three ___ match
38 "Anybody home? . . . home? . . . home? . . ."
42 "God Bless America" composer
47 Drink that might come with a mint leaf
50 Japanese site of the 1972 Winter Olympics
51 Lon ___ of Cambodia
52 Greek portico
55 "You said it, ___!"
56 Elite roster
58 Cook, as steaks in an oven
60 Indy 500, e.g.
61 "The Call of the Wild" author
66 Chief Norse god
67 The "A" in U.S.A.: Abbr.
68 Seeing Eye dog, e.g.
69 Light bulb unit
70 Nothing, in Juárez
71 Pegasus, e.g.

DOWN

1 Speedometer reading: Abbr.
2 ___ carte
3 Dog prone to biting
4 From ___ Z
5 One who changes form during a full moon
6 Beginner
7 Mentally unclear
8 French military force
9 Go out with
10 Auto financing inits.
11 Childbirth training method
12 Undoes pencil marks
13 Scope
18 Sturm und ___
21 Kind of sax

22 Hurried
23 Pairs suburb
24 Theme song of bandleader Vincent Lopez
25 Gift-giver's urging
27 Fall behind
30 "The Time Machine" people
32 Dweebs
34 The Beach Boys' "Barbara ___"
35 Is low around the waist, as pants
39 Blood circulation problem
40 Put on the payroll
41 ___ off (light switch option)
43 Remainder

44 Industrial container
45 Pesto seasoning
46 Ends of some novels
47 Lined up
48 Piña ___
49 Bring out
53 First president born in Hawaii
54 Followed a curved path
57 E-mail folder
59 Gumbo pod
61 First mo.
62 Hickory ___
63 What immortals never do
64 Shelley's "___ to the West Wind"
65 ___ Flanders of "The Simpsons"

by Randy Sowell

ACROSS

1 "What did Delaware?" "I don't know, but ___" (old joke)
7 "I ___ bored!"
11 Score components: Abbr.
14 Decorate flamboyantly, in slang
15 Simon ___
16 Noisy fight
17 King who was the son of Pepin the Short
19 "___ Rocker" (Springsteen song)
20 Electron's path
21 River that ends at Cairo
22 Cinematographer Nykvist
23 Post-copyright status
26 Sister of Snow White
29 Smack hard
30 Intuition, maybe: Abbr.
31 Darkens
34 Big name in vacuums
37 La Choy product
41 Russian country house
42 F.B.I. guys
43 Ming of the N.B.A.
44 Puts away plates
46 French carmaker
49 Easternmost U.S. capital
53 Graph paper pattern
54 Food thickener
55 For face value
59 Cabinet dept. overseeing farm interests
60 Fancy equine coif
62 No. on a calling card
63 Zealous
64 Not polished
65 Pothook shape
66 Till compartment
67 Like Dracula

DOWN

1 Classic record label for the Bee Gees and Cream
2 Bert who played a cowardly lion
3 Emirate dweller
4 Indicator of rank
5 Civilization, to Freud
6 Distant cousin of humans
7 Sapporo competitor
8 ___ Johnson
9 Church councils
10 Sugar suffix
11 Philip Marlowe or Sam Spade
12 Actress Marisa
13 Ex-Steeler Lynn
18 Crown ___
22 Unctuous flattery
24 "Venerable" monk
25 "Geez! That stings!"
26 Shipping dept. stamp
27 Dept. of Labor arm
28 Scary, Baby, Ginger, Posh and Sporty
32 Year McKinley was elected to a second term
33 First American in space
35 "Gotta go!"
36 Muscle malady
38 Hot: Fr.
39 Kit ___ (candy bars)
40 "Dedicated to the ___ Love"
45 Excessively fast
47 Japanese eel and rice dish
48 Lose patience and then some
49 Ornamental quartz
50 Earnestly recommends
51 "To repeat . . ."
52 Dust busters
56 Peel
57 Jug handle, in archaeology
58 Stalk in a marsh
60 Face the pitcher
61 Old French coin

by Paula Gamache

ACROSS

1 Navajo's neighbor in Arizona
5 Edinburg native
9 Defect
13 Racetrack shapes
15 Many millennia
16 Parks who received the Presidential Medal of Freedom
17 Tendon
18 Common advice to travelers
20 Terminus
21 Seed with a licoricelike flavor
23 Beginning
24 Race that finishes in a tie
26 Warm embrace
27 Worms, to a fisherman
28 Early Fords that "put America on wheels"
32 Say "C-A-T" or "D-O-G," e.g.
34 Boathouse gear
36 "___ don't say!"
37 Doing something risky . . . or a hint to the last words of 18-, 24-, 49- and 58-Across
41 Avis or Alamo offering
42 Misfortunes
43 Uncles' mates
44 Being risked, as in a bet
47 Cassini of fashion
48 Cubes from the freezer
49 Bygone love interest
53 Digging tool
56 Weak-___ (easily intimidated)
57 Candlemaking supply
58 "Omigosh!"
60 Oven brand
62 Language of Pakistan
63 What Yale became in 1969
64 Hayseed
65 Vault (over)
66 "The ___ the limit"
67 Crème de la crème

DOWN

1 Cleaned with water, as a sidewalk
2 Sheeplike
3 Adorable zoo critters from China
4 Suffix with percent
5 Tone of many old photos
6 Where a hurricane makes landfall
7 ___ in a blue moon
8 "For shame!"
9 Outer edge
10 Hearth contents
11 U.S. tennis legend on a 37¢ stamp
12 The "W" of kWh
14 Widespread language of East Africa
19 Earsplitting
22 Ping-Pong table divider
25 Tyne of "Cagney & Lacey"
26 Party giver
28 CT scan alternatives
29 Suffering from insomnia
30 Wrong that's adjudicated in court
31 Takes to court
32 Org. for cat and dog lovers
33 Builder's map
34 Look at lustfully
35 Hole-making tool
38 Athletics brand with a swoosh
39 9:00 a.m. to 12:30 p.m., say, for a worker
40 Gasoline or peat
45 Neaten
46 Unreturned tennis serves
47 Keats's "___ to Psyche"
49 Not sharp or flat
50 Textile city of north-central England
51 Grooms comb them
52 Praise mightily
53 Place for a bar mitzvah service
54 Skin opening
55 Alan of "M*A*S*H"
56 Nutcase
59 Introducers of a show's acts, e.g.
61 "The Godfather" crowd, with "the"

by Lynn Lempel

184

ACROSS

1 Tiny
7 End of a Shakespeare play
11 MP3 holders
14 Artist Diego
15 One who talks only about himself, say
16 Egg layer
17 Genesis duo
19 Historical time
20 Fish-fowl connector
21 It's found on a nightstand
23 ___-Wan with the Force
26 Chum
28 "Enough!"
29 Certain mustache shape
33 Not great, but not awful either
34 TV part
35 Computer capacity, informally
38 Means of staying toasty at night
43 Yankee nickname starting in 2004
44 Control, as expenses
46 Treated, as a sprained ankle
50 American symbol
52 "Let's play!"
55 Major coll. fraternity
56 Sunburned
57 Made possible
59 "___ moment!" ("Don't rush me!")
61 French pronoun
62 Street weapon . . . or a hint to the circled letters in this puzzle
68 Under the weather
69 Bond girl Kurylenko
70 Spotted feline
71 Profs.' helpers
72 Wall Street inits.
73 Darcy's Pemberley, e.g., in "Pride and Prejudice"

DOWN

1 Parabola, e.g.
2 ___ Maria
3 Prefix with duct
4 Target audience of Details magazine
5 Country with a Guardian Council
6 One use of a Swiss Army knife
7 Lawyers' org.
8 Ty with batting titles
9 Sequoias, e.g.
10 Open grassland
11 Penny-pincher, slangily
12 Skin layer
13 Wake with a start
18 Blah
22 ___ Lonely Boys (rock band)
23 Cries of surprise
24 "The Well-Tempered Clavier" composer
25 Memo starter
27 Greek L's
30 Org. monitoring narcotics smuggling
31 "___ thousand flowers bloom"
32 Bible study: Abbr.
36 Tool you can lean on
37 Snick's partner
39 When you entered this world: Abbr.
40 Seoul-based automaker
41 Hwy. planner
42 10-point Q, e.g.
45 Actor Beatty
46 "That's clear"
47 Kind of oil
48 Contacts via the Net
49 Girl with a coming-out party
51 Secular
53 Johnny who used to cry "Come on down!"
54 As of late
58 Shovels
60 Rudimentary education
63 ___ Bo
64 Redo, in tennis
65 ___ mode
66 Half of a colon
67 Summer on the Seine

by Oliver Hill

ACROSS

1 Vision that isn't real
6 Areas of urban decay
11 Country singer Ritter
14 Ahead of time
15 Vietnam's capital
16 Vietnam ___
17 A-team
19 Provision for old age, in brief
20 Footballers' measures: Abbr.
21 Pay attention to
22 Excellent, in slang
24 Abruptly dump, as a lover
25 Curly-haired dogs
26 Composer's work for a film
30 Caribbean resort island
31 "Sesame Street" airer
32 Realtor's favorite sign
36 Five-digit postal number, informally
37 Slow-moving primates
41 ___ de Janeiro
42 Canadian gas brand
44 Former Mideast inits.
45 "Come on!" and "Go!"
47 Portuguese, for Brazilians, e.g.
51 Waltz composer
54 Love god
55 Fireplace floor
56 Spew
57 Drunk's road offense, for short
60 "Star Trek" rank: Abbr.
61 Really steamed . . . or what the ends of 17-, 26- and 47-Across are?
64 Conk
65 Map close-up
66 "Boléro" composer
67 "___ questions?"
68 Show just a little bit of leg, say
69 Winding

DOWN

1 Go against, as someone's will
2 Antibug spray
3 Makes a boo-boo
4 Gore and Green
5 Like dragons and centaurs
6 Yiddish for "small town"
7 Cooking fat
8 Prefix with cycle
9 Kipling's Rikki-tikki-tavi, for one
10 Milan mister
11 Band majorette's move
12 Country star Steve
13 Pictures at a dentist's
18 Actress Ward
23 Fruity drinks
24 Triangular sail
25 Banned pollutants, briefly
26 Labyrinth
27 Literary Leon
28 Dines
29 Church feature seen from a distance
33 Not a copy: Abbr.
34 In ___ of (replacing)
35 One teaspoonful or two caplets, maybe
38 Surpass
39 Stadium cheers
40 Relatives of mopeds
43 "The Rubáiyát" poet ___ Khayyám
46 E.R. or O.R. workers
48 Barbie doll purchase
49 What a couch potato probably holds
50 Oakland paper, informally
51 Biblical queendom
52 It's inserted in a mortise
53 Hoarse
56 Hot times on the Riviera
57 One who might receive roses at the end of a performance
58 Timespan for The Economist
59 How thumbs are twiddled
62 Airport worker's org.
63 Light brown

by Susan Gelfand

ACROSS

1 Dudley Do-Right's org.
5 Banjo sound
10 Video recorders, briefly
14 Anticipatory cry
15 Tend to, as plants
16 "So true!"
17 Disk-shaped sea creature
19 Bit of dialogue
20 Oral hesitations
21 Bruins' sch.
22 High-I.Q. crew
23 Actress Carrere
24 Shift blame to another
27 More posh
29 Approx. takeoff hour
30 Bashful
31 Routing abbr.
32 Immeasurably vast
35 Chowder ingredient
40 Tater Tots brand
41 Santa ___ (hot California winds)
43 Exclamation in Berlin
46 Leatherworker's tool
47 Current unit
49 Hit that just clears the infield
53 Short smoke?
54 Turkish money
55 Jean who wrote "The Clan of the Cave Bear"
56 Hydroelectric project
57 "He loves," in Latin
58 Auto-racing designation
61 "Scrubs" actor Braff
62 Not abridged
63 Baseball great Musial

64 Ones who've been through divorce court
65 Horseshoers' tools
66 Pain in the neck

DOWN

1 Stone discovery site
2 "Ben-Hur" racers
3 Global agricultural company
4 Advanced deg.
5 Kind of garage
6 Masons' creations
7 Muscular Charles
8 Union with 3+ million members, in brief
9 Junkyard dog's greeting
10 Novelist Carr
11 Pretty good grade
12 Stand-up guy
13 Deceitful
18 Hornswoggle
22 Battlefield doc
25 Rival of Edison
26 WWW code
28 "For more ___ . . ."
32 Hot dog topper
33 U.K. lexicon
34 Sound of thunder
36 Golf hazards
37 Wields a needle
38 Short reminiscence
39 ___ Trench (deepest point on Earth's surface)
42 Orange part, e.g.
43 In flames
44 Part of a book where you're unlikely to stop
45 Poet who originated the phrase "harmony in discord"
47 Indigenous Alaskans
48 Pell-___
50 Courtroom rituals
51 Feds who make busts
52 Ruin, informally
58 Stole material
59 "Not ___ bet!"
60 African slitherer

by Doug Peterson

ACROSS

1 2006 boorish film character from Kazakhstan
6 Castle-defending ditches
11 David Letterman's network
14 Smells
15 Suffer ignominious defeat, in slang
16 Feedbag tidbit
17 Second- or third-string player
19 Actress Hagen
20 Cyclotron particles
21 Interest-grabbing
23 "Apologies"
27 "As old as the hills" and others
28 What wheels do on an axis
29 Talk to flirtatiously
30 Screwballs
31 "God ___ America"
32 Photo ___ (when pictures may be taken)
35 Son of Seth
36 Audio censor's sound
37 Molecule component
38 Broadband connection inits.
39 Lewis's partner in an expedition
40 Stiller and ___ (comedy duo)
41 One-horse town
43 Explorer Hernando
44 One showing diners to their tables
46 Indian baby on a back
47 Spider's cocoon, e.g.
48 Suspect, to a cop
49 "Norma ___"
50 Presider at a meeting
56 Stock debut, for short
57 Newsstand
58 Decorative fabric
59 Highest non-face card
60 Spread, as the legs
61 Assail

DOWN

1 Dylan or Dole
2 Praiseful poem
3 Director Howard
4 Lob's path
5 Gift shop apparel
6 George who was the first president of the A.F.L.-C.I.O.
7 Items fitting in rowlocks
8 Place to enter a PIN
9 Man's jewelry item
10 Narrow passageways
11 Boob tube lover
12 Wash oneself
13 Remains
18 Had on
22 Fort Worth sch.
23 Annoyed
24 Time periods lasting about 29½ days
25 Police informant
26 Acorn producers
27 Where rouge goes
29 Office worker
31 Lacking individuality
33 Skin openings
34 Some air pollution
36 Kind of stock
37 Prefix with dynamic
39 Music store fixtures
40 Tots
42 Tie-breaking play periods: Abbr.
43 Complain
44 ___ badge
45 Open-mouthed
46 Cheerful
48 Leaning Tower site
51 Yahoo! competitor
52 ___ v. Wade
53 Use the start of 17- or 50-Across or 11- or 25-Down?
54 Suffix with schnozz
55 What 51-Down connects to, with "the"

by Randy Sowell

188

ACROSS

1 Defeat, barely
5 Word on a bar worker's jar
9 Gem
14 Pasta or potato, for short
15 Savoie sweetheart
16 Still in the game
17 Brag
18 Beekeeper played by Peter Fonda
19 Recurring melody
20 Tiger and Elin Woods's 37-Across order?
23 Super, slangily
24 Sign on a locked lavatory
25 Vast amounts
27 It might start "E FP TOZ LPED"
30 Party that's a wow
31 Posh
32 One pitied by Mr. T
33 Doo-___ music
36 Actor's rep: Abbr.
37 Cocktail called "the elixir of quietude" by 4-Down
40 1950s campaign nickname
41 ___'easter
42 Apple originally marketed to schools
43 New car sticker fig.
44 Figure of Greek myth with a statue at Rockefeller Center
46 1889 statehood achievers, with "the"
49 Ringtoss game
51 A marathon has about 26 of these
52 Runnin' Rebels' sch.
53 Paula Abdul's 37-Across order?
58 "Later, amigo!"
60 French cleric
61 Foot: Prefix
62 It's not good to run one
63 Potter's oven
64 Mineral in hemoglobin
65 The hapless Corleone
66 Things that modest people lack
67 "Peter Pan" fairy, for short

DOWN

1 Shoe company founded in Denmark
2 "Phooey!"
3 Small cavern, in poetry
4 "The Elements of Style" updater
5 Sign after Aries
6 "Please help me with directions!"
7 Jigsaw puzzle element
8 Be "it," in a game
9 Wing it, musically
10 Skips the dos before the I do's?
11 O. Henry's 37-Across order?
12 Aquafina rival
13 Some turns and boxing punches
21 Opposite WSW
22 Wise old Athenian
26 City known as Colombia's sports capital
27 Pizazz
28 "Car Talk" dubbed it "the worst car of the millennium"
29 Popeye's 37-Across order?
30 Avril Lavigne's "Sk8er ___"
32 Consumer protection agcy.
34 Vegetable in Cajun cuisine
35 Livens, with "up"
37 Cheesy sandwich
38 Collect
39 Dorm figures, for short
43 Frenzied place at a rock club
45 Recorded for later viewing
46 Cisco Kid's horse
47 "The X-Files" figures
48 Big beer buy
49 Hearty drink
50 Hypnotized or anesthetized
51 Head honcho
54 Help oneself to
55 Garr of "Tootsie"
56 Noodles with tempura
57 Medium-rare steak color
59 B'way success sign

by Keith Talon

ACROSS

1 Listings in a dr.'s calendar
6 Number of Muses
10 Best guesses: Abbr.
14 Nary ___ (no one)
15 Grandson of Adam
16 March Madness org.
17 Parting words from the Everly Brothers
19 Unrestrained revelry
20 "Clean up your ___!"
21 "___ Baba and the 40 Thieves"
22 "___ me, Father" (confessional phrase)
23 Parting words from the Lone Ranger
28 Card game for two
29 "Telephone Line" rock grp.
30 Diminutive suffix
31 ___-Coburg-Gotha, former British royal house
32 Heavenly body
33 Gorillas
34 Parting words from the Terminator
38 Degs. for corporate types
41 ___ Lingus
42 Hula dancers wiggle them
45 Building wing
46 Suffix with labyrinth
47 Reply to "Am not!"
49 Parting words from the von Trapps
52 Laughs
53 Forbid
54 Bowling stat.
56 Western Indian tribe
57 Parting words from Donald Trump
61 Halliwell of the Spice Girls
62 Claudia ___ Taylor (Lady Bird Johnson)
63 Director Kurosawa
64 Fruity drinks
65 Dennis the Menace, for one
66 Not tidy

DOWN

1 Four-line rhyme scheme
2 Human spirits
3 Horace's "Ars ___"
4 Bath site
5 Foxy
6 Nervous ___
7 How French fries are fried
8 Oct. follower
9 Language suffix
10 W.W. II bomber ___ Gay
11 Homer Simpson type
12 Common house event before moving
13 Agrees
18 Sunrise direction
22 Pal
24 Vertical line on a graph
25 Hershiser on the mound
26 Subject follower
27 Isle of exile
32 "___ the ramparts . . ."
33 "Go fly ___!"
35 Fritz who directed "Metropolis"
36 Hamburger meat
37 "___ your food" (mother's admonition)
38 Yiddish for "crazy"
39 Like a stomach after an all-you-can-eat buffet
40 Fully focused and attentive
43 North Star
44 Crossword doers
46 ___ and outs
47 Mount where Noah landed
48 Artist Magritte
50 Place for camels to water
51 Touches
55 "Hello" Down Under
57 Talk noisily
58 Bullfight cheer
59 Clan: Abbr.
60 '50s prez

by Jay Kaskel

190

ACROSS

1 You might fix one yourself at a bar
6 Abbr. after a lawyer's name
9 Blog additions
14 Dance partner for Fred
15 Little, in Lille
16 "99 and $^{44}/_{100}$% pure" soap
17 Place for knickknacks
18 "What ___ to do?"
19 Link
20 Thief in a western
23 Rm. coolers
24 ___-de-sac
25 Suffix with Orwell
26 Bard's "before"
29 Some metal frames
32 "Dancing Queen" group
35 Penn, e.g.: Abbr.
36 They're red or blue, on some maps
37 Emergency strategy
39 N.L. cap letters
41 "All About ___," 2009 Sandra Bullock bomb
42 Main lines
44 Canon camera line
46 "___ Tú" (1974 hit)
47 Parliamentary procedure guide, familiarly
50 Outcomes of some QB sneaks
51 Bacon runoff
52 Suffix with penta-
53 ___ few rounds (spar)
56 Unclear outcome . . . or what can be found literally in 20-, 29- and 47-Across
59 Hip-hopper's headgear
62 Battery for many penlights
63 Modular elements
64 PayPal money, e.g.
65 Chain part: Abbr.
66 Little Munster
67 SALT subject
68 To date
69 Accomplish, biblically

DOWN

1 The younger Obama girl
2 Specially formed, as a committee
3 Lascivious looks
4 Tell-___ (some bios)
5 Reason for a merchandise return
6 Adornments on officers' shoulders
7 Coll. terms
8 "Knock that off!"
9 Pesto ingredients
10 In the strike zone
11 Beantown or Chi-Town team
12 Play about Capote
13 Part of CBS: Abbr.
21 They intersect in Montréal
22 TV husband of Phyllis
26 Perfumery compound
27 Christopher of "Somewhere in Time"
28 Slalom paths
29 "À votre ___!"
30 "I'm outta here!"
31 Fills to the gills
32 In pieces
33 Red Cross supply
34 Verbal digs
38 A bouncer might break one up
40 TV boss of Mary Richards
43 Record label for Booker T. & the M.G.'s
45 Gin flavoring
48 Like a Turkish bath
49 Came next
53 Go like a flying squirrel
54 Super Bowl XXV M.V.P. ___ Anderson
55 Item in the plus column
56 Communion service
57 See socially
58 "Go back," on an edit menu
59 TV room
60 World Food Day mo.
61 "Norma ___"

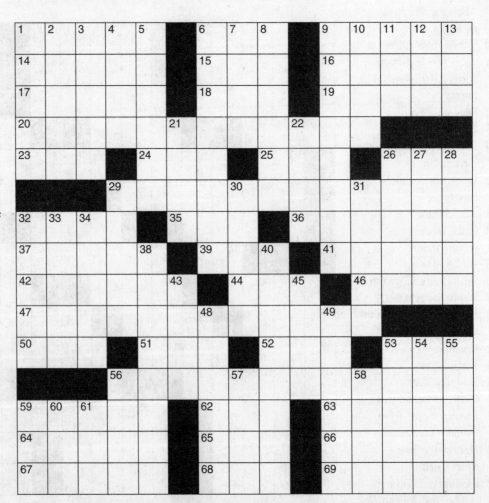

by Peter A. Collins

ACROSS

1 Cow's offspring
5 U.C.L.A. player
10 Bank no.
14 Margarine
15 Copy, for short
16 What's seen in "Saw"
17 Football alignment named for its shape
19 "___ a Song Go Out of My Heart"
20 Impertinent
21 Bed-and-breakfast
22 Muslim's God
23 Elvis ___ Presley
25 Drug that's a downer
26 Top choice
31 Sign in a boardinghouse window
32 "Yes, captain!"
33 Good "Wheel of Fortune" purchase for STRING BIKINI
34 Drano ingredient
35 Undeveloped
38 Heckle or Jeckle of cartoons
42 Lay waste to
45 "Light" dessert?
48 Went nuts
49 School near Windsor Castle
50 11th-century conqueror of Valencia
51 Number on a golf hole
53 Starbucks size that's Italian for "twenty"
57 Fruity drinks
58 Sci-fi hero in the 25th century
60 Circus shelter
61 Stan's pal in old films
62 Puccini's "Nessun dorma," for one
63 Captain Hook's henchman
64 To the point, ironically
65 Classic theater name

DOWN

1 Foldable beds
2 ___ Romeo (Italian car)
3 Ones born before Virgos
4 Abandon
5 Item under a blouse
6 Color again, as the hair
7 Go ___ smoke
8 Do a post-washing chore
9 Oui's opposite
10 Nimbleness
11 Property securing a loan
12 Manufacture
13 Restraining cord
18 Ancient Athenian sculptor
22 Samoan capital
24 Frequent, in poetry
25 Cheer for a bullfighter
26 School org.
27 Charged particle
28 It might be marked off with police tape
29 Rutherford B. ___
30 Ogle
34 Big fib
36 Biographical datum
37 Itsy-bitsy
39 Skilled entertainer
40 Where to enter this puzzle's answers
41 Indy 500 service area
42 Same old same old
43 From the beginning: Lat.
44 The "sour" in sweet-and-sour
45 Shoe grippers
46 Poker variety
47 Sleeveless jacket
51 Word on a door handle
52 Org. protecting individual rights
54 Literary Wolfe
55 "___ are for kids" (ad slogan)
56 "___, old chap!"
58 Go up and down, as in the water
59 On Social Security: Abbr.

by Bob Johnson

192

ACROSS

1 Deep-six
5 Crosswise, on deck
10 Movie lot sights
14 "Beat it!"
15 Martini's partner in wine
16 Turkish title of old
17 Not stuffy
18 Pesky swarm
19 H.S. math class
20 Keypad forerunner
22 Safecracker
23 They, in Thiers
24 Coarse, as humor
26 Knock down in rank
30 Term of address from a hat-tipper
32 Seat of Marion County, Fla.
33 Ghana, once
38 Company that makes Lincoln and Mercury
39 Afternoon fare . . . or a hint to the ends of 20-, 33-, 41- and 52-Across
40 Eliciting a "So what?"
41 Body suit shade, perhaps
43 Community of plant and animal life
44 Blossoms-to-be
45 Glossy fabric
46 Absolutely perfect
50 Mineo of "Exodus"
51 Zap in the microwave
52 One of two in a Christmas song
59 "Axis of evil" land
60 Stiller's partner in comedy
61 Like thrift shop wares
62 Snowman's prop
63 Vows locale
64 Came into a base horizontally
65 Give off
66 Down and out
67 Broadway honor

DOWN

1 Peter the Great, e.g.
2 Kent State locale
3 Do a laundry chore
4 ___ beans (miso ingredients)
5 Pattern named for a Scottish county
6 Wall Street buys
7 Morales of "La Bamba"
8 Terrier in whodunits
9 Isn't completely honest with
10 Lecherous figure of Greek myth
11 Everglades wader
12 Chicken piece
13 Drooping
21 Meter maid of song
25 Onetime Jeep mfr.
26 Tip, as a hat
27 Earth Day subj.
28 Foal's mother
29 Cutlass or 88
30 Haunted house sounds
31 Mont Blanc, par exemple
33 Well-behaved
34 Article that may list survivors, in brief
35 Burn soother
36 Common bar order, with "the"
37 "That was ___ . . ."
39 Movie double, often
42 "Def Comedy Jam" channel
43 Seat at a barn dance
45 Job interview topic
46 Take potshots (at)
47 Jewish holiday when the book of Esther is read
48 Cousin of a giraffe
49 Basic belief
50 Fine fiddle, for short
53 River to the Ubangi
54 Credit card statement figure
55 Do some housecleaning
56 Capital on a fjord
57 Way to a man's heart?
58 Whirling water

by Sarah Keller

ACROSS

1 AARP or the National Rifle Association
6 Without: Fr.
10 French city in 1944 fighting
14 "Bird on ___" (1990 film)
15 Lafayette's state?
16 Singer India.___
17 Kind of code
18 Super star
19 Poetic foot
20 Asian cat
23 Blue Jays, on a scoreboard
24 Net
25 Heroine of Verdi's "Il Trovatore"
27 Euro forerunner
29 Slo-o-ow leak
31 Santa ___ winds
32 Makeshift seat at a rodeo
34 Penn, for one: Abbr.
35 Alarm bell
39, 41 & 43 Cop cruiser . . . or a description of the five animals named in this puzzle
44 Form of many a diploma
46 Smidge
48 Sign to be interpreted
49 "The dog ate my homework," maybe
50 "You love," to Livy
52 Thurman of "Pulp Fiction"
53 Some track-and-field training
57 Move stealthily
59 Decorative pond fish
60 Shamu, for one
64 "Back in the ___"
66 Porky Pig, e.g.
67 Building usually without a 13th floor
68 Penury
69 "La Belle et la ___" (French fairy tale)
70 At ___ for words
71 Actress Sedgwick of "The Closer"
72 Cornerstone abbr.
73 Like the review "Hated it," e.g.

DOWN

1 Track units
2 Wilson of "Wedding Crashers"
3 Like some vision
4 Melee
5 Bellowed
6 Potential enamorada
7 On
8 Like some exercises
9 Ogle
10 ___ tai (drink)
11 Poetic Muse
12 Island near Java
13 Equus quagga
21 Prominent features of Alfred E. Neuman
22 "What should I ___?"
26 ___ cheese
27 Wanes
28 Class after trig
30 One of the 2008 Olympic mascots
33 Cause of a beach closure, maybe
36 Flight training equipment
37 Thing
38 "99 Red Balloons" singer, 1984
40 "Hogan's Heroes" colonel
42 Made less intense
45 1970 #1 hit whose title follows the lyric "Speaking words of wisdom . . ."
47 Bob ___, 2008 Libertarian candidate for president
51 "Who cares?"
53 Polecat
54 Actress Parker
55 Choir support
56 Tart fruits
58 Intact
61 Former Mississippi senator Trent
62 Minus
63 Ultimatum ender
65 Nutritional abbr.

by Peter A. Collins

ACROSS

1 No-no
6 Football star and FTD pitchman Merlin
11 Driver's lic. and such
14 Take forcibly
15 Sluggo's comics pal
16 Thing to pick
17 BAD
19 Buck's mate
20 Two cents' worth
21 Morales of "La Bamba"
22 Capitol Hill worker
23 BED
27 Name to the cabinet, say
30 Comic-strip light bulb
31 Van Susteren of Fox News
32 Ajax or Bon Ami
36 Weed whacker
37 BID
39 Movie pal of Stitch
40 Strange
42 River pair
43 At the drop of ___
44 "Animal House" beanie sporters
46 BOD
50 Exclude
51 Late singer Horne
52 F.D.R. power project: Abbr.
55 Blood-type abbr.
56 BUD
60 Versatile vehicle, for short
61 For all to see
62 Not quite round
63 Place that's "up the river"
64 Hobbyist's knife brand
65 Doesn't hoof it

DOWN

1 Rolaids alternative
2 Province of ancient Rome
3 Like the proverbial beaver
4 Tolkien beast
5 Shakespeare character who goes insane
6 Having no intermission

7 "___ en Rose" (Edith Piaf song)
8 ___-cone
9 Old French coin
10 Albany is its cap.
11 The movie "Wordplay," for one
12 L.E.D. part
13 High, pricewise
18 "This ___ outrage!"
22 "Shane" star
23 Slow-cooked beef entree
24 Some flooring
25 Wroclaw's river
26 Neptune's realm
27 Ottoman Empire chief
28 "No ___!" ("Easy!")
29 Hammer part

32 North-of-the-border grid org.
33 Rat on the Mob
34 Sommer in cinema
35 Woman depicted in "The Birth of Old Glory"
37 Neighbor of Yemen
38 Some are saturated
41 Letter after pi
42 Beat to death, so to speak
44 ___ Vallarta, Mexico
45 Checkout annoyance
46 Like some toasters and children's books
47 Overdo it onstage
48 "Christ is ___!" (Easter shout)
49 Say without thinking

52 Fly-catching creature
53 Show of hands, e.g.
54 Spy Aldrich
56 Symbol of slyness
57 Sch. founded by Thomas Jefferson
58 Gumshoe
59 56, in old Rome

by Sarah Keller

195

ACROSS
1 Angers, with "up"
6 Forest
11 Protrude
14 Disney's "little mermaid"
15 Facing the pitcher
16 French "a"
17 Recipe guideline for a hot dish
19 Railroad stop: Abbr.
20 Cozy lodging
21 Lure for Simple Simon
22 Smidgens
24 Persian Gulf leader
26 Family divided by divorce
30 Barbers' tools
32 Deep hole
33 Fat used for tallow
34 Captain of Jules Verne's Nautilus
35 Name in a family restaurant chain
37 Football scores, for short
38 High-stakes draw in Las Vegas
41 Place for a baby to sit
44 Fish often destined for cans
45 Medical success
48 Gear for gondolas
50 Gradually slowing, in music: Abbr.
51 Pacific island garment wrapped around the waist
53 Pastrami, for one
56 Greek liqueur
57 Fainthearted
58 Spain's Costa del ___
60 Ob-___ (med. specialty)
61 Rope-a-dope boxer
62 "Sure, go ahead" . . . and a literal hint to what's found in 17-, 26-, 38- and 53-Across
67 IV adjusters
68 Oil directly from a well
69 12" stick
70 Golf peg
71 Entered via a keyboard
72 Chasm

DOWN
1 More risqué
2 Certain triathlete
3 Treat as a celebrity
4 "Yikes!"
5 Sales receipt
6 Transaction at a racetrack
7 Slugger Mel
8 Kimono closer
9 Hoover ___
10 Gertrude who wrote "Rose is a rose is a rose is a rose"
11 Hot off the press
12 Wild
13 Dishes for doll parties
18 Penpoints
23 Cries of excitement
25 Frolic
27 Do surgery
28 Old Testament books labeled I and II
29 Sicilian erupter
31 Tooth or plant part
35 Jeans fabric
36 Family rec facility
39 Many a northern Iraqi
40 Continental currency
41 Skill that no one has anymore
42 "Now We Are Six" poet
43 Declaration sometimes made with crossed fingers behind the back
46 More or less
47 They help digest food
49 Vacation at Vail, maybe
51 Store (away)
52 Dead ducks
54 Formal decree
55 Queried
59 Turkey's currency
63 Give it a shot
64 Dine
65 "___ on a Grecian Urn"
66 Rubber ducky's spot

by Lynn Lempel

ACROSS

1 Muscat's land
5 Asset
9 Coffee choices
14 Clinton's 1996 opponent
15 Woodcarver's tool
16 Tortoise or hare
17 Actress Swenson of "Benson"
18 ___ de vivre
19 Milo of "Romeo and Juliet"
20 Astronomer's aid
22 Means
24 With 41- and 54-Across, group with a 1967 ballad version of 39-/41-/42-Across
26 Word after "does" and "doesn't" in an old ad slogan
27 Glass on a radio
28 Audio input location
33 Wraps (up)
36 One who can't keep off the grass?
38 One of the Mannings
39, 41 & 42 1964 Beatles hit
44 "The Star-Spangled Banner" preposition
45 Join the staff
48 Pinnacle
49 Keeps from happening
51 Western defense grp.
53 Broadcast
54 See 24-Across
59 Women, quaintly, with "the"
63 12:30 a.m. or p.m., on a ship
64 Bubbling
65 Cord material
67 Et ___
68 Zellweger of "My One and Only"
69 Button between * and #
70 Fronted, in a way
71 Piglike
72 Look inside?
73 Some jeans

DOWN

1 Keats, for one
2 The 6 in 6/8/10, e.g.
3 Pond buildup
4 Close call
5 Some are flannel
6 Parkinsonism drug
7 Israeli arm
8 Appear
9 See 40-Down
10 Having less forethought
11 Repeated message?
12 Thistle or goldenrod
13 Ladies of Spain: Abbr.
21 Damage
23 Villa d'___
25 Earliest time
29 Edit menu option
30 Job rights agcy.
31 Grad
32 Marriage, for one
33 Word before "You're killing me!"
34 Fancy pitcher
35 Bra insert
37 Lemony
40 With 9-Down, group with a 1962 hit version of 39-/41-/42-Across
43 Really enjoys oneself
46 About, on a memo
47 "Private—keep out"
50 Isn't all the same
52 O'Neill's "The Hairy ___"
55 Old Testament prophet who married a harlot
56 Martinique volcano
57 Dior-designed dress
58 Strips in front of a window?
59 Old MacDonald had one
60 Busy as ___
61 Table salt is composed of them
62 PlayStation 2 competitor
66 Auto loan inits.

by Peter A. Collins

ACROSS

1 The Crimson Tide, informally
5 Swiss peaks
9 Rand McNally product
14 Author Haley of "Roots" fame
15 "___ Caesar!"
16 Result of an armistice
17 1980s TV series starring Michael Landon
20 Confused
21 Fill to excess
22 Sail holder
23 A sharpshooter needs a good one
25 Golf pro Ernie
27 2002 Tom Hanks/Paul Newman film
36 Easter roast
37 Actress Sorvino
38 Organization for geniuses
39 Japanese port
42 Catch red-handed
43 Cranium contents
44 Parking space adjunct
45 Elevator inventor Elisha
47 Big Japanese computer maker: Abbr.
48 Onetime Alaska boondoggle
52 One in a blue state majority: Abbr.
53 A pair
54 Yard entrance
57 Time of danger for Caesar
61 Occupied, as a lavatory
65 Traveler's option . . . or what you won't get on a 17-, 27- or 48-Across?
68 Near the center
69 Burden
70 Rough-___ (not smoothly finished)
71 Impoverished
72 Reserved parking space for an exec, maybe
73 Bones, anatomically

DOWN

1 ___ Men ("Who Let the Dogs Out" group)
2 Touched down
3 Computer capacity, in brief
4 Cutting part of a lumberjack's tool
5 Idea person's exclamation
6 Puts down
7 ___ bread
8 One-armed bandit
9 Animal that beats its chest
10 Professional truck driver
11 Volcano's output
12 King beaters
13 Already in the mail
18 Word repeated before "Don't Tell Me!"
19 Obey
24 Pop's partner
26 What a do-it-yourself swing may hang from
27 Oblique-angled, four-sided figure
28 Western, in slang
29 Classic violin maker
30 ___ grigio (wine)
31 Muse of love poetry
32 Israel's Yitzhak
33 Nonsensical
34 Willow whose twigs are used in basketry
35 F.D.R. veep John ___ Garner
40 Blushed
41 Encourage
46 Drunkard
49 Send out, as rays
50 Hitler started it: Abbr.
51 Top dog
54 Sheepish look, maybe
55 Popular steak sauce
56 Something to sing along to
58 Go south, as a stock market
59 "___ kleine Nachtmusik"
60 Thing on a cowboy's boot
62 Hawaiian instruments, informally
63 Stitches
64 Sicily's Mt. ___
66 Drought-stricken
67 "Shame on you!"

by Mark Feldman

198

ACROSS

1 Pet rocks, once
4 Prebirth event
10 Message runner
14 Top-of-the-charts number
15 It may come before the end of a sentence
16 Not get merely by accident
17 Intermittent, as a relationship
20 Host of a nightly TV show taped in Burbank
21 Sunburned
22 Lift the spirits of
23 Spearheaded
25 Plumlike fruit
27 Leaves the main topic temporarily
35 Playground retort
36 Pub deliveries
37 Apply brakes to
38 Org. with audits
39 Gearbox option
42 Day of anticipation
43 ___-do-well
45 One you dig the most
46 More exquisite
48 Start to exit an Interstate
51 Old El ___ (food brand)
52 Simile connection
53 Fall bloom
56 Resinous tree
58 Stick it in your ear
62 Trade places . . . or a hint to parts of 17-, 27- and 48-Across
66 Smuggler's unit
67 Francis of old game shows
68 Show hosts, for short
69 Dish simmered in a pot
70 Negotiator's refusal
71 Dig in

DOWN

1 Jester
2 Rice who wrote "The Vampire Chronicles"
3 College V.I.P.
4 Place to relax
5 Arrangement of locks
6 River of Normandy
7 Alternative to an iron
8 Little help?
9 Whistle blower, in brief
10 Limbs for movie pirates
11 Tiny battery
12 Sand
13 Feminine suffix
18 Uses an iron or a 7-Down, say
19 Time in earth's history
24 Get an ___ effort
25 Quadraphonic halved
26 Scottish miss
27 Last step at a bakery
28 Delhi wrap: Var.
29 Beginning
30 Arizona tribe
31 Pain reliever brand
32 ___ Kagan, Obama nominee to the Supreme Court
33 Caesar's nine
34 Impudent nobody
40 Terrestrial salamanders
41 Bad grades
44 Aid for skiing uphill
47 Modern dweller in ancient Ur
49 Crack officer?
50 Hot breakfast cereal
53 Questions
54 Loretta of "M*A*S*H"
55 Scrabble piece
56 Bow out of a poker hand
57 "Now it's clear"
59 Big book
60 Member of a Pre-Columbian empire
61 It's attention-getting
63 ___ Solo, Harrison Ford role
64 Voting yes
65 ___ Aviv

by Jill Winslow

ACROSS

1 Leftover bit of cloth
6 "The Zoo Story" playwright Edward
11 Manx or Siamese
14 "Remember the ___!" (cry of 1836)
15 Sounds SSTs made
16 Color shade
17 "It ain't hard!"
19 Ill temper
20 Go like a bunny
21 Wedding dress material
22 Kind of sleeve named after a British baron
24 With 46-Across, "It ain't hard!"
25 Chop-chop
26 Nadir's opposite
29 School time when kids aren't studying
30 Without an escort
31 Irritated
32 Potpie vegetable
35 Playful bites
36 Tennis great Monica
37 Source of linen
38 Big beagle feature
39 Farm tracts
40 Work like a dog
41 Be against
43 Hung around
44 Singer Flack or Peters
46 See 24-Across
47 Mama Cass ___
48 Autobiographer's subject
49 Follow the coxswain's calls
52 Sidewalk stand quaff
53 "It ain't hard!"
56 Not Rep. or Ind.
57 "The Odd Couple" slob
58 Bird on a U.S. quarter
59 B'way sellout sign
60 Attempts at baskets
61 Live in fear of

DOWN

1 Pageant entrant's wear
2 Advertising award
3 Multistory parking garage feature
4 Guitarist's accessory, for short
5 Foul the water, e.g.
6 Taken ___ (surprised)
7 Get whipped
8 Drag queen's wrap
9 Hugs tightly
10 Made a getaway
11 "It ain't hard!"
12 Hearing-related
13 Pint-size
18 To ___ his own
23 U.S.O. show audience members
24 Rackets
25 T. ___ (fearsome dinos)
26 Grey who wrote westerns
27 Charles Lamb alias
28 "It ain't hard!"
29 C.S.A. general
31 Vice ___
33 Roof overhang
34 Abruptly dismissed
36 Like many tartan wearers
37 Pajamas' rear opening
39 Pertinent
40 Like a taxidermist's work
42 Rock and Roll Hall of Fame architect I. M. ___
43 Without an escort
44 Uses a Kindle, e.g.
45 Like a big brother
46 Tarot card readers, e.g.
48 Ad-libbing vocal style
49 Violent 19-Across
50 State with a panhandle: Abbr.
51 Whacked plant
54 ___-friendly (green)
55 Indy 500 entry

by Fred Piscop

200

ACROSS

1 Fresh talk
4 Female TV dog played by males
10 Alphabet enders, to Brits
14 Letters on a wanted poster
15 Sitcom pal of 46-Down
16 Plains Indians
17 Kitten call
18 Governing body of a municipality
20 South-of-the-border outlaws
22 Conductor Zubin
23 12:50 or 1:50
24 Bay Area law enforcement org.
26 1965 Vivien Leigh movie
29 Gateways or Dells, briefly
32 Georgia home of the Allman Brothers
33 Baseball Triple Crown stat
34 Excellent, slangily
35 Safe havens
36 Word game . . . or a word that can precede the starts of 18-, 26-, 43- and 54-Across
38 Suffix for the wealthy
39 ___-Ball (arcade game)
40 Rawls of R&B
41 Strait of Hormuz vessel
42 "The buck stops here" prez
43 Old comics boy with the dog Tige
46 Rope fiber
47 Board game turns
48 Briquette residue
51 Delivery entrance, maybe
54 Center of attention around a campfire, say
57 Palm Treo, e.g.
58 Deborah of "The King and I"
59 Deck treatments
60 Often-replaced joint
61 Swing in the breeze
62 Hallucinogen-yielding cactus
63 To this point

DOWN

1 Souvlaki meat
2 Swedish home furnishings chain
3 Hockshop receipt
4 Make privy to, as a secret
5 Many
6 Remove, as a branch
7 Confessional list
8 Abbr. in co. names
9 Fair-hiring letters
10 Like most urban land
11 Impress deeply
12 Two-thirds of D.I.Y.
13 Ward of "The Fugitive," 1993
19 Stereotypically "blind" officials
21 Topple from power
24 Cries out loud
25 Move like a moth
26 Box-office hit
27 Pays attention
28 "Are you in ___?"
29 Field of Plato and Aristotle
30 Rod with seven batting championships
31 Howard of satellite radio
34 Like sorted socks
36 Market surplus
37 Nozzle site
41 "Heads" side of a coin
43 At it
44 The Brat Pack's Estevez
45 Porcupine or gopher
46 Former boyfriend of 15-Across
48 Queries
49 Ratatouille or ragout
50 Bar mitzvah dance
51 Leave in stitches
52 Occasionally punted comics canine
53 Totally absorbed
55 Dose amt.
56 Summer on the Seine

by Barry C. Silk

The New York Times

SMART PUZZLES

Presented With Style

Available at your local bookstore or online at www.nytimes.com/nytstore

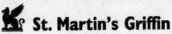 St. Martin's Griffin

1

```
L I T U P ■ M A S T ■ F A N S
A R O S E ■ O K R A ■ O V A L
G E N E R A T I O N ■ R O S A
E N G ■ ■ W O N ■ L E E W A Y
R E A C T O R ■ H I T S ■ ■ ■
■ ■ A W L ■ P A N A T E L A
T E T R A ■ L I V E S A L I E
A T O B ■ S E X E S ■ T I E R
M A J O R E D I N ■ P I A N O
S T O N E A G E ■ R E O ■ ■ ■
■ ■ A S H E ■ S E A N C E S
B L O T T O ■ A P E ■ O V O
R A V I ■ R E V E L A T I O N
O R E O ■ S P I N ■ S A N K A
W A R N ■ E A S T ■ P O S E R
```

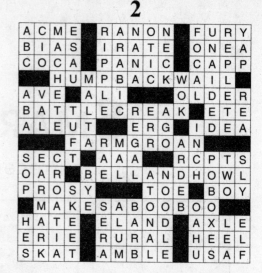

2

```
A C M E ■ R A N O N ■ F U R Y
B I A S ■ I R A T E ■ O N E A
C O C A ■ P A N I C ■ C A P P
■ ■ H U M P B A C K W A I L ■
A V E ■ A L I ■ ■ O L D E R
B A T T L E C R E A K ■ E T E
A L E U T ■ E R G ■ I D E A
■ ■ F A R M G R O A N ■ ■
S E C T ■ A A A ■ R C P T S
O A R ■ B E L L A N D H O W L
P R O S Y ■ T O E ■ B O Y
■ M A K E S A B O O B O O ■
H A T E ■ E L A N D ■ A X L E
E R I E ■ R U R A L ■ H E E L
S K A T ■ A M B L E ■ U S A F
```

3

```
P A T T I ■ R I F F ■ A S E A
A V I A N ■ O M A R ■ P A T S
J A L F R E D P R U F R O C K
A L L T I M E ■ ■ G O O P ■
M O E ■ ■ T O S S ■ O N A I R
A N D I E ■ A W E D ■ U R I
■ ■ P I L S N E R ■ U L A N
■ J J O N A H J A M E S O N ■
P I E D ■ L E O T A R D ■
A M T ■ B A A S ■ R A F T S
Z I P P O ■ F E A R ■ R I P
■ L O F T ■ S E R R A T E
J D A N F O R T H Q U A Y L E
L A N D ■ O B O E ■ S T E E D
O D E S ■ N I P S ■ T E D D Y
```

4

```
L O F T ■ E B O L A ■ O M S K
I D I O ■ N O R A D ■ M U N I
F I V E S T A R G E N E R A L
T E E T E R ■ ■ A L A I N
■ ■ C O E ■ F I V E B E L L S
S T E T S ■ A F I R S T ■
H A N O I ■ T S A R ■ G A D
E X T E N T ■ S I C I L Y
D I S ■ G U L F ■ N O M D E
■ ■ T A I P E I ■ P U M A S
T A K E S F I V E ■ O N E ■
O D E T S ■ ■ A R T F U L
Q U A R T E R P A S T F I V E
U L N A ■ R A B B I ■ O V E N
E T E S ■ A T S E A ■ R E A D
```

5

```
B O S C ■ P I G S T Y ■ G R A S
A N K A ■ E N A M O R ■ L A S T
D R I V I N G M I S S D A I S Y
M E T ■ S T O U T S ■ A N S E L
O P T ■ M A T T E ■ E N C O R E
V O I C E D ■ ■ C L I E N T S
E R S E ■ P A T O I S ■ ■
■ T H E B L A C K D A H L I A
■ ■ R O D E O S ■ E S P N
V A S S A L S ■ T R O U P E
A R E T H A ■ M E D I A ■ P E T
S C R A M ■ P O L I T Y ■ P A Z
T H E N A M E O F T H E R O S E
L I N D ■ O N S I T E ■ U S E R
Y E A S ■ S T E N O S ■ N E R O
```

6

```
A T M O ■ R A T E D ■ B O O M
B R I S ■ A G A P E ■ E R M A
C U S S ■ D E N I M ■ A D E N
■ S H O W I N G C O N C E R N
A T M ■ O U T ■ ■ I H A T E
L E A S E S ■ J O E S ■ L A D
P E S T ■ V A R L E T ■ ■
■ ■ H O L D I N G F I R M ■
■ ■ P A U L E Y ■ E A T S
A L T ■ N E A T ■ I B E R I A
S O U S A ■ ■ S N O ■ I N D
P A R T I N G C O M P A N Y ■
E T N A ■ O M A N I ■ R A T S
C H I N ■ M E G A N ■ T R I O
T E N D ■ S N E R D ■ Y A M S
```

7

```
WISP  CRIPES  TIM
ALOE  DENALI  ONE
FIFTHCOLUMN  PAL
TETRA  ELI  VILE
  TOILETARTICLE
TROLLED  AVA
IOU  SAGES  ALIBI
LOCH  PAPER  SNUB
ETHAN  RADIO  TRI
  IFS  GOPHERS
SCARLETLETTER
MANY  ROE  ISLAM
INN  BESTPICTURE
TOE  UNCOOL  ODIE
HEX  BEANIE  NEAT
```

8

```
HOFFA  SKI  VIBES
ABDUL  PAL  USURP
GIANTBILL  LAINE
  NOIRE  ACACIA
EBAY  COLTPACKER
DALLAS  RIN
IBEAM  SEAS  MAYO
CARDINALCHARGER
TROY  OUST  LORNE
  XIN  ETCETC
CHIEFSAINT  TEAK
RONNIE  LOTTO
AWFUL  SUPERBOWL
STORE  OVA  AERIE
SORES  BUR  PREGO
```

9

```
GARB  BROW  APPLE
OREO  OENO  FRIES
HACKYSACK  LAPSE
OBE  ACRE  LANES
MISSYOU  HECKLER
EASY  PLUG  SINK
  NAG  ABUT  NEO
HICKORYSMOKED
ROD  ALOT  EGO
ALES  DROP  LAWS
HOCKNEY  ROMANIA
GLEAN  RISE  GPS
BRAIN  HUCKABEES
EARNA  ASEA  BLUE
AMESS  TERR  SAPS
```

10

```
OWING  ICU  POTS
RODEO  RIND  OMEN
AVERS  ORZO  LENO
LEADPENCIL  IGOR
  EXS  PEASANT
DOUBLETS  DUH
EDNA  COOP  FJORD
NOTS  SNARL  OUSE
GROSS  EPEE  KITE
  GAP  SCARESUP
VACUOUS  LSU
AGRI  MINUTEMAID
LOOT  PLOD  FARSI
INCA  SORE  UNCLE
DYER  SAD  LOSES
```

11

```
ATOM  ECON  COLAS
LIMO  MOLE  ORALS
ALAN  IAGO  EGRET
STRONGLANGUAGE
  LARS  LORNE
DOTIME  LIN  SPUR
EVITA  RAGES  RTE
MIGHTYAPHRODITE
ONE  HEIST  NINES
BERG  ANE  SARTRE
  WEARS  MITT
POTENTPOTABLES
ROOST  OLLA  IONA
OLDEN  REAR  KNOW
ZESTA  MARS  EELS
```

12

```
SHARP  CAVED  PAT
EAGER  ALERO  OLE
CLOSEFRIEND  PAM
  NEVER  GRUMP
OBTUSE  ZEALOT
JULEPS  DHARMA
OTOES  HOOPS  RBI
KISS  CARBS  TBAR
YES  FOLIO  MARLA
OLIVES  SATEEN
ERMINE  MACAWS
MITZI  OHARA
ELO  COMICABBOTT
NEB  KNACK  RETRO
DYE  YANKS  EATUP
```

The missing clue: Bud

13

```
W A L S H . . K E N . P S S T
A T A R I . A R C H . A L T O
S P R I N G R O L L . D I A N
H A G . T O S C A . S U N N Y
. R O T A T E . I D T A G .
. . S T I N G R A Y . S P A
E L S A . T A R . M E S H E S
D O W R Y . L E A . S T O R K
A R I S E S . G U M . A T M S
M E N . S I N G S O N G .
. G E E S E . T R U S T S
D I V A S . S C R O D . W P A
A M O S . S T R I N G B E A N
D A T E . P L E A . E R E C T
A X E D . Y E W . D A N E S
```

14

```
L A C Y . A D M I T . D I K E
O B I E . R E I N S . E R L E
B U T T H A T S N O T F A I R
E T E . A R E S . O A T E S
. . C H A R . N U T M E G .
O L D H A T . B A S I E
M O R E . A R D E N . V I A
E V E R Y O N E I S G O I N G
N E W . O R D E R . W E R E
. G U A R D . S P E W E D
. L I A B L E . B A L D
L O R R E . H I Y A . D U O
I C A N T D O A N Y T H I N G
P A N E . S U R G E . E M I R
S L I T . L I M O S . P E T E
```

15

```
A L M A . I B A R . S I D E B
M U O N . R I L E . P R A D A
S A R A T O G A S P R I N G S
O U T L A N D S . R A S C A L
. G O T O . N O W H E R E
N I A G A R A F A L L S .
O R G . R E L I N E . E S A U
M E E T S . T E T . S A I L S
E S S O . T E R E S A . L A P
. L A R R Y S U M M E R S
C A M E R A S . L O A N .
A D O R E S . A T L A N T I S
J O N A T H A N W I N T E R S
U S O N E . O K I E . A R A T
N E S T S . L A G S . S A N S
```

16

```
J E S T . J A C O B . S C A M
A C N E . U N I T E . T A R O
W H O C A N I T B E . E L E V
S O B . D K N Y . P R A I S E
. S A Y . F E E L F O R
W H A T M A T T E R S .
O O N A . R B I S . A P S O S
W H E R E D O E S I T H U R T
S O W E D . N O U S . A R E A
. W H E N P I G S F L Y
S T U D I O S . T R E .
T O R E N T . L I S A . F I G
A M B I . W H Y P A Y M O R E
I M A C . A I R O F . O X E N
D Y N E . R E E S E . M Y S T
```

17

```
J A M B S . I M P E I . B O X
A W A I T . N A I L S . O H M
P A R T Y A N I M A L . R I A
A R I S E N . T E L . A N O N
N E O . D E A N . H S T
. C R E D I T R E P O R T
R A P P E R S . O E R . R E O
A C R O S S . S E G U E S
I T O . H E S . A T T E N D S
L I F E I N P R I S O N .
. E S P . L O T T . P D A
L O S T . P I C . O S I R I S
I R S . P I C K U P T R U C K
N C O . A T E I N . D O N E E
E A R . W A R N S . S N E R D
```

18

```
H A F T S . W A G E . A D Z E
A R L E N . O V A L . I R O N
J O Y E U X N O E L . R E O S
I M B I B E . C A S A B A .
. A Y N . N R A . L A M P S
. G L A E D E L I G J U L
A R G U E . D O S O . O R U
B I O P I C S . P L U M B E R
A D D . N E E R . M U S E S
F E L I Z N A V I D A D .
T R I N I . E T A . B A M
. N E T M E N . R E A P E D
E L E V . B U O N N A T A L E
D O S E . A R F S . S H R E K
U S S R . S O F A . E S T E E
```

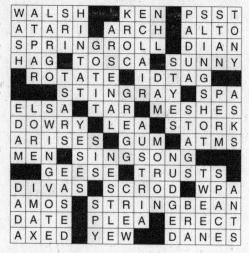

19

```
SCADS . VAST . BLEW
KOREA . ARIA . LEAH
IRONFILING . ONCE
DAM . ENID . SOOTHE
SLANTED . LAUD . .
. . AIR . SPLITSUP
THEMET . AGE . YORE
HEXES . CIA . SPLAT
ERIC . CON . SPIELS
NOTAWHIT . WIN . .
. . LOON . CARGOES
ANGLER . COMA . MRI
BALI . TOPBILLING
EDEN . LIAR . EATIN
TANG . ELSA . DOSES
```

20

```
ABBA . DRIVE . LOAN
COEN . EATEN . OPIE
HEADINTHECLOUDS
ERN . RISER . ASSET
. . TAR . ONE . .
HEARTOFDARKNESS
ALBEE . LAITY . NAT
REOS . FOURH . ANTI
SNO . TOWNE . BRUIN
HANDSONTRAINING
. . OLD . TKO . .
CARGO . SUITE . ASK
HEALTHINSURANCE
ERIE . ADDON . STAG
WONG . LEONE . HERS
```

21

```
PARERS . BYE . CBS
ABILENE . OAKTREE
POPFOUL . OPERATE
EDU . BALMS . ISAN
REPEL . NET . RAH .
. SAIDNO . ADDED
DOCTOR . SWAN . IDO
ERRATIC . NESTEGG
ALA . ISLE . ROUTES
LYCRA . APLOMB .
. KIN . PEA . SEEMS
BASS . STEMS . VII
ACHEFOR . BIGBANG
DIORAMA . SPIEDON
EDT . REP . SNEERS
```

22

```
ICON . SCTV . OCCAM
CUBA . CRUE . RHETT
BRIM . OUST . WOOLS
METEORSHOWER .
. . TACO . ELAPSE
. WEATHERBALLOON
RIDGE . AER . ECUA
EMI . SHUTEYE . ORC
APTS . USE . AMNOT
CLOUDFORMATION .
TERRIF . ASSN .
. FLYINGSAUCER
CILIA . MUNI . SIZE
ARENT . ADES . ETRE
BADGE . YETI . SEAL
```

23

```
UMASS . PLUMS . JAW
TENTH . HOSEA . USE
ENDROADWORK . SSE
. AVIS . LENTEN
WAFTED . VII . OMNI
ABRADE . ANNOTATE
DUE . SPCA . ORR .
STEPS . LAP . HERBS
. KEY . ANTS . IRA
TRIASSIC . UPBEAT
EATS . ANY . SLEDGE
ATTEST . THUS .
STE . PRIZEINSIDE
EEN . AARON . KILOS
TDS . SPEED . SEEMS
```

24

```
GALAS . VOCAL . IRS
ALANA . AISLE . VIC
ZESTFORLIFE . OVA
ACHIEVE . ASTRAL
. RASCAL . KYLE
TACO . LEADFOOT .
EXODUS . MOAT . ORC
CLASS . LES . RAWER
HES . EZIO . GAZEBO
. TODIEFOR . TRAP
OLGA . PUFFIN .
COURIC . NEONGAS
TRA . TONEOFVOICE
ERR . ADEPT . ALLOW
TED . RETIE . SOAPS
```

25

L	E	W	D		D	W	A	R	F		J	E	S	T
A	R	E	A		R	A	R	E	R		U	T	A	H
W	I	N	B	Y	A	N	O	S	E		M	A	U	I
N	E	T		A	M	E	S		E	B	B	I	N	G
	F	A	C	A	D	E	S		A	L	L	A	H	
S	M	I	R	K	S		T	U	B	E				
T	O	R	T		R	E	U	S	E		U	S	N	
L	O	S	E	O	N	E	S	B	A	L	A	N	C	E
O	T	T		C	O	N	E	S		A	D	O	S	
	N	E	W	T		C	A	R	E	T	S			
S	A	M	O	A		S	O	B	E	R	E	R		
A	L	U	M	N	I		C	O	D	A		O	U	I
V	I	S	A		D	R	A	W	A	B	L	A	N	K
E	K	E	D		O	I	L	E	R		E	T	T	E
R	E	D	S		L	O	A	D	S		W	H	O	A

26

S	E	E	P		O	K	L	A		C	H	A	S	E
H	U	L	A		N	A	I	L		L	O	G	I	N
O	B	I	T		E	R	N	E		E	R	O	D	E
W	I	Z		L	A	N	E	C	H	A	N	G	E	S
S	E	A		A	L	A		O	N	E				
	B	E	T		K	E	N	T	S	T	A	T	E	
C	R	E	P	E	S		L	O	D	E		D	A	B
R	A	T	A		C	H	I	N	O		D	A	T	A
A	S	H		R	H	O	S		G	E	R	M	A	N
W	H	I	T	E	L	I	E	S		R	E	A		
	U	T	E		E	R	A		N	A	P			
D	A	I	L	Y	P	L	A	N	E	T		D	I	E
A	S	C	A	P		A	L	A	S		M	E	M	O
S	T	O	N	E		D	O	T	E		O	V	E	N
H	O	N	E	D		S	T	E	T		W	E	D	S

27

M	A	M	M	A		A	D	S		A	B	U	T	S
A	B	E	A	T		L	E	T		N	E	P	A	L
T	E	R	R	A		T	A	I		T	A	S	T	Y
A	L	V	I	N	T	O	F	F	L	E	R			
	N	E	O		F	E	N		T	L	C			
S	I	M	O	N	W	I	E	S	E	N	T	H	A	L
E	M	O		D	I	V	A		A	R	O	M	A	
D	I	O	R		T	E	R	M	S		I	M	A	M
A	G	R	E	E		L	O	T	T		A	Z	O	
T	H	E	O	D	O	R	E	D	R	E	I	S	E	R
E	T	D		W	W	I		E	R	N				
	T	H	E	C	H	I	P	M	U	N	K	S		
A	T	A	R	I		H	A	N		I	R	E	N	E
R	O	G	E	T		E	S	T		T	E	H	E	E
M	O	O	S	E		R	H	O		E	D	I	E	S

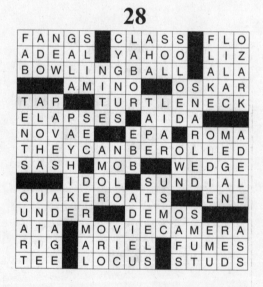

28

F	A	N	G	S		C	L	A	S	S		F	L	O
A	D	E	A	L		Y	A	H	O	O		L	I	Z
B	O	W	L	I	N	G	B	A	L	L		A	L	A
	A	M	I	N	O			O	S	K	A	R		
T	A	P		T	U	R	T	L	E	N	E	C	K	
E	L	A	P	S	E	S		A	I	D	A			
N	O	V	A	E		E	P	A		R	O	M	A	
T	H	E	Y	C	A	N	B	E	R	O	L	L	E	D
S	A	S	H		M	O	B		W	E	D	G	E	
	I	D	O	L		S	U	N	D	I	A	L		
Q	U	A	K	E	R	O	A	T	S		E	N	E	
U	N	D	E	R		D	E	M	O	S				
A	T	A		M	O	V	I	E	C	A	M	E	R	A
R	I	G		A	R	I	E	L		F	U	M	E	S
T	E	E		L	O	C	U	S		S	T	U	D	S

29

O	N	C	E		I	D	E	A	L		F	A	S	T
L	E	I	A		R	E	T	R	O		O	N	T	O
D	O	N	T	B	E	A	S	T	R	A	N	G	E	R
	M	U	D	D		E	N	D	Z	O	N	E		
P	A	V	E	S		E	S	S	E	S		L	O	U
A	T	E		B	N	A	I		R	A	S	P		
C	A	E	S	A	R		R	A	D	I	O			
	D	R	O	P	I	N	A	N	Y	T	I	M	E	
	L	T	C	O	L		A	O	L	E	R	S		
L	O	G	O		B	E	I	N		N	A	P		
A	L	A		T	I	L	E	S		B	O	S	S	Y
W	E	L	F	A	R	E		O	D	I	N			
Y	A	L	L	C	O	M	E	B	A	C	K	N	O	W
E	R	O	O		N	A	V	A	L		E	A	R	P
R	Y	N	E		S	N	A	R	E		Y	M	C	A

30

P	A	L	E		O	G	E	E		A	M	B	E	R
E	L	E	E		R	U	L	E		L	O	O	S	E
P	A	R	K	E	D	I	L	L	E	G	A	L	L	Y
S	R	O		N	E	D		L	I	T				
I	M	I	N	T	R	O	U	B	L	E		H	E	P
	O	R	S		N	A	I	R		O	X	O		
E	M	O	R	Y		D	R	E	S	C	H	E	R	
M	A	R	M		H	E	R	B	S		H	O	C	K
C	R	E	A	T	U	R	E		B	O	S	S	Y	
E	C	O		I	R	I	S		P	E	R			
E	O	S		P	R	E	S	S	A	G	E	N	T	S
	U	S	A		P	R	E		I	I	I			
L	E	N	G	T	H	Y	M	E	E	T	I	N	G	S
O	V	U	L	E		E	B	A	N		M	E	R	S
S	A	T	Y	R		P	A	R	T		P	R	E	Y

31

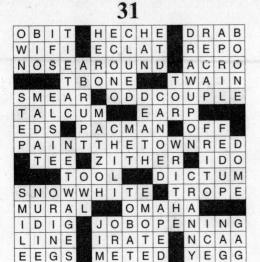

```
O B I T   H E C H E   D R A B
W I F I   E C L A T   R E P O
N O S E A R O U N D   A C R O
      T B O N E     T W A I N
S M E A R   O D D C O U P L E
T A L C U M     E A R P
E D S   P A C M A N   O F F
P A I N T T H E T O W N R E D
  T E E   Z I T H E R   I D O
  T O O L     D I C T U M
S N O W W H I T E   T R O P E
M U R A L     O M A H A
I D I G   J O B O P E N I N G
L I N E   I R A T E   N C A A
E E G S   M E T E D   Y E G G
```

32

```
M E D A L   E G A D   A S I F
A L E X A   M O L E   F A T E
R E M E M B E R P R O F I L E
A N O   B O R I S   M O L L S
T A C T   N I L   S I R
    R E C O L L E C T D U S T
G L A R E   A K A   S O U
O A T M E A L   G R A M M A R
E M I   B A M   L E A R N
R E C A L L W A I T I N G
    C U E   R N A   S A G O
C L A R A   T A C I T   Z E N
R E C O U N T C A L O R I E S
A G E S   B O A S   M A N S E
B O D S   A P S E   S W E E T
```

33

```
B O B U P   F L U B   G E A R
A B A S E   I O T A   O M N I
L I B E R A L B E N E F I T S
K E Y   F L I E S   V E R S E
    L E I A     P E R
R A D I C A L S I G N   A L T
A L E R T S   M E A T S T E W
I L I A   O A R   L A N A
N O T S O F A R   P O U R I N
S T Y   L E F T H A N G I N G
    A D Z     A Y E S
S T Y L E   P A T T Y   H A T
P R O G R E S S I V E L E N S
I O W A   L A I N   A O R T A
N Y S E   S T A G   R Y D E R
```

34

```
Y I P S   L E E J   G L A R E
A R I A   O B L A   O O Z E S
K A T Y   G R A F   S Q U A T
O N T H E G O L F C O U R S E
V I S I N E   A L F A
    L R O N   A T C O S T
S E L M A   L O R N   I N T O
P L A Y I N G E I G H T E E N
A L U M   Y A N G   E Y I N G
R A D I A L   D A W G
    S L O E   R E V I S E
H I T T I N G T H E L I N K S
A S I A N   R A I N   L O I S
S T A K E   E X E C   L I L A
H O S E D   T I S H   A L L Y
```

35

```
P O P S   C O A S T   H A L F
A N E W   A L L A H   O L I O
S T R I P T E A S E   M E S A
T O U P E E   S H E   E X A M
    E A R L     N R A
S K A   S A N D D O L L A R
C I T E D   R E O   B O O Z E
A T A L E   E G G   I N C U R
M E R I T   D E L   N E H R U
P R I M E M O V E R   S E N
    I R A     G O B S
W O O D   G O T   T A P O U T
A L V A   P A I N T H O R S E
S E A T   I R E N E   T E S S
H O L E   E S S E N   S O R T
```

36

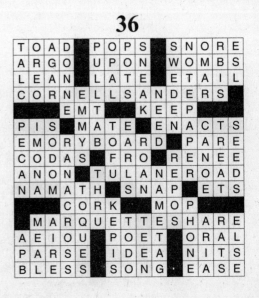

```
T O A D   P O P S   S N O R E
A R G O   U P O N   W O M B S
L E A N   L A T E   E T A I L
C O R N E L L S A N D E R S
    E M T     K E E P
P I S   M A T E   E N A C T S
E M O R Y B O A R D   P A R E
C O D A S   F R O   R E N E E
A N O N   T U L A N E R O A D
N A M A T H   S N A P   E T S
    C O R K   M O P
M A R Q U E T T E S H A R E
A E I O U   P O E T   O R A L
P A R S E   I D E A   N I T S
B L E S S   S O N G   E A S E
```

37

M	A	R	I	E	░	░	A	D	D	S	░	A	C	T
A	M	A	N	D	A	░	N	U	D	E	░	R	H	O
T	O	N	S	I	L	░	G	E	T	A	G	R	I	P
E	N	G	░	T	E	A	L	░	░	E	O	N	S	
░	G	E	T	O	U	T	O	F	T	H	E	W	A	Y
░	░	E	R	T	E	░	R	E	A					
U	R	S	A	░	H	E	A	D	G	E	A	R		
G	E	T	T	H	I	S	S	T	R	A	I	G	H	T
H	O	U	S	E	S	A	T	░	░	R	O	S	E	
░	L	A	G	░	M	A	S	T	░					
G	E	T	A	L	O	A	D	O	F	T	H	A	T	
A	N	O	N	░	░	Y	O	U	R	░	F	U	N	
G	E	T	A	L	I	F	E	░	S	O	N	A	T	A
O	R	E	░	O	V	E	R	░	E	N	A	C	T	S
N	O	D	░	B	Y	E	S	░	░	G	E	T	I	T

38

G	O	L	F	░	A	C	I	D	S	░	S	C	A	R
A	R	E	A	░	C	U	M	I	N	░	M	E	M	O
F	E	A	T	H	E	R	B	O	A	░	A	L	B	A
F	O	R	C	E	░	B	U	R	P	░	S	L	E	D
░	░	A	R	I	S	E	░	A	B	H	O	R	S	
D	E	B	T	O	R	░	S	T	R	E	P	░		
R	U	E	S	░	A	C	M	E	░	A	S	H	E	N
A	R	E	░	U	N	L	O	A	D	S	░	A	X	E
G	O	F	A	R	░	A	M	M	O	░	A	N	E	W
░	F	E	I	G	N	░	░	D	E	T	E	C	T	
S	P	A	R	S	E	░	B	O	O	Z	E	░		
M	O	J	O	░	N	A	R	C	░	R	A	T	E	S
I	S	I	S	░	T	H	A	T	S	A	W	R	A	P
T	I	T	O	░	L	E	V	E	E	░	A	U	R	A
E	T	A	L	░	E	M	O	T	E	░	Y	E	N	S

39

F	L	A	G	░	F	O	C	I	░	S	A	L	U	T
E	A	R	L	░	R	A	I	N	░	A	L	O	N	E
S	P	E	A	K	O	F	T	H	E	D	E	V	I	L
S	P	A	D	E	░	Y	A	P	S	░	E	T	E	
░	░	T	E	A	S	░	L	E	O	░	L	E	X	
S	I	T	O	N	T	H	E	F	E	N	C	E		
A	S	H	░	S	O	A	P	░	G	O	T	O	N	
G	L	I	B	░	P	H	O	T	O	░	O	T	T	O
A	E	S	O	P	░	C	I	R	C	░	E	I	N	
░	S	T	A	Y	T	H	E	C	O	U	R	S	E	
E	P	I	░	R	O	W	░	R	A	M	P			
C	O	D	░	T	R	E	E	░	I	S	L	I	P	
O	B	E	D	I	E	N	C	E	S	C	H	O	O	L
L	O	U	I	E	░	T	H	E	E	░	O	C	T	O
E	X	P	O	S	░	Y	O	G	A	░	T	H	A	W

40

A	L	T	A	R	░	I	R	I	S	░	S	M	E	E
G	U	A	V	A	░	S	U	C	H	░	L	Y	N	N
E	X	P	E	C	T	S	T	H	E	W	O	R	S	T
S	E	A	S	C	O	U	T	░	S	O	T	R	U	E
░	░	O	B	E	Y	S	░	U	S	H	E	R		
C	A	T	T	O	Y	░	A	U	K					
A	L	I	E	N	░	F	E	N	G	░	E	T	A	S
H	O	P	E	S	F	O	R	T	H	E	B	E	S	T
N	E	S	S	░	A	G	R	A	░	X	A	C	T	O
░	░	G	N	U	░	░	S	P	Y	H	O	P		
W	A	S	T	E	░	P	L	U	T	O	░			
A	V	A	I	L	S	░	O	N	A	S	P	R	E	E
C	O	U	L	D	N	T	C	A	R	E	L	E	S	S
K	I	T	E	░	A	S	A	P	░	R	O	M	P	S
O	D	E	S	░	P	E	L	T	░	S	T	O	N	E

41

E	S	A	U	░	S	O	D	░	A	T	L	A	S	T
B	A	N	S	░	C	R	Y	░	R	O	A	D	I	E
B	Y	G	E	O	R	G	E	░	T	E	N	U	R	E
S	A	L	░	Y	E	A	R	░	░	G	L	E	N	
░	H	E	A	V	E	N	S	T	O	B	E	T	S	Y
░	░	B	E	N	░	░	O	L	E	░				
S	A	T	B	Y	░	G	O	O	D	G	O	L	L	Y
A	T	I	E	░	I	R	A	T	E	░	N	E	M	O
O	H	M	Y	S	T	A	R	S	░	G	E	T	N	O
░	░	I	A	M	░	░	H	I	T	░				
W	E	L	L	B	L	O	W	M	E	D	O	W	N	
A	X	E	L	░	░	H	A	R	D	░	H	U	E	
R	E	V	A	M	P	░	O	H	M	Y	W	O	R	D
T	R	E	M	O	R	░	L	E	A	░	H	O	S	E
S	T	E	A	D	Y	░	E	R	N	░	O	P	E	N

42

A	N	D	I	E	░	B	U	S	H	░	E	G	G	S
C	O	I	N	S	░	A	S	I	A	░	T	O	O	L
H	E	A	V	E	N	S	E	N	T	░	C	A	N	E
E	L	L	E	░	O	E	R	░	R	E	E	L	E	D
░	░	S	T	U	░	░	R	E	S	T	░			
N	O	T	O	N	E	R	E	D	C	E	N	T		
B	O	D	░	A	S	S	E	T	S	░	R	O	O	T
S	T	E	A	D	░	T	A	I	░	M	A	M	A	S
A	C	T	S	░	S	A	C	R	E	D	░	A	S	P
░	H	O	T	O	N	T	H	E	S	C	E	N	T	
░	░	O	B	O	E	░	░	S	I	X	░			
A	L	L	N	E	W	░	O	W	E	░	T	A	I	L
L	E	O	I	░	M	A	K	E	S	S	E	N	S	E
A	V	I	S	░	A	B	L	E	░	A	N	K	L	E
W	I	S	H	░	N	E	A	P	░	O	T	H	E	R

43

```
SEEP  SCALA  ACES
PLEA  PERIL  FOGG
ALLSHOOKUP  ALOT
    SITS   HARI
HAWKS   PSAT  NAG
ALEE  STRATA  PSI
ITSY  HAILED  OTB
ROTS  ELVIS  AWOL
COG  PLIANT  PERU
UNE  ELATES  PLIE
TAR  EASE  HALAS
   MARC   APER
REAR  KINGCREOLE
CONE  EVERT  NAIL
ANYA  DEGAS  TREK
```

44

```
ISMS  TEMPE  WRAP
REAP  ACORN  HIYA
AMIE  BOREDROARD
SIZES  NNE  ALTER
 MEDIA  INCREASE
GEM  SCAN  ASH
UTAH  ELGAR  OILS
LAZE  TEMPO  LSAT
FLEA  AFOOT  ELSA
   RIT  UPIN  EEG
HEADGEAR  DEBAR
ALTHO  RNA  BRIBE
SWEETSUITE  USER
TEAR  ABNER  SLAG
ESTD  PAGER  HEMS
```

45

```
CRAB  OCTET  PLOT
HOLA  ARISE  LEGO
AMOS  FORCEFIELD
DATELINE  SLAKED
   BOSE  CHAN
SPLASH  SHOWTIME
LULLS  SLAT  SOD
ORAL  AIR  SANG
TEM  HUNT  SPATE
HEADLOCK  MEEKER
   OILY  WALE
PALTRY  MAILDROP
SPACECRAFT  WAKE
ASTO  OATER  ACRE
TEEM  WHERE  YEAR
```

46

```
 STUD  QID  NOMAD
 WORE  UNA  OPINE
FOOLFAINT  BILGE
ARKS  ERIE  OUTER
REN  FREE  ADMIRE
GOOGOO  PRY  ESS
 OFTWO  PURIST
 FEELLIKEAFOOL
  NIECES  ERVIN
MIT  NIK  GENEVA
INRAGS  IDOL  REV
ACETO  KNOB  ASWE
SHARK  APRILFEEL
MEDIA  YUM  ITLL
ASSAY  OTS  TALL
```

47

```
AMIN  CRAW  ZAPPA
SANE  ANNA  ADORN
FIRSTLADY  NOSED
ONETO  SASE  SSE
RES  SECONDGUESS
   EDSEL  SIRS
ACRE  LUX  EASEL
COVERSEVERYBASE
CREPE  IDO  LISA
   EDIT  ELLEN
THIRDDEGREE  TSK
OAR  WINO  DIJON
GRETA  HOMEALONE
ASNER  UNIT  SAIL
SHELF  TYRA  ANAT
```

48

```
GABE  ADDUP  ZOLA
OWES  IRATE  OMIT
BEDTIMEFORBONZO
IDEAS  STP  ELIAN
   THUS  IMHO
ARNE  PAJAMAGAME
SAO  SAGA  EVIGAN
CIVIC  EBB  ECOLI
AMELIE  BIRD  REA
PILLOWTALK  MASC
   TREY  LOCO
TOERR  CAY  IRISH
IDREAMOFJEANNIE
EDNA  ROTOS  IFFY
ASST  INSET  NOTS
```

49

```
FANG  AGATE  EVER
AREA  MOTOR  XENA
ATOZ  OTERI  IRAN
   AUCTIONBLOCK
YUM GOIN   YENTL
INOIL   IST  ASE
PICNICHAMPER
ESSO  HOSEA  UPAT
  REALITYCHECK
SAN  LTD   ORTHO
TRASH   SOTS  SYS
ALUMINUMFOIL
MESA  ANITA  YEAR
ONER  MILES  NEMO
SEAT  EVENT  XRAY
```

50

```
ALOOF  SEMIS  MOP
LARUE  ABASH  AVE
MISTERMAGOO   SIP
SCOW  GENA  WATTS
   ASTA  ZAMBEZI
ADMIT  SKIWEAR
DIETED  INA  AMOK
OAT  MIDTERM  IRE
SLED  NEE  EISNER
  RUTGERS  RADON
GUMDROP  AEON
ERASE  EAUX  DRIP
OBI  MONSTERMASH
DAD  OLDIE  CANED
ENS  RESTS  ANTES
```

51

```
REAP  EARS  GLASS
AXLE  STEP  AUDIE
YEAR  CLEANSLATE
SCRUBOAK  ALLIED
   IRS  EVA  RDS
HAZMAT  SWIMS
ALOES  SWEEPHAND
ROOS  MEALS  ERIE
DUSTDEVIL  PLANE
  ARDEN  RIFLED
ESP  AIR  NET
APERCU  WASHSALE
VACUUMTUBE  AJAX
ETAIL  ASEA  MAGI
SENNA  PSST  ERST
```

52

```
HARDG  BABAR  PEW
EMAIL  OMANI  URI
NETEARNINGS  MIN
CEO  DES  DRIPPED
ERN  HAAS  INTS
  CAPITALGAINS
SEDANS  ANY  REO
ONEND  ART  FLOAT
AYE  SID  SAINTS
PAPERPROFITS
  SOIL  MINT  ARA
ICINGUP  RAE  RED
SAX  GROSSINCOME
APE  EGRET  UHAUL
YES  DEKES  PERSE
```

53

```
SASH  CAPOS  BABA
ARTY  ANIME  ENOS
ROOMSTOLET  ATOP
ASONE  NOGO  GINS
NEPALI  TANGLE
  LANA  RELAX
PUNS  PREVUE  ISM
ERA  NECKING  TEA
ADS  UNSEAL  PEAS
LUCID  LICE
  ACETIC  THRALL
CARE  AVOW  IGLOO
ALFA  NOVASCOTIA
STAG  GRECO  LARD
HONE  SYNOD  ARES
```

54

```
SKIBUM  ROLL  JAG
HADAGO  ASIA  ASH
ALLTHATJAZZ  CHI
SKIT  BEAK  EWOK
TANYA  CHAR  ABED
ANG  LAH  NEWLINE
  SEINE  TARTAN
  ALEXRODRIGUEZ
BLARED  TUNES
MCGUIRE  PAR  SFC
WARM  YUMA  SLYER
  TASK  ROUT  EZRA
URN  APOLLOSOYUZ
ZAG  TYPE  JINGLE
IZE  EXES  OBEYED
```

55

```
S P A M | M A C S | S E G A R
T A D A | A L A W | I R E N E
O N U S | D O M E | C I T G O
W E L C O M E P A C K E T |
E L T O R O | R A D | O P S
| T E N N I S R A C K E T
L B J | S E E P | Y E N T L
I O U S | Y E A S T | L O R E
B R I A R | N O A H | W O O
Y E L L O W J A C K E T |
A S L | A H A | E R A S E S
| I N C O M E B R A C K E T
C O A C H | M I L O | T O R I
A U R A E | E R O O | I S I N
M I D A S | D E B T | C H E T
```

56

```
C I R C | M E O W S | E D A M
A L O U | A T E A M | L E G O
D E L T A F O R C E | P I U S
S A L A M I | S A R A L E E
| R E A L (M) | R A S A |
M O D U S | (A) (G) (O) | C O R G I
O N E G | (I) (M) (M) (U) (N) (E) | E I N
V A L | (D) R E | T A (D) | E N S
I I I | Y E N T A (S) | P S S T
E R N I E | (T) (E) (T) | S O E U R
| Q T R S | (A) E S O P |
H A U L S I N | U P S A L A
A B E L | D E L I G H T F U L
L E N D | E R I C A | A R N E
O T T O | D O V E R | R O T S
```

57

```
A M I N | T A M P A | A S P S
C A N T | A L I A S | S A L E
H I G H C H U R C H | S P I N
E N O | A I M | D U P E D
D E T E C T | S P E E C H |
W H I C H I S W H I C H
T H R E E | H E N S | R O O
B O O S T | A A A | I D E A L
A B A | M I T T | N A S T Y
R O S H H A S H A N A H |
T O U P E E | I S L A N D
A R B O R | A C E | C O O
D E E P | F O U R H C L U B S
O P E L | C A R N E | A T E E
S O F A | C R I E S | G E L S
```

58

```
I D E A L | B A A | A G O G
C I R R I | U R N S | C E D E
B L A C K S M I T H | I T E M
M A S S E U R | S E E D S |
S T E | B A R | L I M I T
E D E L | P E T T Y C A S H
M I T | C O O S | R I O
U N I T E D A R T I S T S
F D A | H A I R | E A T
Y O U N G L O V E | N A R C
I N T O O | E A N | E L I
I O W A S | R O O S T E D
B A L D | B R O W N S T O N E
A Z U L | S A R A | L O R C A
N O S E | S A X | O A T H S
```

59

```
T O M B S | P S S T | J I M
A M O R Y | H O W E | A O N E
V A C A N T A P A R T M E N T
I N K N O T S | G R O U P I E
N O E L | P L I E D
E M P T Y P R O M I S E S
R E A I M | W A V Y | C S I
G A T E | G I D D Y | G O A S
O T C | F I D O | A M P U P
H O L L O W V I C T O R Y
A L A M O | N O T E
S I D E C A R | R E H E A T S
B L A N K C A R T R I D G E S
A L M S | O K I E | G I A N T
D Y S | G E N X | H E R D S
```

60

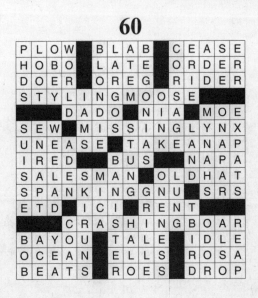

```
P L O W | B L A B | C E A S E
H O B O | L A T E | O R D E R
D O E R | O R E G | R I D E R
S T Y L I N G M O O S E |
D A D O | N I A | M O E
S E W | M I S S I N G L Y N X
U N E A S E | T A K E A N A P
I R E D | B U S | N A P A
S A L E S M A N | O L D H A T
S P A N K I N G G N U | S R S
E T D | I C I | R E N T
C R A S H I N G B O A R
B A Y O U | T A L E | I D L E
O C E A N | E L L S | R O S A
B E A T S | R O E S | D R O P
```

61

```
A C T O R ■ O P A L ■ B O Z O
S A R D I ■ P A V E ■ L I A R
K N E E B R A C E S ■ A N N E
S E X ■ C O R E ■ S I S K E L
■ ■ T A U T ■ G E N T ■ ■ ■
C H A R G E ■ D E N T I S T S
A E R I E ■ P O N E ■ N O A H
L I M P ■ D A V I D ■ G A T E
I D O L ■ A L E E ■ S C R U B
F I R E A R M S ■ M I A S M A
■ ■ C A K E ■ S U M P ■ ■ ■
Z E B R A S ■ J O N I ■ T I S
A B O O ■ P I E F I L L I N G
C R A W ■ O S S A ■ E B E R T
H O R N ■ T H U R ■ S O R E S
```

62

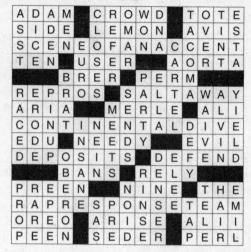

```
A D A M ■ C R O W D ■ ■ T O T E
S I D E ■ L E M O N ■ A V I S
S C E N E O F A N A C C E N T
T E N ■ U S E R ■ ■ A O R T A
■ ■ B R E R ■ P E R M ■ ■ ■
R E P R O S ■ S A L T A W A Y
A R I A ■ M E R L E ■ A L I
C O N T I N E N T A L D I V E
E D U ■ N E E D Y ■ E V I L
D E P O S I T S ■ D E F E N D
■ ■ B A N S ■ R E L Y ■ ■ ■
P R E E N ■ N I N E ■ T H E
R A P R E S P O N S E T E A M
O R E O ■ A R I S E ■ A L I I
P E E N ■ S E D E R ■ P E R L
```

63

```
V E A L ■ O C T A D ■ K A O S
A R L O ■ M E H T A ■ O G R E
T I E S ■ E Y E O N ■ J E E Z
S E X T O N ■ F I R E A R M
■ ■ C A S I O ■ A S K ■ ■ ■
C A R A T ■ D U S T S ■ A S A
L U A U ■ E A R T H O R B I T
A R T S ■ S H E R E ■ O O Z E
W A T E R C O L O R ■ Y V E S
S L Y ■ E A S E D ■ B R E S T
■ ■ G A L ■ M E T O O ■ ■ ■
■ A I R D A T E ■ R A G T A G
J U D O ■ T O N T O ■ E A R L
A T O P ■ O N T A P ■ R I T A
M O L E ■ R E S E E ■ S L E D
```

64

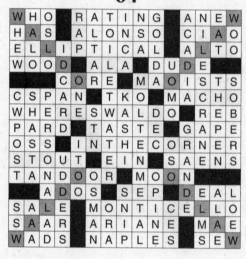

```
W H O ■ R A T I N G ■ A N E W
H A S ■ A L O N S O ■ C I A O
E L L I P T I C A L ■ A L T O
W O O D ■ A L A ■ D U D E ■
■ ■ C O R E ■ M A O I S T S
C S P A N ■ T K O ■ M A C H O
W H E R E S W A L D O ■ R E B
P A R D ■ T A S T E ■ G A P E
O S S ■ I N T H E C O R N E R
S T O U T ■ E I N ■ S A E N S
T A N D O O R ■ M O O N ■ ■
■ A D O S ■ S E P ■ D E A L
S A L E ■ M O N T I C E L L O
S A A R ■ A R I A N E ■ M A E
W A D S ■ N A P L E S ■ S E W
```

65

```
H A L F ■ M A J A ■ S P C A
A L A I ■ E L I H U ■ H O O F
T O U R I S T M A P ■ A L S O
S E D E R S ■ S T C R O I X
■ ■ P A R K A ■ I L K ■ ■ ■
M C M L ■ S A N D C A S T L E
O R O U T ■ R E E K S ■ A E S
S A N G R I A ■ A S P I R E S
E M T ■ A N T I C ■ S T O R E
S P E E D D E M O N ■ S T Y X
■ ■ N E O ■ E N O L A ■ ■ ■
S H U T S U P ■ T A T L E R
H O P I ■ B O O B Y P R I Z E
A M O R ■ T O R R E ■ A F R O
G O N E ■ P E R T ■ P E A S
```

66

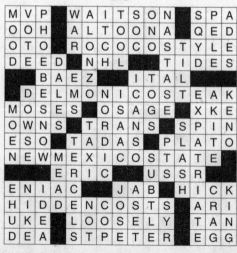

```
M V P ■ W A I T S O N ■ S P A
O O H ■ A L T O O N A ■ Q E D
O T O ■ R O C O C O S T Y L E
D E E D ■ N H L ■ T I D E S
■ ■ B A E Z ■ I T A L ■ ■ ■
■ D E L M O N I C O S T E A K
M O S E S ■ O S A G E ■ X K E
O W N S ■ T R A N S ■ S P I N
E S O ■ T A D A S ■ P L A T O
N E W M E X I C O S T A T E
■ ■ E R I C ■ U S S R ■ ■ ■
E N I A C ■ J A B ■ H I C K
H I D D E N C O S T S ■ A R I
U K E ■ L O O S E L Y ■ T A N
D E A ■ S T P E T E R ■ E G G
```

67

A	D	O	S		B	A	L	S	A		N	E	S	T
R	O	T	H		O	C	E	A	N		I	T	C	H
A	L	T	O		S	T	A	L	K		I	H	O	U
B	L	O	W	I	N	I	N	T	H	E	W	I	N	D
			C	O	I	N	S			D	I	C	E	S
A	R	C	A	N	A			B	A	I	T			
C	E	O	S			S	L	A	N	T		A	C	E
H	E	R	E	C	O	M	E	S	T	H	E	S	U	N
E	L	K		A	V	O	W	S			G	I	R	D
			S	T	A	G			S	T	O	A	T	S
A	S	P	I	C			A	S	C	O	T			
R	H	Y	T	H	M	O	F	T	H	E	R	A	I	N
S	A	R	I		A	R	I	E	L		I	S	L	A
O	M	E	N		C	A	R	R	E		P	E	L	T
N	E	S	S		S	L	E	E	P		S	A	S	S

68

M	R	S		G	O	T	I	T		S	P	A	T	E
E	O	N		O	P	I	N	E		A	L	L	A	Y
A	L	A		D	I	N	N	E	R	T	A	B	L	E
D	E	F		S	E	E	S	T	O		Y	A	K	S
E	X	U	D	E				H	O	P	S			
			O	N	S	E	T		K	I	T	S	C	H
C	L	O	U	D	O	V	E	R		T	A	H	O	E
H	E	R	B		P	E	N	A	L		T	I	D	E
A	G	I	L	E		N	O	S	E	D	I	V	E	D
R	O	G	E	T	S		R	H	I	N	O			
			A	C	H	E			A	N	G	S	T	
S	M	U	G		I	N	S	P	O	T		A	T	E
D	A	T	E	A	N	D	T	I	M	E		T	E	N
A	G	I	N	G		O	A	S	I	S		O	A	T
K	I	L	T	S		W	Y	A	T	T		R	M	S

69

S	A	N	T	A		P	A	C	E		A	C	M	E
A	L	I	E	N		I	B	E	T		B	L	I	P
W	I	N	S	O	M	E	L	O	S	E	S	O	M	E
S	T	A	T		I	R	E	S		B	O	G	I	E
			T	I	N			H	E	R				
	Y	O	U	D	I	D	Y	O	U	R	B	E	S	T
S	A	M	B	A		R	O	U	S	T		R	H	O
K	L	E	E		W	I	D	T	H		P	A	A	R
E	I	N		R	I	L	E	D		E	A	T	M	E
W	E	S	T	I	L	L	L	O	V	E	Y	O	U	
			E	N	D			E	L	S				
S	A	G	A	S		H	E	A	T		L	E	N	T
C	L	O	S	E	B	U	T	N	O	C	I	G	A	R
A	I	R	E		A	R	N	O		U	P	O	N	E
B	E	E	T		A	L	A	N		E	S	S	A	Y

70

W	A	R	N		I	D	I	O		A	M	A	T	I
E	T	A	T		W	O	M	B		G	A	B	O	N
B	A	T	H	T	O	W	E	L		O	R	B	I	T
T	R	E		C	U	R	T	A	I	N	C	A	L	L
V	I	S	I	B	L	Y			D	I	I			
			C	Y	D		A	M	A	Z	E	D	A	T
B	E	S	O			A	M	O	R	E		A	P	E
B	L	A	N	K	E	X	P	R	E	S	S	I	O	N
Q	E	D		E	M	I	L	E			E	S	P	N
S	E	R	E	N	E	L	Y		P	A	M			
			A	T	E			P	E	T	I	T	E	S
P	I	C	T	U	R	E	S	H	O	W		U	L	T
A	D	H	O	C		G	U	N	P	O	W	D	E	R
A	N	O	U	K		G	E	O	L		A	O	N	E
R	O	O	T	Y		O	R	M	E		D	R	A	W

71

P	R	E	K		B	E	N	C	H		C	A	L	L
H	O	N	E		E	C	O	L	I		O	R	E	O
D	U	R	A	N	D	U	R	A	N		S	T	E	W
S	T	A	T	U	S			S	D	I		U	R	I
		G	O	D		M	O	S	U	L	I	R	A	Q
I	T	I	N	E	R	A	R	Y		L	O	O	T	S
S	A	N		E	N	D		S	E	T				
H	I	G	H	W	A	Y	E	N	T	R	A	N	C	E
			T	I	P		R	C	A			A	H	A
S	P	I	T	Z		T	E	A	T	A	S	T	E	R
G	R	A	P	E	S	O	D	A		H	O	I		
T	A	G		N	I	B			D	E	N	O	T	E
M	I	R	O		F	O	U	N	D	M	O	N	E	Y
A	S	E	A		T	O	S	C	A		R	A	R	E
J	E	E	R		S	T	O	R	Y		A	L	M	S

72

A	V	I	L	A		T	E	L	E		R	D	A	S
V	I	D	A	L		A	X	E	L		A	E	R	O
A	R	E	S	T	I	N	G	O	F	F	I	C	E	R
S	T	A	T		D	A	I	S		E	L	K		
T	U	L	S	A	O	K			E	B	B	E	T	S
			B	L	A	R	E	D			I	D	Y	L
	H	I	H	O			I	V	Y		R	O	P	Y
	A	C	O	U	N	T	P	A	S	T	D	U	E	
E	L	E	M		E	S	O			A	S	T	A	
R	O	S	E		S	O	N	I	C	S				
A	S	H	P	I	T			T	A	K	E	A	I	M
	E	L	L		P	E	C	S		E	L	O	I	
A	P	E	A	L	T	O	T	H	E	C	R	O	W	D
M	A	T	T		A	D	U	E		S	I	N	A	I
P	O	S	E		P	S	I	S		T	E	E	N	S

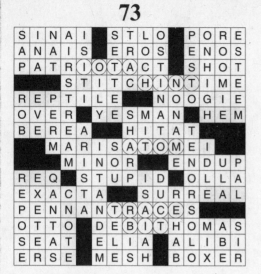

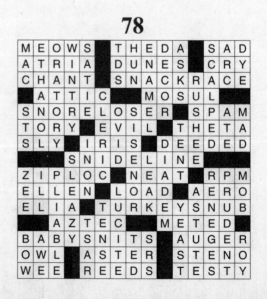

73

```
S I N A I   S T L O   P O R E
A N A I S   E R O S   E N O S
P A T R I O T A C T   S H O T
    S T I T C H I N T I M E
R E P T I L E   N O O G I E
O V E R   Y E S M A N   H E M
B E R E A   H I T A T
    M A R I S A T O M E I
    M I N O R   E N D U P
R E Q   S T U P I D   O L L A
E X A C T A   S U R R E A L
P E N N A N T R A C E S
O T T O   D E B I T H O M A S
S E A T   E L I A   A L I B I
E R S E   M E S H   B O X E R
```

74

```
  G E D   G A B S   E D S E L
P O U R   A U R A   D O U S E
A I R J O R D A N   I N B E D
S T A   F B I   S T O P
H E I R T O T H E T H R O N E
A R L O   S O N Y   S E E R
    A L T   N O L O   N O R
    E R E I S A W E L B A
I Q S   W A H L   S E A
R U T S   R U E S   E Z R A
A I R E D A L E T E R R I E R
    A X I S   A L B   N C O
M O N T E   A E R L I N G U S
A R G O T   D O V E   S E S E
C O E N S   O N E S   A R E
```

75

```
D E L H I   C A P E   I B E T
I V I E D   A L E E   C O D A
F E N W A Y P A R K   E G G O
    S H A R I F   J A D E S
A I M   O R I   O M E G A
S T A T E N   P R E T E N D S
P A R E S   B R A S S   O M E
E L S E   K E A T S   O V I D
N I H   A L L Y E   T W I N E
S C A N D A L S   R A N C O R
    M O U N T   A U K   H R S
S H A N E   O N S P E C
L O S E   S W A M P S C O T T
A L O E   G E N A   T U D O R
W A N D   T R O D   O P E R A
```

76

```
R A G A   V O I L A   F A Z E
E R A S   A R R A U   O N I T
P E R K   M E A N S   R A P S
O N C E U P O N A T I M E
S A I D H I   I R S   R A I
E S A   U R I S   I M C O L D
    W H E N I W A S A B O Y
A L S O   I K E   R E E L
B A C K I N T H E D A Y
C R I S T O   S P E C   U T A
S A M   S S W   I R O N O N
    I N Y E A R S G O N E B Y
J E T E   O R I O N   E V A H
A G A R   U N C L E   L E G O
W O R D   T S K E D   S N O W
```

77

```
R E B   C O M A S   P E A L S
U S O   A D E L A   E D G A R
S T D   B A N A L   T U R K S
T H E G A Y D I V O R C E E
L E G A L   O U I   E V A
E R A S   A T E S T   F D I C
    A M A N   S L A T E S
    T H E M E R R Y W I D O W
C A E S A R   O M I T
A L A S   I S L A M   C A S H
B L T   S C I   L E N T O
    T H E H A P P Y H O O K E R
M A R I E   H O M E R   A P T
A L O N E   O S C A R   R I O
S E W E R   N E A L E   A N N
```

78

```
M E O W S   T H E D A   S A D
A T R I A   D U N E S   C R Y
C H A N T   S N A C K R A C E
  A T T I C   M O S U L
S N O R E L O S E R   S P A M
T O R Y   E V I L   T H E T A
S L Y   I R I S   D E E D E D
    S N I D E L I N E
Z I P L O C   N E A T   R P M
E L L E N   L O A D   A E R O
E L I A   T U R K E Y S N U B
  A Z T E C   M E T E D
B A B Y S N I T S   A U G E R
O W L   A S T E R   S T E N O
W E E   R E E D S   T E S T Y
```

79

80

81

82

83

84

85

```
ROTC  TVS     ASONE
ITAL  HIE   CLIMAX
BODYHEAT    ATBEST
SHADOW   ALVA   GAO
     ETAL   AIRBALL
BTU   EVE   SASE
LASTLETTER    VIDA
EXPOS   MER   MERRY
WISP   CENTERLINE
     AMAS   ACT   SOS
ENDZONE   GOOP
NOR   UVEA   CASTLE
JOANNA    DEADHEAD
ONMEDS   APR   ACNE
YEATS     MAS   WHEN
```

86

```
BEAST   SCAT   ABEL
WELCH   CORA   TITO
AROAR   OVEN   ONTO
YOUREBREAKINGUP
     ETC     ARC
CANYOUHEARMENOW
AGAIN   DADA   AMY
COOP   ARIAS   ETNA
TOM   OPEN   TACIT
IDIDNTCATCHTHAT
     AOL   ORE
ILLTRYREDIALING
DAYS   PUMA   ROPER
ECRU   UNIT   TOSCA
SEEN   TETE   SMOKY
```

87

```
ANTI   SHIN   AFAR
MEAN   STINT   LALA
PACKAPUNCH    BRIT
SRO   LINDA   PEEVE
     PECKINGORDER
POLICE      ONT
OMAN   LAPAZ   STP
PICKOFTHELITTER
STY   CEDAR   OLEO
     STA   AARONS
POCKETCHANGE
UNLIT   HESSE   ADO
TEAM   PUCKEREDUP
TARP   ETHEL   RANT
SLAY   NEED   AMES
```

88

```
DABS   MBAS   BLASS
UTAH   ARNO   LOCAL
OLDE   GOWN   ULTRA
 AMERICANBEAUTY
TNOTE   CREEL   ARE
BTU   OTO   TRILLED
SITS   ALT   MPS
 CHARLIEHUSTLE
   AOL   CYD   SATE
BUSBOYS   SAD   NCO
ATT   SHOOT   EMCEE
TOOKTOONESFEET
OPINE   TERI   OLEG
NICER   HAIL   WORE
SASES   ELAL   STAT
```

89

```
NAPS   PSIS   ALIVE
ODIC   ETTU   MINEO
SILENCEISGOLDEN
ADANO   TSHIRT
LATENT   INA   MIA
ESE   CAMP   ALPERT
   NORUSH   ELSE
  MUMSTHEWORD
MAID   TARIFF
TVSETS   WOLF   SRO
SAT   ROD   LISTEN
  CITRUS   CLOVE
MYLIPSARESEALED
GOTTO   IGGY   BERG
MUSED   NEAR   SNEE
```

90

```
RCMP   SHOE   ABCTV
ELAL   CURB   DELHI
MANAGINGEDITORS
AROSE   ARID   CEO
PERMANENTMARKER
     AROD   ESE
PEA   TRACI   NASA
TENCOMMANDMENTS
ALTO   STORE   YUK
     MOP   NANU
REFERENCEMANUAL
AXE   ETON   CANTO
MIDDLELOWGERMAN
PLODS   ATOP   MERE
SENSE   NEWS   STIR
```

91

B	A	S	H		G	A	L	S		V	A	L	L	I
O	J	A	I		E	P	E	E		A	Z	T	E	C
Z	A	N	Y		W	A	V	E		N	U	D	G	E
O	R	G	A	N	G	R	I	N	D	E	R			
			E	A	T			U	S	E	R	I	D	
K	O	W	T	O	W		L	A	M	S		E	N	E
A	L	I	E	N		G	E	R	M	A	N	S	U	B
N	E	N	E		R	A	T	T	Y		C	H	I	A
S	A	N	D	W	E	D	G	E		B	A	I	T	S
A	T	O		A	H	S	O		E	L	A	P	S	E
S	E	W	A	G	E			S	L	O				
		R	O	M	A	N	T	I	C	H	E	R	O	
E	G	G	O	N		H	O	A	X		A	L	I	A
S	U	E	M	E		A	N	T	I		Z	E	S	T
S	M	E	A	R		B	E	E	R		Y	V	E	S

92

S	P	A	M		A	B	I	T		R	S	V	P	S
S	O	H	O		L	O	R	E		A	T	E	A	T
T	O	M	D	I	C	K	A	N	D	H	A	R	R	Y
S	H	E	E	S	H		Q	U	I		R	A	T	E
			L	O	E	B		R	E	N	T			
N	E	A	T		M	A	L	E	T	U	R	K	E	Y
A	L	T		P	Y	R	O		S	T	E	E	L	E
A	G	A	V	E		D	R	J		S	K	E	I	N
C	A	R	A	T	S		N	A	T	O		N	E	T
P	R	I	V	A	T	E	E	Y	E		S	E	L	L
			A	L	O	U		Z	E	B	U			
B	E	A	V		I	R	S		N	O	N	E	E	D
A	N	N	O	Y	C	O	N	S	T	A	N	T	L	Y
M	I	N	O	R		P	O	P	S		E	A	S	E
A	D	A	M	S		E	B	A	Y		R	T	E	S

93

A	S	A	P		A	T	A	D		P	U	R	R	S
L	O	C	O		N	O	V	A		A	M	A	H	L
B	U	C	K	N	A	K	E	D		S	A	M	O	A
A	R	T	I	E		E	N	A	C	T		C	N	N
			E	W	I	N	G		S	A	C	H	E	T
C	O	B	R	A	S		E	L	I	S	H	A		
A	P	U		G	L	A	R	E		I	R	A	N	
V	A	L	J	E	A	N		A	T	I	N	G	L	E
E	L	L	E		E	P	S	O	N		E	A	R	
		M	E	A	N	T	O		U	S	E	R	I	D
S	T	A	P	L	E		P	O	R	T	S			
T	O	R		L	E	A	S	H		E	T	A	I	L
A	S	K	E	W		S	T	A	G	P	A	R	T	Y
G	E	E	S	E		T	A	R	A		T	A	L	E
E	A	T	A	T		A	R	E	S		E	L	L	S

94

V	A	L	E	T		D	R	O	O	L		E	S	S
A	R	E	N	A		V	A	N	N	A		V	O	L
S	T	E	A	M	E	D	C	R	A	B		I	F	I
T	E	R	M		U	S	E	U	P		A	T	T	N
			E	E	R			S	A	D	S	A	C	K
G	R	I	L	L	E	D	S	H	R	I	M	P		
R	O	C		S	K	E	E		G	U	E	S	S	
A	L	E	S		A	B	N	E	R		D	R	I	P
D	E	B	T	S		S	N	I	T		O	T	O	
	R	O	A	S	T	E	D	P	E	A	N	U	T	
I	N	E	R	T	I	A		E	E	L				
R	O	A	M		E	X	P	O	S		D	E	L	E
I	L	K		F	R	I	E	D	T	U	R	K	E	Y
S	T	E		I	R	E	N	E		S	I	E	G	E
H	E	R		R	A	D	A	R		A	N	D	O	R

95

M	A	N	I	C		O	M	A	H	A		T	H	E
E	N	O	L	A		C	A	N	O	N		R	O	M
M	O	T	E	T		C	R	A	M	S		O	R	A
O	N	A		C	R	U	I	S	E	A	L	O	N	G
		S	A	H	A	R	A		P	R	O	P	S	
A	R	A	R	A	T			S	O	A	R			
R	E	B	E	L		I	N	O	R		E	C	O	N
E	E	L		L	U	G	N	U	T	S		A	V	A
A	L	E	C		N	O	E	L		N	A	M	E	S
			A	M	U	R		C	O	V	E	R	T	
	A	P	R	E	S		T	R	O	W	E	L		
I	L	L	B	E	A	R	O	U	N	D		A	R	R
N	E	A		T	B	O	N	E		A	R	T	I	E
E	R	N		U	L	N	A	R		Y	I	E	L	D
Z	O	O		P	E	A	L	S		S	O	R	E	S

96

S	P	A	M		G	L	E	N	S		G	A	Z	E
A	L	S	O		R	E	L	A	Y		R	I	O	T
L	A	W	B	R	E	A	K	E	R		A	R	E	A
I	N	A		A	C	R	E	S		E	D	W		
V	E	R	S	I	O	N			C	R	E	A	S	E
A	D	M	A	N		T	E	A	L	E	A	V	E	S
			R	E	S		N	R	A		E	X	T	
		D	I	R	T	Y	D	I	S	H	E	S		
S	C	I		R	E	A		H	O	I				
S	P	A	G	H	E	T	T	I		W	R	I	N	G
W	A	L	L	O	P		D	I	N	E	D	O	N	
	T	I	P		A	S	I	D	O		O	V	A	
M	O	O	D		I	N	H	O	T	W	A	T	E	R
A	N	N	E		A	N	I	T	A		L	O	L	L
J	E	E	R		N	O	M	S	G		P	O	S	Y

97

```
O R E O   I O N I C   S T A T
P I C K   S P E L T   H O L E
T O R I   S E W E R S E W E R
S T U N G U N S   O P I U M
    A L E E   T Y R A N T S
D R A W E R D R A W E R
R O M A N   H I C   D A T A
A T E   S C H O L A R   V A C
G E N E   E O N   E M O T E
    S H O W E R S H O W E R
M A L T E S E   E T A L
A M E E R   I C E B E R G S
T O W E R T O W E R   S O O T
T R I M   A B I D E   T O N E
S E S S   M I N E O   S K E W
```

98

```
A M A H L   F U E L   P A C T
M E D E A   A N T I   O M A R
I R V I N   L I T E   W A R Y
G E I G E R C O U N T E R
A S C H   I O N   A R E A S
S T E T S O N   E M U   T H O
    E A R   I R A   T T O P
J O H N W I L K E S B O O T H
P A Y S   T O E   O I L
E T D   C A W   U N D E R G O
G H E N T   A N I   R E A D
  P E R I O D I C T A B L E
C Z A R   M M E S   E N O L S
H E R D   P I L E   A C R E S
I N K S   S T A X   K E N Y A
```

99

```
O N E G   L E S   D O L L A R   H B O   Z O N E
P O T R O A S T   E U G E N E   E A R L O B E S
T H E U N I T E D S T A T E S O F A M E R I C A
    N O R   R I P     O S T   E B B
S S T   I N G O D W E T R U S T     A M S
E A U   E S C   T E A A C T   Y O W   A A H
G R E A T S E A L   W I S E   B A L D E A G L E
G A M M A R A Y S   E V E L   S T E E L D O O R
O N E A L   X E D   Y E L L   A E R   D O O N E
```

100

```
B R I T   D W A R F   B A W L
M E N U   R A V E L   O H I O
W A F F L E C O N E   Y A N K
S M O T E   C O W L   M O I
    S I M B A   B O Z O
A N D   F O O D P Y R A M I D
B O O S   O B O E   N I E C E
O C T A N T S   L E A R N O F
M A C R O   U S T A   E T N A
B L O G O S P H E R E   S S T
    M E I N   O R N O T
J A B   L O E W   N A G A T
A T O Z   R U B I K S C U B E
I T O O   E R I K A   E R I N
L A M E   D O Z E N   T U T S
```

101

```
B A S I C   S N A P S   Q E D
O L L A S   C O V E Y   U S A
S P A N I S H M A I N   A T M
C H I   O O O   O G D E N
H A N S O L O   C I D E R
    T H E L I O N S M A N E
S E R U M   N I T   S T A T
C L O D   J E L L O   T I N A
A B L Y   O N A   V O C A L
B E E F C H O W M E I N
    M O O N S   I M M E R S E
S T O R M   A M I   H O V
P A D   B A N G O R M A I N E
A X E   A L O E S   U L N A R
N I L   T E R R A   G L O R Y
```

102

```
W A T T S   M E S H   S H I P
I N H O T   E L M O   H E R O
K E E N E   E L I S   O M A R
I N T E R S T A T E   R I N K
  T A R O T   T A C T
    L E N N Y   P E A C E
L O S T   P R O   B A N J O S
A V O W   P A R D O   E A R P
D E F I N E   S U N   D R A Y
D R A C O   W E B M D
    E V A H   O R O N O
N C A A   N I N E T Y F I V E
S C U D   I T A R   O F O U R
E L S A   S E G A   F A B L E
C I T Y   E R S T   F L E E S
```

103

```
S T O R M . E S O S . . A P E D
T Y P E A . T I V O . . E R G O
I N E S T . C L E O . . R A G F
N O R T H T H O R N . . I G O R
T S A R . B E S S . G E M . .
. . A J A R . E T O . . A B A
A S C I I . . W E S T S T E W
C H A N G E D I R E C T I O N
E A S T S E A T . . H O C K S
D Y E . A L F . D R A C . .
. . S A W . F L E A . K A T S
P A T S . S O U T H S H O U T
E Q U I . E D I E . H O R D E
R U D D . W I G S . E L T O N
K A Y E . S L I T . S M A R T
```

104

```
G A L A S . T E S L A . S S E
A L A R M . E X C O N . I N A
S I X T E E N T H L E T T E R
. . A R O O M . . E A R L
R I V E R O F L O M B A R D Y
O N E L S . . E A R .
C L E O . H E R B A L . C S T
C A P I T O L H I L L T Y P E
O W S . O N I O N S . I C A N
. . A M O . . B E L I E
F O R M E R P R E S I D E N T
L A O S . A U N T S . .
O K T O B E R F E S T T U N E
R I O . O P I U M . R A Z O R
A E R . S A S S Y . O R I N G
```

105

```
O L G A . C A G E D . G A P S
N E A T . A B A T E . U N I T
E A R L . P A S T A . S T A R
S P R A Y O F S U N S H I N E
. . N U T T Y . A E S O P
B E A T L E . O I L S .
A S T I . S A B R E . K I A
S P A C E O F D I A M O N D S
E N D . D E P O T . N E A P
. . B I R D . E X C E S S
A S P I C . A I R E R .
S P U T T E R N O N S E N S E
P E R T . L O E W E . D O P E
E L S E . L I R A S . I M I N
N L E R . S L A N T . T O N Y
```

106

```
S H E L F . A F T E R . T E T
H E N I E . T O R S O . E L O
O L I V E R T W I S T . A I M
V I A . H E L M E T . R M S
E X C I S E S . . E O S I N
. . S H E T L A N D P O N Y
E N T R E . U M A . S P A D
L E O . D A N C I N G . E T E
E T T U . V I I . A S N E R
C L E A N A N D J E R K .
T O M E I . . E X P A R T E
I S P . M I N E T A . A W L
V S O . B R A S S M O N K E Y
E E L . L O T T E . F R E E S
S S E . E C L A T . T A S T E
```

107

```
A C R E S . B R A T . C A L F
C A U L K . R O M A . O V A L
E M I L Y P O S T S . Y O K E
D E N . D E W Y . M E O W E D
. . R I D S . W A N T
S T E V I E W O N D E R S
S H A V E . I R I S . I K E
E R R S . M E D E A . A V I V
X E S . P A G O . S W E D E
. W I N S L O W H O M E R S
. . E A T S . I D A S
G H O S T S . S K I S . O A T
N E X T . H E L E N H U N T S
A X E L . O V E R . E S T O P
W A N E . P A W S . R O O M S
```

108

```
A D E S . A C R O S S . F A T
T E R I . L E A N T O . A L E
E L E C T I O N D A Y . N I L
A I M E E . T O R . A B E S
S L I M M E D . P R E V E N T
E A T . L O W E . V O L T A
. H E M L I N E . V I C T O R
. . C A S T A V O T E
L O U V R E . V A C A T E S
A N N I V . V E N A . Y E N
B E R E A V E . E L G R E C O
C P A S . I I I . A H E R O
O A T . B A L L O T B O X E S
A G E . O N E I D A . D A T E
T E D . O D D E S T . A M E S
```

109

```
M I S T Y _ D R A M A _ O A T
A M U S E _ I O T A S _ N I A
C H E E S E C L O T H _ I S P
H I D _ S N E E Z E _ S O L E
O P E N I T _ Y A W N E D _ _
_ _ A R R A Y _ S K I D _ _ _
S I S I _ A S I S _ A N O D E
E T A L _ P A P E R _ G M A N
W O L F S _ P E T E _ S E N D
_ _ S I T S _ S H A D E _ _ _
C H A L E T _ D E T E R S _ _
R A C E _ R E C I T E _ V I A
A I L _ T A C O T O P P I N G
B T U _ A T O N E _ E R A S E
S I B _ S A L E M _ R E N E S
```

110

```
S P R Y _ S C H S _ _ T H O R
A L E E _ P O E T _ _ W O U K
W A I L _ I S A A C _ I N T O
T I N P A N _ D I O N N E _ _
O D E S S A _ I N R I _ Y M A
_ _ _ K L M N _ N E T M A N _
H A W S E _ I G G Y _ H O S T
I L I A D _ R D A _ A R O S E
T O N S _ Y O U I _ D U N E S
A N D H O W _ E T N A _ _ _ _
T E Y _ N C O S _ A G L E A M
_ _ C H E A P O _ S E A R L E
M A I M _ S T U N S _ T W O S
A L T O _ I T B E _ K I A S _
L A Y S _ C H A R _ A N D Y _
```

111

```
P A W _ A L P S _ P E T I T E
R B I _ L E A P _ E M I N E M
O D S _ S A D E _ C A R A T S
S U E F O R D A M A G E S _ _
E C T O _ N I K O N _ N O D _
_ T O G A _ N O N _ A M A N A
_ _ B E G F O R M E R C Y _ _
G A S B A G _ _ O O D L E S _
P R A Y F O R R A I N _ _ _ _
A L L O T _ E E L _ G A Z E _
S O S _ A N T I C _ P E N D _
_ A S K F O R T R O U B L E _
O R D E A L _ A T O P _ R I G
P O I N T A _ C L O T _ A S A
S E P T E T _ T E N S _ S T S
```

112

```
T A G U P _ _ S S R _ A T O Z
A D L A I _ A T M E _ L A N E
F I E R O _ R O A D B L O C K
T E A _ N A B I S C O _ S E E
S U M M E R S C H O O L _ _ _
_ _ _ M E T _ _ A N E M I C _
O T T E R _ S T A T E B I R D
F A Y _ N A I F S _ _ C A R _
F I R E P O W E R _ B E A N S
S L O T H S _ _ B A M _ _ _ _
_ _ D O L L C A R R I A G E _
E S P _ T O I L S A T _ R O D
T W O H O U S E S _ E C O L E
N A P E _ C A A N _ N O M A N
A P E X _ H S T _ D E A N S _
```

113

```
R I O T _ A B L E _ A J A R
U N P E G _ C R A M _ M A D E
G R E E N T H U M B _ A W O L
S E N S O R _ T A R P _ E R A
_ _ _ M I S E R Y I N D E X _
M A C H E T E _ R O U E _ _ _
O S L O _ O N S _ S E E M S _
M E E T I N T H E M I D D L E
S C O O T _ E X O _ N I L E _
_ _ N E T S _ G O A T E E S _
G I V E M E A R I N G _ _ _ _
A D O _ S E T A _ E A T O U T
R E I N _ H I N K Y P I N K Y
B A L E _ E R I E _ E N T E R
O L A V _ E E N Y _ S O S O _
```

114

```
K A F K A _ S Q F T _ T R A P
E M A I L _ T A L E _ R E B A
P E N A L P A N E L _ I G O R
I N S _ W I L D E _ S P A D E
_ _ _ C E L L A R C A L L E R
M R M O T O _ _ O L E _ _ _ _
R I A L _ T E X A S T A X E S
S C I _ V I P _ _ _ B A H _ _
C O N A N C A N O N _ R O S E
_ _ _ N E D _ A M E X E S _ _
T I C T A C T A C T I C _ _ _
A L O F T _ I D L E D _ O H O
C O R A _ D A V I S D I V A S
O V E R _ E R I N _ A C U R A
S E A M _ M A L E _ Y U M M Y
```

115

```
AGNES █ BATCH █ LBJ
LEAST █ ADELE █ IOU
BETTEMIDLER █ LIN
USA █ RUNS █ RARELY
MELANIE █ OGLES █
█ NURSEMIDWIFE
SCRAM █ LEES █ ZOO
ALIT █ OWENS █ KERN
MUG █ IVAN █ BIDES
SEMIDETACHED █
█ AVERT █ OARSMEN
THREAT █ ACHE █ ALE
WOO █ TURNONADIME
AWL █ ERATO █ VINED
SEE █ SETIN █ EMERY
```

116

```
CREWS █ ACLU █ BOOM
LEGIT █ CLAP █ IONA
INGIF █ HUSH █ SONY
NEEDED █ CHOOCHOO
KERPLUNK █ LOU █
█ ISLA █ ADMIRED
PING █ ACAT █ PTERO
SOU █ SCREECH █ DIN
SWISH █ ESAI █ PONG
TATTOOS █ STAT █
█ RAP █ BEEPBEEP
SPLATTER █ DOOMTO
OLAF █ FLEE █ GAMAL
HOME █ OINK █ ETYPE
OPED █ RATE █ ESSES
```

117

```
SATE █ HASTA █ OPAL
ECOL █ ICIER █ RIME
CHAINSTORE █ ENOS
TONTO █ SUR █ WINKS
SODIUM █ XANADU █
█ SNOB █ ENAMEL
PSST █ MANUAL █ BRO
LOT █ JEWELRY █ EGO
EAU █ UNDONE █ TROT
ARDENT █ ASHE █
█ PUTSON █ TENDON
AHORA █ VIA █ MARCO
MAKO █ RINGBINDER
PREP █ INNER █ TRAM
SIRE █ MEYER █ SENS
```

118

```
ARYANS █ DATE █ MAP
PEORIA █ INON █ ALE
PLUMPUDDING █ ITT
█ PTAS █ RAZES
SCARLETTANAGER █
LADIES █ NAVE █
ATOMS █ WHITESALE
NEB █ ERASE █ WON
GREENMILE █ BEARD
█ ROME █ ERMINE
█ MUSTARDPLASTER
CONTE █ ALEC █
LOB █ PEACOCKBLUE
USA █ ARCH █ TERESA
EER █ DATA █ STREET
```

119

```
APER █ AMEX █ PSHAW
TERI █ MOLE █ UTICA
LAIC █ POUNDCAKES
ACCEDE █ LOOK █ ESP
SEAPORT █ NOEL █
█ UVEAS █ DROWSY
BLADE █ TORA █ NONO
RIND █ QUAID █ DOUG
OMNI █ UMPS █ VOLGA
SEANCE █ SETIN █
█ GENT █ SUNBATH
CDS █ ACRO █ SERBIA
LAMBSHANKS █ OILY
AZURE █ ITAL █ IDLE
DEGAS █ TONE █ LESS
```

120

```
OSHA █ BATH █ ABODE
APER █ ABOO █ BAGEL
FARMERINTHEDELL
STRAW █ TIDE █ PETS
█ DEA █ OMAR █
█ GARDENGATEWAY
AKA █ SRI █ NOSHOW
SERBS █ AXE █ NSYNC
ANNULS █ ETO █ MEA
POISONEDAPPLE █
█ DEES █ TEE █
ALOE █ RTES █ RAGON
COMPUTERCOMPANY
TRIOS █ EGAD █ ARCS
VETTE █ MOBS █ TREE
```

121

T	E	M	P		T	A	P	S		T	R	A	M	P
A	L	O	U		N	I	L	E		H	A	N	O	I
R	A	B	B	I	T	R	U	N		O	W	N	U	P
O	L	S	E	N			M	A	R		D	O	S	E
		C	R	I	C	K	E	T	P	L	A	Y	E	R
	M	E	T	T	L	E		E	M	I	T			
D	E	N	Y		E	L	M		N	A	S	T	Y	
O	N	E		H	O	P	T	O	I	T		P	I	E
G	U	S	T	O		S	P	A		H	I	P	S	
		A	R	A	B		E	G	R	E	T	S		
K	A	N	G	A	R	O	O	C	O	U	R	T		
A	L	A	S		C	O	D			T	B	O	N	E
P	I	T	A	S		T	O	A	D	S	T	O	O	L
U	N	C	L	E		E	R	M	A		E	N	D	S
T	E	H	E	E		E	S	P	N		A	S	E	A

122

T	E	D		S	A	T			R	A	T	E	R
I	L	E		E	N	I	D		T	A	R	A	R	A
M	I	N		D	I	D	I		R	E	T	R	A	P
E	D	I	S	O	N		A	M	O		P	T	S
R	E	M	A	N		S	P	I	T	O	N
		S	A	I	L	E	D		N	O	N	E	T
E	R	I	E		D	A	R		L	A	M	I	N	A
T	E	S		N	O	V		V	O	N		S	E	T
A	N	I	M	A	L		R	A	D		E	I	R	E
T	E	N	O	N		D	E	L	I	A	S
		N	O	T	I	P	S		N	A	M	E	R
S	T	P		O	M	A		N	O	S	I	D	E
P	A	R	T	E	R		I	D	I	D		N	I	M
A	R	A	R	A	T		D	I	N	E		E	L	I
R	E	T	A	R		T	A	S		D	E	T

123

F	E	I	G	N		C	L	A	R	A		P	T	A
C	E	L	L	O		A	A	R	O	N		R	O	N
C	L	O	U	D		R	U	M	M	Y	H	A	N	D
		M	O	P	E	D	S		T	U	T	T	I
	S	A	M	U	E	L		B	I	G	T	O	E
B	A	S	E	B	A	L	L	G	A	M	E
E	X	I	S	T	S		A	O	N	E		T	I	N
T	O	A	T		A	C	T		R	E	D	O
A	N	N		A	C	H	E		T	H	E	S	E	S
		B	R	O	A	D	W	A	Y	P	L	A	Y
P	O	P	A	R	T		A	L	P	H	A	S
U	H	U	R	A		B	U	T	L	E	R
P	A	N	T	Y	H	O	S	E		D	A	R	T	S
I	R	K		E	I	D	E	R		U	S	U	A	L
L	E	S		D	E	E	D	S		P	E	N	N	Y

124

S	H	A	M		W	E	B	E	R		T	Y	K	E
L	O	R	I		A	G	I	L	E		R	A	I	L
A	L	E	X		R	A	B	I	D		O	W	L	S
S	E	N	I	O	R	D	I	S	C	O	U	N	T
H	Y	A	N	N	I	S		E	R	G
		G	T	O		L	I	N	C	H	P	I	N
J	U	N	I	O	R	M	I	N	T	S		A	D	O
A	N	O	N		E	S	C		O	L	E	O
G	P	S		T	H	E	T	H	I	R	D	M	A	N
S	C	H	N	O	O	K	S		W	A	Y
		I	S	M		N	O	N	S	L	I	P
	F	A	T	H	E	R	S	A	N	D	S	O	N	S
B	L	O	W		R	O	U	N	D		E	T	N	A
L	O	K	I		O	N	I	C	E		U	T	I	L
T	E	S	T		W	A	T	E	R		S	E	E	M

125

T	R	A	I	T		C	E	D	E		C	A	S	A
A	A	R	G	H		A	L	O	E		A	L	I	S
W	I	L	L	I	A	M	M	C	K	I	N	L	E	Y
S	L	O	U	C	H	E	S			N	A	I	V	E
			K	E	R		D	A	T	A	S	E	T
J	A	M	E	S	M	A	D	I	S	O	N
E	L	A	T	E		I	S	H			A	C	H
R	I	G	H	T	O	N	T	H	E	M	O	N	E	Y
K	A	I		G	O	T		A	S	K	E	D
		S	A	L	M	O	N	P	C	H	A	S	E
M	U	S	T	S	E	E		O	R	A
A	N	N	O	Y		P	R	O	R	A	T	E	D
G	R	O	V	E	R	C	L	E	V	E	L	A	N	D
M	I	R	E		B	O	A	S		N	A	F	T	A
A	G	E	S		I	S	N	T		A	N	T	S	Y

126

E	R	I	K		O	M	N	I		O	C	C	A	M
R	A	M	A		R	E	A	M		E	L	L	I	S
I	S	M	Y		C	A	M	P	G	R	O	U	N	D
S	P	O	O	R		D	E	A	L		S	E	G	O
	B	L	E	E	D		R	E	C	E	D	E	S
H	E	A	D	Q	U	A	R	T	E	R	S
A	R	T		D	O	Z	E		Y	E	C	C	H
I	R	E	D		S	T	I	L	T		T	H	R	O
R	Y	D	E	R		N	O	A	H		A	A	A
		T	H	A	N	K	S	G	I	V	I	N	G
S	P	A	R	E	M	E		S	T	I	N	K
A	O	K	I		O	U	T	S		S	P	E	C	S
B	L	I	T	Z	K	R	I	E	G		E	D	A	M
L	A	R	U	E		O	R	C	A		R	U	S	E
E	R	A	S	E		N	E	T	S		S	P	E	E

127

R	A	Y		G	A	L	L		E	V	E	N	U	P
E	W	E		O	W	I	E		V	A	L	I	S	E
T	A	M		S	W	I	M	M	I	N	G	B	A	N
A	R	E	S	O			M	E	L	B	A			
G	E	N	T	L	E	B	E	N		U	R	G	E	S
		R	O	X	Y		D	O	R		A	L	T	
L	I	L	I		U	N	O		R	E	I	L	L	Y
U	S	E	D	C	L	O	T	H	I	N	G	B	I	N
M	O	D	E	L	T		T	I	E		E	A	S	E
P	U	T		A	S	A		S	N	I	T			
S	T	O	M	P		C	E	S	T	S	I	B	O	N
		A	T	S	E	A			I	T	A	L	Y	
H	O	T	C	R	O	S	S	B	U	N		R	I	M
A	R	A	R	A	T		T	A	F	T		E	V	E
D	R	O	O	P	S		S	H	O	O		S	E	T

128

M	A	M	A	S		G	A	D		M	I	S	S	
A	M	A	N	A		I	P	O	S		A	C	T	A
L	I	T	T	L	E	J	O	H	N		R	F	A	I
		A	S	T	R	O	S		E	A	S	T	L	A
A	S	H	Y		L	E	T	T	E	R	H	E	A	D
S	H	A		N	E	S		O	R	T		A	G	A
C	U	R	I	O		A	B	A	S	E				
H	E	I	R	T	O	T	H	E	T	H	R	O	N	E
				T	A	P	E	S		O	R	I	O	N
U	S	A		B	E	T		C	O	W		L	I	Z
S	A	R	D	I	N	E	C	A	N		A	G	R	O
E	X	C	I	T	E		O	N	E	I	D	A		
R	O	A	D		R	O	Y	A	L	F	L	U	S	H
I	N	D	O		S	U	E	R		S	E	G	A	R
D	Y	E	S		T	R	Y		O	R	E	O	S	

129

L	I	M	O		B	A	W	L		W	H	I	M	
O	D	O	R		O	B	O	E		S	H	O	N	E
B	O	O	N	D	O	C	K	S		H	O	O	D	S
		N	O	R	M	S		S	E	R	A	P	E	S
C	O	S	T	A		S	E	G	A		L	E	E	
A	S	H		N	E	U	T	R	O	N		A	D	S
B	L	O	C	K	A	G	E		I	K	E			
S	O	T	S		S	H	E	D	S		A	B	E	D
			T	E	E		P	E	T	S	T	O	R	E
N	E	T		G	O	U	L	A	S	H		U	S	C
E	D	U		R	U	N	E		O	R	F	E	O	
P	I	C	K	E	T	S		S	E	R	I	F		
A	S	S	E	T		O	O	H	A	N	D	A	A	H
L	O	O	N	S		L	E	I	S		E	N	D	S
I	N	N	S		D	R	A	T		S	T	A	T	

130

W	E	I	L	L		H	O	O	P		F	A	C	T
A	M	T	O	O		E	D	N	A		E	S	A	U
R	O	S	E	G	A	R	D	E	N		S	I	R	S
		A	B	I	T	E			T	O	T	A	L	S
D	A	D		C	H	I	V	A	S	R	E	G	A	L
O	R	E	L		N	I	P		A	R	O	S	E	
C	L	A	S	S	A		N	A	A	N				
	O	L	D	T	I	M	E	R	S	G	A	M	E	
				O	R	I	G		H	E	R	A	L	D
A	R	E	U	P		C	A	T		M	I	S	O	
S	A	U	S	A	G	E	R	O	L	L		N	E	T
S	T	R	A	T	A			F	E	T	A	L		
T	H	O	U		S	H	I	F	T	G	E	A	R	S
D	E	P	S		P	A	V	E		E	R	N	I	E
A	R	E	A		S	T	Y	E		N	O	D	O	Z

131

R	O	L	F	E		A	S	S	N		S	A	C	K
O	P	E	R	A		S	H	O	O		A	U	R	A
M	A	X	E	S		F	O	X	M	U	L	D	E	R
A	L	L	E	Y	C	A	T		A	L	T	I	M	A
		U	B	O	L	T		H	A	S	B	E	E	N
L	A	T	I	N	I		A	I	M	T	O			
A	C	H	E		F	A	L	L		E	X	T	R	A
P	R	O		X	F	A	C	T	O	R		E	E	L
P	E	R	O	T		H	O	S	T		E	X	G	I
			N	E	M	E	A		H	E	A	R	O	F
C	O	V	E	R	E	D		V	E	N	T	I		
O	S	I	E	R	S		P	E	R	M	I	T	M	E
M	A	X	Y	A	S	G	U	R		E	N	T	R	Y
A	G	E	E		U	R	N	S		S	T	E	E	R
S	E	N	D		P	O	K	E		H	O	R	D	E

132

P	E	A	K	S		I	A	M	B	S		R	I	B
I	N	U	I	T		V	I	O	L	A		E	T	A
T	E	T	R	A	H	E	D	R	O	N		C	U	R
		O	K	I	E		S	O	M	E	O	N	E	
S	Y	L		R	A	H	M	E	M	A	N	U	E	L
W	O	O	D		D	U	E	L		T	I	P	S	Y
I	R	A	E		P	E	W		L	E	G			
G	E	N	E	S	I	S		B	O	O	M	E	R	S
			P	U	N		S	O	W		A	X	E	S
A	D	M	E	N		B	L	O	B		S	T	A	T
G	R	A	N	D	P	O	O	B	A	H		E	M	S
H	A	R	D	E	S	T		L	Y	N	N			
A	W	L		C	H	E	E	R	L	E	A	D	E	R
S	E	E		K	A	R	M	A		N	I	T	R	O
T	R	Y		S	W	O	O	P		A	F	O	R	E

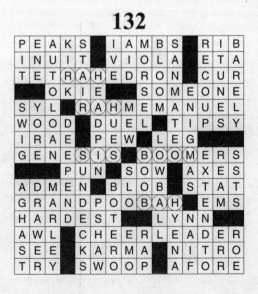

133

```
F E M A   S N A P   H A S T A
A X E S   P O L E   A C T O R
R I S K   E D I T   S Q U A T
  T H E E A S T E R B U N N Y
    D I K     E R I
S T P   G O B   F L O T S A M
T O O T H F A I R Y   T I N E
I N L E T   H O O   S A L O N
C Y A N   S A N T A C L A U S
K A R A C H I   H B O   S T A
    C H I     D U E
B E L I E V E I T O R N O T
E Y E O N   S P A M   T O U R
A R G U E   T O M E   E Z R A
M E S S Y   E D E N   R E N T
```

134

```
M A R I O   B A R G E   K P S
A M E N D   E T H E L   W A C
C A C T I   C O A T S   A T A
  Y O U C A M P A I G N I N
P F C   M U M   S N E E Z E D
D E L A   Z E R O G   L A N A
Q U E L L   A D R Y   A T L
  P O E T R Y Y O U
D A T   S L O E   S A C K S
I N R E   S W E E P   R H E A
S T E N C I L   X E S   E G G
G O V E R N I N P R O S E
U N I   I O N I A   N U R S E
S I N   E R E C T   I L I A D
T A O   D E S K S   C U O M O
```

135

```
A G E N T   C A S T   O G L E
T O N E R   O T T O   L I E S
H A S T Y   C O U G H D R O P
E L I   A O L   A T I L T
N I G H T F A L L   M E T A L
S E N I O R S   E S L   A R E
  T R I   T A U   A L D A
  K I T C H E N S I N K
E M I T   A A A   P V T
P E N   C N N   W E A S E L S
A N G L O   S K I N N Y D I P
  T S A R S   A N D   I N A
T H I N K T A N K   A M B E R
O O Z E   E D G E   M I L N E
O L E S   T O A D   P R E S S
```

136

```
S I C E M   S A G   S A W I N
I N A D V A N C E   A G O N Y
T A K E P L A C E   T O M E S
O W E N   O P T   S U R E
N E D   T H E S O P R A N O S
  B O A   Z E N   S P H
A L I E N   M O O N   E L I A
M O N E Y L A U N D E R I N G
E G O S   E D I E   V I B E S
B A R   I R T   H E N
A N D I L O V E H E R   R D A
  E L L Y   Q A S   S U E R
L U R I D   R U N S C A R E D
A F T E R   R I D E S H A R E
W O O D Y   S P Y   A L L E N
```

137

```
L A M B S   O R G A N   L T D
U S A I R   L E A S E   I R A
C O C K A N D B U L L   F U R
K N E E   O P A L   S L E E K
Y E S D E A R   B O A S
  S H O C K A N D A W E
J A B B A   L I B   I V E S
E L L A   P R E X Y   D E E P
E T A S   A A A   T A R D Y
R O C K A N D R O L L
  K E N T   F I C T I O N
Y A L T A   I S L E   A F R O
A L I   L O C K A N D L O A D
L E S   O R B I T   N O L T E
E X T   G I M M E   A N D E S
```

138

```
  A D E N   P E T   D U B S
O C U L I   E L I   E N L A I
D U R A N   P O D   B L I N G
O R A T O R S   E N T E N T E
R A N I   G I T M O   A G A R
    O J S   W A V E S
B O O N E   W I R E P H O T O
U S A   T W I N K L E   N E W
C U F F L I N K S   E R O D E
    R I G E L   A S O
E S S O   A L E R T   S K U A
S P U M O N I   I M E A N N O
S U G A R   S O N   K N O C K
A R A G E   T A G   E N C L S
  T R E O   S R O   D E K E
```

139

R	A	J		D	I	G	I	N		A	B	B	E	Y
O	N	O		I	R	A	T	E		Q	U	O	T	E
P	O	I		P	O	L	E	V	A	U	L	T	E	R
E	D	N	A		N	A	M	E	T	A	G			
R	E	T	Y	P	E	S		O	S	I	R	I	S	
		H	E	L	D		M	A	N		N	E	S	T
T	H	E	S	E		L	A	I	C		G	A	T	E
W	A	N		B	E	A	T	L	E	S		D	O	W
E	L	A	L		L	I	E	S		T	R	I	O	S
R	A	V	I		T	R	Y		N	E	O	N		
P	S	Y	C	H	O			D	A	M	A	G	E	D
		E	A	R	P	L	U	G		D	R	E	W	
A	G	E	N	T	O	R	A	N	G	E		O	R	E
W	O	R	S	E		O	W	N	E	D		O	I	L
L	O	R	E	S		S	N	O	R	T		M	E	L

140

G	U	M	T	R	E	E		S	L	Y		P	I	C	A
E	N	C	H	A	N	T		T	E	E		I	D	O	L
A	D	D	E	D	I	N		A	T	T	H	E	E	N	D
R	O	L	F		G	A	V	E		I	P	A	N	A	
			I	B	M		A	L	A	S	K	A			
A	L	A	N	B	A	L	L		W	H	E	N	A	L	L
R	E	H	A	B		E	I	T	H	E	R		S	E	A
E	V	E	L		I	S	S	A	I	D		A	K	I	N
N	I	A		C	O	S	E	L	L		V	N	E	C	K
A	N	D	D	O	N	E		K	E	E	P	A	W	A	Y
			U	N	S	E	A	T		D	S	L			
L	A	I	R	D		B	O	R	E		Y	O	D	A	
O	F	T	H	E	D	A	Y		O	N	A	S	S	I	S
A	R	E	A		I	R	S		S	I	M	I	L	E	S
D	O	R	M		G	A	S		A	C	E	S	O	U	T

141

W	E	S	T		E	Q	U	A	L		A	S	U
A	V	E	R		N	U	R	S	E	D		P	E	P
R	I	G	A		L	I	G	H	T	S	P	E	E	D
P	L	A	Y	M	A	T	E		S	T	E	R	N	A
		F	O	C	I				S	C	A	T		
A	S	Q	U	I	E	T	A	S	A	M	O	U	S	E
P	A	U	L		G	A	L	A	S				
E	X	O		A	L	D	E	N	T	E		Z	I	T
		C	R	O	O	N				N	O	N	O	
B	L	U	E	F	O	O	T	E	D	B	O	O	B	Y
O	O	P	S				B	A	I	T			
U	N	M	A	S	K		R	O	D	C	A	R	E	W
G	E	O	R	G	E	S	A	N	D		B	E	T	E
H	R	S		T	R	E	N	D	Y		I	A	T	E
S	S	T		R	A	T	S	O		T	R	A	P

142

C	A	I	R	O		O	R	E		E	L	B	O	W
A	L	L	E	N		F	E	Z		G	O	O	S	E
R	O	O	S	T		F	A	I	R	Y	D	U	S	T
A	M	I	E			I	N	A	P	E	T			
F	A	L	C	O	N	C	R	E	S	T		I	R	E
E	R	O	T	I	C	A				A	Q	U	A	
			L	A	S	E	S		A	L	U	M	S	
F	A	T	H	E	R	K	N	O	W	S	B	E	S	T
I	L	I	A	D		S	L	O	A	N			
R	E	E	D				T	W	E	E	Z	E	S
E	X	O		F	A	L	L	H	A	R	V	E	S	T
	N	E	A	R	L	Y				O	R	C	A	
B	R	E	A	K	F	A	S	T		F	L	O	O	R
A	B	O	V	E		M	O	O		A	V	E	R	T
D	I	N	E	D		A	L	E		N	E	S	T	S

143

S	A	M	S		A	C	H	E		H	A	I	T	I
A	S	A	P		R	O	U	T		O	D	D	E	R
Y	O	G	U	R	T	S	M	O	O	T	H	I	E	S
O	N	D	R	A	F	T		N	I	C	E			
K	E	A		Y	U	L	E		L	A	R	O	S	A
		H	O	L	Y	M	A	C	K	E	R	E	L	
B	R	I	A	N		B	R	A	E		M	A	I	
L	O	T	S		P	L	A	I	N		B	A	R	K
A	B	S		T	A	I	L		T	E	N	S	E	
H	O	M	E	R	S	I	M	P	S	O	N			
S	T	E	N	O	S		S	O	O	N		C	E	Y
		T	U	G	S		O	B	T	R	U	D	E	
A	N	D	A	B	O	T	T	L	E	O	F	R	U	M
B	R	O	I	L		E	W	E	R		D	I	C	E
E	A	G	L	E		P	O	D	S		S	E	E	N

144

L	E	S		M	A	R	V		A	N	I	T	A
A	R	T		L	O	U	I	E		D	E	N	I	S
I	D	A		O	R	S	O	N		W	A	N	D	A
R	E	G	I	N	A		S	A	R	A		I	A	N
			N	E	L	L		A	R	I	E	L	
S	T	A	N	L	E	Y		A	L	E	C		
C	O	R	E	Y		C	A	R	L		E	R	M	A
O	M	A	R		P	E	R	R	Y		C	H	E	T
P	E	T	E		L	U	K	E		I	R	E	N	E
			A	D	A	M		A	N	N	E	T	T	E
	K	A	R	E	N		R	O	S	A			
A	N	N		M	E	R	L		T	A	M	A	R	A
R	E	N	E	E		A	A	R	O	N		R	O	D
C	L	A	R	A		I	L	E	N	E		A	L	I
A	L	L	E	N		N	A	T	E		B	E	N

145

```
A M B I . A T H O S . L I S A
W E A N . T E M P O . A R I D
E A S T E R N M E D I C I N E
S N E E Z E S . . A M U S E S
. . R I S E . A S S N .
. C E N T R A L H E A T E R
W H O S E . S P O T . I V E
H A R T . R E T O P . C L A N
A L F . S O L O . A R E N T
M O U N T A I N B I K E R .
. . A I D E . E N I D
S C A R F S . S P R E A D S
P A C I F I C I S L A N D E R
E R A T . D O R I A . Z O L A
X E N A . E L R E Y . A G T S
```

146

```
S I M P . A N A L O G . A D Z
E S S O . M A R I N A . F R A
E A G E R B E A V E R . I O N
M O R T A R . L I F T . C I I
. I C O N . N O H . I D E
P L A C E S T O G O . B O S S
R A F . W E S T . T M A N
O S T I A . B T U . I M A G E
. E L Y S . O S A S . D O G
S O R E . T H I N G S T O D O
E N S . L O O . A R E S .
A S H . A R N O . E N T I T Y
M I A . P E O P L E T O S E E
A T V . P U R I S T . P E A T
N E E . S P E E D O . S E M I
```

147

```
R O A L D . B O A T S . J E T
A R N I E . R O L E S . A X E
M A D M A G A Z I N E . S I X
. A R M I E S . R O S A
S C H . M E D S T U D E N T S
C H O S E N . R A S .
A A R P . H E A D T O T O E
M I D A I R R E F U E L I N G
P R E T T I E S T . E T R E
. T A T . A I S L E S
M O D E L T R A I N S . E D T
O D O R . A U N T I E
R I G . M U D S L I N G I N G
S U E . A N O S E . T A L I A
E M S . C A N I T . O N E N D
```

148

```
D E N I M . L E G O . P I S A
A N I T A . O R A L . A N O N
H O P S T E W A R D . R U L E
. M I N K S . A K R O N
E L F E S T E E M . S P E N T
S A L . S O Y . E T A L .
S T O L E . S L I P U P S
E C R U . B R I D E . G L E N
. H A S B E E N . U S A G E
. H A N A . K A T . N N E
W A I F S . P I N D O C T O R
I N D U S . S O A P Y .
S K I N . M A L L M I N D E D
P L O D . A B E L . A D A G E
S E T S . P E T S . N I N O N
```

149

```
D E N Z E L . L P G A . D A S
I C E A X E . A R A W . E S P
C O C K A N D B U L L . A T E
E L K . M O U R N S . T R I X
D I S K . M E I . A H S
. R O O M A N D B O A R D
V I S I B L Y . G A R . N A E
O N E S I E . R U S T I C
I T A . W A C . P E P T A L K
D O W N A N D D I R T Y .
. O O N . R O Z . X R A Y
B I R D . B A N Z A I . O T O
A N T . R O C K A N D R O L L
I C H . B A K E . K A R N A K
T H Y . I T S Y . A S S E S S
```

150

```
J I V E . C A G E Y . R E B
E B O N . A B O V E . M E R E
R O L L E D O V E R . A T I T
K S U . L E D . S T A T S
. M I S T E R N I C E G U Y
A L E V E . P E D R O .
R O T O . A U S S I E . F O P
L O W R E N T . T O W L I N E
O N O . I C I E S T . O X E N
. A N O L D . B L E S S
B R A V E N E W W O R L D .
I O W A N . I C I . C U R
R A M S . A N O T H E R O N E
D R A T . D E N T E . A S T I
S S N . S A T Y R . E T O N
```

151

```
GAME  SCRAP  LEMS
AVON  PIETA  SMEE
SOURGRAPES  DELA
 CRONY  RUSH  RIB
MANNA  TOPBANANA
ODE  WAH  YIELDS
SODA  LOOT  TADAS
  BEARFRUIT
ABHOR  NAES  OOHS
TRAVIS  SAG  NOT
LEMONLAWS  OCALA
AWS  SASH  BRADY
RETD  CHERRYPICK
GREY  KOREA  OMOO
EYRE  STEAM  SEWS
```

152

```
SCOFF  TBAR  SLOW
AUDIO  RITA  KEPI
STOREDETECTIVES
HERE  AVE  IODINE
  DRNO  SEE
SNAREDRUMS  DUMA
WARILY  BUT  ASIN
EVILS  FOG  BRINK
DEAL  PEA  CLENCH
ELLS  OUTEREDGES
  RED  LODE
AFLOAT  PIC  VISA
TEACHEREDITIONS
ITCH  SORE  ALLAH
TEES  STUD  OSAGE
```

153

```
WAVER  JAMS  BASH
ECOLI  EMIR  OMOO
BRIDGETONOWHERE
BEDE  DLII  HEXED
  RHEA  STEM
FILLINGSTATION
OBEYS  WED  ATON
GMC  SAHARAN  TRE
SPAN  NAM  ATOMS
 CROWNVICTORIAS
  THEE  OAHU
AGGIE  APEX  MBAS
BRACESFORIMPACT
BALE  WISC  AETNA
ABED  ETTE  ETHER
```

154

```
LOBE  APPT  ARBYS
OKRA  PAAR  HERON
COOTIEPIE  ALOHA
AKISS  ARES  INOR
 LARRY  AMECHE
AFEW  FAMILYFOOD
BARACK  AMEN
EASYA  OMS  ASSET
  SCAB  ASTERS
FOSSILFOOL  ARGO
AHCHOO  PAIGE
TSAR  GASP  VENTI
CURED  BOOTYMARK
AREWE  BASE  ODIE
TEDDY  APEX  MEGA
```

155

```
SOLID  POME  BIKE
SPARE  ELAL  USES
RENEW  RACE  DEEP
 CANIBUYAVOWEL
  ETA  WAKE
ARG  TRAP  TAICHI
MERC  SURVEYSAYS
ICAHN  LEO  SEPAL
COMEONDOWN  ROTE
INMATE  PSAT  STS
  TIVO  THO
 THEPASSWORDIS
BEAD  DALI  EERIE
ORZO  AKIN  ETATS
XMEN  NAME  DONUT
```

156

```
ACME  ASPER  SSNS
TRAM  DOLED  OTOE
BINOCULARS  BAMA
ATA  REIN  DIGIT
TINGE  DETERGENT
SCARABS  ESE  MAL
 ASI  ACT  COTE
 NAMEOFTHEGAME
BOTS  LAM  EAU
AST  PAZ  SMUSHES
HEARTBEAT  GEESE
ADIOS  RAZE  LAD
MINI  QUESADILLA
EVEL  BRAIN  ANET
NEDS  SISSY  NONE
```

157

```
HUNG · ATALE · HIED
OLEO · BOGEY · TOFU
ONER · ATONE · TWOS
PARENT · BALLPARK
· · DATA · SEE · · ·
STP · COLO · TESTED
TRASHIEST · HOSE
PARFORTHECOURSE
ALEC · · AEROMETER
TARSAL · AIDA · SSE
· · LOC · SINS · ·
PARABOLA · FIESTA
ONES · MERCI · PARD
UKES · EAGLE · TWOD
RAFT · DROID · SSTS
```

158

```
BOTH MINT ESQUE
ATRA IDEA VAUNT
COUNTDOWN ALICE
HESSIAN SADIE
STOPIT DENTED
LTR TAO ATNO
TABOO SILL SIGN
IRA PACEOFF MEN
DICE DART ADELE
ASKS HRS TRE
LETSGO SERBIA
REACH NEATNIK
PLANT OPENHOUSE
BOCCE LARS RILE
JOKES ARTY STEP
```

159

```
RAMIS STEEL KAT
ALACK NOWAY WOE
PICKYEATERS INN
INAYEAR SMOCKED
DEW SEW ALOE
SST HUR OMSK
JAVAN RICKILAKE
AVILA ENL ACRED
WIKIPEDIA MATES
SAKE MSN FAT
INRE GRO MRE
LECTERN EXCLAIM
ERA MICKEYMOUSE
AIR ETAIL OGDEN
HER TARTS NOEND
```

160

```
LISA HEAR APART
ONCE ELLE TYLER
SAUR LIES TRACE
SPLITDECISION
EELER NHL ACE
STY EARS HALLOW
BASICS ADZE
DIVIDEDHIGHWAYS
EGAD SMORES
COGENT ONON POR
IRA OED NIOBE
BROKENHEARTED
STOAS RAIL WAYS
TENSE MEGS ISEE
EDDAS ASHE NHRA
```

161

```
MBAS MEGA SEXY
EURO ASOF SACRO
STOLENCAR CLOAK
ATWORK DICE LYE
NIL CONFESS
BOILINGWATER
AGREEDTO YIELDS
GROG HOT SUCK
SENATE DELICACY
TABASCOSAUCE
PALOMAR SNL
LUI AYES DEARME
ADVIL THIRDRAIL
NIECE HIKE NICK
BODY APES ONES
```

162

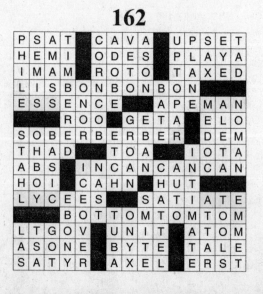

```
PSAT CAVA UPSET
HEMI ODES PLAYA
IMAM ROTO TAXED
LISBONBONBON
ESSENCE APEMAN
ROO GETA ELO
SOBERBERBER DEM
THAD TOA IOTA
ABS INCANCANCAN
HOI CAHN HUT
LYCEES SATIATE
BOTTOMTOMTOM
LTGOV UNIT ATOM
ASONE BYTE TALE
SATYR AXEL ERST
```

163

```
D O R M ▮ D A D A ▮ E N D O W
E D I E ▮ O P A L ▮ M I A M I
M I N D I N I H E G U T T E R
I N D I R A ▮ L S U ▮ W A N E
▮ ▮ C O L D ▮ S K I ▮ ▮
▮ H A N D I N T H E T I L L ▮
S C A R Y ▮ R O U E N ▮ C I A
E L S E ▮ S E R F S ▮ G I N S
L E T ▮ D E C A F ▮ T R E K S
F O O T I N T H E D O O R ▮ ▮
▮ O D D ▮ T O W S ▮ ▮
C A M P ▮ O A T ▮ T E S T E E
H E A D I N T H E C L O U D S
A R D O R ▮ M A Y O ▮ U N I T
D O D G E ▮ S T E M ▮ T A T A
```

164

```
G R A N ▮ B A S S ▮ S A P P Y
R I M E ▮ O C T A ▮ C U R E D
I D I G ▮ L A O S ▮ I D E A S
M E T A M O R P H O S I S ▮ ▮
M A Y T A G ▮ S A C S ▮ I N A
▮ ▮ E I N S ▮ H O T D O G
E O S ▮ M A T E F O R L I F E
A L P E ▮ E X E ▮ C O E N
T E A M C A P T A I N ▮ S E T
A O R T A S ▮ R T E S ▮ ▮
T S K ▮ B E L A ▮ S E A R C H
▮ P R O C E S S E D M E A T
F O L I O ▮ N C A A ▮ P A N E
L O U T S ▮ D O N S ▮ A D O S
O H G E E ▮ S T A Y ▮ N Y E T
```

165

```
A L E C ▮ F A R S I ▮ A M P S
M A Y O ▮ O L E O S ▮ N O A H
O V E N ▮ O L D H I C K O R Y
N E W C A L E D O N I A ▮ ▮
G R E E T S ▮ ▮ T R O V E
S N A R E ▮ T S E ▮ R A D I O
T E R N ▮ G H E T T O ▮ D A N
▮ S O M E T H I N G ▮ ▮
A S S ▮ R A M O N E ▮ E S A I
P A P U A ▮ E N O ▮ S M E L L
E G Y P T ▮ ▮ D I S M A L
▮ B O R R O W E D T I M E
B L U E R I B B O N ▮ O N E G
R O S A ▮ P I L O T ▮ N A D A
A B E T ▮ A S A L E ▮ E L A L
```

166

```
A P E R T U R E S ▮ S A B O T
V A L E N T I N E ▮ C L I M E
I L L A T E A S E ▮ A L F I E
S P A M ▮ U P D R A F T S
▮ V A S E ▮ Y I N ▮ ▮
E T A L I A E ▮ E E N ▮ M A T
M E S S C A L L S ▮ G L A C E
M P A A ▮ S E A T S ▮ E R I N
Y E N T A ▮ C H A P L A I N S
S E A ▮ N O T ▮ T E E N A G E
▮ G N U ▮ C E D E ▮ ▮
A L O U E T T E ▮ M U I R
L E O I X ▮ A L L U D E S T O
A M P L E ▮ L I O N E S S E S
S A S E S ▮ L A N D F O R M S
```

167

```
B O B ▮ I T E M S ▮ M C C O Y
E T A ▮ M O X I E ▮ I H O P E
R E C ▮ P A P E R P R O F I T
T R O N ▮ S O N I A ▮ P F U I
H I N T A T ▮ N N E ▮ E M S
▮ S H A M U S ▮ C E D E ▮
F I R ▮ H I G H F A L U T I N
O N E I ▮ S H A R K ▮ B A D E
R A B B I T S F E E T ▮ B O Z
▮ E M I R ▮ T I M B A L ▮
P A L ▮ N E T ▮ A S P E C T
A R L O ▮ S A J A K ▮ T B A R
W E I G H S C A L E S ▮ O N O
E N O L A ▮ O N E U P ▮ O T T
D A N E S ▮ S E E P Y ▮ K O S
```

168

```
L I O N ▮ A L T O ▮ F A U N S
O S L O ▮ L O O N ▮ O R S O N
U T E P ▮ B O O N ▮ B A D T O
T H A R P ▮ S T O A ▮ B O O B
S E N O R A ▮ S H E L ▮ ▮
▮ B O M B ▮ S H E L L A C
S O T ▮ L E A S T ▮ L L A M A
T H E M O N T H O F M A R C H
A N S O N ▮ T A I L S ▮ S S N
G O T O G U Y ▮ C O M B ▮
▮ A N S A ▮ P E R U S E
C O M P ▮ L U C A ▮ N A V E S
A T E I T ▮ C A M P ▮ S U I T
E R N E S ▮ L A M P ▮ I L S A
N O T S O ▮ A N O S ▮ L A M B
```

169

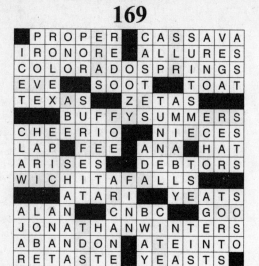

```
  P R O P E R   C A S S A V A
I R O N O R E   A L L U R E S
C O L O R A D O S P R I N G S
E V E     S O O T     T O A T
T E X A S     Z E T A S
      B U F F Y S U M M E R S
C H E E R I O     N I E C E S
L A P   F E E   A N A   H A T
A R I S E S     D E B T O R S
W I C H I T A F A L L S
      A T A R I     Y E A T S
A L A N     C N B C     G O O
J O N A T H A N W I N T E R S
A B A N D O N   A T E I N T O
R E T A S T E   Y E A S T S
```

170

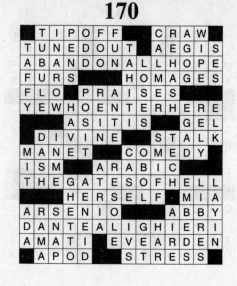

```
  T I P O F F   C R A W
T U N E D O U T   A E G I S
A B A N D O N A L L H O P E
F U R S     H O M A G E S
F L O   P R A I S E S
Y E W H O E N T E R H E R E
    A S I T I S   G E L
  D I V I N E   S T A L K
M A N E T     C O M E D Y
I S M   A R A B I C
T H E G A T E S O F H E L L
    H E R S E L F   M I A
A R S E N I O     A B B Y
D A N T E A L I G H I E R I
A M A T I   E V E A R D E N
  A P O D   S T R E S S
```

171

```
H O L E D   F L A P   S P A M
O L I V E   A I R E   W A G E
P A R A M O U N T S   A R E A
I N A S E N S E   T E N A N T
      R U T   G E T T Y
C A P R I S   J I G G E R
A W A I T   M O N E Y   O A R
N O R M   B U T T E   H O L Y
A L A   G U S T O   L A P S E
  G H E T T O   L A S S O S
A A R O N   E A U
S M A R T S   E M I G R A T E
L O P S   P A R A C H U T E S
A C H E   A G O G   E L I A S
N O S Y   T O S S   R E T R O
```

172

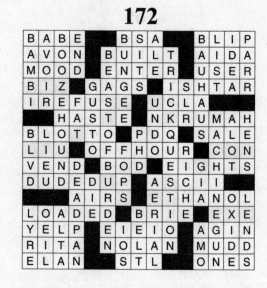

```
B A B E   B S A   B L I P
A V O N   B U I L T   A I D A
M O O D   E N T E R   U S E R
B I Z   G A G S   I S H T A R
I R E F U S E   U C L A
  H A S T E   N K R U M A H
B L O T T O   P D Q   S A L E
L I U   O F F H O U R   C O N
V E N D   B O D   E I G H T S
D U D E D U P   A S C I I
  A I R S   E T H A N O L
L O A D E D   B R I E   E X E
Y E L P   E I E I O   A G I N
R I T A   N O L A N   M U D D
E L A N   S T L   O N E S
```

173

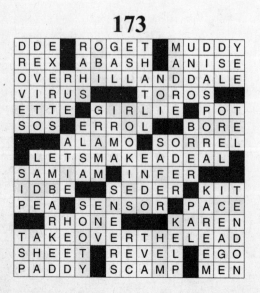

```
D D E   R O G E T   M U D D Y
R E X   A B A S H   A N I S E
O V E R H I L L A N D D A L E
V I R U S   T O R O S
E T T E   G I R L I E   P O T
S O S   E R R O L   B O R E
  A L A M O   S O R R E L
  L E T S M A K E A D E A L
S A M I A M   I N F E R
I D B E   S E D E R   K I T
P E A   S E N S O R   P A C E
  R H O N E   K A R E N
T A K E O V E R T H E L E A D
S H E E T   R E V E L   E G O
P A D D Y   S C A M P   M E N
```

174

```
F U M E S   S W A P S   J F K
T R I T T   P A B L O   E L I
D I S C O V E R C O D   M O N
  T H R E E   T A P I R S
T H E   M E D I A   A M I E
G I R D   P O T C O M P A N Y
I D E E S   S E P I A
F E D E R A L   D E N Y I N G
  P A P A L   N A V E L
T A K E S U P O M S   S E M I
O M A N   P L E A S   G O B
W I N D O W   A S T R O
I D S   S H O P S H O O T E R
N S A   H A M E L   M A I N E
G T S   A T B A Y   A R T O O
```

175

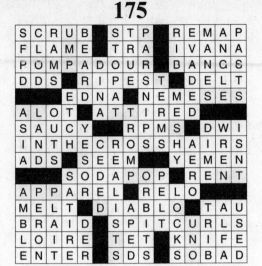

S	C	R	U	B	■	S	T	P	■	R	E	M	A	P
F	L	A	M	E	■	T	R	A	■	I	V	A	N	A
P	O	M	P	A	D	O	U	R	■	D	A	N	C	E
D	D	S	■	R	I	P	E	S	T	■	D	E	L	T
■	■	E	D	N	A	■	N	E	M	E	S	E	S	■
A	L	O	T	■	A	T	T	I	R	E	D	■	■	■
S	A	U	C	Y	■	R	P	M	S	■	D	W	I	■
I	N	T	H	E	C	R	O	S	S	H	A	I	R	S
A	D	S	■	S	E	E	M	■	Y	E	M	E	N	■
■	■	S	O	D	A	P	O	P	■	R	E	N	T	■
A	P	P	A	R	E	L	■	R	E	L	O	■	■	■
M	E	L	T	■	D	I	A	B	L	O	■	T	A	U
B	R	A	I	D	■	S	P	I	T	C	U	R	L	S
L	O	I	R	E	■	T	E	T	■	K	N	I	F	E
E	N	T	E	R	■	S	D	S	■	S	O	B	A	D

176

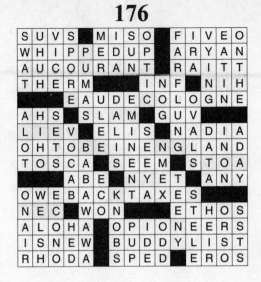

S	U	V	S	■	M	I	S	O	■	F	I	V	E	O
W	H	I	P	P	E	D	U	P	■	A	R	Y	A	N
A	U	C	O	U	R	A	N	T	■	R	A	I	T	T
T	H	E	R	M	■	■	I	N	F	■	N	I	H	■
■	■	■	E	A	U	D	E	C	O	L	O	G	N	E
A	H	S	■	S	L	A	M	■	G	U	V	■	■	■
L	I	E	V	■	E	L	I	S	■	N	A	D	I	A
O	H	T	O	B	E	I	N	E	N	G	L	A	N	D
T	O	S	C	A	■	S	E	E	M	■	S	T	O	A
■	■	A	B	E	■	N	Y	E	T	■	A	N	Y	■
O	W	E	B	A	C	K	T	A	X	E	S	■	■	■
N	E	C	■	W	O	N	■	■	E	T	H	O	S	■
A	L	O	H	A	■	O	P	I	O	N	E	E	R	S
I	S	N	E	W	■	B	U	D	D	Y	L	I	S	T
R	H	O	D	A	■	S	P	E	D	■	E	R	O	S

177

A	L	L	I	N	■	B	E	A	R	D	■	C	F	O
L	O	O	I	E	■	A	R	T	O	O	■	A	R	R
T	O	W	N	A	N	D	G	O	W	N	■	R	I	B
A	P	P	S	■	I	G	O	R	■	A	N	D	E	S
■	S	H	I	I	T	E	■	■	I	L	I	E	D	■
■	■	■	S	T	A	R	S	A	N	D	B	A	R	S
S	P	I	T	S	■	H	M	O	■	L	I	P	■	■
I	O	N	■	Y	O	K	O	O	N	O	■	E	C	O
N	O	T	■	M	A	E	■	B	E	R	E	T	■	■
G	L	O	O	M	A	N	D	D	O	O	M	■	■	■
■	T	O	W	I	N	■	O	R	E	I	D	A	■	■
F	A	D	E	D	■	N	O	T	A	■	T	U	B	A
A	B	E	■	W	E	A	R	A	N	D	T	E	A	R
I	L	E	■	A	L	T	A	R	■	D	E	L	T	A
R	E	P	■	Y	I	E	L	D	■	E	D	S	E	L

178

D	I	S	C	O	S	■	A	T	E	■	A	G	O	G
E	N	T	A	I	L	■	S	U	R	■	W	I	P	E
N	E	A	T	L	Y	■	S	P	A	C	E	B	A	R
S	P	I	N	■	■	C	O	A	T	I	■	E	L	M
■	■	T	R	A	F	F	I	C	C	O	N	E	■	■
■	■	■	P	L	A	N	■	■	E	N	D	I	N	■
O	U	T	■	A	U	D	I	T	S	■	O	R	N	E
K	N	U	C	K	L	E	S	A	N	D	W	I	C	H
A	T	T	U	■	T	R	I	X	I	E	■	P	H	I
Y	O	U	L	L	■	■	I	F	A	T	■	■	■	■
■	■	P	A	R	A	D	E	F	L	O	A	T	■	■
A	S	S	■	H	E	W	E	D	■	M	O	W	S	■
I	C	E	C	R	E	A	M	■	E	N	T	R	E	E
D	A	M	P	■	S	R	O	■	R	O	O	T	E	R
A	R	I	A	■	E	D	S	■	A	R	M	A	D	A

179

E	R	G	O	■	D	O	L	E	D	■	E	W	O	K
D	E	A	N	■	E	B	O	L	A	■	M	A	G	E
I	M	T	E	R	R	I	B	L	Y	S	O	R	R	Y
T	I	E	G	A	M	E	S	■	L	A	T	T	E	S
■	■	A	V	A	S	■	J	I	V	E	■	■	■	■
L	E	N	T	I	L	■	W	A	G	E	■	G	P	S
A	T	E	I	N	■	S	A	S	H	■	S	A	L	T
I	H	A	V	E	N	T	G	O	T	A	C	L	U	E
R	O	L	E	■	A	R	O	N	■	D	R	A	M	A
S	S	E	■	T	M	A	N	■	W	E	A	S	E	L
■	■	■	B	R	E	W	■	R	A	S	P	■	■	■
V	E	T	O	E	D	■	P	A	S	T	I	M	E	S
I	T	S	W	O	R	T	H	T	H	E	R	I	S	K
E	T	A	L	■	O	R	D	I	E	■	O	C	T	A
W	A	R	S	■	P	E	S	O	S	■	N	E	A	T

180

S	A	M	S	O	N	■	S	A	Y	■	M	A	D	D
I	C	E	A	X	E	■	P	G	A	■	O	L	A	Y
P	O	W	D	E	R	R	O	O	M	■	J	I	M	I
S	P	L	E	N	D	O	R	■	■	G	A	B	O	N
■	■	■	■	■	S	K	Y	D	I	V	I	N	G	■
N	A	T	A	L	I	E	■	O	R	N	E	■	■	■
A	N	A	L	O	G	■	W	H	Y	S	■	S	S	N
B	A	B	Y	O	N	E	M	O	R	E	T	I	M	E
S	T	U	■	S	O	L	D	■	U	N	I	T	E	S
■	■	T	E	R	I	■	U	N	G	L	U	E	S	■
N	A	V	Y	S	E	A	L	S	■	■	■	■	■	■
A	L	E	R	T	■	A	E	R	A	T	I	O	N	■
M	E	G	A	■	K	I	N	D	O	F	B	L	U	E
E	V	A	N	■	I	N	K	■	T	R	A	I	T	S
D	E	N	T	■	A	N	Y	■	S	O	R	E	S	T

181

M	A	C	A	W		T	W	A	S		G	L	E	E
P	L	U	T	O		Y	O	R	E		M	A	R	X
H	A	R	O	L	D	R	O	M	E		A	M	A	T
			F	R	O	Z	E		A	C	A	S	E	
S	O	N	O	M	A		Y	E	L	L		Z	E	N
P	R	O	P	A	N	E		A	T	T	E	S	T	
E	L	L	E	N	G	L	A	S	G	O	W			
D	Y	A	N		O	N	A		E	C	H	O		
		I	R	V	I	N	G	B	E	R	L	I	N	
I	C	E	T	E	A		S	A	P	P	O	R	O	
N	O	L		S	T	O	A		S	I	S	T	E	R
A	L	I	S	T		B	R	O	I	L				
R	A	C	E		J	A	C	K	L	O	N	D	O	N
O	D	I	N		A	M	E	R		G	U	I	D	E
W	A	T	T		N	A	D	A		S	T	E	E	D

182

A	L	A	S	K	A		A	M	S	O		P	T	S
T	A	R	T	U	P		S	A	Y	S		R	O	W
C	H	A	R	L	E	M	A	G	N	E		I	M	A
O	R	B	I	T		O	H	I	O		S	V	E	N
			P	U	B	L	I	C	D	O	M	A	I	N
R	O	S	E	R	E	D			S	W	A	T		
E	S	P		D	I	M	S		O	R	E	C	K	
C	H	I	C	K	E	N	C	H	O	W	M	E	I	N
D	A	C	H	A		G	M	E	N		Y	A	O	
		E	A	T	S		P	E	U	G	E	O	T	
A	U	G	U	S	T	A	M	A	I	N	E			
G	R	I	D		A	G	A	R		A	T	P	A	R
A	G	R		B	R	A	I	D	E	D	M	A	N	E
T	E	L		A	V	I	D		C	O	A	R	S	E
E	S	S		T	E	N	S		U	N	D	E	A	D

183

H	O	P	I		S	C	O	T		F	L	A	W	
O	V	A	L	S		E	O	N	S		R	O	S	A
S	I	N	E	W		P	A	C	K	L	I	G	H	T
E	N	D		A	N	I	S	E		O	N	S	E	T
D	E	A	D	H	E	A	T		H	U	G			
		B	A	I	T		M	O	D	E	L	T	S	
S	P	E	L	L		O	A	R	S		Y	O	U	
P	L	A	Y	I	N	G	W	I	T	H	F	I	R	E
C	A	R		I	L	L	S		A	U	N	T	S	
A	T	S	T	A	K	E		O	L	E	G			
		I	C	E		O	L	D	F	L	A	M	E	
S	P	A	D	E		K	N	E	E	D		W	A	X
H	O	L	Y	S	M	O	K	E		A	M	A	N	A
U	R	D	U		C	O	E	D		Y	O	K	E	L
L	E	A	P		S	K	Y	S		B	E	S	T	

184

A	T	O	M	I	C		A	C	T	V		C	D	S
R	I	V	E	R	A		B	O	R	E		H	E	N
C	A	I	N	A	N	D	A	B	E	L		E	R	A
			N	O	R		B	E	D	L	A	M	P	
O	B	I		P	A	L		S	T	O	P	I	T	
H	A	N	D	L	E	B	A	R		S	O	S	O	
S	C	R	E	E	N		M	E	G	S				
		H	E	A	T	E	D	B	L	A	N	K	E	T
			A	R	O	D		R	E	I	N	I	N	
I	C	E	D		B	A	L	D	E	A	G	L	E	
G	A	M	E	O	N		S	A	E		R	E	D	
E	N	A	B	L	E	D		I	N	A				
T	O	I		S	W	I	T	C	H	B	L	A	D	E
I	L	L		O	L	G	A		O	C	E	L	O	T
T	A	S		N	Y	S	E		E	S	T	A	T	E

185

D	R	E	A	M		S	L	U	M	S		T	E	X
E	A	R	L	Y		H	A	N	O	I		W	A	R
F	I	R	S	T	S	T	R	I	N	G		I	R	A
Y	D	S		H	E	E	D		G	N	A	R	L	Y
		J	I	L	T		P	O	O	D	L	E	S	
M	U	S	I	C	A	L	S	C	O	R	E			
A	R	U	B	A		P	B	S		S	O	L	D	
Z	I	P		L	O	R	I	S	E	S		R	I	O
E	S	S	O		U	A	R		C	R	I	E	S	
		M	O	T	H	E	R	T	O	N	G	U	E	
S	T	R	A	U	S	S		E	R	O	S			
H	E	A	R	T	H		E	M	I	T		D	W	I
E	N	S		F	I	T	T	O	B	E	T	I	E	D
B	O	P		I	N	S	E	T		R	A	V	E	L
A	N	Y		T	E	A	S	E		S	N	A	K	Y

186

R	C	M	P		T	W	A	N	G		C	A	M	S
O	H	O	H		W	A	T	E	R		A	M	E	N
S	A	N	D	D	O	L	L	A	R		L	I	N	E
E	R	S		U	C	L	A		M	E	N	S	A	
T	I	A		P	A	S	S	T	H	E	B	U	C	K
T	O	N	I	E	R		E	T	D		S	H	Y	
A	T	T	N		C	O	S	M	I	C				
		S	O	F	T	S	H	E	L	L	C	L	A	M
		O	R	E	I	D	A		A	N	A	S		
A	C	H		A	W	L		A	M	P	E	R	E	
B	L	O	O	P	S	I	N	G	L	E		C	I	G
L	I	R	A	S		A	U	E	L		D	A	M	
A	M	A	T		F	O	R	M	U	L	A	O	N	E
Z	A	C	H		U	N	C	U	T		S	T	A	N
E	X	E	S		R	A	S	P	S		P	E	S	T

187

```
BORAT  MOATS  CBS
ODORS  EATIT  OAT
BENCHWARMER  UIA
   IONS  CATCHY
IMSORRY CLICHES
ROTATE  CHATUP
KOOKS  BLESS  OPS
ENOS  BLEEP  ATOM
DSL  CLARK  MEARA
  PODUNK  CORTEZ
MAITRED  PAPOOSE
EGGSAC  PERP
RAE  CHAIRPERSON
IPO  KIOSK  TOILE
TEN  SPLAY  SETAT
```

188

```
EDGE  TIPS  JEWEL
CARB  AMIE  ALIVE
CNOW  ULEE  MOTIF
ONTHEROCKS  PHAT
   INUSE  OCEANS
EYETEST  BLAST
LUXE  FOOL  WOP
AGT  MARTINI  IKE
NOR  EMAC  MSRP
  ATLAS  DAKOTAS
QUOITS  MILES
UNLV  STRAIGHTUP
ADIOS  ABBE  PEDI
FEVER  KILN  IRON
FREDO  EGOS  TINK
```

189

```
APPTS  NINE  ESTS
ASOUL  ENOS  NCAA
BYEBYELOVE  ORGY
ACT  ALI  BLESS
HIYOSILVERAWAY
ECARTE  ELO  ULE
SAXE  ORB  APES
  ILLBEBACK
MBAS  AER  HIPS
ELL  INE  ARETOO
SOLONGFAREWELL
HAHAS  BAN  AVG
UTES  YOUREFIRED
GERI  ALTA  AKIRA
ADES  PEST  MESSY
```

190

```
SALAD  ESQ  POSTS
ADELE  PEU  IVORY
SHELF  AMI  NEXUS
HORSERUSTLER
ACS  CUL  IAN  ERE
  STEELTRUSSES
ABBA  STA  STATES
PLANB  STL  STEVE
AORTAS  EOS  ERES
ROBERTSRULES
TDS  FAT  GON  GOA
  MIXEDRESULTS
DORAG  AAA  UNITS
ECASH  MTN  EDDIE
NTEST  YET  DOEST
```

191

```
CALF  BRUIN  ACCT
OLEO  REPRO  GORE
TFORMATION  ILET
SASSY  INN  ALLAH
  ARON  OPIATE
PICKOFTHELITTER
TORENT  AYEAYE
ANI  LYE  RAW
  MAGPIE  RAVAGE
CHERRIESJUBILEE
LOSTIT  ETON
ELCID  PAR  VENTI
ADES  BUCKROGERS
TENT  OLLIE  ARIA
SMEE  BLUNT  ROXY
```

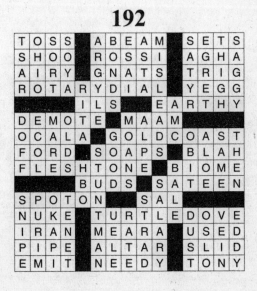

192

```
TOSS  ABEAM  SETS
SHOO  ROSSI  AGHA
AIRY  GNATS  TRIG
ROTARYDIAL  YEGG
   ILS  EARTHY
DEMOTE  MAAM
OCALA  GOLDCOAST
FORD  SOAPS  BLAH
FLESHTONE  BIOME
  BUDS  SATEEN
SPOTON  SAL
NUKE  TURTLEDOVE
IRAN  MEARA  USED
PIPE  ALTAR  SLID
EMIT  NEEDY  TONY
```

193

L	O	B	B	Y	■	S	A	N	S	■	M	E	T	Z
A	W	I	R	E	■	E	T	A	T	■	A	R	I	E
P	E	N	A	L	■	N	O	V	A	■	I	A	M	B
S	N	O	W	L	E	O	P	A	R	D	■	T	O	R
■	C	L	E	A	R	■	L	E	O	N	O	R	A	■
E	C	U	■	D	R	I	P	■	A	N	A	■	■	■
B	A	L	E	■	S	T	A	■	T	O	C	S	I	N
B	L	A	C	K	■	A	N	D	■	W	H	I	T	E
S	C	R	O	L	L	■	D	A	B	■	O	M	E	N
■	■	L	I	E	■	A	M	A	S	■	U	M	A	■
S	P	R	I	N	T	S	■	P	R	O	W	L	■	■
K	O	I	■	K	I	L	L	E	R	W	H	A	L	E
U	S	S	R	■	T	O	O	N	■	H	O	T	E	L
N	E	E	D	■	B	E	T	E	■	A	L	O	S	S
K	Y	R	A	■	E	S	T	D	■	T	E	R	S	E

194

T	A	B	O	O	■	O	L	S	E	N	■	I	D	S
U	S	U	R	P	■	N	A	N	C	Y	■	N	I	T
M	I	S	C	H	I	E	V	O	U	S	■	D	O	E
S	A	Y	■	E	S	A	I	■	■	A	I	D	E	■
■	■	■	P	L	A	C	E	T	O	S	L	E	E	P
A	P	P	O	I	N	T	■	I	D	E	A	■	■	■
G	R	E	T	A	■	■	C	L	E	A	N	S	E	R
H	O	E	R	■	O	F	F	E	R	■	L	I	L	O
A	B	N	O	R	M	A	L	■	■	B	A	N	K	S
■	■	■	A	H	A	T	■	P	L	E	D	G	E	S
P	E	R	S	O	N	S	B	U	I	L	D	■	■	■
O	M	I	T	■	■	■	L	E	N	A	■	T	V	A
P	O	S	■	F	U	T	U	R	E	B	L	O	O	M
U	T	E	■	O	V	E	R	T	■	O	V	A	T	E
P	E	N	■	X	A	C	T	O	■	R	I	D	E	S

195

R	I	L	E	S	■	W	O	O	D	S	■	J	U	T
A	R	I	E	L	■	A	T	B	A	T	■	U	N	E
C	O	O	K	I	N	G	T	I	M	E	■	S	T	A
I	N	N	■	P	I	E	■	I	O	T	A	S	■	■
E	M	I	R	■	B	R	O	K	E	N	H	O	M	E
R	A	Z	O	R	S	■	P	I	T	■	S	U	E	T
■	N	E	M	O	■	D	E	N	N	Y	■	T	D	S
■	■	P	O	K	E	R	G	A	M	E	■	■	■	■
L	A	P	■	T	U	N	A	S	■	C	U	R	E	■
O	A	R	S	■	R	I	T	■	S	A	R	O	N	G
S	M	O	K	E	D	M	E	A	T	■	O	U	Z	O
T	I	M	I	D	■	■	S	O	L	■	G	Y	N	■
A	L	I	■	I	T	S	O	K	W	I	T	H	M	E
R	N	S	■	C	R	U	D	E	■	R	U	L	E	R
T	E	E	■	T	Y	P	E	D	■	A	B	Y	S	S

196

O	M	A	N	■	P	L	U	S	■	B	R	E	W	S
D	O	L	E	■	A	D	Z	E	■	R	A	C	E	R
I	N	G	A	■	J	O	I	E	■	O	S	H	E	A
S	T	A	R	M	A	P	■	M	E	T	H	O	D	S
T	H	E	M	A	M	A	S	■	S	H	E	■	■	■
■	■	■	I	R	A	■	O	U	T	E	R	E	A	R
S	E	W	S	■	S	T	O	N	E	R	■	E	L	I
T	W	I	S	T	■	A	N	D	■	S	H	O	U	T
O	E	R	■	H	I	R	E	O	N	■	A	C	M	E
P	R	E	V	E	N	T	S	■	O	A	S	■	■	■
■	■	■	A	I	R	■	T	H	E	P	A	P	A	S
F	A	I	R	S	E	X	■	O	N	E	B	E	L	L
A	B	O	I	L	■	B	A	S	T	■	A	L	I	A
R	E	N	E	E	■	O	P	E	R	■	L	E	N	T
M	E	S	S	Y	■	X	R	A	Y	■	L	E	E	S

197

B	A	M	A	■	A	L	P	S	■	A	T	L	A	S
A	L	E	X	■	H	A	I	L	■	P	E	A	C	E
H	I	G	H	W	A	Y	T	O	H	E	A	V	E	N
A	T	S	E	A	■	S	A	T	E	■	M	A	S	T
■	■	■	A	I	M	■	■	E	L	S	■	■	■	■
R	O	A	D	T	O	P	E	R	D	I	T	I	O	N
H	A	M	■	■	M	I	R	A	■	M	E	N	S	A
O	T	A	R	U	■	N	A	B	■	B	R	A	I	N
M	E	T	E	R	■	O	T	I	S	■	N	E	C	■
B	R	I	D	G	E	T	O	N	O	W	H	E	R	E
■	■	■	D	E	M	■	■	T	W	O	■	■	■	■
G	A	T	E	■	I	D	E	S	■	I	N	U	S	E
R	O	U	N	D	T	R	I	P	T	I	C	K	E	T
I	N	N	E	R	■	O	N	U	S	■	H	E	W	N
N	E	E	D	Y	■	P	E	R	K	■	O	S	S	A

198

F	A	D	■	S	H	O	W	E	R	■	P	A	G	E
O	N	E	■	P	A	R	O	L	E	■	E	A	R	N
O	N	A	G	A	I	N	O	F	F	A	G	A	I	N
L	E	N	O	■	R	E	D	■	■	E	L	A	T	E
■	■	■	L	E	D	■	■	S	L	O	E	■	■	■
I	S	O	F	F	O	N	A	T	A	N	G	E	N	T
C	A	N	S	O	■	A	L	E	S	■	S	L	O	W
I	R	S	■	R	E	V	E	R	S	E	■	E	V	E
N	E	E	R	■	F	A	V	E	■	F	I	N	E	R
G	E	T	O	N	T	H	E	O	F	F	R	A	M	P
■	■	■	P	A	S	O	■	■	A	S	A	■	■	■
A	S	T	E	R	■	■	F	I	R	■	Q	T	I	P
S	W	I	T	C	H	P	O	S	I	T	I	O	N	S
K	I	L	O	■	A	R	L	E	N	E	■	M	C	S
S	T	E	W	■	N	O	D	E	A	L	■	E	A	T

199

S	C	R	A	P	■	A	L	B	E	E	■	C	A	T
A	L	A	M	O	■	B	O	O	M	S	■	H	U	E
S	I	M	P	L	E	A	3	A	D	C	■	I	R	E
H	O	P	■	L	A	C	E	■	R	A	G	L	A	N
■	■	D	U	C	K	■	R	A	P	I	D	L	Y	■
Z	E	N	I	T	H	■	R	E	C	E	S	S	■	■
A	L	O	N	E	■	V	E	X	E	D	■	P	E	A
N	I	P	S	■	S	E	L	E	S	■	F	L	A	X
E	A	R	■	A	C	R	E	S	■	S	L	A	V	E
■	■	O	P	P	O	S	E	■	S	T	A	Y	E	D
R	O	B	E	R	T	A	■	S	O	U	P	■	■	■
E	L	L	I	O	T	■	S	E	L	F	■	R	O	W
A	D	E	■	P	I	E	C	E	O	F	C	A	K	E
D	E	M	■	O	S	C	A	R	■	E	A	G	L	E
S	R	O	■	S	H	O	T	S	■	D	R	E	A	D

200

L	I	P	■	L	A	S	S	I	E	■	Z	E	D	S
A	K	A	■	E	L	A	I	N	E	■	O	T	O	E
M	E	W	■	T	O	W	N	C	O	U	N	C	I	L
B	A	N	D	I	T	O	S	■	M	E	H	T	A	■
■	T	E	N	O	F	■	S	F	P	D	■	■	■	■
S	H	I	P	O	F	F	O	O	L	S	■	P	C	S
M	A	C	O	N	■	R	B	I	■	P	H	A	T	■
A	R	K	S	■	G	H	O	S	T	■	A	I	R	E
S	K	E	E	■	L	O	U	■	O	I	L	E	R	■
H	S	T	■	B	U	S	T	E	R	B	R	O	W	N
■	■	J	U	T	E	■	M	O	V	E	S	■	■	■
A	S	H	E	S	■	S	I	D	E	D	O	O	R	■
S	T	O	R	Y	T	E	L	L	E	R	■	P	D	A
K	E	R	R	■	S	T	A	I	N	S	■	H	I	P
S	W	A	Y	■	P	E	Y	O	T	E	■	Y	E	T

The New York Times

Crossword Puzzles

The #1 Name in Crosswords

Available at your local bookstore or online at nytimes.com/nytstore

Coming Soon!

Big, Bad Book of Crosswords	978-0-312-58841-0
Midsummer Night's Crosswords	978-0-312-58842-7
Early Morning Crosswords	978-0-312-58840-3
Day at the Beach Crossword Puzzle Omnibus	978-0-312-58843-4
Snuggle Up Sunday Crosswords	978-0-312-59057-4
Pop Culture Crosswords	978-0-312-59059-8
Mad Hatter Crosswords	978-0-312-58847-2
Crosswords to Unwind Your Mind	978-0-312-68135-7
Easy Crossword Puzzle Omnibus Vol. 7	978-0-312-59058-1

Special Editions

Crossword Lovers Only: Easy Puzzles	978-0-312-54619-9
Crossword Lovers Only: Easy to Hard Puzzles	978-0-312-68139-5
Little Pink Book of Crosswords	978-0-312-65421-4
Little Black & White Book of Holiday Crosswords	978-0-312-65424-5
Brilliant Book of Crosswords	978-0-312-59004-8
Little Black (and White) Book of Sunday Crosswords	978-0-312-59003-1
Will Shortz's Wittiest, Wackiest Crosswords	978-0-312-59034-5
Little Luxe Book of Crosswords	0-312-38622-2
Double Flip Book of Crosswords and Sudoku	0-312-38635-4
Crosswords to Keep Your Brain Young	0-312-37658-8
Little Black (and White) Book of Crosswords	0-312-36105-X
The Joy of Crosswords	0-312-37510-7
Little Red and Green Book of Crosswords	0-312-37661-8
Little Flip Book of Crosswords	0-312-37043-1
How to Conquer the New York Times Crossword Puzzle	0-312-36554-3
Will Shortz's Favorite Crossword Puzzles	0-312-30613-X
Will Shortz's Favorite Sunday Crossword Puzzles	0-312-32488-X
Will Shortz's Greatest Hits	0-312-34242-X
Will Shortz Presents Crosswords for 365 Days	0-312-36121-1
Will Shortz's Funniest Crossword Puzzles Vol. 2	0-312-33960-7
Will Shortz's Funniest Crossword Puzzles	0-312-32489-8
Will Shortz's Xtreme Xwords	0-312-35203-4
Vocabulary Power Crosswords	0-312-35199-2

Easy Crosswords

Easy Crossword Puzzles Vol. 12	978-0-312-68137-1
Easy Crossword Puzzles Vol. 11	978-0-312-60826-2

Volumes 2–10 also available

Tough Crosswords

Tough Crossword Puzzles Vol. 13	0-312-34240-3
Tough Crossword Puzzles Vol. 12	0-312-32442-1

Volumes 9–11 also available

Sunday Crosswords

Stay in Bed Sunday Crosswords	978-0-312-68144-9
Relaxing Sunday Crosswords	978-0-312-65429-0
Finally Sunday Crosswords	978-0-312-64113-9
Crosswords for a Lazy Sunday	978-0-312-60820-0
Stress-Free Sunday Crosswords	0-312-56537-2
Big Book of Sunday Crosswords	0-312-56533-X
Forever Sunday Crosswords	0-312-54167-8
Sunday Delight Crosswords	0-312-38626-5
Sunday in the Sand Crosswords	0-312-38269-3
Simply Sunday Crosswords	0-312-34243-8
Sunday in the Park Crosswords	0-312-35197-6
Sunday Morning Crossword Puzzles	0-312-35672-2
Everyday Sunday Crossword Puzzles	0-312-36106-8
Sunday Brunch Crosswords	0-312-36557-8
Sunday at the Seashore Crosswords	0-312-37070-9
Sleepy Sunday Crossword Puzzles	0-312-37508-5
Sunday's Best	0-312-37637-5
Sunday at Home Crosswords	0-312-37834-3
Sunday Crossword Puzzles Vol. 36	978-0-312-65431-3

Omnibus

Easy to Not-So-Easy Crossword Puzzle Omnibus Vol. 5	978-0-312-68138-8
Garden Party Crossword Puzzles	978-0-312-60824-8
Easy to Not-So-Easy Crossword Puzzle Omnibus Vol. 4	978-0-312-60825-5
Lazy Day Crossword Puzzle Omnibus	0-312-56532-1
Weekend in the Country	0-312-38270-7
Crosswords for Two	0-312-37830-0
Crosswords for a Relaxing Weekend	0-312-37829-7
Crosswords for a Lazy Afternoon	0-312-33108-8
Lazy Weekend Crossword Puzzle Omnibus	0-312-34247-0
Lazy Sunday Crossword Puzzle Omnibus	0-312-35279-4
Ultimate Crossword Omnibus	0-312-31622-4
Tough Crossword Puzzle Omnibus Vol. 1	0-312-32441-3
Crossword Challenge	0-312-33951-8
Crosswords for a Weekend Getaway	0-312-35198-4
Biggest Beach Crossword Omnibus	0-312-35667-6
Weekend Away Crossword Puzzle Omnibus	0-312-35669-2
Weekend at Home Crossword Puzzle Omnibus	0-312-35670-6
Holiday Cheer Crossword Puzzles	0-312-36126-2
Crosswords for a Long Weekend	0-312-36560-8
Crosswords for a Relaxing Vacation	0-312-36694-9
Will Shortz Presents Fun in the Sun Crossword Puzzle Omnibus	0-312-37041-5
Sunday Crossword Omnibus Vol. 10	0-312-59006-7
Sunday Crossword Omnibus Vol. 9	0-312-35666-8
Easy Crossword Puzzle Omnibus Vol. 6	0-312-38287-1

Crossword Puzzle Omnibus Vol. 16	0-312-36104-1
Supersized Book of Easy Crosswords	0-312-35277-8
Supersized Book of Sunday Crosswords	0-312-36122-X

Previous volumes also available

Portable Size Format

Keep Calm and Crossword On	978-0-312-68141-8
Light and Easy Crosswords	978-0-312-68142-5
Hot and Steamy Crosswords	978-0-312-68140-1
Big and Bold Crosswords	978-0-312-68134-0
Cup O'Joe Crosswords	978-0-312-68136-4
Cozy Crosswords	978-0-312-65430-6
Weekends with Will	978-0-312-65668-3
Every Day with Crosswords	978-0-312-65426-9
Clever Crosswords	978-0-312-65425-2
Everyday Easy Crosswords	978-0-312-64115-3
Puzzle Doctor Presents Crossword Fever	978-0-312-64110-8
Poolside Puzzles	978-0-312-64114-6
Sunny Crosswords	978-0-312-61446-0
Mild Crosswords	978-0-312-64117-7
Mellow Crosswords	978-0-312-64118-4
Mischievous Crosswords	978-0-312-64119-1
Wake Up with Crosswords	978-0-312-60819-4
Simply Soothing Crosswords	978-0-312-60823-1
Simply Satisfying Crosswords	978-0-312-60822-4
Simply Sneaky Crosswords	978-0-312-60821-7
Soul-Soothing Crosswords	0-312-59032-6
Crosswords in Bed	0-312-59009-1
Crosswords by the Seaside	0-312-56534-8
Easy, Breezy Crosswords	0-312-56535-6
Ferociously Fun Crosswords	0-312-56538-0
Fearsomely Frightful Crosswords	0-312-56539-9
Fascinatingly Fierce Crosswords	0-312-56540-2
Will Shortz Presents the Dangerous Book of Crosswords	0-312-56536-4
Coffee and Crosswords: Whipped Wednesday	978-0-312-60799-9
Coffee and Crosswords: Thirsty Thursday	978-0-312-60800-2
Coffee and Crosswords: Mocha Monday	0-312-54164-3
Coffee and Crosswords: Tea Time Tuesday	0-312-54165-1
Stress-Free Crosswords	0-312-54166-X
Tame Crosswords	0-312-54168-6
Wild Crosswords	0-312-54169-4
Ferocious Crosswords	0-312-54170-8
Ready, Set, Solve! Crosswords	0-312-38623-0
Crosswords 101	0-312-38619-2
Tension-Taming Crosswords	0-312-38624-9
The Crossword Connoisseur	0-312-38627-3
The Puzzlemaster's Choice	0-312-38271-5
In the Kitchen Crosswords	0-312-38259-6
Think Outside the Box Crosswords	0-312-38261-8
Big Book of Easy Crosswords	0-312-38268-5
Real Simple Crosswords	0-312-38254-5
Crosswords By the Bay	0-312-38267-7
Crosswords for Your Coffee Break	0-312-28830-1
Sun, Sand and Crosswords	0-312-30076-X
Crosswords for Your Beach Bag	0-312-31455-8
Crosswords to Boost Your Brainpower	0-312-32033-7
Cuddle Up with Crosswords	0-312-37636-7
C Is for Crosswords	0-312-37509-3
Crazy for Crosswords	0-312-37513-1
Crosswords for a Mental Edge	0-312-37069-5
Afternoon Delight Crosswords	0-312-37071-9
Crosswords Under the Covers	0-312-37044-X
Crosswords for the Beach	0-312-37073-3
Will Shortz Presents I Love Crosswords	0-312-37040-7
Will Shortz Presents Crosswords to Go	0-312-36695-7
Favorite Day Crosswords: Wednesday	0-312-59033-4
Favorite Day Crosswords: Tuesday	0-312-37072-5
Favorite Day Crosswords: Monday	0-312-36556-X
Crosswords in the Sun	0-312-36555-1
Expand Your Mind Crosswords	0-312-36553-5
After Dinner Crosswords	0-312-36559-4
Groovy Crossword Puzzles from the '60s	0-312-36103-3
Piece of Cake Crosswords	0-312-36124-6
Carefree Crosswords	0-312-36102-5
Fast and Easy Crossword Puzzles	0-312-35629-3
Backyard Crossword Puzzles	0-312-35668-4
Brainbuilder Crosswords	0-312-35276-X
Stress-Buster Crosswords	0-312-35196-8
Super Saturday Crosswords	0-312-30604-0
Café Crosswords	0-312-34854-1
Crosswords for Your Lunch Hour	0-312-34857-6
Easy as Pie Crossword Puzzles	0-312-34331-0
Crosswords to Soothe Your Soul	0-312-34244-6
Beach Blanket Crosswords	0-312-34250-0
Crosswords for Stress Relief	0-312-33953-4
Crosswords for a Brain Workout	0-312-32610-6
A Cup of Tea Crosswords	0-312-32435-9
Crosswords for Your Bedside	0-312-32032-9
Coffee Break Crosswords	0-312-37515-8
Rise and Shine Crossword Puzzles	0-312-37833-5
Coffee, Tea or Crosswords	0-312-37828-9
Sweet Dreams Crosswords	0-312-37836-X

Other volumes also available

St. Martin's Griffin